John Warner Barber

Thrilling incidents in American history

Being a selection of the most important and interesting events which have transpired since the discovery of America to the present time. Compiled from the most approved authorities

John Warner Barber

Thrilling incidents in American history
Being a selection of the most important and interesting events which have transpired since the discovery of America to the present time. Compiled from the most approved authorities

ISBN/EAN: 9783337282080

Printed in Europe, USA, Canada, Australia, Japan

Cover: Foto ©ninafisch / pixelio.de

More available books at **www.hansebooks.com**

INCIDENTS IN AMERICAN HISTORY.

BY J. W. BARBER.

PHILADELPHIA:
G. G. EVANS, PUBLISHER,
No. 439 CHESTNUT STREET.

THRILLING INCIDENTS

IN

AMERICAN HISTORY;

BEING A SELECTION OF THE

Most Important and Interesting Events

WHICH HAVE TRANSPIRED

SINCE THE DISCOVERY OF AMERICA TO THE
PRESENT TIME.

COMPILED FROM THE MOST APPROVED AUTHORITIES,
BY J. W. BARBER.

NEW EDITION, ENLARGED.

PHILADELPHIA:
G. G. EVANS, PUBLISHER,
No. 439 CHESTNUT STREET.
1860.

Entered according to the Act of Congress, in the year 1860, by

G. G. EVANS,

in the Clerk's Office of the District Court for the Eastern District of Pennsylvania.

PREFACE.

AUTHENTIC accounts of important events which have taken place in past ages, are of much utility; especially to the countries and people whose affairs are related. In a country like ours, it seems necessary to the existence of true and enlightned patriotism, that every person should possess some knowedge of the history of his own country. By the aid of history we can call up past scenes and events in review—we can see the effects they have had upon the nations before us, and from thence we can learn wisdom for the future. It is, in reality, interesting and instructive to every intelligent mind, to be transported back to the time of the first settlement of our country, to observe the courage, fortitude, and self-denial of our forefathers, amidst many surrounding dangers, difficulties, and privations,—their unconquerable love of freedom,—the resistance they manifested to tyranny in all its shapes,—and the final success of their efforts to preserve the freedom and independence of their country entire.

This work is not designed for the information of those who are conversant with the history of our country in all its parts, (this class of community is comparatively small;) but for those who cannot spare the time or expense of reading or procuring a full and complete history. The object of the work is to give an account, in a short but comprehensive manner, of the most important and interesting events which have taken place in our country, nearly all of which are arranged in chronological order. Those events which are deemed of minor importance, are inserted in the Chronological Tables, at the end of the book, as every event which is mentioned could not be detailed, without swelling the book to an expensive size.

PREFACE.

It is believed that this work will be found useful as a reference book, for events recorded in American history; there being, it is presumed, no event of any very considerable importance, which is not noticed in its pages.

In making the selection of events, care has been taken to consult the most approved authorities; and the compiler would here state, that he feels himself under particular obligations to HOLMES' AMERICAN ANNALS, the most valuable work of the kind which has ever appeared in this country,—a work from which a great proportion of the late Histories of the United States have been benefited, either directly or indirectly.

Other authors have also been consulted, and extracts made from them in many instances, as will be perceived on examination of the work. A short outline sketch of the History of the United States is prefixed; the Constitution of the United States, and the Farewell Address of Washington, are added; and other interesting additions have been made. The engravings interspersed throughout the book will, it is thought, be of utility in fixing more firmly in the mind many important facts, and in rendering the work interesting.

J. W. B.

CONTENTS.

Outline History of the United States,	PAGE 7
North American Indians,	27
Expeditions of Ferdinand de Soto and M. de la Salle,	32
Introduction of the use of Tobacco,	33
Settlement of Jamestown, Va.,	34
Pocahontas,	36
Plymouth settlers,	38
Discovery of Indian corn,	39
Massasoit, the Indian Sachem,	40
Exploits of Capt. Standish,	41
First settlements in Connecticut,	43
Blue Laws of Connecticut,	44
Earthquakes,	47
Indian cunning and sagacity,	49
Expedition against the Pequots,	49
Elliot, the Indian Missionary,	52
King Philip's War.—Attack on Brookfield,	53
Swamp fight with the Narragansetts,	54
Death of King Philip,	56
Bacon's Insurrection in Virginia,	57
The Regicides, Goffe and Whalley,	58
William Penn,	60
Tyranny of Andros,	61
Preservation of the Charter of Connecticut,	62
Destruction of Schenectady,	64
First culture of Rice in the Colonies,	64
Salem Witchcraft,	65
Captain Kidd, the Pirate,	66
Great Snow Storm,	68
Dark Days,	71
Northern Lights,	72
Gov. Fletcher and Capt. Wadsworth,	74

CONTENTS.

War with the Tuscaroras, PAGE 75
War with the Yamasees, 76
Inoculation introduced, 78
Father Ralle, the French Jesuit, 80
Natchez Indians extirpated, 81
Negro Insurrection in Carolina, 82
Invasion of Georgia, 83
Capture of Louisburg, 85
D'Anville's Expedition, 86
Tumult in Boston, 88
Braddock's Defeat, 89
Massacre at Fort William Henry, 90
Abercrombie's Defeat, 92
Capture of Quebec, 93
War with the Cherokees, 95
Expeditions against the Spanish settlements in the W. Indies, 99
Dr. Franklin's Experiment in Electricity, 100
Whitefield, the celebrated Preacher, 102
Col. Boon's first settlement of Kentucky, 103
Stamp Act, 107
Massacre in Boston, 108
Destruction of Tea in Boston, 110
First Continental Congress, 111
Battle of Lexington, 113
Taking of Ticonderoga by Col. Allen, 115
Battle of Bunker Hill, 117
Arnold's march through the Wilderness, 125
Death of Gen. Montgomery, 126
Washington Commander in Chief of the American Army, 128
Attack on Sullivan's Island, 130
Declaration of Independence, 132
Battle on Long Island, 134
Death of Capt. Hale, 137
Battle of Trenton, 139
Battle of Princeton, 141
Battle of Brandywine, 142
Battle of Germantown, and attack on Red Bank, 144
Murder of Miss McCrea, 145

CONTENTS.

Battle of Bennington and Capture of Burgoyne, PAGE	146
Treaty with France,	150
Battle of Monmouth or Freehold,	151
Taking of Savannah and Charleston,	152
Paul Jones' Naval Battle,	154
Gen. Putnam's Escape at Horseneck, and Wolf Den,	155
Storming of Stony Point,	157
Battle of Camden,	158
Murder of Mrs. and Mr. Caldwell,	159
Massacre of Wyoming,	161
Distress and mutiny of the American Army,	162
Capture of Andre and Treason of Arnold,	165
Battle at King's Mountain,	167
Battle of the Cowpens,	170
Battle of Guilford,	171
Battle of Eutaw Springs,	172
Storming of Fort Griswold,	174
Siege of Yorktown and Surrender of Cornwallis,	175
Washington taking leave of the Army,	178
Continental Money,	178
Shays' Insurrection in Massachusetts,	180
Adoption of the Federal Constitution,	181
Inauguration of President Washington,	183
Whiskey Insurrection in Pennsylvania,	184
Yellow Fever in Philadelphia in 1793,	185
St. Clair's Defeat and Wayne's Victory,	187
Difficulties with the French,	189
Death of Washington,	191
Invention of Steamboats,	193
Wars with the Barbary States,	196
Burr's Conspiracy,	200
Expeditions of Captains Lewis and Clark to the Pacific Ocean,	204
Burning of the Theatre at Richmond, Va.,	205
Second War with Great Britain,	207
Mob in Baltimore,	209
Gen. Hull's Surrender,	211
Capture of the Guerriere,	213
Battle of Queenstown,	214

CONTENTS.

Massacre at Fort Mimms,	PAGE 216
Capture of York, U. C.,	217
Battle on Lake Erie,	219
Death of Tecumseh,	220
Barbarities of the British at Hampton, Va.,	222
Battle of Niagara,	225
Burning of Washington City,	228
Battle of Plattsburg,	230
Hartford Convention,	236
Gen. Jackson's Victory at New Orleans,	237
Bank of the United States,	240
Conspiracy of the Blacks in Charleston, S. C.,	247
Western Antiquities,	254
Erie Canal,	258
Gen. Lafayette's Visit,	260
Insurrection and Massacre in Virginia, (1831,)	262
Riot in Providence, R. I., (1831,)	268
Florida or Seminole War,	274
Revolution in Texas,	278
Difficulties on the Canadian Frontier,	281
Account of the Mormons,	283
War with Black Hawk,	286
Cholera in the United States,	290
Great fire in New York,	292
Captain Wilke's Exploration Expedition,	294
Dorr Insurrection in Rhode Island,	297
Riots in Philadelphia,	299
Mexican War	303
Battle of Palo Alto and Resaca de la Palma,	305
Capture of Monterey,	308
Battle of Buena Vista,	311
Expedition against New Mexico,	313
Military Operations in California,	315
Taking of Vera Cruz,	317
Battle of Cerro Gordo,	319
Battle of Contreras,	322
Battle of Cherubusco,	323
Battle of Molina del Rey, and Storming of Chapultepec,	325
California,	328
Gold Digging in California,	329
First Steamer Across the Atlantic,	331
Lynch's Expedition to the River Jordan and the Dead Sea	333
Death of Ex-President Adams,	338
Mob at the Opera House, New York,	341
Col. Fremont's Expeditions,	344
Reception of Father Mathew	352
APPENDIX—	
Chronological Table,	3
Declaration of Independence,	19
Constitution of the United States,	23
Farewell Address of Washington,	42
Circular Letter to the Governors of the States,	59
Farewell Orders to the Army of the United States,	70
Indian Speeches,	75

INCIDENTS IN AMERICAN HISTORY.

OUTLINE HISTORY.

AFTER the first daring and successful voyage of Coumbus, the attention of the European governments was directed towards exploring the "new world." In the year 1497, John Cabot, a Venetian in the service of Henry VII. of England, first discovered the Island of Newfoundland, and from thence ranged the coast of the United States to Florida. The country was peopled by uncivilized nations, who subsisted chiefly by hunting and fishing. The Europeans who first visited our shores, treated the natives as wild beasts of the forest, which have no property in the forests through which they roam; and therefore planted the standard of their respective masters on the spot where they first landed, and in their names took possession of the country, which they claimed by right of discovery. Previous to any settlement in North America, many titles of this kind were acquired by the English, Dutch, French, and Spanish navigators. Slight as these claims were, they were afterwards the causes of much dispute and contention between the European governments. These contentions arose from the fact of the subjects of different princes laying claim to the same tract of country, because both had discovered the same river or promontory; or because the extent of the claims of each party was undefined.

The first permanent English settlements in the United States were at Jamestown in Virginia, in 1607, and at Plymouth in Massachusetts in 1620. While the European settlements were few and scattered in this vast and uncultivated country, and the trade of it confined to the bartering of a few trinkets, &c. for furs, the interfering of different claims produced no important controversy among the Europeans. But in proportion as the settlements were extended, and in proportion as the trade with the natives became valuable, the jealousies of the nations who had made discoveries and settlements on the coast were alarmed, and each power took measures to secure and extend its possessions, at the expense of its rivals.

From the earliest settlement of the Colonies to the treaty of Paris in 1763, they were often harassed by frequent wars with the Indians, French, Spaniards, and Dutch. During the Indian wars, the savages were often instigated by the French and Dutch to fall on the English settlements, in order to exterminate the colonists, or drive them from the country. These wars were by far the most distressing; the first settlers lived in continual fear and anxiety, for fear their Indian foes would fall upon them in some unguarded moment, and oftentimes they had to struggle to prevent their entire extermination. After the colonies had subdued the Indians in their immediate vicinity, they were assailed by the *French* and *Indians.* The French possessed Canada, and had made a number of settlements in Florida, and claimed the country on both sides of the Mississippi. To secure and extend their claims they established a line of forts back of the English settlements, from Canada to Florida. They used much art and persuasion to gain over the Indians to their interest, in which they were generally successful. Encroachments were accordingly made on the English possessions, and mutual injuries succeeded, which soon broke out into open war.

In order to put a stop to the depredations of the French and Indians, it was contemplated to conquer Canada. In 1690 the Commissioners of the Colonies projected an expedition against Quebec. The land forces ordered for this invasion consisted of 850 men, raised from the Colonies of New England and New York, and commanded by Gen. Winthrop. At the same time a fleet of armed ships and transports, with 1800 men under Sir William Phipps, was ordered to sail up the St. Lawrence, and co-operate with the land forces in the reduction of Quebec But owing to the delay of the fleet, and the want of boats and provisions among the land forces, the expedition was unsuccessful. The next expedition against Canada took place in 1709, in Queen Anne's reign. The Colonies of New England and New York, raised about 2,500 men, who were placed under the command of Gen. Nicholson, who proceeded to Wood Creek, south of Lake George. Here they waited to hear of the arrival of the fleet which was to co-operate with them. The fleet did not arrive, and the army at Wood Creek were attacked with a malignant disease, which occasioned a great mortality, which compelled them to withdraw, and the expedition was abandoned. In 1711, another attempt under Gen. Nicholson with the land forces, and a fleet under Admiral Walker, was made for the conquest of Canada. But this failed by the loss of eight or nine transports, with about 1000 men, by shipwreck. The peace of *Utrecht*, signed March 3d, 1713, put an end to hostilities, and continued till 1739.

In 1744, Great Britain declared war against France, and the next year Louisburg, a strong fortress on Cape Breton, was taken from the French. The French government soon fitted out a large fleet, with a large body of land forces, for the purpose of recovering Louisburg, and attacking the English Colonies. But this expedition, by means of storms, sickness among the troops, &c. failed of accomplishing any thing, and the Colonies were relieved from consternation and dismay. This war closed by a treaty of peace, signed at *Aix la Chapelle*, in 1748.

In 1755, hostilities again commenced between Great Britain and France, and in 1756, four expeditions were undertaken against the French. One was conducted by Col. Monckton and Gen. Winslow, against Nova Scotia. This expedition was attended with success. The country was subdued, and the inhabitants, about 2,000 in number, were transported to New England, and dispersed and incorporated with their conquerors. Gen. Johnson was ordered, with a body of troops, to take possession of Crown Point but he did not succeed. Gen. Shirley commanded an expedition against the fort at Niagara, but lost the season by delay. Gen. Braddock was sent against Fort du Quesne, but in penetrating through the wilderness fell into an ambuscade of French and Indians, where he was killed, and his troops suffered an entire defeat.

In 1758, great efforts were made to subdue the French in America. Three armies were employed—one commanded by Gen. Amherst, to take possession of Cape Breton—one under Gen. Abercrombie, destined against Crown Point—and a third under Gen. Forbes, to drive the French from the Ohio. Gen. Amherst was successful in taking Louisburg, after a warm siege. The inhabitants of Cape Breton were sent to France, and the fortifications of Louisburg reduced to a heap of ruins.

Gen. Abercrombie, who was sent against Crown Point and Ticonderoga, attacked the French at the latter place, and was defeated with a terrible slaughter of his troops. Gen. Forbes was successful in taking possession of Fort du Quesne, which the French thought proper to abandon.—The next year the efforts of the British and Americans to reduce the French were more successful. Gen. Prideaux and Sir William Johnson began the operations of the campaign, by taking possession of the French fort near Niagara. Gen. Amherst took possession of the forts at Crown Point and Ticonderoga, which the French had abandoned.

But the decisive blow which proved the destruction of the French power in America, was the *taking of Quebec* by Gen. Wolfe. The loss of Quebec was soon followed by the capture of Montreal by Gen. Amherst, and Canada became a province of the British Empire. " Thus, after a century of wars, massacres, and destruction, committed by the French and savages, the colonies were secured from ferocious invaders, and Canada, with a valuable trade in furs, came under the British dominion."

The conquest of Canada, and the expulsion of the French from the Ohio, put an end to all important military operations in the American Colonies. In Europe, however, the war continued to rage; and in the **West Indies**, the British, aided by the Americans, took Havana from the Spaniards. But in 1762, "a definitive treaty of peace was signed at Paris, by which the French king ceded Nova Scotia, Cape Breton, and Canada, to the British king; and the middle of the Mississippi, from its source to the river Ibberville, and the middle of that river to the sea, was made the boundary between the Brit:sh and French dominions in America. Spain ceded to Great Britain, Florida, and all her possessions to the east of the Mississippi. Such was the state of the European possessions in America, at the commencement of the Revolution."

Before the Revolution, there were three kinds of government established in the British American Colonies. "The first was a charter government, by which the powers of legislation were vested in a governor, council, and assembly, chosen by the people. Of this kind were the governments of Connecticut and Rhode Island. The second was a proprietary government, in which the proprietor of the province was governor; although he generally resided abroad, and administered the government by a deputy of his own appointment; the assembly only being chosen by the people. Such were the governments of Pennsylvania and Maryland; and, originally, of New-Jersey and Carolina. The third kind was that of royal government, where the governor and council were appointed by the crown, and the assembly by the people. Of this kind were the governments of New-Hampshire, Massachusetts, New-York, New-Jersey, after the year 1702, Virginia, the Carolinas, after the resignation of the proprietors in 1728, and Georgia. This variety of governments created different degrees of dependence on the crown. To render laws valid, it was constitutionally required that they should be ratified by the king; but this formality was often dispensed with, especially in the charter governments.

"At the beginning of the last war with France, commissioners from many of the colonies had assembled at Albany, and proposed that a great council should be formed by deputies from the several colonies, which, with a general governor, to be appointed by the crown, should be empowered to take measures for the common safety, and to raise money for the execution of their designs. This proposal was not relished by the British ministry; but in place of this plan it was proposed, that the governors of the colonies, with the assistance of one or two of their council, should assemble and concert measures for the general defence; erect forts, levy troops, and draw on the treasury of England for moneys that should be wanted; but the treasury to be reimbursed by a tax on the colonies, to be laid by the English parliament. To this plan, which would imply an avowal of the right of parliament to tax the colonies, the provincial assemblies objected with unshaken firmness. It seems, therefore, that the British parliament, *before* the war, had it in contemplation to exercise the right they claimed of taxing the colonies at pleasure, without permitting them to be represented. Indeed it is obvious that they laid hold of the alarming situation of the colonies, about 1754 and 1755, to force them into an acknowledgment of the right, or the adoption of measures that might afterwards be drawn into precedent. The colonies, however, with an uncommon foresight and firmness, defeated all their attempts. The war was carried on by requisitions on the colonies for supplies of men and money, or by voluntary contributions.

"But no sooner was peace concluded, than the English parliament resumed the plan of taxing the colonies; and, to justify their attempts, said, that the money to be raised was to be appropriated to defray the expense of defending them in the late war."*

The first attempt of the British government to raise a revenue in America, appeared in the memorable *Stamp Act;* but such was the opposition of the colonies to this act, that it was shortly after repealed. The parliament, however, persisted in their right to raise a revenue from the colonies, and accordingly passed an act, laying a certain duty on glass, tea, paper, and painters' colours—

* Dr. Morse.

articles which were much wanted, and not manufactured in America. This act was so obnoxious to the Americans, that the parliament thought proper, in 1770, to take off these duties, except three pence a pound on tea. But this duty, however trifling, kept alive the jealousies of the colonies, and their opposition continued and increased. It was not the inconvenience of paying the duty which raised their opposition, but it was the *principle*, which, once admitted, would have subjected the colonies to unlimited parliamentary taxation, without the privilege of being represented.

After a series of oppressive acts on the part of the British government, and of opposition on the part of the colonies, General Gage was sent over with an armed force to Boston, in 1774, to overawe and reduce the rebellious colonies to submission. But these measures did not intimidate the Americans. The people generally concurred in a proposition for holding a Congress by deputation from the several colonies, in order to concert measures for the preservation of their rights. Deputies were accordingly appointed, and the *first Congress* met at Philadelphia, in October, 1774. The proceedings of the American Congress had a tendency to confirm the people in a spirited and unanimous determination to resist the oppressive acts of the mother country, and to defend their just and constitutional rights. On the other hand, the British Parliament declared that a *rebellion* actually existed, and besought his Britannic Majesty to take the most effectual measures to enforce due obedience to the laws and authority of his government; and assured him that they were determined to support him in maintaining the just rights of the crown. " From this moment an appeal to arms became unavoidable, and both parties prepared for the conflict."

The first scene of this sanguinary contest opened at Lexington, on the morning of the 19th of April, 1775. Here was spilt the first blood in a war of seven years duration, a war which severed these United States from the British Empire, and ended in the establishment of the independence of a nation of freemen.

1775

[The first year of the Revolution.]

The principal operations of the war during this year took place in the northern States. As the province of Massachusetts had been foremost in opposition, the British government sent their forces to Boston, the capital, and held it in possession during the year. Soon after the battles of *Lexington* and *Bunker's Hill*, Gen. Washington, who was appointed commander in chief of the American forces, arrived at Cambridge, and took the command of the army in July. The army investing Boston amounted to about 15,000 men. They were mostly destitute of good arms, ammunition, clothing, and experienced officers. Washington's first and most difficult task was to organize and discipline the troops. Owing to his uncommon exertions and influence, he succeeded in bringing high-minded freemen to know their respective places, and to have the mechanism as well as the movements of a regular army.

In the autumn of this year, a body of troops under the command of Gen. Montgomery, besieged and took the garrison at St. John's, which commanded the entrance into Canada. Gen. Montgomery pursued his success, and took Montreal. At Quebec being joined by Gen. Arnold, who had marched a body of men through the wilderness to his assistance, Montgomery made an assault on Quebec, on the last day of the year. In this attack he was killed, his troops defeated, and the American army was finally compelled to evacuate Canada.

During this year nearly all the old governments of the colonies were dissolved; and the royal governors, and the crown officers adhering to British measures, were obliged to leave the country, or suspend their functions. From that time temporary conventions were held, for the purpose of administering the laws, and making regulations to meet the public exigences. In some of the colonies, however, the British adherents (who were called *tories*) were numerous and powerful, which weakened the opposition to the British arms.

1776.

This year was opened by the burning of the large and flourishing town of Norfolk in Virginia, by order of Lord Dunmore, the royal governor of that province.

The British King entered into treaties with some of the German States for about 17,000 men who were to be sent to America this year, to assist in subduing the colonies. These troops were generally called *Hessians*, from the circumstance of many of them being raised in Hesse Cassel in Germany. Gen. Washington who still continued before Boston, in the opening of the spring planted his batteries so judiciously before that town, that the British General Howe, on the 17th of March abandoned the place, and Gen. Washington marched into the place in triumph.

During the summer a squadron of ships commanded by Sir Peter Parker, and a body of troops under Generals Clinton and Cornwallis, attempted to take Charleston, the capital of South Carolina. The fort on Sullivan's Island, near Charleston, was attacked with great fury by the ships of the squadron, but the British were repulsed with great loss, and the expedition was abandoned.

On the 4th of July, Congress published the *Declaration of Independence.* Soon after the declaration, Gen. Howe with a powerful force arrived near New-York; and landed the troops on Staten Island. Gen. Washington at this time was in New-York with about 13,000 men, who were encamped either in the city, or the neighbouring fortifications. The operations of the British began by attacking the Americans on Long Island. The Americans were defeated with severe loss, and Gen. Washington probably saved the remainder of his troops by ordering them to retreat in the night after the battle.

In September, New-York was abandoned by the Americans, and taken by the British, and in November, fort Washington on York Island was taken, and more than 2,000 men made prisoners: about the same time Gen. Clinton took possession of Rhode Island.

The American army being greatly diminished by the loss of men taken prisoners, and the departure of large bodies of others whose term of enlistment had expired, General Washington was obliged with the remnant of his army which had been reduced from 25,000, to scarcely 3,000, to retreat towards Philadelphia, pursued by their victorious enemies. This was the most gloomy period of the Revolution. Washington saw the necessity of striking some successful blow, to reanimate the expiring hopes of his countrymen. The battles of *Trenton* and *Princeton* revived the hopes of America, and confounded their enemies. Congress also made great exertions to rouse the spirits of the people, and sent agents to solicit the friendship and aid of foreign powers.

1777.

The plan of the British Ministry during this year was to separate the northern from the southern States, by sending an army under Gen. Burgoyne from Canada, to penetrate into the northern States, and endeavour to effect a communication with the British at New-York. If this plan had been successful, it would probably have had a fatal effect on the American cause. But the defeat of Burgoyne at *Bennington* and *Saratoga*, and the surrender of his army at the latter place, produced important results in favour of the Americans. At the South the British were more successful. Gen. Howe embarked his forces at New-York, sailed up the Chesapeake, landed at the head of Elk river, and began his march to Philadelphia. Gen. Washington endeavoured to stop his progress, and a battle was fought near *Brandywine* Creek, but the Americans were overpowered by superior numbers and discipline, and Gen. Howe took possession of Philadelphia. The American **Congress** now retired to Yorktown in Virginia.

1778.

The beginning of this year was distinguished by a *Treaty of Alliance with France*, whereby the Americans obtained a powerful ally. When the British Ministry were informed that this treaty was in agitation, they despatched commissioners to America to attempt a reconciliation.—But the Americans had now gone too far to accept their offers. The British evacuated Philadelphia in June and marched for New-York; on their march they were annoyed by the Americans, and at *Monmouth* an action took place, in which, had Gen. Lee obeyed his orders, a signal victory would have been obtained.

In July, Count D'Estaing arrived at Newport, R. I. with a French fleet for the assistance of the Americans. In August, Gen. Sullivan, with a large body of troops, attempted to take possession of Rhode Island, but did not succeed. In December, Savannah, the then capital of Georgia, was taken by the British under the command of Col. Campbell. About this time an insurrection of the Royalists in North Carolina, was crushed by the spirited exertions of the Militia. During this year a more regular discipline was introduced into the American army by Baron Steuben, a German officer.

1779.

The campaign of 1779 was distinguished for nothing decisive on the part of the Americans or British. "The British seemed to have aimed at little more than to distress, plunder, and consume—it having been, early in the year, adopted as a principle upon which to proceed, to render the Colonies of as little avail as possible to their new connexions." In accordance with these views, an expedition was sent from New-York to Virginia for the purpose of distressing the Americans

They landed at Portsmouth, and destroyed the shipping and valuable stores in that vicinity. After enriching themselves with various kinds of booty, and burning several places, they returned to New-York. Soon after this expedition, a similar one, under the command of Governor Tryon, was sent against Connecticut. New-Haven and East-Haven were plundered; Fairfield. Norwalk, and Green's Farms, were wantonly burned. About this time *Stony Point* was taken by Gen. Wayne. In October, Gen. Lincoln (who commanded the southern American army) and Count D'Estaing made an assault on Savannah, but they were repulsed with considerable loss. During the summer, Gen. Sullivan was sent against the *Six Nations*, and laid waste their country;—these Indians had been induced by the British to take up arms against the Americans. Forty villages were consumed, and 100,000 bushels of corn were destroyed.

1780.

On the opening of the campaign of this year, the British troops left Rhode Island, and Sir Henry Clinton finding it more easy to make an impression on the Southern States, which were less populous than the Northern, determined to make them the seat of war. Clinton, with Lord Cornwallis, undertook an expedition against Charleston, South Carolina, where Gen. Lincoln commanded. This place, after a close siege of about six weeks, surrendered to the British commander; and Gen. Lincoln, and the whole garrison, were made prisoners on the 12th of May.

Gen. Gates was now appointed to the command of the southern American army. In August, Lord Cornwallis (who was left in the command of the British forces at the South) attacked Gen. Gates, and entirely routed his army. He afterwards marched through the southern States, and supposed them entirely subdued. During the summer, the British troops made frequent incursions into New-Jersey, ravaging and plundering the country. This year was also distinguished for the infamous *treason* of Gen. Arnold, which stamped his name with lasting infamy.

1781.

The beginning of this year was distinguished by a mutiny in the American army: this was occasioned by their severe sufferings and privations, and the depreciation of the *Continental Money* with which they were paid. But the punishment of the ringleaders, and the exhortation of the officers, prevailed to bring them back to their duty.

After the defeat of Gen. Gates in Carolina, Gen. Greene was appointed to the command of the American troops in that quarter. From this period the aspect of the war was more favourable. On the 17th of January, at the *Cowpens*, Gen. Morgan, the intrepid commander of riflemen, signally defeated Col. Tarleton, the active commander of the British Legion. After a variety of movements, the main armies met at *Guilford* in Carolina on the 15th of March. Gen. Greene and Lord Cornwallis exerted themselves at the head of their respective armies; and although the Americans were obliged to retire from the field of battle, yet the British army suffered a severe loss, and could not pursue the victory. After the battle of Guilford, Gen. Greene moved towards South Carolina to drive the British from their posts in that State, and by a brilliant action at *Eutaw Springs*, forced Lord Cornwallis to withdraw his forces, and fortify himself in Yorktown, in Virginia.

In the Spring of this year, *Arnold* the traitor, with a number of British troops, sailed to Virginia and plundered the country, and at the time Cornwallis was at Yorktown made an incursion into Connecticut, burnt New-London, took fort Griswold by storm, and put the garrison to the sword.

About the last of August, Count de Grasse with a large French fleet arrived in the Chesapeake and blocked up the British troops at Yorktown. Gen. Wash ington previous to this had moved the main body of his army to the southward, and when he heard of the arrival of the French fleet, made rapid marches to the head of Elk river, where embarking, his army soon arrived at *Yorktown*. A vigorous siege now commenced, and was carried on with such effect by the combined forces of America and France, that Cornwallis was forced to surrender. This important event took place on the 19th of October, 1781, and decided the Revolutionary war.

On the 30th of November, 1782, the provisional articles of peace were signed at Paris; by which Great Britain acknowledged the Independence and sovereignty of the United States of America; and these articles were afterwards ratified by a definitive treaty.

" Thus ended a long and arduous conflict, in which Great Britain expended near a hundred millions of money, with a hundred thousand lives, and won nothing. America endured every cruelty and distress; lost many lives and much treasure; but delivered herself from a foreign dominion, and gained a rank among the nations of the earth."

After peace was restored to the country, the next and most difficult object was to organize and establish a general Government. Articles of confederation and perpetual union had been framed in Congress, and submitted to the consideration of the States in 1778, and in 1781 were agreed to by all the State legislatures.

The articles, however, were framed during the rage of war, when principles of common safety supplied the place of a coercive power in the government. To have offered to the people, at that time, a regular system of government, armed with the necessary power to regulate the conflicting interests of thirteen States, might have raised a jealousy between them or the people at large, that would have weakened the operations of war, and perhaps have rendered a union impracticable. Hence the numerous defects of the confederation. On the con clusion of peace the defects began to be felt. Each State assumed the right of disputing the propriety of the resolutions of Congress, and the interests of an individual State were often placed in opposition to the common interest of the union. In addition to this, a jealousy of the powers of Congress began to be excited in the minds of many of the people.

Without a union that was able to form and execute a general system of commercial regulations, some of the States attempted to impose restraints upon the foreign trade that should indemnify them for the losses they had sustained. These measures, however, produced nothing but mischief. The States did not act in concert, and the restraints laid on the trade of one State operated to throw the business into the hands of its neighbour. Thus divided, the States began to feel their weakness. Most of the Legislatures had neglected to comply with the requisitions of Congress for supplying the Federal Treasury; the resolves of Congress were disregarded; the proposition for a general impost to be laid and collected by Congress was negatived by Rhode Island and New-York.

In pursuance of the request of Virginia, most of the States appointed delegates who assembled at Annapolis in 1786, to consult what measures should be taken in order to unite the States in some general and efficient government. But as the powers of these delegates were limited, they adjourned, and recommended a general Convention to meet at Philadelphia the next year. Accordingly in May, 1787, delegates from all the States, except Rhode Island, assembled at Philadelphia, and appointed Gen. Washington their president. "After four months deliberation, in which the clashing interests of the several States appeared in all their force," the convention agreed to a frame of government which was finally agreed to by all the States; and on the 30th of April, 1789, Gen. Washington was inaugurated the first President of the United States. From this auspicious moment the American Republic has steadily advanced in a tide of prosperity and growing power.

WASHINGTON'S ADMINISTRATION.

This period continued for eight years. Washington, the leader of the armies of the United States, who conducted them through the perilous and successful struggle for Independence, now received the unanimous suffrages of his countrymen to administer their national government. "His administration, partaking of his character, was mild and firm at home; noble and prudent abroad." The principal events which took place during this period were, the *Indian war* on our Western frontiers—the *Whiskey Insurrection*, in Pennsylvania—Jay's treaty with Great Britain,—and the establishment of a National Bank and Mint.

"During this period, the arts and manufactures attracted the attention of Government. Mr. Hamilton, Secretary of the Treasury, made a report to Congress on the subject, in which he set forth their importance to the country, and urged the policy of aiding them. Since that time the revenue laws have been framed, with a view to the encouragement of manufactures, and their promotion has been considered as a part of the policy of the United States." The United States at the close of this period, contained about 5,000,000 of inhabitants

J. ADAMS' ADMINISTRATION.

In 1796, Mr. Adams was elected President, and continued in the office four years. The principal events during this time, were—the *difficulties* with the *French* Government—the *death of Washington*, and the *transfer* of the seat of the national government to *Washington*. The greater part of Mr. Adams' administration was the subject of much popular clamour, owing to several imprudent laws which were passed during his presidency. Such were the "*Alien*" and "*Sedition Laws*," the act for raising a standing army, and the act for imposing a direct tax, and internal duties These causes, with some others, caused so much opposition to Mr. Adams, that it prevented his re-election to the presidency

JEFFERSON'S ADMINISTRATION.

Mr. Jefferson's administration commenced in 1801 and continued for eight years. The most prominent events during this period were—the purchase of Louisiana—the *War with Tripoli*—*Burr's conspiracy*, the outrage upon the *Chesapeake*, and the laying of an *Embargo*.

The bitterness of party spirit during this time raged with some violence, and it interrupted in some degree that general harmony which it is always important to the welfare of our union to cultivate. Trade and commerce progressed with great rapidity. The European nations being at war with each other, and the United States remaining neutral, our vessels carried to Europe the produce of our own country, and the produce of other countries. This is commonly called the *carrying trade*, and was very profitable to our citizens. After the year 1807, the commercial restraints laid by France by her *Berlin* and *Milan* decrees, and by Great Britain by her *Orders in Council*, began to curtail our trade, and the *Embargo* laid by our Government at the close of the year interrupted it still more.—The Arts and Manufactures still progressed, and the population of the United States, at the close of Mr. Jefferson's administration, amounted to about 7,000,000.

MADISON'S ADMINISTRATION.

On the 4th of March, 1809, Mr. Madison was inducted into the office of President, and continued in office eight years. This period was distinguished for the *Second War with Great Britain*. When Mr. Madison entered upon his office, the state of the country was in some respects gloomy and critical. France and England were at war, and they issued against each other the most violent commercial edicts, in violation of the laws of nations, and injurious to those nations who wished to remain neutral. After a series of injurious and insulting acts, on the part of the government of Great Britain and its agents, the government of the United States declared war against that power, June 18th, 1812, which continued about three years.

The seat of war on the land, was principally on the frontiers of *Canada*, of which province it was the object of the Americans to take possession. The war at that point continued with various success on the part of the Americans and British. The Americans, however, were able to effect but little towards accomplishing the designs of their government. The situation of the contending parties at the close of the war was nearly the same as it was at the commencement; on the ocean, however, it was different. The splendid success of the American navy in various engagements, raised it to a high elevation, and taught her proud rival a lesson which will not be forgotten. During Mr. Madison's Presidency, in 1816, a *National Bank* was established with a capital of thirty-five millions of dollars.

MONROE'S ADMINISTRATION.

Mr. Monroe commenced his administration in 1817, under many favourable circumstances,—the country was fast recovering from the depression of commerce and a three years' war. The political feuds, which had, since the revolution, occasioned so much animosity, were now gradually subsiding, and there appeared in the administration a disposition to remove old party prejudices, and to promote union among the people. A spirit of improvement was spreading throughout the country: roads and canals were constructed in various parts of the union. The principal events which took place in Mr. Monroe's administration were—the war with the *Seminole Indians* —the passage of an act by Congress granting a *pension* to the indigent officers and soldiers of the revolution— the *cession of Florida* to the United States by the Spanish government, and the *visit of Gen. Lafayette* to the United States.

J. Q. ADAMS' ADMINISTRATION.

Mr. Adams was elected President in 1825, and continued in office four years. The principal events during this period were—the *Treaty with Colombia*—the *Panama Mission*, and the death of the two venerable patriarchs of the revolution, *John Adams* and *Thomas Jefferson*, on the fiftieth anniversary of Independence. During this period, the people of the United States were divided into two parties in reference to the Presidential election; one party desirous of retaining Mr. Adams during another term of office, the other upholding General Andrew Jackson as a suitable candidate for the office of President. Party spirit now raged with violence, each party upholding their favourite candidate, and traducing the other. Upon counting the votes, it appeared that a large majority were in favour of Andrew Jackson; and on the 4th of March, 1829, he was inducted into the office of President of the United States, according to the form prescribed by the Constitution.

JACKSON'S ADMINISTRATION.

General Jackson took the oath of office as president of the United States, March 4th, 1829, and was continued in office eight years. The leading measures of his administration were carried out with an uncommon degree of energy and determination. In 1832, the bill to recharter the United States bank was passed by Congress, but being vetoed by the president, it was lost. In 1832, also, Congress passed a new *tariff* bill. This act was considered so grievous in South Carolina, that a convention was assembled, who published an " ordinance," *nullifying* or forbidding the operation of the tariff laws within the limits of that state. This act called forth a proclamation from President Jackson, stating that " such opposition must be repelled." Hostile preparations were now made on both sides. The gathering storm was allayed by the passage of the *compromise act*, introduced into Congress by Mr. Clay, which reduced the duties on certain articles and limited the operation of the tariff to the 30th of September, 1842.

In 1835, serious apprehensions were entertained of a war with France. Our government for many years had urged in vain upon that country the claims of our citizens, for spoliations upon American commerce during the wars of Napoleon. These claims amounting to *twenty-five millions* of francs, had been acknowledged by the French government, but for various reasons payment was delayed. Certain measures were now proposed, which it was feared would involve the two nations in war. Happily all differences were amicably settled.

In 1835, the national debt was extinguished, and such was the financial state of the nation, that several millions of surplus revenue, at the beginning of 1836 remained in the treasury.

VAN BUREN'S ADMINISTRATION.

Martin Van Buren, succeeded General Jackson in the presidency, in 1837, and continued in office four years During the administration of his predecessor, the public moneys were removed from the United States bank and deposited in the state banks. These institutions thus had their facilities for lending money increased, speculation was encouraged, large debts were contracted, and the common beaten track of honest industry in order to acquire wealth, was in a measure abandoned. This unnatural state of things of course could not continue; it had its crisis in 1837. Such was the revulsion in business transactions, that the banks suspended specie payments. Those where the public funds were deposited, shared the common fate, and the government expected embarrassment. The president convened a special session of Congress, September 4th, 1837, and recommended a mode of keeping the public money called the "*sub-treasury*" scheme. This was rejected by Congress, and treasury notes were ordered to be issued in order to supply the wants of government.

HARRISON'S AND TYLER'S ADMINISTRATIONS.

After a long and exciting political contention with regard to candidates for the presidential office, General Wm. H. Harrison was by a large majority elected president, and John Tyler vice-president. General Harrison was inaugurated March 4th, 1841, and died April 4th, just one month afterward; and Mr. Tyler, by the constitution, became president. Some of the leading measures of Mr. Tyler's administration were not in accordance with the wishes of the political party who elevated him to office, and much dissatisfaction was thereby given. The most important political event during his administration was the *annexation of Texas* to the United States. In 1842, after a long and exciting controversy for some years, respecting the northeastern boundary of the United States, dividing the state of Maine from Canada, a treaty was negotiated between the British envoy Lord Ashburton, and Daniel Webster the American secretary. After another exciting political struggle, James K. Polk having received a majority of electoral votes, was on the 4th of March, 1845, inducted into the presidential office.

POLK'S ADMINISTRATION.

The principal events and measures which signalized the administration of Mr. Polk, were: the admission of Texas as a state; the division of Oregon; the Mexican war; the occupation of Mexico; the treaty; and the acquisition of California with its mines of gold. In consequence of the measures of the American government in relation to Texas, difficulties took place with the government of Mexico, which resulted in open war. For a long period the boundaries of Oregon, owing to conflicting claims remained undefined, and it was feared that hostilities would arise on this account, but in 1846, all differences were adjusted. The acquisition of California, extending the limits of the United States from the Atlantic to the Pacific, will undoubted prove an important event in the history of the world. After another political struggle, General Zachary Taylor having received a majority of thirty-six votes in the electoral college over his competitor, General Cass, was on the 5th of March, 1849, inaugurated as president.

INTERESTING EVENTS, &c.

1. *North American Indians.*

It has long been a question agitated among the learned, how America was first peopled. The opinion best supported is, that the Indians of this country emigrated from the north-eastern parts of Asia, crossing over to this continent at Bhering's straits. It having been established by the discoveries of Captain Cook, that at Kamschatka, in about latitude 66 degrees north, the continents of Asia and America, are separated by a strait only eighteen miles wide, and that the inhabitants on each continent are similar, and frequently pass and repass in canoes from one continent to another: from these and other circumstances, it is rendered highly probable that America was first peopled from the north-east parts of Asia.

But since the Esquimaux Indians are manifestly a separate species of men, distinct from all the nations of the American continent, in language, disposition, and habits of life; and in all these respects bear a near resemblance to the northern Europeans, it is believed that the Esquimaux Indians emigrated from the northwest parts of Europe. Several circumstances confirm this belief. As early as the ninth century, the Norwegians discovered Greenland, and planted colonies there.

With regard to the number of Indians inhabiting our country, at the time of the arrival of the European settlers, no correct estimate can be made; but, according to the estimate of Dr. Trumbull, they could not much exceed 150,000, within the compass of the thirteen original states. It is believed that they were formerly much more numerous, particularly on the Ohio river and its branches, and in New-England.

A few years before the arrival of the Plymouth settlers, a very mortal sickness raged with great violence among the Indians inhabiting the eastern parts of New-England. "Whole towns were depopulated. The living were not able to bury the dead; and their bones were found lying above ground many years after. The Massachusetts Indians are said to have been reduced from 30,000 to 300 fighting men. In 1633, the small pox swept off great numbers."

The Indians of this country were divided into many small tribes, governed by their sachems, or kings, and were often at war with each other.

In their persons, the Indians were tall, straight, and well proportioned; in their councils, they were distinguished for their gravity and eloquence; in war, for bravery, stratagem, and revenge.

Hunting, fishing, and war, were the employment of the men. The women were compelled to till the field and to perform the common drudgery of their domestic affairs.

Their dress in summer consisted chiefly of a slight covering about the waist; in winter they clothed themselves with the skins of wild animals.

They were extremely fond of ornaments, and on days of festivity and show, they were painted with various colours, and profusely ornamented with shells, beads, and feathers.

Their habitations, which were called by the English *wigwams*, were constructed by erecting a strong pole for the centre, around which other poles, a few feet distant, were driven, and fastened to the centre pole at the top, then covered with mats and bark of trees, which rendered them a shelter from the weather.

Their warlike instruments and domestic utensils were few and simple;—a *tomahawk*, or hatchet of stone, bows and arrows, sharp stones and shells, which they used for knives and hoes, and stone mortars for pounding their corn. For money they used small beads, curiously wrought from shells, and strung on belts, or in chains, called *wampum*.

The Indians of this country were generally Polytheists, or believed in a plurality of gods. Some were considered as local deities; yet they believed that there was one Supreme God, or *Great Spirit*, the creator of the rest, and all creatures and things. Him the natives of New-England called Kichtan. They believed that good men, at death, ascended to Kichtan, above the heavens, where they enjoyed their departed friends and all good things; that bad men also went and knocked at the gate of glory, but Kichtan bade them depart, for there was no place for such, whence they wandered in restless poverty. This Supreme Being they held to be good, and prayed to him when they desired any great favour, and paid a sort of acknowledgment to him for plenty, victory, &c. The manner of worship in many tribes, was to sing and dance around a large fire.

There was another power which they called *Hobbamock*, in English, the Devil, of whom they stood in greater awe, and worshipped him merely from a principle of fear, and it is said that they sometimes even sacrificed their own children to appease him.[*] They prayed to him to heal their wounds and diseases. When found curable, he was supposed to be the author of their complaints; when they were mortal, they were ascribed to Kichtan, whose diseases none were able to remove; therefore they never prayed to him in sickness. Their priests, which were called *Powaws*, and their chief warriors, pretended often to see Hobbamock in the shape of a man, fawn, or eagle, but generally of a *snake*, who gave them advice in their difficult undertakings. The duty and office of the Powaws, was to pray to Hobbamock for the removal of evils; the common people said amen. In his prayer the Powaw promised skins, kettles, hatchets, beads, &c., as sacrifices, if his request should be granted.

The apparent insensibility of the Indians under pains

[*] Morse and Parish's Hist.

and wounds is well known; yet they had awful apprehensions of death.

When sick, and all hope of recovery was gone, their bursting sobs and sighs, their wringing hands, their flowing tears, and dismal cries and shrieks, were enough to excite sympathy from the hardest heart. Their affection was very strong for their children, who by indulgence were saucy and undutiful. A father would sometimes, through grief and rage for the loss of a child, stab himself. Some tribes of Indians would not allow of mentioning the name of a friend after death. When a person died, they generally buried him with his bow and arrows, dogs, and whatever was valuable to him while living, supposing he would want them in another world, as their ideas of the happiness of heaven consisted in finding plenty of game, feasting, &c.

Of their bravery and address in war we have many proofs. The fortitude, calmness, and even exultation which they manifest while under the extremest torture from the hand of their enemies, is in part owing to their savage insensibility, but more to their high notions of military glory, and their rude notions of future happiness, which they shall forfeit by the least manifestation of fear, or uneasiness under their sufferings. They are sincere and faithful in their friendships, remembering the smallest favour done them to the latest period, but bitter and determined in their resentments, and often pursuing their enemies hundreds of miles through the wilderness, encountering every difficulty in order to be revenged. This spirit oftentimes descended from the father to the son, who felt bound to revenge the injuries done his father when living. In their public councils they observe the greatest decorum. In the foremost ranks sit the old men who are the counsellors of the tribe, the warriors, and next the women and children. "Their kindness and hospitality is seldom equalled by any civilized society. Their politeness in conversation is even carried to excess, since it does not allow them to contradict any thing that is asserted in their presence."

The Indians appear to have distinct traditions of the creation and deluge, and some of their words, rites, and ceremonies, bear a strong affinity to those of the ancient Hebrews.

---

2. *Expeditions of Ferdinand de Soto and M. de la Salle.*

The Mississippi was first discovered by Ferdinand de Soto in 1541, and Father Hennepin, (a French Catholic Missionary,) and Monsieur de la Salle, were the first Europeans that traversed it. Soto had served under Pizarro in the conquest of Peru, with such reputation, that the King of Spain intrusted him with the government of Cuba, with the rank of General of Florida, and Marquis of the lands he should conquer.

Soto collected a body of 900 foot and 350 horse, for an expedition into Florida, where he landed in May, 1539. From the Gulf of Mexico he penetrated into the country northward, and wandered about in search of gold, exposed to famine, hardships, and the opposition of the natives. He pursued his course north to the country inhabited by the Chickasaws, where he spent a winter. He then crossed the Mississippi, being the first European that had discovered that vast river. After a long march into the country westward, in which Soto died, the remains of his troops returned to the Mississippi. Here they built a number of small vessels, in which they sailed down the stream, and made the best of their way to Panuco, in Mexico, where they arrived in September, 1543. In this extraordinary expedition of more than four years' duration, in search of gold in the wilderness, and among hostile savages, more than half the men perished.*

Father Hennepin, a missionary of the Franciscan order, and M. de la Salle, with a party of men, embarked from Fort Frontenac, in Canada, in Nov 1678 After having passed through Lakes Ontario, Erie, Hu-

* Webster's Elements of Useful Knowledge, Vol. I.

ron, and Michigan, and carried their canoes over land to the head of the Illinois river, Hennepin passed down to the mouth of the Mississippi. He set out upon his return to Canada, where he arrived in 1681, after having passed through many hardships and difficulties in this perilous enterprise among the savages, who for some time detained him as a prisoner.

M. de la Salle returned to France; and from the flattering account he gave of the country, and the advantages that would accrue from settling a colony in those parts, Louis XV. was induced to establish a company for that purpose. Salle embarked, with an intention to settle near the mouth of the Mississippi. But through mistake, he sailed 100 leagues to the westward of it, where he attempted to settle a colony; but through the unfavourableness of the climate, most of his men miserably perished, and he himself was villanously murdered, not long after, by two of his own men.

3. *Introduction of the use of Tobacco.*

This singular native American plant, appears to have been used by the Indians in all parts of America. It is said it was first discovered by the Spaniards, in 1520, near the town of *Tobasco*, in Mexico. The Mexicans used it copiously, not only in smoke in the mouth, but also in snuff at the nose.

" In order to smoke it," says the historian, "they put the leaves, with the gum of liquid amber, and other hot odorous herbs, into a little pipe of reed or wood, or some other more valuable substance. They received the smoke by sucking the pipe, and shutting the nostrils with their fingers, so that it might pass more easily by the breath into the lungs." It was such a luxury that the lords of Mexico were accustomed to compose themselves to sleep with it.

In the account of Cartier's voyage in 1535, we find it used in Canada: it is thus described:—" There grow eth a certaine kind of herbe, whereof in sommer they make great provision for all the yeer, making great account of it, and onely men use of it, and first they cause it to be dried in the sunne, then were it about their necks wrapped in a little beast's skinne, made like a little bagge, with a hollow piece of stone or wood like a pipe: then when they please they make a pouder of it, and then put it in one of the ends of said cornet, or pipe, and laying a cole of fire upon it, at the other ende, sucke so long that they fill their bodies full of smoke, till it cometh out of their mouth and nostrils, even as out of the tonnell of a chimney."

Tobacco was carried into England from Virginia, by Mr. Lane, in 1536. Sir Walter Raleigh, a man of gayety and fashion, adopted the Indian usage of smoking, and by his interest and example, introducing it at court, the pipe soon became fashionable. It was in vain that parliament discouraged the use of this "*vile Indian weed.*" In vain King James assured his subjects, that the custom of smoking it was loathsome to the eyes, hateful to the nose, harmful to the brain, and dangerous to the lungs. Opposition made proselytes; and the united influence of fashion and habit, extended the practice through the kingdom.*

Tobacco was first cultivated by the English in Virginia, about the year 1616;—from that time to the present, it has ever been one of the staple productions of that state.

---

4. *Settlement of Jamestown, Va.*

"North America was discovered in a period when the Arts and Sciences had made very considerable progress in Europe. Many of the first adventurers were men of genius and learning, and were careful to preserve authentic records of such of their proceedings as would be interesting to posterity. These records afford

* Holmes' Annals.

ample documents for American historians. Perhaps no people on the globe, can trace the history of their origin and progress with so much precision, as the inhabitants of North America; particularly that part of them who inhabit the territory of the United States."

The first European who discovered the coast of the United States, was John Cabot, a Venetian, who was employed by Henry VII. of England to make discoveries. What is now called the Island of Newfoundland was first seen by him, and sailing thence in a westerly direction, he ranged the coast to Florida. This was in the year 1497—about five years after the first discoveries of Columbus.

In 1584, Queen Elizabeth of England, by patent, granted to Sir Walter Raleigh authority to discover, occupy, and govern " remote, heathen, and barbarous countries." Under this commission, two ships commanded by Amidas and Barlow, arrived in America in July, 1584. These men landed at Roanoke, and took possession of the country for the crown of England, calling it *Virginia*, in honour of the virgin Queen. The next year a company of 107 adventurers, under Sir Richard Grenville, came over to Virginia, and fixed their residence on the islands of Roanoke. The settlers were left here under the command of Mr. Lane. It appears that these persons, by rambling into the country without due caution, or provoking the Indians by their lawless conduct, many of them were killed by the natives, while others perished by want. The survivors were taken to England the next year by Sir Francis Drake. In a fortnight, however, after they had departed, Sir Richard Grenville arrived with provisions, and an additional number of colonists. Not finding the former colonists, he left a few of his people, and returned to England. A third expedition, in 1587, went out under Mr. White with 115 persons, who were left at Roanoke. Three years had elapsed before Gov. White arrived with supplies and an additional number of colonists. Upon their arrival, they found no Englishmen, and it was evident they had been slain by the savages, or perished by hunger. The last adventurers returned disheartened and all farther attempts to establish a colony at that time were laid aside.

Under the authority of the first patent, Capt. Christopher Newport was sent out by the London Company, with a number of adventurers, who entered Cheanpeake bay after a voyage of four months,—sailed into the Powhattan, or James River, and landed 150 colonists, who began a plantation at Jamestown. Newport returned to England, and the next year carried 120 persons, with supplies of provisions.

In 1609, Sir George Somers and Sir Thomas Gates, with 500 adventurers, sailed for Virginia, and finding the colony reduced by sickness and want, they resolved to abandon the country, and actually sailed for England. But meeting the next day Lord Delaware with fresh supplies, they returned, and established the first permanent English Colony in North America.

5. *Pocahontas.*

Among the most enterprising and brave of the Virginia settlers, was Capt. John Smith. Under pretext of commerce, he was drawn into an ambush of a numerous body of Indians, who seized and carried him in triumph to Powhattan their king. Powhattan sentenced him to death.—Capt. Smith was led out, and his head placed upon a large stone, to receive the fatal blow. At this moment, Pocahontas, the youngest and darling daughter of Powhattan, then thirteen years old, rushed to the spot where Capt. Smith lay, threw her arms about his neck, and placed her own head on his, declaring that if the cruel sentence was executed, the first blow should fall on her. The sachem was moved—yielded to the entreaties of his daughter, and consented to spare his victim upon the conditions of a ransom. The ransom was paid—Capt. Smith was then released, and returned, unhurt, to Jamestown.

In 1609, two or three years after Pocahontas saved the life of Capt. Smith, Powhattan formed a horrid scheme for the entire destruction of the colony at Jamestown. His project was to attack them in time of peace and cut the throats of the whole colony.

In a dark and stormy night, Pocahontas, like an angel of mercy, hastened alone to Jamestown, and discovered the inhuman plot of her father. The colonists, thus warned, took proper measures to repel the insidious attack.

Soon after this, Governor Dale concluded a treaty of friendship with the Powhattans, one of the most powerful tribes in Virginia. This important event for the colonies was brought about by means not very honourable to the governor. Pocahontas, who had saved the life of Capt. Smith, persevered in her attachment to the English, and frequently visited the settlements. On one of these occasions, she was decoyed on board a vessel, and there held in confinement. Her father, who loved her with ardent affection, was now obliged to discontinue hostilities, and conclude a treaty on such terms as the colonists dictated. The beauty of Pocahontas made such an impression on Mr. Rolfe, a young gentleman of rank, that he offered her his hand in marriage. Her father consented to the union, and the marriage was celebrated with great pomp; and from that period harmony prevailed between the colony and the tribes subject to Powhattan, or that were under the influence of his power. Rolfe and his princess went to England, and was received at court with the respect due her birth. Here she embraced the Christian religion, and was baptized by the name of Rebecca. She died at Gravesend, in 1617, as she was on the point of embarking for America. "She left one son: from whom are sprung some of the most respectable families in Virginia; who boast of their descent from this celebrated female, the daughter of the ancient rulers of the country."

6. *Plymouth Settlers.*

The colony of Plymouth, Mass., (the first European settlement in New-England,) was planted principally for the sake of the free and undisturbed enjoyment of religious and civil liberty. The colonists were originally from the north of England, and were of that class of people in those days called *Puritans*, so named from their uncommon zeal in endeavouring to preserve the purity of divine worship.

Being persecuted by their enemies, during the reign of James I., they fled with their pastor to Amsterdam, in Holland, in 1608. They afterwards removed to Leyden, where they remained till they sailed for America.

Having resolved upon a removal, they procured two small ships, and repaired to Plymouth, (Eng.,) and from thence they proceeded about 100 leagues on their voyage, when they were compelled to return, in consequence of one of the ships being leaky. The ship was condemned, and the other, called the *May Flower*, being crowded with passengers, again put to sea, September 6: on the 9th of November, after a dangerous passage, they arrived at Cape Cod, and the next day anchored in the harbour which is formed by the hook of the cape.

Before they landed, having devoutly given thanks to God for their safe arrival, they formed themselves into a "body politic," and chose Mr. John Carver their Governor for the first year.

The next object was, to fix on a convenient place for settlement. In doing this, they encountered many difficulties—many of them were sick, in consequence of the fatigues of a long voyage—their provisions were bad—the season was uncommonly cold—the Indians, though afterwards friendly, were now hostile—and they were unacquainted with the coast. These difficulties they surmounted, and on the 22d of December, 1620, they safely landed at a place which they named *Plymouth*. The anniversary of their landing is still celebrated, by the descendants of the *Pilgrims*, as a religious festival.

The whole company that landed consisted of but 101 souls. Their situation and prospects were truly dismal and discouraging. The nearest European settlement was 500 miles distant, and utterly incapable of affording them relief in time of famine or danger. Wherever they turned their eyes, distress was before them. "Persecuted in their native land—grieved for the profanation of the holy Sabbath, and other licentiousness in Holland—fatigued by their long and boisterous voyage—forced on a dangerous and unknown shore in the advance of a cold winter—surrounded with hostile barbarians, without any hope of human succour—denied the aid or favour of the court of England—without a patent—without a public promise of the peaceable enjoyment of their religious liberties—without convenient shelter from the rigours of the weather. Such were the prospects, and such the situation of these pious and solitary Christians. To add to their distress, a very mortal sickness prevailed among them, which swept off forty-six of their number before the ensuing spring.

" To support them under these trials, they had need of all the aids and comforts which Christianity affords; and these were found sufficient. The free and unmolested enjoyment of their religion, reconciled them to their lonely situation—they bore their hardships with unexampled patience, and persevered in their pilgrimage of almost unparalleled trials, with such resignation and calmness, as gave proof of great piety and unconquerable virtue."

7. *Discovery of Indian Corn.*

Before the settlers landed at Plymouth, they sent out a number of parties to explore the country. One of these parties consisted of sixteen men, under Captain Miles Standish. In their route, they discovered several small hillocks, which they conjectured to be the graves of the Indians; but, proceeding still farther, they discovered many more, and, on closer, examination, each hillock was found to contain a considerable quantity of *Indian Corn!* It was buried in the ear, and excited no small degree of their curiosity. By a few of the company i was thought a valuable discovery; others, who had tasted the corn in its raw state, thought it indifferent food, and of but little value.

This corn served them for seed in the ensuing spring. They were instructed by *Squanto*,* a friendly Indian how to raise it, and it was probably the means of preserving them from famine.

---

8. *Massasoit, the Indian Sachem.*

The infant colony of Plymouth was much indebted to the friendship and influence of Massasoit, a powerful prince, or sachem, in those parts. About three months after their establishment, they received a visit from Massasoit, with sixty of his men. They were conducted to the Governor, who received them with military parade. The Governor and Massasoit kissed each other's hands, as a salutation, and both sat down. "*Strong water*" was then given to the sachem, "who drank a great draught, that made him sweat all the while after." After eating, they entered into a friendly treaty. They agreed to avoid injuries on both sides, to restore stolen goods, to assist each other in all just wars, and to endeavour to promote peace and harmony among their neighbours.

* This friend of the English was one of the twenty Indians whom a Capt. Hunt perfidiously carried to Spain, where he sold them for slaves; whence he found his way to London, and afterwards to his native country, with the Plymouth colony. Forgetting the perfidy of those who sold him a captive, he was a warm friend to the English till the day of his death. He rendered an essential service to the English, by inspiring his countrymen with a dread of their power. One of the arts he used for this purpose, was his informing the natives, that the English kept the *plague* buried in a cellar, which was their magazine of powder, which they could send forth to the destruction of Indians, while they remained at home. He died in 1622. A few days before his death, he desired the Governor to pray that he might go to the "Englishman's God" in heaven.

This treaty was faithfully observed by Massasoit and his successors, for more than forty years. At the time of the treaty, he is described as "a very lusty man, in his best years; an able man, grave of countenance and spare of speech; in his attire, little or nothing different from the rest of his followers, only in a great chain of white bone beads about his neck; and at it, behind his neck, hangs a little bag of tobacco. His face was painted with a sad red, like murrey, and oiled both head and face, that he looked greasy. All his followers likewise were, in their faces, in part or in whole, painted, some black, some red, some yellow, and some white: some with crosses and other antic works. Some had skins on them, and some naked; all tall and strong men in appearance. The king had in his bosom, hanging in a string, a great long knife."

In the year 1623, Massasoit was taken sick, and sent information of it to the Governor, who sent two of his friends to make him a visit. Their visit, and the presents which they brought, were gratifying to Massasoit, and the medicines they administered were successful in restoring his health. Gratitude for their kindness prompted him to disclose a conspiracy of the Indians, which had for its object the total destruction of the English. This timely notice averted the calamity.

9. *Exploits of Capt. Standish.*

Capt. Miles Standish, the hero of New-England, came over with the first Plymouth settlers, in 1620. He was allied to the noble house of Standish of Lancashire, (Eng.,) and was heir apparent to a great estate, unjustly detained from him, which compelled him to depend on himself for support.

"He was small in stature, but of an active spirit, a sanguine temper, and a strong constitution." These qualites led him to the profession of arms. He entered into the service of Queen Elizabeth, in the aid of the

Dutch,—and after the truce, he settled with Mr. Robinson's people, in Leyden. When they emigrated to America, he commanded the detachment for making discoveries after their arrival. He was chosen by the settlers as their military commander, and has since been considered as the *Washington* of the Plymouth colony.

One of the most celebrated exploits was the breaking up of a plot, in 1623, which the Indians had formed to murder the English settlers at Wessagusset, now Weymouth. The Governor of Plymouth having learned from Massasoit the plot of the natives, sent Capt. Standish to their relief, and, if a plot should be discovered, to fall on the conspirators. Standish made choice of eight men, refusing to take any more. When he arrived at Wessagusset, he found the settlers scattered, and insensible of the destruction which awaited them. Standish was careful not to excite the jealousy of the natives till he could assemble the people of the plantation. An Indian brought him some furs, whom he treated "smoothly," yet the Indian reported that he "saw by the Captain's eyes that he was angry in his heart." This induced *Pecksuot*, a chief of courage, to tell *Hobbamock*, Standish's guide and interpreter, that he "understood the Captain had come to kill him and the rest of the Indians there; but tell him," said he, "we know it, but fear him not; neither will we shun him; let him begin when he dare, he shall not take us unawares." Others whetted their knives before him, using insulting gestures and speeches. Pecksuot, being a man of great stature, said to Standish, "Though you are a great captain, yet you are but a little man; and though I be no sachem, yet I am a man of great strength and courage." The next day, seeing he could get no more of them together, Pecksuot, and Wittowamat, and his brother, a youth of eighteen, and one Indian more, being together, and having about so many of his own men in the room, he gave the *word*, the door was fast; he seized Pecksuot, snatched his knife from him, and killed him with it; the rest killed Wittowamat and the other Indian. The youth they took and hanged. Dreadful was the scene; incredible the number of wounds they bore; without any noise, catching at the weapons, and striving till death.*

10. *First Settlements in Connecticut.*

In 1635, October 15th, about sixty men, women, and children, from Dorchester, Mass., with their horses, and cattle, and swine, took up their march across the wilderness to Connecticut River. Their dangerous journey, over mountains and rivers, and through swamps, they were two weeks in performing. "The forests through which they passed, for the first time resounded with the praises of God. They prayed and sang psalms and hymns; the Indians following them in silent admiration." It was so late in the season when they reached the place (now called Windsor) of their destination, that they were unable to find feed for their cattle, most of which died the ensuing winter.

Disappointed in receiving their provisions, famine threatened them; and those who remained through the winter, were obliged to subsist on acorns, malt, and grains.

The congregation at Newton, (now Cambridge,) consisting of about one hundred men, women, and children, with the Rev. Mr. Hooker, their pastor, at their head, also emigrated more than one hundred miles, through a howling wilderness, to Hartford. They had no guide but their compass: on their way they subsisted on milk, for they drove before them one hundred and sixty head of cattle. They were obliged to carry Mrs. Hooker upon a litter.

They began a plantation, and called it *Newtown*, which name was afterwards exchanged for Hartford.

In the fall of 1637, a small party from Massachusetts journeyed to Connecticut to explore the lands and harbours on the sea-coast. They chose *Quinnipiac* for

---
* Morse and Parish's Hist.

the place of their settlement, and erected a poor hut, in which a few men subsisted through the winter. And on the 30th of March following, a large party sailed from Boston for *Quinnipiac*, where they arrived in about two weeks. This began the settlement of New-Haven.

---

11. *Blue Laws of Connecticut.*

The following is a transcript of the principal part of the celebrated judicial code, known by the name of *Blue Laws*, under which, it is said, the first colonists of Connecticut remained for a considerable time. They are as follows:

"The Governor and magistrates, convened in general assembly, are the supreme power, under God, of this independent dominion.

From the determination of the assembly no appeal shall be made.

The Governor is amenable to the voice of the people.

The Governor shall have only a single vote in determining any question, except a casting vote when the assembly may be equally divided.

The assembly of the people shall not be dismissed by the Governor, but shall dismiss itself.

Conspiracy against this dominion shall be punished with death.

Whoever attempts to change or overturn this dominion, shall suffer death.

The Judges shall determine controversies without a Jury.

No one shall be a freeman, or give a vote, unless he be converted, or a member in free communion in one of the churches in this dominion.

No food or lodging shall be afforded to a Quaker, Adamite, or other heretic.

No one shall cross a river without an authorized ferry man.

No one shall run of a Sabbath day, or walk in his garden, or elsewhere, except reverently to and from the church.

No one shall travel, cook victuals, make beds, sweep houses, cut hair, or shave, on the Sabbath day.

No woman shall kiss her child on the Sabbath or fasting day.

A person accused of trespass in the night, shall be judged guilty, unless he clear himself by his oath.

No one shall buy or sell lands without permission of the select men.

Whoever publishes a lie to the prejudice of his neighbour, shall sit in the stocks, or be whipped fifteen stripes.

Whoever wears clothes trimmed with silver, or bone lace, above two shillings a yard, shall be presented by the grand jurors, and the select men shall tax the offender at the rate of 300$l.$ estate.

Whoever brings cards or dice into this dominion shall pay a fine of 5$l.$

No one shall read Common Prayer, keep Christmas or Saint's day, make minced pies, dance, play cards, or play on any instrument of music, except the drum, the trumpet, and jews-harp.

When parents refuse their children suitable marriages, the magistrates shall determine the point.

The select men, on finding children ignorant, may take them away from their parents and put them into better hands, at the expense of the parents.

A man that strikes his wife shall pay a fine of 10$l.$; a woman that strikes her husband shall be punished as the court directs.

Married persons must live together, or be imprisoned.

Every male shall have his hair cut round according to a cap."

This curious code appears never to have been written, but was declared and interpreted by the select men, the judges, and the pastors of the different congregations.*

In 1647 the colony of Connecticut passed a law for the regulation or suppression of the use of tobacco. It

* Analectic Magazine, vol. 1, p. 57.

was ordered by the general Assembly "That no person under the age of twenty, or any other who had not already accustomed himself to the use of it, should take any tobacco until he had obtained a certificate from under the hand of an approved physician that it was useful for him, and until he had also obtained a license from the court. All others, who had addicted themselves to the use of it, were prohibited from taking it in any company, or at their labours, or in travelling, unless ten miles, at least, from any company; and though not in company not more than once a day, upon pain of six-pence for every such offence. One substantial witness was to be sufficient proof of the crime. The Constables of the several towns were to make presentments to the particular courts, and it was ordered that the fine should be paid without gainsaying."

In 1658, the general court of New-Haven passed a severe law against the Quakers. They introduced their law with this preamble—"Whereas there is a cursed sect of heretics lately sprung up in the world, commonly called Quakers, who take upon them that they are immediately sent from God, and infallibly assisted by the Spirit, who yet speak and write blasphemous opinions, despise government, and the order of God in church and commonwealth, speaking evil of dignities, &c.," ordered—"That whosoever shall bring, or cause to be brought, any known Quaker or Quakers, or other blasphemous heretics, shall forfeit the sum of 50l." Also, "If any Quaker come into this jurisdiction on civil business, the time of his stay shall be limited by the civil authority, and he shall not use any means to corrupt or seduce others; on his first arrival he shall appear before the magistrate, and from him have license to pass on to his business. And (for the better prevention of hurt to the people) have one or more to attend upon them at their charge, &c."

The penalties, in case of disobedience, were, whipping, imprisonment, labour, and a deprivation of all converse with any person. For the second offence, the person was to be branded in the hand with the letter

H—to suffer imprisonment—and to be put to labour. For the third, to be branded in the other hand, imprisoned, &c. as before. For the fourth, the offender was to have his tongue bored through with a red hot iron—imprisoned—and kept to labour, until sent away at their own charge. Any person who should attempt to defend the sentiments of the Quakers, was, for the third offence, sentenced to banishment.*

---

12. *Earthquakes.*

The first Earthquake since the settlement of this country, took place in New England, on the first day of June, 1638. The earth shook with such violence, that in some places, the people could not stand, without difficulty, in the streets; and most moveable articles in their houses were thrown down.† It occurred between the hours of three and four, P. M. The weather was clear and warm, and the wind westerly. "It came with a noise like continued thunder, or the rattling of coaches in London, but was presently gone." It was felt at Massachusetts, Connecticut, Narraganset, Piscataqua, and the circumjacent parts. It shook the ships which rode in Boston harbour, and all the adjacent islands. "The noise and shaking continued about four minutes. The earth was unquiet twenty days after by times."‡

On Jan. 6th, 1663, a great earthquake was felt in the northern parts of America. It was felt throughout New England and New Netherlands, (now New York;) but Canada was the chief seat of its concussions. It be-

---

* Though these severe laws cannot be justified, yet we ought to make much allowance for the framers of these laws: they endured many hardships, privations, and sufferings, in order to establish a settlement in the wilderness, and a civil and religious government, under which they could enjoy their civil and religious privileges in peace and tranquillity. The principles of the Quakers were considered by the Colonists not only as destructive to true religion, but also destructive to their civil government, and hazarding their existence as a people.

† Holmes' Annals.   ‡ Winthrop's Journal.

gan there about half past five o'clock, P. M. While the heavens were serene, there was suddenly heard a roar like that of fire. The buildings were shaken with violence. "The doors opened and shut themselves—the bells rang without being touched—the walls split asunder—the floors separated and fell down—the fields put on the appearance of precipices—and the mountains seemed moving out of their places." The first shock continued nearly half an hour. Several violent shocks succeeded this the same evening, and the next day; nor did the earthquake cease till the following July. The effects of the first, in January, were remarkable. "Many fountains and small streams were dried up. In others, the water became sulphurous. Many trees were torn up, and thrown to a considerable distance; and some mountains appeared to be much moved and broken."

On the 29th of October, 1727, there was a great earthquake in New England. This earthquake commenced with a heavy rumbling noise about half past ten o'clock, P. M. when the weather was perfectly calm and tranquil. The motion was undulatory. Its violence caused the houses to shake and rock, as if they were falling to pieces. Stone walls, and the tops of several chimneys, were shaken down. The duration appears to have been about two minutes. Its course appears to have been from northeast to southwest.

The most violent earthquake ever known in this country, took place November 18th, 1755. It was felt at Boston a little after four o'clock, in a serene and pleasant night, and continued nearly four and a half minutes. In Boston, about one hundred chimneys were levelled with the roofs of the houses; and about fifteen hundred shattered and thrown down in part. Many clocks were stopped. "At New-Haven, the ground, in many places, seemed to rise like the sea; and the houses shook and cracked." The motion of the earthquake was undulatory. Its course was nearly from northwest to southeast

Slight shocks of earthquakes have occurred in many instances since the first settlement of this country.

13. *Indian Cunning and Sagacity.*

The Indians have ever been remarkable for their cunning and sagacity.

The following will serve to illustrate this part of their character.

A Pequot Indian, in time of war, was pursued by a Narraganset. Finding it difficult to escape, he had recourse to the following stratagem. Retiring behind a rock, he elevated his hat upon his gun just above the rock, so that nothing but his hat appeared. The Narraganset, who was some distance off, perceiving this, crept up softly, within a few feet, and fired, and supposed that he had shot his enemy through the head. But he soon found out his mistake, for the Pequot immediately sprung around the rock, and shot him before he had time to load his gun.

Such is the sagacity and habits of nice observation which an Indian possesses, that it is said, he can tell whether his enemy has passed any place—will discern foot-marks which an European could not see; he will tell what tribe it was, and what were their numbers.

On the smoothest grass, on the hardest earth, and even on the very stones, will he discern traces. In the pursuit of game they will track their prey in the same manner, and see which way to go in pursuit.

14. *Expedition against the Pequots.*

The year 1637 is memorable in the history of Connecticut for the war with the Pequot Indians—one of the most warlike and haughty tribes in New England. Previous to the breaking out of the war, the Pequots had much annoyed the English, and murdered a number of them, whereupon a court was summoned at Hartford who determined upon a war with the Pequots. Ninety men were mustered from the towns of Hartford,

Windsor, and Wethersfield, being about half of the effective force of the whole colony. This expedition was commanded by Capt. Mason, assisted by Capt. Underhill. Previous to their marching, the Rev. Mr. Hooker, of Hartford, addressed them in the following manner:

"Fellow Soldiers, Countrymen, and Companions, you are this day assembled by the special Providence of God; you are not collected by wild fancy, nor ferocious passions. It is not a tumultuous assembly, whose actions are aborted, or if successful, produce only theft, rapine, rape, and murder: crimes inconsistent with nature's light, inconsistent with a soldier's valour. You, my dear hearts, were selected from your neighbours, by the godly fathers of the land, for your known courage to execute such a work.

"Your cause is the cause of heaven; the enemy have blasphemed your God, and slain his servants; you are only the ministers of his justice. I do not pretend that your enemies are careless or indifferent; no, their hatred is inflamed, their lips thirst for blood; they would devour you, and all the people of God; but, my brave soldiers, their guilt has reached the clouds; they are ripe for destruction; their cruelty is notorious; and cruelty and cowardice are always united.

"There is nothing, therefore, to prevent your certain victory, but their nimble feet, their impenetrable swamps and woods; from these your small numbers will entice them, or your courage drive them. I now put the question—Who would not fight in such a cause? figh with undaunted boldness? Do you wish for more en couragement? more I give you. Riches awaken th soldier's sword; and though you will not obtain silver and gold on the field of victory, you will secure wha is indefinitely more precious; you will secure the *liberties, the privileges, and the lives of Christ's Church in this new world.*

"You will procure safety for your affectionate wives, safety for your prattling, harmless, smiling babes; you will secure all the blessings enjoyed by the people of

God in the ordinances of the gospel. Distinguished was the honour conferred upon David, for fighting the battles of the Lord: this honour, O ye courageous soldiers of God, is now prepared for you. You will now execute his vengeance on the heathen; you will bind their kings in chains, and their nobles in fetters of iron.

"But perhaps some one may fear that a fatal arrow may deprive him of this honour. Let every faithful soldier of Jesus Christ be assured, that if any servant be taken away, it is merely because the honours of this world are too narrow for his reward; an everlasting crown is set upon his head, because the rewards of this life are insufficient. March, then, with Christian courage, in the strength of the Lord; march with faith in his divine promises, and soon your swords shall find your enemies; soon they shall fall like leaves of the forest under your feet."

Being now joined by *Uncas*, the sachem of the Mohegans, they all proceeded down the river to Saybrook, where they formed their plan of operations. It was determined to attack the enemy in one of their principal forts, (in the present town of Stonington,) where Sassacus, their chief sachem, had retired. Previous to the attack, Capt. Mason was joined by about five hundred Narraganset Indians, who, when they understood that they were to fight Sassacus, betrayed much fear, and retired to the rear, saying, "*Sassacus was all one a god, and nobody could kill him.*"

The time fixed at length arrived—the dawn of the 26th of May, which was to decide the fate of the colony of Connecticut. The barking of a dog, when within a few rods of the fort, announced their approach, and aroused the Pequot sentinel, who cried out, *Owannux! Owannux!* i. e. Englishmen! Englishmen! The captains, followed by their men, courageously pressed forward, found an entrance, and fired upon the enemy in the fort, who made a desperate resistance. The destruction of the Pequots was terrible, yet the victory seemed doubtful. Captain Mason (who with his men were now nearly exhausted) seized a firebrand, and set fire to a wigwam, of which there were many in the fort, covered with mats and other combustible materials. The fire, assisted by the wind, spread rapidly, and directly the whole fort was in a flame. The roar and crackling of the flames, with the yells of savages, and the discharge of musketry, formed an awful and terrific scene! The troops who had now formed outside of the fort, with the friendly Indians, who had by this time gathered courage to approach, surrounded the enemy, and fired upon those who attempted to escape.

The work of destruction was complete; of five or six hundred Pequots, only seven or eight escaped—the rest were either shot or perished in the flames. The loss of the English was only two killed, and sixteen wounded.

15. *Elliot, the Indian Missionary.*

In 1650, the society in England, instituted for propagating the gospel, began a correspondence with the commissioners of the colonies of New-England, who were employed as agents of the society. In consequence, exertions were made to christianize the Indians. Mr. John Elliot, minister of Roxbury, distinguished himself in this pious work. He collected the Indian families, and established towns; he taught them husbandry, the mechanic arts, and a prudent management of their affairs, and instructed them with unwearied attention, in the principles of Christianity. For his uncommon zeal and success, he has been called the *Apostle of New-England.*

Mr. Elliot began his labours about the year 1646. His first labour was to learn the language, which was peculiarly difficult to acquire; for instance, the Indian word *Nammatchechodtantamoonganunnonash,* signifies no more in English than *our lusts.** Elliot having finished a grammar of this tongue, at the close of which he wrote, "*Prayers and pains through faith in Jesus*

* Mather's Magnalia, Vol. I.

Christ will do any thing!" With very great labour he translated the whole Bible into the Indian language. This Bible was printed in 1664, at Cambridge, and was the first Bible ever printed in America. He also translated the *Practice of Piety, Baxter's Call to the Unconverted,* besides some smaller works, into the Indian tongue. Having performed many wearisome journeys, and endured many hardships and privations, this indefatigable missionary closed his labours in 1690, aged eighty-six years.

The ardour and zeal of Elliot, Mayhew, and others, were crowned with such success. that in 1660, there were ten towns of Indians in Massachusetts who were converted to the Christian religion. In 1695, there were not less than three thousand adult converts in the islands of Nantucket and Martha's Vineyard.

---

16. *King Philip's War.*

(ATTACK ON BROOKFIELD.)

In the year 1675, Philip, sachem of the Wampanoags, and grandson of Massasoit, began the most destructive war ever waged by the Indians upon the infant colonies. He resided at Mount Hope, in the present town of Bristol, in Rhode Island.

It is supposed that his object was the entire extinction of the colonists, who were now rapidly extending their settlements. The immediate cause of the war was this: Sausaman, an Indian missionary,* had made a discovery of Philip's plots to the English, for which Philip caused him to be murdered. The murderers were tried and executed by the English. This roused the anger of Philip, who immediately commenced hostilities, and by

---

* Philip always opposed the introduction of Christianity among his people. When Mr. Elliot urged upon him its great importance, he said, "he cared no more for the Gospel than he did for a button upon his coat."—*Mather's Magnalia.*

his influence, drew into the war most of the Indian tribes in New-England.

Philip fled to the Nipmucks, a tribe of Indians in that part of Massachusetts which is now called Worcester county, and persuaded them to assist him. The English sent a party also to this tribe, to renew a former treaty; but Philip's influence prevailed, and this party were waylaid, and eight of their number killed. The remainder fled to Brookfield, pursued by the Indians into the town. Every house in this place was burnt by the Indians except one, into which the inhabitants had fled for refuge; and this was soon surrounded by their foes, and for two days they poured into its walls a shower of musket balls. Only one person, however, was killed. Brands and rags, dipped in brimstone, attached to the ends of long poles, were used to fire the house; arrows of fire were shot against it; and a carriage of tow and other combustibles, was with long poles, pushed against the house, and the savages stood ready to slaughter all who should attempt to escape.

At this awful and critical moment, a sudden torrent of rain extinguished the kindling flames. Major Willard soon after came to their assistance, raised the siege, and, after some slaughter of the enemy, compelled them to retreat.

---

17. *Swamp Fight with the Narragansets.*

Lest Philip should increase his power, by an alliance with the Narraganset Indians, the English had made a friendly treaty with them in July, 1675. But notwithstanding this, in December of the same year, it was discovered that they were secretly aiding Philip's party. This determined the English to undertake a winter expedition against them. For this object, the colony of Massachusetts furnished five hundred and twenty-seven men, Plymouth one hundred and fifty-nine, and Connecticut three hundred; to all these were attached one hundred and fifty Mohegan Indians. After electing Josiah Winslow, Governor of Plymouth colony, to be their commander, the whole party met at Pettyquamsquot. About sixteen miles from this place, it was found that the Narragansets had built a strong fort in the midst of a large swamp, upon a piece of dry land of about five or six acres. The fort was a circle of pallisadoes surrounded by a fence of trees, which was about one rod thick.

On the 19th of December, 1675, at dawn of day, the English took up their march through a deep snow, and at 4 o'clock in the afternoon attacked the Indians in their fortress. The only entrance which appeared practicable was over a log, or tree, which lay up five or six feet from the ground, and this opening was commanded by a sort of a block house in front. The Massachusetts men, led on by their captains, first rushed into the fort, but the enemy, from the block house and other places, opened so furious a fire upon them, that they were obliged to retreat. Many men were killed in this assault, and among them Captains Johnson and Davenport. The whole army then made a united onset. The conflict was terrible. Some of the bravest captains fell, and victory seemed very doubtful. At this crisis some of the Connecticut men ran to the opposite side of the fort, where there were no pallisadoes; they sprang in, and opened a brisk and well directed fire upon the backs of the enemy. This decided the contest. The Indians were driven from the block house, and from one covert to another, until they were wholly destroyed or dispersed in the wilderness. As they retreated, the soldiers set fire to their wigwams, (about six hundred in number,) which were consumed by the flames. In this action it was computed that about seven hundred fighting Indians perished, and among them twenty of their chiefs. Three hundred more died from their wounds;—to these numbers may be added many old men, women, and children, who had retired to this fort as a place of undoubted security.

"The burning of the wigwams, the **shrieks of the**

women and children, the yelling of the warriors, exhibited a most horrid and affecting scene, so that it greatly moved some of the soldiers. They were much in doubt whether the burning of their enemies alive could be consistent with humanity and the benevolent principles of the gospel."

From this blow the Indians never recovered. The victory of the English, though complete, was dearly purchased: six of their captains, and eighty of their men, were killed or mortally wounded; and one hundred and fifty were wounded and afterwards recovered. About one half of the loss of this bloody fight fell upon the Connecticut soldiers.

18. *Death of King Philip.*

The finishing stroke was given to the Indian power in New-England, by the death of Philip, August 12th, 1676.

Failing in his attempts to rouse the *Mohawk* tribe to war with the English, he returned to Mount Hope— the tide of war against him. The English had killed or captured his brother, counsellors, and chief warriors, his wife and family, and he was obliged to flee from one lurking place to another, from the pursuit of his foes. Firm and unbroken amidst all his misfortunes, he would listen to no proposals of peace. He even shot one of his own men for daring to suggest it.

Captain Church, who, for his courage and enterprise in this war, had acquired renown, received information that Philip was in a swamp near Mount Hope. To this place he marched immediately, with a party of men, whom he placed in ambush about the swamp, with orders not to move until daylight, that they might distinguish Philip. Captain Church, confident of success, took Major Sanford by the hand, exclaiming, "It is scarcely possible that Philip should escape;" at this moment a bullet whistled over their heads, and a volley followed. Immediately Philip, with his powder horn and gun, ran fiercely towards a spot where lay concealed a white man and a friendly Indian. The Englishman levelled his gun at Philip, but it missed fire. The Indian ally then fired. The bullet entered the heart of Philip, and he fell on his face in the mire of the swamp. By the order of Captain Church, his body was drawn from the place where he fell, and beheaded and quartered.* The Indian who executed this order, taking his hatchet, thus addressed the body of Philip:—"You have been one very great man—you have made a many a man afraid of you—but so big as you be, I will chop you in pieces."

"Thus fell a brave chieftain, who defended himself, and what he imagined to be the just rights of his countrymen, to the last extremity."

After the death of Philip, the war continued in the province of Maine, till the spring of 1678. But westward, the Indians having lost their chiefs, wigwams and provisions, and perceiving farther contest vain, came in singly, and by tens, and by hundreds, and submitted to the English.

Thus closed a melancholy period in the annals of New-England history; during which, 600 men, in the flower of their strength, had fallen; 12 or 13 towns had been destroyed, and 600 dwelling houses consumed. Every 11th family was houseless, and every 11th soldier had sunk to the grave.†

---

19. *Bacon's Insurrection in Virginia.*

Virginia, while a colony of Great Britain, often suffered from the oppressive acts of the mother country, and their essential interests were often sacrificed to individuals in Great Britain. These proceedings gave

* The head of Philip was sent to Plymouth, where it was exposed for twenty years on a gibbet; his hands to Boston, where they were exhibited in triumph; and his mangled body was denied the right of sepulture.

† Goodrich.

rise to a spirit of opposition in many of the colonists, which sometimes broke out into open acts of resistance.

"The malcontents in Virginia, in 1676, taking advantage of a war with the Susquehanna Indians, excited the people to insurrection. Nathaniel Bacon, a bold, seditious, and eloquent young man, who had been concerned in a recent insurrection, now offered himself as a leader of the insurgents, was chosen their general, and soon after entered Jamestown with six hundred armed followers. Having besieged the grand assembly, then convened in the capital, he compelled them to grant whatever he demanded. On finding himself denounced, after his departure, as a rebel, by a proclamation of Governor Berkely, he returned indignantly to Jamestown. The aged governor, unsupported, and almost abandoned, fled precipitately to Accomack, on the eastern shore of the colony; and collecting those who were well affected towards his government, began to oppose the insurgents. Several skirmishes were fought, with various success. A party of the insurgents burned Jamestown. Those districts of the colony which adhered to the old administration, were laid waste. The estates of the loyalists were confiscated. Women, whose fathers and husbands obeyed what they deemed the legal government, were carried forcibly along with the soldiers. The governor, in retaliation, seized the estates of many of the insurgents, and executed several of their leaders by martial law. In the midst of these calamities, Bacon, the author of them, sickened and died; and the flames of war expired. This rebellion cost the colony one hundred thousand pounds.*

---

20. *The Regicides.*

Soon after the restoration of monarchy in England, many of the judges who had condemned King Charles I. to death, were apprehended. Thirty were condemned,

* Holmes' Annals.

and ten were executed as traitors; two of them, Colonels Goffe and Whalley, made their escape to New-England, and arrived at Boston, July, 1660. They were gentlemen of worth, and were much esteemed by the colonists for their unfeigned piety. Their manners and appearance were dignified, commanding universal respect. Whalley had been a Lieutenant General, and Goffe, a Major General in Cromwell's army. An order for their apprehension, from Charles II., reached New-England soon after their arrival. The King's commissioners, eager to execute this order, compelled the Judges to resort to the woods and caves, and other hiding places; and they would undoubtedly have been taken, had not the colonists secretly aided and assisted them in their concealments. Sometimes they found a refuge in a cave on a mountain near New-Haven, and at others, in cellars of the houses of their friends, and once they were secreted under the Neck bridge in New-Haven, while their pursuers crossed the bridge on horseback.

While in New-Haven, they owed their lives to the intrepidity of Mr. Davenport, the minister of the place, who, when the pursuers arrived, preached to the people from this text, "*Take council, execute judgment, make thy shadow as the night in the midst of the noon day, hide the outcasts, bewray not him that wandereth. Let my outcasts dwell with thee. Moab, be thou a covert to them from the face of the spoiler.*" Large rewards were offered for their apprehension, or for any information which might lead to it. Mr. Davenport was threatened, for it was known that he had harboured them. Upon hearing that he was in danger, they offered to deliver themselves up, and actually gave notice to the deputy governor of the place of their concealment; but Davenport had not preached in vain, and the magistrate took no other notice than to advise them not to betray themselves. After lurking about for two or three years in and near New-Haven, they found it necessary to remove to Hadley,* where they were received by Mr.

* While Goffe was secreted in Hadley, in 1675, the Indians attacked the town while the inhabitants were at public worship. The peo-

Russell, with whom they were concealed fifteen or sixteen years. After many hair-breadth escapes, the pursuit was given over, and they were finally suffered to die a natural death in their exile.

21. *William Penn.*

The territory of Pennsylvania was granted to William Penn, from whom it derives its name. This grant was made by King Charles II. of England, in 1681, in consideration of service rendered to the crown by the father of Penn, who was an admiral in the English navy. In October, 1682, William Penn arrived in the Delaware, with his colony of Friends or Quakers. He purchased of the natives the land where he proposed to build his capital, which he called Philadelphia, or the *seat of brotherly love.* William Penn gave the Indians a satisfactory equivalent for all lands which he obtained: and when he paid them, he administered such wholesome counsel and advice, as proved salutary to the natives, and greatly endeared him to their affections. The treaty of peace which he concluded with them in 1682, lasted more than seventy years. He parcelled out lands at moderate rents, gave free toleration to all religious sects, enacted mild and equitable laws, and thus invited a rapid settlement of the colony. The respect and affection which the natives had for Penn, and those of his religious tenets, was so great, that it is related as a fact, that in their wars with the whites, they never killed a *Quaker*, knowing him to be such.

Though Penn was a strictly conscientious and peace-

---

ple were thrown into the utmost confusion, till Goffe, entirely unknown to them, white with age, of a venerable and commanding aspect, and in an unusual dress, suddenly presented himself among them, encouraging the affrighted inhabitants, put himself at their head, and by his military skill, led them on to an immediate victory. After the dispersion of the enemy, he instantly disappeared. The wondering inhabitants, alike ignorant whence he came, and where he had retired, imagined him to be an angel sent for their deliverance.—*Stiles' Hist. Judges.*

able man, and the people he brought to Pennsylvania were in general orderly and well disposed, yet there existed almost constantly bickerings. He three times altered the form of government for the satisfaction of the people. Notwithstanding all the efforts which he made, there seldom was an harmonious feeling between the people and their governor. From the difficulties in Pennsylvania, and the opposition he met with in England, Penn's life was a scene of vexation. In order to promote the infant settlement, and to preserve harmony with the Indians, he materially injured his private fortune. For a time he was deprived of his personal liberty by his creditors. But though he was necessitous during his life, yet at its termination he was wealthy. He died at London in 1718, at the age of 74; leaving an inheritance to his children, which ultimately proved of immense value; which they possessed till the Revolution, when it was assigned to the commonwealth for an equitable sum in money.

22. *Tyranny of Andros.*

In the year 1684, it was decided in the high court of Chancery, that Massachusetts had forfeited her charter, and that henceforth her government should be placed in the hands of the King. This event was brought about chiefly by the instrumentality of Edmund Andros. This man had been sent over as a kind of spy on the colonies; he made it his business to collect charges against the colonies, and return to England and excite the jealousy of the British government. In this manner, the way was prepared for annulling the colonial charters. In December, 1686, Andros arrived at Boston, being commissioned, by King James, as Governor General, and Vice-Admiral, over New-England, New-York, and the Jerseys. Like all tyrants, Sir Edmund began his administration with professions of high *regard for the public welfare.* In a few months, however, the prospect was changed. The press was restrained, liberty of conscience infringed, and exorbitant taxes were levied. The charters being vacated, it was pretended all titles to land were destroyed; farmers, therefore, who had cultivated their soil for half a century, were obliged to take new patents, giving large fees, or writs of intrusion were brought, and their lands sold to others. To prevent petitions or consultations, town meetings were prohibited, excepting once in a year for the choice of town officers. Lest cries of oppression should reach the throne, he forbade any to leave the country without permission from the government.*

In 1689, King James having abdicated the throne, William, Prince of Orange, and Mary, daughter of James, were proclaimed in February. A report of the landing of William in England, reached Boston, but before the news of the entire revolution in the British government arrived, a most daring one was effected in New-England.

The Colonists had borne the impositions of Andros' government about three years. Their patience was now exhausted. On the morning of April 18th, the public fury burst forth like a volcano. The inhabitants of Boston were in arms, and the people from the country poured in to their assistance. Andros and his associates fled to a fort; resistance was in vain, he was made a prisoner, and sent to England.

---

23. *Preservation of the Charter of Connecticut.*

Sir Edmund Andros being appointed the first governor General over New-England, arrived at Boston in December, 1686. From this place he wrote to the colony of Connecticut to resign their charter, but without success. "The Assembly met as usual, in October, and the government continued according to charter, until the last of the month. About this time, Sir Edmund, with his suite, and more than sixty regular

* Morse's Hist. New-England.

troops, came to Hartford when the assembly were sitting, and demanded the charter, and declared the government under it to be dissolved. The assembly were extremely reluctant and slow with respect to any resolve to surrender the charter, or with respect to any motion to bring it forth. The tradition is, that Governor Treat strongly represented the great expense and hardships of the colonists in planting the country; the blood and treasure which they had expended in defending it, both against the savages and foreigners; to what hardships and dangers he himself had been exposed for that purpose; and that it was like giving up his life, now to surrender the patent and privileges so dearly bought, and so long enjoyed. The important affair was debated and kept in suspense until the evening, when the charter was brought and laid upon the table, where the assembly were sitting. By this time great numbers of people were assembled, and men sufficiently bold to enterprise whatever might be necessary or expedient. The lights were instantly extinguished, and one Captain Wadsworth, of Hartford, in the most silent and secret manner, carried off the charter, and secreted it in a large hollow tree, fronting the house of Hon. Samuel Wyllys, then one of the magistrates of the colony. The people appeared all peaceable and orderly. The candles were officiously relighted, but the patent was gone, and no discovery could be made of it, or the person who carried it away. Sir Edmund assumed the government, and the records of the colony were closed in the following words:

"At a General Court at Hartford, Oct. 31st, 1687, his excellency Sir Edmund Andros, knight, and captain general and governor of his Majesty's territories and dominions in New-England, by order of his Majesty James II. King of England, Scotland, France, and Ireland, the 31st of October, 1687, took into his hands the government of the Colony of Connecticut, it being by his majesty annexed to Massachusetts, and other colonies under his Excellency's government. FINIS."*

* Trumbull's Hist. Connecticut.

24. *Destruction of Schenectady.*

In the war between England and France, in the year 1689, the French, who then possessed Canada, instigated the Indians to hostilities against the Colonies. A detachment of between two and three hundred French and Indians, were sent from Montreal against the frontiers of New-York. A march of more than twenty days, in the depth of winter, brought them to Schenectady, February 18th, 1690.

In this march they had been reduced to such straits, that they had thoughts of surrendering themselves prisoners of war. But their scouts brought them information that the inhabitants were in a state of unsuspecting security. Upon this they determined to attack them. On Saturday night, about eleven o'clock, they entered the town through an unguarded point, and that they might invest every house at the same time, they divided into parties of six or seven men each. The inhabitants were in a profound sleep, and unalarmed, until the enemy had broken open their doors. In this dreadful surprise and consternation, successful resistance was impossible; and this wretched people were aroused from their midnight slumbers, to endure the perpetration of savage and inhuman barbarities, too shocking to record. Sixty of the inhabitants were killed, and twenty taken off captives. To crown their work, the enemy set on fire the village, killed most of the cattle and horses, and those which they spared, they drove off laden with plunder. Those of the people who escaped, fled, almost naked, through a deep snow, and in a heavy storm; twenty-five of whom lost the use of their limbs by the severe frost.

25. *First culture of Rice in the Colonies.*

The planting of Rice was introduced into Carolina about the year 1695. Incidents, apparently small, are often productive of important consequences. A brigantine from Madagascar, touching at Carolina on her way to Great Britain, came to anchor off Sullivan's Island. Landgrave Smith, on invitation of the Captain, paid him a visit on board his vessel, and received from him a present of a bag of seed rice, with information of its growth in eastern countries; of its suitableness for food; and of its incredible increase. The Governor divided his bag of rice among some of his friends; who, agreeing to make an experiment, planted their parcels in different soils. The success fully equalled their expectation; and from this small beginning arose the staple commodity of Carolina, which soon became the chief support of the Colony, and the great source of its opulence.*

---

26. *Salem Witchcraft.*

The year 1692 is memorable in New-England for the convulsion produced in Salem, and its vicinity, by the supposed prevalence of *witchcraft*. Many were supposed to be *bewitched*, and would complain of being bitten, pinched, pricked with pins, &c.; some declared that they beheld a spectral representation of the person whom they said was the cause of their affliction. Some were struck dumb, others had their limbs distorted in a shocking manner, sometimes running on their hands and feet, creeping through holes, and under chairs, tables, &c.; barking like a dog, with other actions equally strange and unaccountable. Upon the accusation and testimony of persons thus afflicted, many were imprisoned, and nineteen were executed for *practising witchcraft*, most of whom died professing their innocence.†

---

* Holmes' Annals.
† A cotemporary writer observes: "As to the method which the Salem justices do take in their examinations, it is truly this: A warrant being issued out to apprehend the persons that are charged and complained of by the afflicted children, as they are called, said persons are brought before the justices, the afflicted being present. The justices ask the apprehended why they afflict those poor children

The evil became awfully alarming; the most respectable persons in the country were accused; but the magistrates finally acquitted those who were accused, and the menacing storm blew over, to the great joy of the inhabitants.

At this period, many learned and eminent men, both in England and America, fully believed in the existence of witchcraft. Sir Matthew Hale, one of the brightest ornaments of the English bench, repeatedly tried and condemned persons as criminals, who were brought before him, charged with this crime. It must be confessed, that notwithstanding all the obloquy and contempt which is now cast upon our forefathers, for believing in the existence of witchcraft, many things took place at that time, (if we can credit the accounts given by many respectable witnesses,) which would be extremely difficult to account for, on natural principles.

---

27. *Captain Kidd, the Pirate.*

Capt. Robert Kidd, in the beginning of King William's war, commanded a privateer in the West Indies, and by several adventurous actions acquired the reputation of a brave man, as well as an experienced seaman. About this time the pirates were very troublesome in those parts; whereupon Capt. Kidd was recommended by Lord Bellamont, (then governor of Barbadoes,) to the British government, as a person very fit to be intrusted with the command of a government ship, for the purpose of suppressing piracy. The proposal, how-

to which the apprehended answer, they do not afflict them. The justices order the apprehended to look upon the said children, which accordingly they do; and at the time of that look (I dare not say *by* that look, as the Salem gentlemen do,) the afflicted are cast into a fit. The apprehended are then blinded, and ordered to touch the afflicted; and at that touch, though not *by* that touch, (as above,) the afflicted do ordinarily come out of their fits. The afflicted persons then declare and affirm that the apprehended have afflicted them; upon which the apprehended persons, though of never so good repute, are forthwith committed to prison, on suspicion of witchcraft."

ever, through some cause, met with no encouragement from the government; whereupon Lord Bellamont, and some others, who knew of great captures which had been made by the pirates, and what prodigious wealth must be in their possession, were tempted to fit out a ship at their own private charge, and to give the command of her to Capt. Kidd; and to give the thing a greater reputation, as well as to keep their seamen under better command, they procured the king's commission for Capt. Kidd. This commission was dated at Kensington, Jan. 26, 1695, in the seventh year of the reign of King William the third. Kidd having received this commission for the suppression of piracy, sailed from Plymouth, England, in the Adventure galley, of 30 guns and 80 men; and arrived in New York, where he had a family. Here he held out great encouragement for others to join him, and he soon increased his company to 155 men.

With this company he proceeded to the Madeiras, and the Cape Verd Islands, and from thence to the East Indies, in order to suppress piracies. After having cruised about in those seas for some time without any success, he formed the resolution of becoming pirate himself. Finding his crew not averse to such a course, they accordingly commenced the practice of robbing. After having taken a number of rich prizes, Kidd returned to America, and, landing at Boston openly, he was taken, sent to England, and executed at Execution Dock, with six of his companions, and afterwards hung in chains, at some distance from each other, down the river, where their bodies hung exposed for many years.

The remembrance of Capt. Kidd is kept alive in the eastern states by the circumstance of his having buried large sums of money, it is believed, somewhere on the coast. There have been many attempts made to discover this treasure by digging, &c. at various places: how much of it has been found, or whether there has been any found at all, is a matter which it would be difficult to ascertain.

28. *Great Snow Storm.*

In February, 1717, fell the greatest snow ever known in this country, or, perhaps, in any other. So deep was it, that people stepped out of their chamber windows on snow shoes. With this fall of snow there was a terrible tempest; eleven hundred sheep, the property of one man, were found dead; one flock of a hundred, on Fisher's Island, were found buried sixteen feet in the snow; two of them only were alive, they having subsisted on the wool of their companions twenty-eight days after the storm.

The following account of this snow storm was written by Dr. *Cotton Mather*, and preserved amongst the *manuscript* volumes of the Massachusetts Historical Society. It is a curious relic, and will serve to show the doctor's method of writing.

AN HORRID SNOW.

Boston, 10*th Dec.* 1717.

Tho' we are gott so far onward as the beginning of another Winter, yett we have not forgott ye last, which at the latter end whereof we were entertained & overwhelmed with a Snow, which was attended with some Things, which were uncommon enough to afford matter for a letter from us. Our winter was not so bad as that wherein Tacitus tells us that Corbulo made his expedition against the Parthians, nor that which proved so fatal to ye Beasts & Birds in ye days of ye Emperor Justinian, & that the very Fishes were killed under ye freezing sea, when Phocas did as much to ye men whom Tyrants treat like ye Fishes of ye Sea. But ye conclusion of our Winter was hard enough, and was too formidable to be easily forgotten, & of a piece with what you had in Europe a year before. The snow was ye chief Thing that made it so. For tho' rarely does a Winter pass us, wherein we may not say with Pliny, *Ingens*

Hyeme Nivis apud nos copia, yet our last Winter brought with it a Snow, that excelled them all. The Snow, 'tis true, not equal to that, which once fell & lay twenty Cubits high, about the Beginning of October, in the parts about y^e *Euxine Sea,* Nor to that which y^e *French Annals* tell us kept falling for twenty Nine weeks together, Nor to several mentioned by *Bœthius,* wherein vast numbers of people, & of Cattel perished, Nor to those that *Strabo* finds upon *Caucasus* & *Rhodiginus* in *Armenia.* But yett such an one, & attended with such circumstances, as may deserve to be remembered.

On the twentieth of the last *February* there came on a *Snow,* which being added unto what had covered the ground a few days before, made a thicker mantle for our Mother than what was usual: And ye storm with it was, for the following day, so violent as to make all communication between ye Neighbors every where to cease.—People, for some hours, could not pass from one side of a street unto another, & ye poor Women, who happened in this critical time to fall into Travail, were putt unto Hardships, which anon produced many odd stories for us. But on y^e *Twenty fourth* day of ye Month, comes *Pelion upon Ossa:* Another Snow came on which almost buried ye Memory of ye former, with a Storm so famous that Heaven laid an Interdict on ye Religious Assemblies throughout ye Country, on this Lord's day, ye like whereunto had never been seen before. The Indians near an hundred years old, affirm that their *Fathers* never told them of any thing that equalled it. Vast numbers of Cattel were destroyed in this Calamity. Whereof some there were, of ye Stranger sort, were found standing dead on their legs, as if they had been alive many weeks after, when ye Snow melted away. And others had their eyes glazed over with Ice at such a rate, that being not far from ye Sea, their mistake of their way drowned them there. One gentleman, on whose farms were now lost above 1100 sheep, which with other Cattel, were interred (shall I say) or *Innived,* in the Snow, writes me word that there were *two Sheep* very singularly circumstanced. For no less than eight and twenty days after the Storm, the People pulling out the Ruins of above an 100 sheep out of a Snow-Bank, which lay 16 foot high, drifted over them, there was two found alive, which had been there all this time, and kept themselves alive by eating the wool of their dead companions. When they were taken out they shed their own Fleeces, but soon gott into good Case again. *Sheep* were not ye only creatures that lived unaccountably, for whole weeks without their usual sustenance, entirely buried in ye Snow-drifts.

The *Swine* had a share with y^e *Sheep* in strange survivals. A man had a couple of young *Hoggs*, which he gave over for dead, But on the twenty seventh day after their *Burial*, they made their way out of a *Snow-Bank*, at the bottom of which they had found a little Tansy to feed upon. The *Poultry* as unaccountably survived as these. Hens were found alive after seven days; Turkeys were found alive after five and twenty days, buried in ye Snow, and at a distance from ye ground, and altogether destitute of any thing to feed them. The number of creatures that kept a *Rigid Fast*, shutt up in Snow for divers weeks together, & were found alive after all, have yielded surprizing stories unto us.

The Wild Creatures of ye Woods, ye outgoings of ye Evening, made their Descent as well as they could in this time of scarcity for them, towards ye Sea-side. A vast multitude of Deer, for ye same cause, taking ye same course, and ye Deep Snow Spoiling them of their only Defence, which is to *run*, they became such a prey to these Devourers, that it is thought not one in twenty escaped. But here again occurred a Curiosity. These carniverous Sharpers, & especially the Foxes, would make their Nocturnal visits to the Pens, where the people had their sheep defended from them. The poor Ewes big with young, were so terrified with the frequent Approaches of ye Foxes, & the Terror had such Impression on them, that most of y^e *Lambs* brought forth in the Spring following, were of Monsieur *Reinard's* complexion, when ye Dam, were either *White* or *Black*.

It is remarkable that immediately after yͤ fall of yͤ Snow an infinite multitude of *Sparrows* made their Appearance, but then, after a short continuance, all disappeared.

It is incredible how much damage is done to yͤ *Orchards*, For the Snow freezing to a Crust, as high as the boughs of yͤ trees, anon split yᵐ to pieces. The Cattel also, walking on yͤ crusted Snow a dozen foot from yͤ ground, so fed upon yͤ Trees as very much to damnify them. The Ocean was in a prodigious Ferment, an after it was over, vast heaps of little shells were driven ashore, where they were never seen before. Mighty shoals of Porpoises also kept a play-day in the disturbed waves of our Harbours. The odd Accidents befalling many poor people, whose Cottages were totally covered with yͤ Snow, & not yͤ very tops of their chimneys to be seen, would afford a Story. But there not being any relation to philosophy in them, I forbear them.

And now *Satis Terris Nivis.* And there is enough of my Winter Tale. If it serve to no other purpose, yett it will give me an opportunity to tell you That nine months ago I did a thousand times wish myself with you in *Gresham Colledge*, which is never so horribly snow'd upon. But instead of so great a Satisfaction, all I can attain to is the pleasure of talking with you in this Epistolary way & subscribing myself

    Syr Yours with an affection
      that knows no Winter,
       COTTON MATHER.

---

29. *Dark Days.*

We find recorded in history, instances of extreme darkness in the daytime, and in some cases this obscurity has lasted for a number of days. The 19th of May, 1780, was distinguished by the phenomenon of a remarkable darkness over all the northern States, and is still called the *Dark Day.**

* At this time the legislature of Connecticut was in session in

The darkness commenced between the hours of ten and eleven, A. M., and continued to the middle of the next night. It was occasioned by a thick vapour, or cloud, tinged with a yellow colour, or faint red, and a thin coat of dust was deposited on white substances.*

The wind was in the south-west; and the darkness appeared to come on with clouds in that direction. Its extent was from Falmouth, Maine, to New-Jersey. The darkness appears to have been the greatest in the county of Essex, Mass., in the lower part of New-Hampshire, and Maine; it was also great in Rhode Island and Connecticut. In most parts of the country where the darkness prevailed, it was so great, that persons were unable to read common print, determine the time of day by their clocks or watches, dine, or manage their domestic business, without additional light; "candles were lighted up in their houses; the birds, having sung their evening songs, disappeared and became silent; the fowls retired to roost; the cocks were crowing all around, as at break of day; objects could be distinguished but a very little distance; and every thing bore the appearance and gloom of night."†

Besides this instance of uncommon darkness, there was one on the 21st of October, 1716; when "people were forced to light candles to eat their dinner by;" but the particulars of it are not preserved.‡

---

30. *Northern Lights.*

From the earliest times, we have some imperfect accounts of lights in the sky; and superstition has repre

---

Hartford. A very general opinion prevailed, that the day of judgment was at hand. The House of Representatives, being unable to transact their business, adjourned. A proposal to adjourn the council was under consideration. When the opinion of Col. Davenport was asked, he answered, "I am against an adjournment. The day of judgment is either approaching, or it is not. If it is not, there is no cause for an adjournment; if it is, I choose to be found doing my duty. I wish therefore that candles may be brought."—*Dwight's Travels*, vol. 3.

* Webster.   † Coll. Hist. Soc. 95—98.
‡ Philosophical Trans. No. 423.

sented them as the forerunners of bloody wars and other calamities. Sometimes historians speak of them as troops of men armed and rushing to battle. For about three hundred years past, our accounts of northern lights are tolerably correct. There was a discontinuance of them eighty or ninety years, anterior to 1707, when a small light was seen by persons in Europe. But they did not re-appear, in full splendour, till the year 1716, when they were observed in England. Their first appearance in America was December 11, 1719, when they were remarkably bright, and as people in general had never heard of such a phenomenon, they were extremely alarmed with the apprehension of the approach of the final judgment. All amusements, all business, and even sleep, was interrupted, for want of a little knowledge of history. From 1719 to 1790, these lights were frequent, when they again disappeared for ten or twelve years.*

A beautiful phenomenon (connected as it is supposed with the Boreal Lights) was seen in the northern States, on the 28th of August, 1827. The following description is taken from the American Journal of Science and Arts, vol. 14th, art. 16. " In this city (New-York) it was first observed at about half past nine, P. M., at which time the light, except as regards its whitish hue, resembled that produced by a fire at some distance. The light soon, however, became more intense, and its outline more distinctly defined, gradually assuming a columnar shape, and extending from about N. N. W. to a point in the opposite horizon, about E. N. E. In about 10 or 15 minutes from the time I first observed it, waves of light, in detached masses, but all in the line of the luminous arch, began to flow from the eastern towards the western part of its course, until the whole were blended, and the heavens were adorned with a beautiful arch, extending from the terminations above named to a point about 15 degrees north of the zenith. The greatest breadth of the arch, at its centre, was about 9 or 10 degrees, tapering from that point to the western

* Webster

extremity, (where the light was much bright and ran to a point. . . . The whole arch moved with a gradual motion towards the south, and passed the zenith, presenting a broad bright band of wavy light. After it passed the zenith towards the south, its eastern limb became less distinct, while the western part became more exact in its outline, and was as well defined as a pencil of rays passed through a prism into a dark room. The colour was a bright white, and slowly faded, until about two hours from the time of its first appearance, when it was no longer visible." About 50 or 60 years since, similar appearances were observed in the northern States.

31. *Gov. Fletcher and Capt. Wadsworth.*

In 1692, Col. Fletcher arrived with the commission of governor of New-York, and was also vested with plenary powers of commanding the whole militia of Connecticut; and insisted on the exercise of that command. The legislature of Connecticut, knowing that authority to be expressly given to the colony by charter, would not submit to his requisition; but the colony, desirous of maintaining a good understanding with Gov. Fletcher, sent William Pitkin, Esq. to New York, to make terms with him respecting the militia, until his majesty's pleasure should be further known. No terms, however, could be made with the governor, short of an explicit submission of the militia to his command. On the 26th of October, 1693, he came to Hartford, while the assembly were sitting, and, in his majesty's name, demanded that submission. The assembly resolutely persisted in a refusal. After the requisitions had been repeatedly made, with plausible explanations and serious menaces, Fletcher ordered his commission and instructions to be read in audience of the trainbands of Hartford, which had been prudentially assembled, upon his order. Capt. Wadsworth, the senior officer, who was at that moment exercising the soldiers, instantly called out, "Beat the drums," which in a moment overwhelmed every voice. Fletcher commanded silence. No sooner was a second attempt made to read, than Wadsworth vociferated, "Drum, drum, I say." The drummers instantly beat again with the greatest possible spirit. "Silence, silence," exclaimed the governor. At the first moment of a pause, Wadsworth called out earnestly, "Drum, drum, I say;" and turning to his excellency, said, "If I am interrupted again, *I will make the sun shine through you in a moment.*" This decision produced its proper effect; and the governor and his suite soon returned to New-York.*

32. *War with the Tuscaroras.*

In 1710, a large number of German emigrants arrived in this country, and settled in North Carolina. Two years after their arrival, the Tuscaroras, Corees, and other tribes of Indians, formed a deep conspiracy for the extermination of the English settlers. Having fortified the chief town in the Tuscarora nation, for the security of their own families, the different tribes met at this place, to the number of 1200 warriors, and laid the horrible plot, which was concerted and executed with stability and great secresy. From this place of rendezvous they sent out small parties, which entered the settlements by different roads, under the mask of friendship. When the night agreed on had arrived, they entered the houses of the settlers, and demanded provisions; and feigning displeasure, fell upon them, and murdered men, women, and children, without distinction. About Roanoke, 137 persons perished in the massacre. A few persons escaping, gave the alarm to their neighbours the next morning, and thus prevented the entire destruction of the colony.

Governor Craven, of South Carolina, as soon as he heard of this massacre, immediately sent Col. Barnwell,

* Holmes' Annals.

with 600 militia and 360 friendly Indians, against these savages. Marching through a hideous wilderness, Barnwell came up with the enemy, and attacked them with great effect. In this action he killed 300 Indians, and took about 100 prisoners. The survivors fled to their fortified town, where Col. Barnwell surrounded them, killed a great number, and compelled the remainder to sue for peace. It is estimated that in this expedition nearly a thousand of the Tuscaroras were killed, wounded, and taken prisoners. Of Barnwell's men, five were killed, and several wounded; of his Indians, thirty-six were killed, and between sixty and seventy wounded.*

"Never had any expedition against the savages in Carolina been attended with such hazards and difficulties; nor had the conquest of any tribe of them been more general and complete." Most of the Tuscaroras who escaped, abandoned their country, settled among the Five Nations, and added a sixth tribe, since which time they have been called the Six Nations.

33. *War with the Yamasees.*

In the year 1715, an Indian war broke out in South Carolina, which threatened a total extirpation of the colony. The numerous and powerful tribe of the Yamasees, possessing a large territory back of Port Royal Island, were the most active in this conspiracy. On the 15th of April, about break of day, the cries of war gave universal alarm; and in a few hours, above ninety persons were massacred in Pocataligo and the neighbouring plantations. A captain of the militia escaping to Port Royal, alarmed the town; and a vessel happening to be in the harbour, the inhabitants repaired precipitately on board, sailed for Charleston, and thus providentially escaped a massacre. A few families of planters on the island, not having timely notice of the danger, fell into the hands of the savages.

* Holmes' Annals.

While some Indian tribes were thus advancing against the southern frontiers, and spreading desolation through the province, formidable parties from the other tribes were penetrating into the settlements on the northern borders; for every tribe, from Florida to Cape Fear, was concerned in the conspiracy. The capital trembled for its own perilous situation. In this moment of universal terror, although there were no more than one thousand two hundred men on the muster roll, fit to bear arms, yet the governor resolved to march with this small force against the enemy. He proclaimed martial law; laid an embargo on all ships, to prevent either men or provisions from leaving the country; and obtained an act of assembly, empowering him to impress men, and seize arms, ammunition, and stores, wherever they were to be found; to arm trusty negroes; and to prosecute the war with the utmost vigour. Agents were sent to Virginia and England, to solicit assistance; and bills were stamped for the payment of the army and other expenses.

The Indians on the northern quarter, about fifty miles from Charleston, having murdered a family on a plantation, Capt. Barker, receiving intelligence of their approach, collected a party of ninety horsemen, and advanced against them. Trusting, however, to an Indian guide, he was led into an ambuscade, and slain, with several of his men. A party of four hundred Indians came down as low as Goose Creek, where seventy men and forty negroes had surrounded themselves with a breast work, with the resolution of maintaining their posts. Discouraged, however, almost as soon as attacked, they rashly agreed to terms of peace; but on admitting the enemy within their works, they were barbarously murdered. The Indians now advanced still nearer to Charleston; but were repulsed by the militia.

In the mean time, the Yamasees, with their confederates, had spread destruction through the parish of St. Bartholomew, and proceeded down to Stono. Governor Craven, advancing towards the wily enemy, with cau tious steps, dispersed their straggling parties, until he reached Saltcatchers, where they had pitched their camp.

Here was fought a severe and bloody battle, from behind trees and bushes; the Indians with their terrible war whoops, alternately retreating and returning with double fury to the charge. The governor, undismayed, pressed closely on them with his provincials; drove them from their territory; pursued them over Savannah river; and thus expelled them from the province.

In this Indian war, nearly four hundred of the inhabitants of Carolina were slain. The Yamasees, after their expulsion, went directly to the Spanish territories in Florida, where they were hospitably received.*

---

34. *Inoculation Introduced.*

The inoculation of small pox was first performed in the English dominions, in April, 1721, upon a daughter of the celebrated Lady M. W. Montague, who had become acquainted with inoculation as practised by Turkish women, during her residence in Constantinople.

About this time, Dr. Zabdiel Boyleston, of Boston, was induced to adopt the same expedient, from reading an account of inoculation, and made his first experiment by inoculating his only son and two negro servants, on the 27th of June, 1721. Probably there never was greater opposition to any measure of real public utility, than was exhibited on this occasion. Dr. Boyleston was execrated and persecuted as a murderer, assaulted in the streets, and loaded with every species of abuse. His house was attacked with violence, so that neither himself nor his family could feel secure in it. At one time he remained fourteen days in a secret apartment of his own house, unknown to any of his family except his wife. The enraged inhabitants patrolled the town in parties, with halters in their hands, threatening to hang him on the nearest tree, and repeatedly entered his

* Holmes' American Annals.

house in search of him during his concealment. Such was the madness of the multitude, that even after the excitement had in some measure subsided, Dr. Boylston only ventured to visit his patients at midnight, and then in disguise. He had also to encounter violent opposition from most of the members of his own profession, and notwithstanding he invited them all to visit his patients, and judge for themselves, received nothing but threats and insults in reply. Indeed, many sober, pious people, were deliberately of opinion, when inoculation was first commenced, that should any of his patients die, the doctor ought to be capitally indicted. He was repeatedly summoned before the select men of Boston, and received their reprehension. His only friends were Dr. Cotton Mather, and other clergymen, most of whom became zealous advocates for the new practice, and consequently drew upon themselves much odium from the populace. Some of them received personal injury; others were insulted in the streets, and were hardly safe in their own dwellings; nor were their services acceptable on Sunday to their respective audiences.

A bill for prohibiting the practice of inoculation, under severe penalties, was brought before the legislature of Massachusetts, and actually passed the house of representatives; but some doubts existing in the senate, it failed to become a law.

Dr. Boyleston lived to see the cause he espoused triumphant, and its utility generally appreciated. So prone are mankind to vacillate from one extreme to the other, that on a subsequent appearance of the small pox in Boston, in the year 1792, the whole town was inoculated *in three days*, to appease the infatuation of the inhabitants respecting the danger apprehended from this deadly pestilence. Persons were inoculated indiscriminately, to the number of 9,152; and such was the hurry and confusion with which it was done, and such the impossibility of rendering proper assistance and attention to so large a number, that 165 deaths were the consequence.*

* Connecticut Journal.

35. *Father Ralle, the French Jesuit.*

During the war between England and France, and while Canada was in possession of the latter power, the Indians were often instigated by them to fall on the frontier settlements of the British colonies. In these proceedings, the French governor of Canada was much assisted by the Roman Catholic missionaries, who had attained a great ascendancy over the Indians.

One of the most celebrated of these missionaries was Father *Sebastian Ralle*, a French Jesuit, who spent thirty-seven years among the Indian tribes, in the interior parts of America, and learned most of their languages. He was a man of learning and address; and by a gentle, condescending deportment, and a compliance with the Indian modes and customs, he obtained a complete ascendancy over the natives; and used his influence to promote the interests of the French among them. "He even made the offices of devotion serve as incentives to their ferocity, and kept a flag, on which was depicted *a cross, surrounded by bows and arrows,* which he used to hoist on a pole at the door of his church, when he gave them absolution, previous to their engaging in any warlike enterprise."

A dictionary of the Norridgewock language was found among Ralle's papers, composed by himself, and was deposited in the library of Harvard College.

The English settlers, having for a number of years suffered from the depredations of the Indians in those parts, in the year 1722 sent Col. Westbrook, with 230 men, to seize Ralle, who was regarded as the principal instigator; but he escaped into the woods, and they merely brought off his strong box of papers. The Indians, to revenge this attempt to carry off their spiritual father, committed various acts of hostility, and at length destroyed the town of Berwick. This last act determined the government to issue a declaration of war, and send an expedition against Norridgewock, and intrust the execution of it to Captains Moulton and Harman. These officers, each at the head of one hundred men, invested and surprised that village, killed the obnoxious Jesuit, with about eighty of his Indians, recovered three captives, destroyed the chapel, brought away the plate and furniture of the altar, and a devotional flag, as trophies of their victory.*

36. *Natchez Indians Extirpated.*

In 1729, the Natchez, an Indian nation on the Mississippi, formed a general conspiracy to massacre the French colonists of Louisiana. M. de Chepar, who commanded at the post of the Natchez, had been somewhat embroiled with the natives; but they so far dissembled as to excite the belief that the French had no allies more faithful than they. The plot having been deeply laid, they appeared in great numbers about the French houses, on the 28th of November, telling the people that they were going a hunting. They sang after the calumet, in honour of the French commandant and his company. Each having returned to his post, a signal was given, and instantly the general massacre began. Two hundred Frenchmen were killed. Of all the people of Natchez, not more than twenty French, and five or six negroes, escaped. One hundred and fifty children, eighty women, and nearly as many negroes, were made prisoners.

M. Perier, governor of Louisiana, resolved on an expedition against the Natchez, to revenge the massacre of the French. M. le Sueur, whom he had sent to the Choctaws, to engage their assistance, arrived in February near the Natchez, at the head of fifteen or sixteen hundred Choctaw warriors; and was joined in March by a body of French troops under M. de Lubois, king's lieutenant, who had the chief command of the expedition. The army encamped near the ruins of the old French settlement and after resting there five days, marched to

* Holmes' American Annals.

the enemy's fort, which was a league distant. After opening the trenches, and firing several days on the fort without much effect, the French at last approached so near, that the Natchez sent conditional proposals of releasing all the French women and children in their possession; but gaining time by negotiation, they silently evacuated the fort in the night, with all their baggage and the French plunder. The French prisoners, however, were ransomed; the stockade fort of the Natchez was demolished; a terrace fort built in its place; and a garrison of one hundred and twenty men left there, with cannon and ammunition.

M. Perier, learning afterwards that the Natchez had retired to the west of the Mississippi, near the Silver Creek, about sixty leagues from the mouth of Red River, applied to the French court for succours to reduce them. M. Perier de Salvert, brother of the governor, arriving from France, with a hundred and fifty soldiers of the marine, the two brothers set out with their army, and arrived without obstruction near the retreat of the Natchez. The enemy, terrified at their approach, shut themselves up in a fort which they had built; but were soon forced, by the fire from the French mortars, to make signals for capitulation. The French army carried the Natchez to New-Orleans, where they were confined in separate prisons; and afterwards were transported as slaves to St. Domingo. Thus that nation, the most illustrious in Louisiana, and the most useful to the French, were destroyed.*

37. *Negro Insurrection in Carolina.*

In 1738, the Spaniards attempted to seduce the negroes of South Carolina, who amounted at that time to the formidable number of forty thousand.

Liberty and protection had long been promised and proclaimed to them by the Spaniards of St. Augustine;

* Holmes' American Annals.

and emissaries had been sent among them, to persuade them to fly from slavery to Florida. The influence of these measures was such as might have been expected. An insurrection of negroes broke out this year in the heart of Carolina. A number of them having collected at Stono, surprised and killed two men in a warehouse, from which they took guns and ammunition, chose a captain, and, with colours and drums, began a march toward the south-west, burning every house, and killing every white person in their way, and compelling the negroes to join them. Governor Bull, returning to Charleston from the southward, and meeting them armed, hastened out of their way and spread the alarm. It soon reached Wiltown, where a large Presbyterian assembly was attending divine service. The men, who, according to a law of the province, had brought their arms to the place of worship, left the women in the church, and instantly marched in quest of the negroes, who by this time had become formidable, and spread desolation above twelve miles. Availing themselves of their superior military skill, and of the intoxication of several of the negroes, they attacked the great body of them in the open field, killed some, and dispersed the rest. Most of the fugitives were taken and tried. They who had been compelled to join the conspirators were pardoned; but all the chosen leaders and first insurgents suffered death.*

38. *Invasion of Georgia.*

In 1742, two years after the declaration of war by England against Spain, the Spaniards attacked Georgia. A Spanish armament, consisting of thirty-two sail, with three thousand men, under command of Don Manuel de Monteano, sailed from St. Augustine, and arrived in the river Altamaha. The expedition, although fitted out at great expense, failed of accomplishing its object.

* Holmes' American Annals.

General Oglethorpe was at this time at Fort Simons. Finding himself unable to retain possession of it, having but about seven hundred men, he spiked his cannon, and destroying his military stores, retreated to his head quarters at Frederica.

On the first prospect of an invasion, General Oglethorpe had applied to the governor of South Carolina for assistance; but the Carolinians fearing for the safety of their own territory, and not approving of General Oglethorpe's management in his late expedition against St. Augustine, declined furnishing troops, but voted supplies.

In this state of danger and perplexity, the general resorted to stratagem. A French soldier belonging to his army deserted to the enemy. Fearing the consequences of their learning his weakness, he devised a plan by which to destroy the credit of any information that the deserter might give.

With this view, he wrote a letter to the French deserter in the Spanish camp, addressing him as if he were a spy of the English. This letter he bribed a Spanish captive to deliver, in which he directed the deserter to state to the Spaniards, that he was in a weak and defenceless condition, and to urge them to an attack.

Should he not be able, however, to persuade them to do this, he wished him to induce them to continue three days longer at their quarters, in which time he expected two thousand men and six British men of war from Carolina. The above letter, as was intended, was delivered to the Spanish general, instead of the deserter, who immediately put the latter in irons.

A council of war was called, and while deliberating upon the measures which should be taken, three supply ships, which had been voted by Carolina, appeared in sight. Imagining these to be the men of war alluded to in the letter, the Spaniards in great haste fired the fort, and embarked, leaving behind them several cannon, and a quantity of provision. By this artful, but justifiable expedient, the country was relieved of its invaders, and

Georgia, and probably a great part of South Carolina, was saved from ruin.*

39. *Capture of Louisburg.*

Great Britain having declared war against France, in March, 1744, the legislature of Massachusetts planned a daring but successful enterprise against Louisburg, a strong fortress belonging to the French, on the island of Cape Breton. The place had been fortified by the French, at an expense of five millions and a half of dollars, and on account of its strength, was sometimes called the "Gibraltar of America." About 4000 troops from Massachusetts, Connecticut, and New-Hampshire, under the command of Col. William Peperell, sailed from Boston in the last week of March, 1745. The expedition was undertaken without the knowledge of the government of England; but a request had been made to Commodore Warren, then in the West Indies, to assist the expedition. He accordingly arrived at Louisburg, with a 60 gun ship, and two or three frigates. In the last of April, the troops, 3,800 in number, landed at Chapeaurogue bay. The transports had been discovered early in the morning from the town, which was the first notice they had of the design. In the night of May 2, 400 men burned the warehouses containing the naval stores. The French were alarmed, spiked the guns, flung their powder into a well, and abandoning the fort, fled to the city. The New England troops cheerfully submitted to extreme hardships; for fourteen nights successively, they were yoked together like oxen, dragging cannon and mortars through a morass of two miles. The commanding artillery of the enemy forbade this toil in the day. No people on earth, perhaps, are more capable of such laborious and daring exploits, than the independent farmers of New England. On the 17th of June the garrison capitulated;

* Goodrich's Hist. of the United States.

but the flag of France was kept flying, which decoyed into the harbour ships of the enemy, to the value of 600,000*l.* sterling. The weather during the siege was fine, but the day following, the rains began, which continued ten days, and must have proved fatal to the provincial troops, had not the capitulation prevented. This expedition was one of the most celebrated and remarkable events in the history of North America. It displayed, in a forcible manner, the enterprising spirit of the New England people; and though it enabled Britain to purchase a peace, yet it excited her jealousy against the colonies by whose exertions it was acquired.

The news of this victory quickly passed through the country. Pious and considerate persons, with emotions of gratitude and admiration, remarked the coincidence of many events and circumstances, on which the success of the expedition essentially depended. While the enterprise, patriotism, and firmness, of the colonists were justly extolled for projecting and executing a great design, attended with hardships and dangers never before paralleled in America, it was also perceived that there was no small degree of temerity in the attempt, and that the propitious agency of divine providence throughout the whole was singularly manifest.*

---

40. *D'Anville's Expedition.*

The capture of Louisburg roused the French government to seek revenge. A very large fleet, in 1746, was sent from France, under the command of the Duke D'Anville, to America. This fleet consisted of about

* The celebrated Mr. Whitefield was preaching in Boston at the time the expedition was fitting out, and one of the officers told him that he must "favour the expedition," otherwise the serious people would be discouraged from enlisting; not only so, but insisted that he should give him a motto for his flag for the encouragement of his soldiers. After considerable hesitation, the officer taking no denial, he at last gave one: *nil desperandum Christo duce*—"If Christ be captain, no fear of defeat." Upon this, great numbers enlisted; and at the request of the officers, he preached a discourse to the soldiers on the occasion.

forty ships of war, besides transports; and brought over between three and four thousand regular troops, with veteran officers, and all kinds of military stores; the most powerful armament that had ever been sent to North America. The object of this armament was supposed to be, to recover Louisburg; to take Annapolis; to break up the settlements on the eastern coast of Massachusetts; and to distress, if not attempt to conquer, the whole country of New England. The troops destined for Canada, had now sufficient employment at home; and the militia were collected to join them. The old forts on the sea coast were repaired; new forts were erected, and military guards appointed. The country was kept in a state of anxiety and fear six weeks, when it was relieved by intelligence of the disabled state of the enemy. The French fleet had sustained much damage by storms, and great loss by shipwreck. An expected junction of M. Conflans, with three ships of the line and a frigate from Hispaniola, had failed. A pestilential fever prevailed among the French troops. Intercepted letters, opened in a council of war, raising the expectation of the speedy arrival of an English fleet, caused a division among the officers. Under the pressure of these adverse occurrences, D'Anville was either seized with an apoplectic fit, or took a poisonous draught, and suddenly expired. D'Estournelle, who succeeded him in the command of the fleet, proposed, in a council of officers, to abandon the expedition, and return to France. The rejection of this proposal, caused such extreme agitation as to bring on a fever, which threw him into delirium, and he fell on his sword. The French, thus disconcerted in their plan, resolved to make an attempt on Annapolis; but having sailed from Chebucto, they were overtaken by a violent tempest, off Cape Sable, and what ships escaped destruction, returned singly to France.

A more remarkable instance of preservation seldom occurs. Had the project of the enemy succeeded, it is impossible to determine to what extent the American colonies would have been distressed or desolated. When man is made the instrument of averting public calamity, the divine agency ought still to be acknowledged; but this was averted without human power. If philosophers would ascribe this event to blind chance, or fatal necessity, Christians will assuredly ascribe it to the operation of that Being who, in ancient times, caused the stars in their courses to fight against Sisera.*

---

41. *Tumult in Boston.*

In the year 1747, a great tumult was raised in the town of Boston. Commodore Knowles, while lying at Nantucket with a number of men of war, losing some of his sailors by desertion, thought it reasonable that Boston should supply him with as many men as he had lost. He therefore sent his boats up to town early in the morning, and surprised not only as many seamen as could be found on board any of the ships, outward bound as well as others, but swept the wharves, taking some ship-carpenters' apprentices, and labouring landmen. This conduct was universally resented as outrageous. A mob was soon collected. As soon as it was dusk, several thousand people assembled in King's-street, below the town-house, where the general court was sitting. Stones and brickbats were thrown into the council chamber through the windows. A judicious speech of the governor from the balcony, greatly disapproving of the impress, promising his utmost endeavours to obtain the discharge of the persons impressed, and gently reprehending the irregular proceedings of the people, had no effect. Equally ineffectual were the attempts of other gentlemen to persuade them to disperse. The seizure and restraint of the commanders and other officers who were in town were insisted on as the only effectual method to procure the release of the inhabitants on board the ships. The militia of Boston was summoned the next day to the aid of the government, but re

* Holmes' Annals.

fused to appear. The governor, judging it inexpedient to remain in town another night, withdrew to Castle William. Letters, in the mean time, were continually passing between him and the commodore. The council and house of representatives now passed some vigorous resolutions; and the tumultuous spirit began to subside. The inhabitants assembled in town meeting, while they expressed their sense of the great insult and injury by the impress, condemned the riotous transactions. The militia of the town the next day promptly made their appearance, and conducted the governor with great pomp to his house. The commodore dismissed most, if not all, of the inhabitants who had been impressed; and the squadron sailed, to the joy and repose of the town.*

42. *Braddock's Defeat.*

The encroachments of the French, and the erection by them of a chain of forts on the back settlements of the colonies, occasioned the British ministry to take measures to possess themselves of these forts, and drive the French from the country.

In the spring of 1755, General Braddock arrived in Virginia, with two regiments, and was soon joined by Colonel Washington, (afterwards General Washington,) with a body of colonial troops; the whole force, two thousand men, took up their march for the French fort on the Ohio. General Braddock, on the 9th July, with twelve hundred of his troops, was within seven miles of Du Quesne, a French fortress, which stood where Pittsburg is now built. Here Colonel Washington, who understood the Indian mode of warfare better than his general, requested him to reconnoitre with his Virginia riflemen. But General Braddock, who held the American officers in contempt, rejected Washington's counsel, and swelling with rage, replied with an oath, "*High*

* Holmes' Annals.

times! high times! when a young buckskin can teach a British General how to fight!" The troops advanced in heavy columns, and passing a narrow defile they fell into an ambush of French and Indians, who opened a deadly fire upon the English and American troops, who were obliged to fire at random, as they could not see their foe.

The slaughter at this crisis was dreadful; particularly among the officers; and Washington was the only one on horseback, who was not either killed or wounded.* He had two horses shot under him, and four bullets passed through his coat. Braddock, if deficient in other military virtues, was not destitute of courage. Amidst a shower of bullets he encouraged his men to stand their ground by his countenance and example. But valour and discipline in this mode of warfare were useless: the action lasted three hours, and seven hundred men were killed on the spot. Braddock, after having three horses killed under him, received a mortal wound; and his troops fled in extreme dismay and confusion. The Virginians, who were the last to leave the field, formed after the action by the prudent valour of Washington, covered the retreat of the regulars, and saved them from entire destruction.

---

43. *Massacre at Fort William Henry.*

In the year 1757, Mons. Montcalm, with a body of 11,000 regular French troops and Canadians, with two thousand Indians, laid siege to Fort William Henry. This fort was defended by a garrison of but 2,300 men, British and Provincials, under the command of Colonel Monro. The garrison made a brave resistance, and would have probably preserved the fort, had they been

* A noted Indian warrior, who acted a leading part in this bloody action, was often heard to swear, that " *Washington was never born to be killed by a bullet!* For," continued he, "*I had seventeen fair fires at him with my rifle, and after all could not bring him to the ground.*"

properly supported by the British army under General Webb, which was then encamped at Fort Edward. The general, however, sent to Colonel Monro, and informed him that he could not assist him, and ordered him to give up the fort on the best terms he could; which was accordingly done. In consideration of the gallant defence the garrison had made, they were to be permitted to march out with all the honours of war, and with a guard to protect them from the fury of the savages. Soon after the capitulation was signed, the whole garrison, besides women and children, were drawn up within the lines, and on the point of marching off, when great numbers of the Indians gathered about and began to plunder, and soon after some of them began to attack the sick and wounded, when such were not able to crawl into the ranks; and notwithstanding they endeavoured to avert the fury of their enemies, by their shrieks and groans, they were soon murdered.

The brave Col. Monro hastened away, soon after the confusion began, to the French camp, to endeavour to procure the guard agreed by stipulation, but his application proved ineffectual. By this time the *war-whoop* was given, and the Indians began to murder those who were nearest them without distinction. "It is not in the power of words," says the narrator, who was one of this ill-fated garrison, "to give any tolerable idea of the horrid scene that now ensued: men, women, and children, were despatched in the most wanton and cruel manner, and immediately scalped. Many of the savages drank the blood of their victims as it flowed warm from the fatal wound."

The garrison now perceived, though too late to avail them, that they were to expect no relief from the French, who, instead of fulfilling their promises to furnish a guard to protect them, seemed tacitly to permit their savage allies to perpetrate these horrid atrocities. A few of the most resolute men, seeing no other probable way of preserving their lives, made a desperate effort, broke their way through the surrounding savages, and escaped.

it was computed that fifteen hundred persons were killed or made prisoners by these savages during this fatal day. Many of the latter were carried off by them, and never returned. A few, through favourable accidents, found their way back to their native country, after having experienced a long and painful captivity.

---

44. *Abercrombie's Defeat.*

The French had erected a fort at Ticonderoga, at the point of communication between Lake George, South Bay, and Lake Champlain. To dispossess them of this important place, an army, under General Abercrombie, was sent against it. His force consisted of 16,000 men, of which 6,000 were British regulars, and 10,000 were colonial troops. On the 5th of July, 1758, he embarked his troops on Lake George, on board 125 whale boats and 900 batteaux. The imposing splendour of the military parade on this occasion, is thus described by Dr. Dwight:—"The morning was remarkably bright and beautiful; and the fleet moved with exact regularity to the sound of fine martial music. The ensigns waved and glittered in the sunbeams, and the anticipation of future triumph shone in every eye. Above, beneath, around, the scenery was that of enchantment. Rarely has the sun, since that luminary was lighted up in the heavens, dawned on such a complication of beauty and magnificence."

After disembarking from the batteaux, the army formed in four columns, and began their march through the woods to Ticonderoga. When approaching the fort, a skirmish took place with the enemy, in which Lord Howe, the idol of the army, was killed; on seeing him fall, the troops moved forward, determined to avenge his death. About 300 of the enemy were killed on the spot, and 148 taken. Abercrombie having received information that the garrison consisted of about 6,000 men, and that a reinforcement of 3,000 more were daily ex pected, determined to attack their lines. Without gaining a proper knowledge of the works of the enemy, or of the proper points of attack, Abercrombie ordered an immediate assault. "The army advanced to the charge with the greatest intrepidity, and for more than two hours, with incredible obstinacy, maintained the attack. But the works, where the principal attack was made, were eight or nine feet high, and impregnable, even by field pieces; and for nearly one hundred yards from the breast work, trees were felled so thick, and wrought together with their limbs pointed outward, that it rendered the approach of the troops in a great measure impossible. In this dreadful situation, under the fire of about three thousand of the enemy, these gallant troops were kept, without the least prospect of success, until nearly two thousand were killed or wounded." After a contest of four hours, Abercrombie ordered a retreat; and the next day resumed his former camp on the south side of Lake George.

45. *Capture of Quebec.*

The capture of Quebec, in 1759, was the most brilliant and important event which took place during the French war; it gave the death blow to the French power in America. The command of the important expedition against Quebec was intrusted to Gen. James Wolfe, a young officer, who had distinguished himself at the capture of Louisburg.

The army, amounting to 8,000 men, landed in June, on the island of Orleans, below Quebec. The city of Quebec stands on a rock, at the confluence of Charles and Iroquois rivers; it is naturally a place of great strength, and was well fortified and defended by a force of 10,000 men, under the command of General Montcalm. Gen. Wolfe had to contend with immense difficulties, and after having failed in several attempts to reduce the city, he conceived the bold project of ascending, with his troops, a steep, craggy cliff, of from 150 to 200 feet, by which he would reach the plains of Abraham, south and west of the city. This almost incredible enterprise was effected in the night; and by daylight, Sept 13, the army was formed, and ready to meet the enemy. The battle which took place, is thus described by Mr. Goodrich, in his History of the United States.

"To Montcalm, the intelligence that the English were occupying the heights of Abraham, was most surprising. The impossibility of ascending the precipice he considered certain, and therefore had taken no measures to fortify its line. But no sooner was he informed of the position of the English army, than he perceived a battle no longer to be avoided, and prepared to fight. Between nine and ten o'clock, the two armies, about equal in numbers, met face to face.

"The battle now commenced. Inattentive to the fire of a body of Canadians and Indians, 1500 of whom Montcalm had stationed in the corn-fields and bushes, Wolfe directed his troops to reserve their fire for the main body of the French, now rapidly advancing. On their approach within 40 yards, the English opened their fire, and the destruction became immense.

"The French fought bravely, but their ranks became disordered, and notwithstanding the repeated efforts of their officers to form them and renew the attack, they were so successfully pushed by the British bayonet, and hewn down by the Highland broadsword, that their discomfiture was complete.

"During the action, Montcalm was on the French left, and Wolfe on the English right, and here they both fell in the critical moment that decided the victory. Early in the battle, Wolfe received a ball in the wrist, but binding his handkerchief around it, he continued to encourage his men. Shortly after, another ball penetrated his groin; but this wound, although much more severe, he concealed, and continued to urge on the contest, till a third bullet pierced his breast. He was now obliged, though reluctant, to be carried to the rear of the line.

"Gen. Monckton succeeded to the command, but was immediately wounded, and conveyed away. In this critical state of the action, the command devolved on Gen. Townsend. Gen. Montcalm, fighting in front of his battalion, received a mortal wound about the same time, and General Jennezergus, his second in command, fell near his side.

"Wolfe died in the field, before the battle was ended; but he lived long enough to know that the victory was his. While leaning on the shoulder of a lieutenant, who kneeled to support him, he was seized with the agonies of death; at this moment was heard the distant sound, 'They fly, they fly.' The hero raised his drooping head, and eagerly asked, 'Who fly?' Being told that it was the French, 'Then,' he replied, 'I die happy,' and expired.

"'This death,' says Professor Silliman, 'has furnished a grand and pathetic subject for the painter, the poet, and the historian; and, undoubtedly, (considered as a specimen of *mere* military glory,) it is one of the most sublime that the annals of war afford.'

"Montcalm was every way worthy of being the competitor of Wolfe. In talents, in military skill, in personal courage, he was not his inferior. Nor was his death much less sublime. He lived to be carried to the city, where his last moments were employed in writing, with his own hand, a letter to the English general, recommending the French prisoners to his care and humanity. When informed that his wound was mortal, he replied, 'I shall not then live to see the surrender of Quebec.'"

---

46. *War with the Cherokees.*

While the British and colonial troops were conquering Canada, the Cherokees, a powerful tribe of Indians, were committing outrages on the frontiers of Virginia and Carolina. During the first years of the war with the French, they espoused the cause of the English. But having been treated with coolness and neglect, and the murder of 12 or 15 of their warriors in the back parts of Virginia, together with the imprudent and perfidious conduct of Gov. Littleton of Carolina, who seized a number of their chiefs as prisoners, while treating for peace, the Cherokees were highly exasperated, and fell upon the frontier settlements, and perpetrated many cruel ravages and murders. Gov. Littleton, with a body of troops, entered the country, and obliged the Indians to sue for peace, which was granted. "But the savages violated the treaty, and attempted to surprise a fort on the frontiers of Carolina. General Amherst, on application, sent Colonel Montgomery, with twelve hundred troops, to protect the southern colonies. This officer penetrated into the heart of the Cherokee country, plundering and destroying all the villages and magazines of corn. In revenge, the savages besieged Fort Loudon, on the confines of Virginia; the garrison, after being reduced to extreme distress, capitulated; but on their march towards Carolina, a body of savages fell upon the party, and murdered five and twenty of them, with all the officers, except Captain Stuart. Colonel Montgomery being obliged by his orders to return to Canada, the Carolinians were alarmed for the safety of the colony, and prevailed with him to leave four companies of men for their defence. Canada being entirely subdued, General Amherst sent Colonel Grant, with a body of troops, who landed at Charleston early in 1761. These troops, being joined by a regiment of colonial forces, under Colonel Middleton, undertook an expedition into the Cherokee country.

"In May, the army, consisting of two thousand and six hundred men, advanced to Fort Prince George. Here Attakullakulla, having heard of the army's advancing against his nation, met Colonel Grant, and repeatedly entreated him, by his friendship, and the many good services he had performed for the English, that he would proceed no farther, until he had once more used his influence with his nation to bring them to an accommodation; but Colonel Grant would not listen to his solicitations. He immediately began his march for the middle settlements. A party of ninety Indians and thirty woodmen, painted like Indians, marched in front of the army, and scoured the woods. After them followed the light infantry, and about fifty rangers, consisting of about two hundred men. By the vigilance and activity of these, the colonel designed to secure the main army from annoyance and surprise. During three days, he made forced marches, with a view to pass a number of dangerous defiles, which might cost him dear, should the enemy first get the possession, and warmly dispute the passage. These he passed safely. But the next day, advancing into suspicious grounds, on all sides, orders were given to prepare for action; and that the guards should advance slowly, doubling their circumspection. While the army was advancing in this cautious manner, about eight o'clock in the morning, the enemy were discovered by the advanced guard, nearly in the same ground where they had attacked Colonel Montgomery the preceding year. Rushing down from the high grounds, they furiously attacked the advanced guard. This was supported, and the action became general. A party of the enemy, driven from the low grounds, immediately ascended the hills, under which the whole line was obliged to pass. On the left was a river, from the opposite bank of which, they received a heavy fire as they advanced. While the line faced and gave their whole fire to the Indians on the bank of the river, a party was ordered to ascend the hills and drive the enemy from their heights. No sooner were they driven from the heights, than they returned with redoubled fury to the charge in the low grounds. These it appeared to be their resolution obstinately to dispute. The situation of the troops soon became critical and distressing. They had been greatly fatigued by forced marches in rainy weather. They were galled by the fire of the enemy, and so compassed with woods, that they neither could discern nor approach them, but with great difficulty and danger. When they were pressed they always kept at a distance; but, rallying, returned again to the charge with the same fierceness and resolution. No sooner were they driven from one place, than they sprung up like furies in another. While the attention of the colonel was directed to the enemy on the banks of the river, and he was employed in driving them from their lurking places on that side, they made so furious an attack on his rear guard, that he was obliged to order a detachment back to its relief, to save his cattle, provisions, and baggage. From nine in the morning to eleven o'clock, did the enemy maintain the fight. Every where did the woods resound with the roar of arms, and with the shouts and hideous yellings of the savages. At length they gave way, but as they were pursued, they kept up a scattering fire until two o'clock; after that they entirely disappeared.

"What loss the enemy suffered, was not known. The loss of Colonel Grant was about sixty men killed and wounded. The army advanced as soon as possible, and about midnight arrived at Etchoe, a large Indian town. The next morning, it was reduced to ashes. There were fourteen towns in the middle settlements, which soon shared the same fate. The enemy's magazines and even their cornfields, which are reported to have amounted to fourteen hundred acres, were utterly destroyed. The miserable inhabitants stood the silent spectators of this general and merciless destruction. They were obliged to retire to starve in the thickets, swamps, and mountains. Nearly the same barbarities were committed against them, by a civilized and Christian people, of which we so much complain when they are perpetrated against us."*

After destroying the Indian towns, the army repaired to Fort Prince George, for rest and refreshment. A short time after, a number of Indian chiefs arrived with proposals of peace, which were gladly received, and peace concluded.

* Dr. Trumbull

47. *Expeditions against the Spanish Settlements in the West Indies.*

In 1740, war having been declared by Great Britain against Spain, expeditions were undertaken against the Spanish West Indies, Porto Bello, Carthagena, and Cuba. Requisitions were made on the colonies to assist in these enterprises. Four regiments were raised from the American colonies, for these expeditions; and the several colonies were at the charge of levy money, provisions, and transports, for their several quotas. An armament from Great Britain, under the command of Lord Cathcart, sailed from the West Indies, and formed a junction with Vice Admiral Vernon's fleet at Jamaica. Lord Cathcart having died in the West Indies before the complete junction of the fleets, Admiral Vernon found himself at the head of the most formidable fleet and army ever sent into those seas. The whole fleet consisted of twenty-nine ships of the line, with nearly the same number of frigates, besides fire-ships and bomb-ketches. The number of seamen amounted to 15,000; the land forces, including the four regiments from the colonies, were not less than 12,000. Vernon having taken and plundered Porto Bello, now proceeded with his fleet, and land forces, under General Wentworth, to attack Carthagena. After demolishing the strong forts and castles in the harbour, an attack was made by Wentworth upon the town; but he was obliged to retire, with the loss of four or five hundred men. In July the combined forces made an attempt on the Island of Cuba. They possessed themselves of a fine harbour, but by reason of an extraordinary sickness and mortality, they were not able to effect any thing of consequence.

"According to the accounts given of the sickness, it was nearly as mortal as the plague. More than a thousand men died in a day, for several days. Of nearly 1000 men from New England, not 100 returned; of 500 men from Massachusetts, 50 only returned."*

* Dr. Trumbull.

In 1762, Admiral Pocock, with a fleet of thirty-seven ships of war, and about one hundred and fifty transports, with a land force of about 15,000 men, under the command of Lord Albemarle, arrived before Havana on the 5th of June. On the 17th the troops landed, and after a siege of more than two months, in which the besieging army showed the most invincible courage, patience, and perseverance, this important place capitulated to his Britannic majesty.

In this siege, before the middle of July, the army in this unwholesome and burning region, was reduced to half its original number. Many of the soldiers dropped down dead under the pressure of heat, thirst, and fatigue. A considerable number of colonial troops enlisted under their own officers, and served in this arduous enterprise.

Of the troops from New England, scarcely any of the private soldiers, and but few of the officers, ever returned. Such as were not killed in the service, were generally swept away by the great mortality which prevailed in the army and navy.

---

48. *Dr. Franklin's Experiment in Electricity.*

In the summer of 1752, Dr. Franklin was enabled to make a grand and unparalleled discovery respecting electricity, by an experiment.

At this time the subject of electricity was a new science, and the philosophers of Europe were busy with it.

Dr. Franklin, in his studies and reasonings on the subject, took up the idea that the thunder and lightning of the heavens were caused by electricity, and conceived the bold idea, that the electric fluid might be conducted, by sharp pointed iron rods, raised upon houses, ships, &c., to the ground or water, and thus preserve them from injury.

"The plan which he had originally proposed, was, to erect or some high tower, or other elevated place, a sentry box, from which should rise a pointed iron rod, insulated by being fixed in a cake of rosin. Electrified clouds passing over this, would, he conceived, impart to it a portion of their electricity, which would be rendered evident to the senses by sparks being emitted, when a key, the knuckle, or other conductor, was presented to it. Philadelphia at this time afforded no opportunity of trying an experiment of this kind. Whilst Franklin was waiting for the erection of a spire, it occurred to him, that he might have more ready access to the region of the clouds by means of a common kite. He prepared one by attaching two cross sticks to a silk handkerchief, which would not suffer so much from the rain as paper. To the upright stick was affixed an iron point. The string was, as usual, of hemp, except the lower end, which was silk. Where the hempen string was terminated, a key was fastened. With this apparatus, on the appearance of a thunder gust approaching, he went out on the commons, accompanied by his son, to whom alone he communicated his intentions, well knowing the ridicule which, too generally for the interest of science, awaits unsuccessful experiments in philosophy. He placed himself under a shed to avoid the rain. His kite was raised. A thunder cloud passed over it. No sign of electricity appeared. He almost despaired of success; when suddenly he observed the loose fibres of the string to move towards an erect position. He now presented his knuckle to the key, and received a strong spark. On this experiment depended the fate of his theory. If he succeeded, his name would rank high amongst those who have improved science; if he failed, he must inevitably be subjected to the derision of mankind, or, what is worse, their pity, as a well meaning man, but a weak, silly projector. The anxiety with which he looked for the result of this experiment, may easily be conceived. Doubts and despair had begun to prevail, when the fact was ascertained in so clear a manner, that even the most incredulous could no longer withhold their assent. Repeated sparks were drawn from the key, a vial was charged, a shock given, and all the experiments made, which are usually performed with electricity."

By this and other experiments, Franklin's theory was established in the most convincing manner. When it was known that an American, an inhabitant of the obscure city of Philadelphia, was able to make discoveries and to frame theories, which had escaped the notice of the enlightened philosophers of Europe, it was quite mortifying to the pride of their scientific societies.

---

49. *Whitefield, the celebrated Preacher.*

The Rev. George Whitefield, a clergyman of the Church of England, first arrived in this country in the year 1738. He landed in Savannah, Geo., and laid the foundation of an orphan house a few miles from Savannah, and afterwards finished it at great expense. He returned to England the same year. On the following year he returned back to America, landed at Philadelphia, and began to preach in different churches. In this, and in his subsequent visits to America, he visited most of the principal places in the colonies. Immense numbers of people flocked to hear him, wherever he preached.

"The effects produced in Philadelphia and other places, were truly astonishing. Numbers of almost all religious denominations, and many who had no connexion with any denomination, were brought to inquire with the utmost eagerness, what they should do to be saved. Such was the eagerness of the multitude in Philadelphia, to listen to spiritual instruction, that there was public worship regularly twice a day for a year: and on the Lord's day it was celebrated thrice or four times.

"During his visit to Philadelphia, he preached frequently after night, from the gallery of the court-house, in Market-street. So loud was his voice at that time, that it was distinctly heard on the Jersey shore, and so distinct was his speech, that every word he said was understood on board a shallop, at Market-street wharf, a distance of upwards of 400 feet from the court-house. All the intermediate space was crowded with his hearers." He was truly remarkable for his uncommon eloquence, and fervent zeal. His eloquence was indeed very great, and of the truest kind. He was utterly devoid of all affectation; the importance of his subject, and the regard due to his hearers, engrossed all his concern. Every accent of his voice spoke to the ear, every feature of his face, every motion of his hands, and every gesture, spoke to the eye; so that the most dissipated and thoughtless found their attention arrested, and the dullest and most ignorant could not but understand. He appeared to be devoid of the spirit of sectarianism; his only object seemed to be to "preach Christ and him crucified."*

Mr. Whitefield died in Newburyport, Mass., on the 30th of September, 1770, in the fifty-sixth year of his age, on his seventh visit to America—having been in the ministry thirty-four years.

---

50. *Col. Boon's Settlement of Kentucky.*

The country now called Kentucky was well known to the Indian traders, many years before its settlement. It, however, remained unexplored by the Virginians, till the year 1769, when Col. Daniel Boon, and a few others, who conceived it to be an interesting object, undertook a journey for that purpose. After a long, fatiguing march, over a mountainous wilderness, in a

---

* The following anecdote respecting his manner of preaching, will serve to illustrate this part of his character. One day, while preaching from the balcony of the court-house, in Philadelphia, he cried out, "Father Abraham, who have you got in heaven; any *Episcopalians?*" "No!" "Any *Presbyterians?*" "No!" "Any *Baptists?*" "No!" "Have you any *Methodists* there?" "No!" "Have you any *Independents* or *Seceders?*" "No! No!" "Why, who have you then?" "We don't know those names here; all that are here are *Christians*—believers in Christ—men who have overcome by the blood of the Lamb, and the word of his testimony!" "O, is this the case? then God help me—God help us all to forget party names, and to become Christians in deed and in truth."

westerly direction, they at length arrived upon its borders, and, from the top of an eminence, "saw with pleasure the beautiful level of Kentucke. For some time," says Col. Boon, "we had experienced the most uncomfortable weather. We now encamped, made a shelter to defend us from the inclement season, and began to hunt and reconnoitre the country. We found abundance of wild beasts in this vast forest. The buffaloes were more numerous than cattle on other settlements, browsing on the leaves of the cane, or cropping the herbage on those extensive plains. We saw hundreds in a drove, and the numbers about the salt springs were amazing. In this forest, the habitation of beasts of every American kind, we hunted with great success till December.

"On the 22d of December, John Stuart and I had a pleasing ramble; but fortune changed the day at the close of it. We had passed through a great forest, in which stood myriads of trees, some gay with blossoms, others rich with fruit. Nature was here a series of wonders, and a fund of delight. Here she displayed her ingenuity and industry in a variety of flowers and fruit, beautifully coloured, elegantly shaped, and charmingly flavoured; and we were diverted with numberless animals, presenting themselves perpetually to our view. In the decline of the day, near Kentucke river, as we ascended the brow of a small hill, a number of Indians rushed out of a thick cane-brake, and made us prisoners. The Indians plundered us, and kept us in confinement seven days. During this, we discovered no uneasiness or desire to escape, which made them less suspicious; but in the dead of night, as we lay by a large fire, in a thick cane-brake, when sleep had locked up their senses, my situation not disposing me to rest, I gently awoke my companion. We seized this favourable opportunity, and departed, directing our course towards our old camp; but found it plundered, and our company dispersed or gone home.

"About this time my brother, Squire Boon. with another adventurer, who came to explore the country shortly after us, was wandering through the forest, and accidentally found our camp. Notwithstanding our unfortunate circumstances, and our dangerous situation, surrounded with hostile savages, our meeting fortunately in the wilderness, gave us the most sensible satisfaction.

"Soon after this, my companion in captivity, John Stuart, was killed by the savages; and the man that came with my brother returned home by himself. We were then in a dangerous, helpless situation; exposed daily to perils and death, amongst savages and wild beasts, not a white man in the country but ourselves.

"Thus, many hundred miles from our families, in the howling wilderness, we did not continue in a state of indolence; but hunted every day, and prepared a little cottage to defend us from the winter storms. We met with no disturbance during the winter.

"On the first of May, 1770, my brother returned home by himself, for a new recruit of horses and ammunition, leaving me alone, without bread, salt, or sugar, or even a horse or dog. I passed a few days uncomfortably. The idea of a beloved wife and family, and their anxiety on my account, would have disposed me to melancholy, if I farther indulged the thought.

"One day I undertook a tour through the country, when the diversity and beauties of nature I met with, in this charming season, expelled every gloomy thought. Just at the close of the day, the gentle gales ceased; not a breath shook the tremulous leaf. I had gained the summit of a commanding ridge, and looking round with astonishing delight, beheld the ample plains and beauteous tracts below. On the one hand I surveyed the famous Ohio, rolling in silent dignity, and marking the western boundary of Kentucke with inconceivable grandeur. At a vast distance, I beheld the mountains lift their venerable brows, and penetrate the clouds. All things were still. I kindled a fire near a fountain of sweet water, and feasted on the loin of a buck, which a few hours before I had killed. The shades of night soon overspread the hemisphere, and the earth seemed to gasp after the hovering moisture. My excursion had fatigued my body and amused my mind. I laid me down to sleep, and awoke not till the sun had chased away the night. I continued this tour, and in a few days explored a considerable part of the country; each day equally pleased as at first; after which I returned to my old camp, which had not been disturbed in my absence. I did not confine my lodging to it, but often reposed in thick canebrakes, to avoid the savages, who, I believe, often visited my camp, but, fortunately for me, in my absence. No populous city, with all the varieties of commerce and stately structures, could afford so much pleasure to my mind, as the beauties of nature I found in this country.

"Until the 27th of July, I spent the time in an uninterrupted scene of sylvan pleasures, when my brother, to my great felicity, met me, according to appointment, at our old camp. Soon after, we left the place, and proceeded to Cumberland river, reconnoitring that part of the country, and giving names to the different rivers. In March, 1771, I returned home to my family, being determined to bring them, as soon as possible, at the risk of my life and fortune, to reside in Kentucke, which I esteemed a second paradise. On my return, I found my family in happy circumstances. I sold my farm at Yadkin, and what goods we could not carry with us, and on the 25th of September, 1773, we bade farewell to our friends, and proceeded on our journey to Kentucke, in company with five more families, and forty men that joined us in Powell's valley.

"On the 10th of October the rear of our company was attacked by a number of Indians, who killed six, and wounded one man; of these, my eldest son was one that fell in the action. Though we repulsed the enemy, yet this unhappy affair scattered our cattle, brought us into extreme difficulty, and so discouraged the whole company, that we retreated forty miles to Clinch river."

In April, 1775, Col. Boon, with a company of enterprising men, after a number of contests with the Indians, erected the fort of Boonsborough, at a salt lick, sixty yards from the river, on the south side. Col. Boon says, "on the 14th of June, having finished the fort, I returned to my family on the Clinch. Soon after, I removed my family to this fort; we arrived safe; my wife and daugh ter being the first white women that stood on the banks of Kentucke river."

51. *Stamp Act.*

The British Parliament, in the year 1765, for the purpose of raising a revenue from the colonies, passed the famous *stamp act;* which ordained that all instruments of writing, as contracts, deeds, notes, &c., should not be valid, unless executed on stamped paper, on which a duty should be paid. This alarmed the colonies, and awakened their indignation. They determined to resist the execution of the law. The 1st of November, 1765, was the day on which this act was to take effect. In Boston, the bells tolled, the shops were shut, effigies of the royalists were carried about in derision, and torn in pieces. At Portsmouth, the bells tolled, a coffin was made, on the lid was inscribed, "*Liberty, aged* 145," and with unbraced drums, and minute guns, a procession followed it to the grave. At the close of an oration, the coffin was taken up, signs of life appeared in the corpse, "*Liberty revived,*" was substituted, the bells struck a cheerful key, and joy sparkled in every countenance.

In New York the stamp act was contemptuously cried about the streets, under the title of " *The Folly of England and Ruin of America.*" The stamp papers having arrived, Gov. Colden took them into the fort in order to secure them. Many of the citizens of New York, offended at the conduct, and disliking the political sentiments of the governor, assembled in the evening, broke open his stable, and took out his coach; and after carrying it about the city, marched to the common, when a gallows was erected, on one end of which they suspended his effigy, with a stamped bill of lading in one hand, and a figure of the devil in the other. After this, the populace took the effigy and the gallows entire, and carried it in procession, the coach preceding, to the gate of the fort, whence it was removed to the bowling green, where the whole pageantry, with the coach, was consumed in a bonfire, amidst the acclamations of thousands of spectators

Similar proceedings occurred in many parts of the country, and the obnoxious act was shortly after repealed.

---

52. *Massacre in Boston.*

The inhabitants of Boston had suffered almost every species of insult from the British soldiery; who, countenanced by the royal party, had generally found means to screen themselves from the hands of the civil officers. Thus all authority rested on the point of the sword, and the partizans of the crown triumphed for a time in the plenitude of military power. Yet the measure and the manner of posting troops in the capital of the province, had roused such jealousy and disgust, as could not be subdued by the scourge that hung over their heads. Continual bickerings took place in the streets, between the soldiers and the citizens; the insolence of the first, which had been carried so far as to excite the African slaves to murder their masters, with the promise of impunity, and the indiscretion of the last, was often productive of tumults and disorder, that led the most cool and temperate to be apprehensive of consequences of the most serious nature.

On the second of March, 1770, a fray took place in Boston, near Mr. Gray's ropewalk, between a private soldier of the 29th regiment and an inhabitant. The former was supported by his comrades, the latter by the rope-makers, till several, on both sides, were involved in the consequences. On the fifth a more dreadful scene was presented. The soldiers, when under arms, were pressed upon, insulted, and pelted, by a mob armed with clubs, sticks, and snow-balls covering stones. They were also dared to fire. In this situation, one of the soldiers, who had received a blow, in resentment, fired at the supposed aggressor. This was followed by a single discharge from six others. Three of the inhabitants were killed, and five dangerously wounded. The town was immediately in commotion. Such was the temper, force, and number of the inhabitants, that nothing but an engagement to remove the troops out of the town, together with the advice of moderate men, prevented the townsmen from falling on the soldiers. The killed were buried in one vault, and in a most respectful manner, in order to express the indignation of the inhabitants at the slaughter of their brethren, by soldiers quartered among them, in violation of their civil liberties. Captain Preston, who commanded the party which fired on the inhabitants, was committed to jail, and afterwards tried. The captain and six of the men were acquitted. Two were brought in guilty of manslaughter. It appeared, on the trial, that the soldiers were abused, insulted, threatened, and pelted, before they fired. It was also proved, that only seven guns were fired by the eight prisoners. These circumstances induced the jury to make a favourable verdict. The result of the trial reflected great honour on John Adams (afterwards President of the United States) and Josiah Quincy, Esqrs. the counsel for the prisoners; and also on the integrity of the jury, who ventured to give an upright verdict, in defiance of popular opinions.

"The people, not dismayed by the blood of their neighbours, thus wantonly shed, determined no longer to submit to the insolence of military power. Colonel Dalrymple, who commanded in Boston, was informed, the day after the riot in King-street, 'that he must withdraw his troops from the town within a limited term, or hazard the consequences.'

"The inhabitants of the town assembled at Faneuil Hall, where the subject was discussed with becoming spirit, and the people unanimously resolved, that no armed force should be suffered longer to reside in the capital; and if the king's troops were not immediately withdrawn by their own officers, the governor should be requested to give orders for their removal, and thereby prevent the necessity of more rigorous steps. A committee from this body was deputed to wait on the governor, and requested him to exert that authority which the exigencies of the times required from the supreme magistrate. Mr. Samuel Adams, the chairman of the committee, with a pathos and address peculiar to himself, exposed the illegality of quartering troops in the town in the midst of peace: he urged the apprehensions of the people, and the fatal consequences that might ensue if their removal was delayed.

"But no arguments could prevail on Mr. Hutchinson, who, from timidity, or some more censurable cause, evaded acting at all in the business, and grounded his refusal on a pretended want of authority. After which, Col. Dalrymple, wishing to compromise the matter, consented that the twenty-ninth regiment, more culpable than any other in the late tumult, should be sent to Castle Island. This concession was by no means satisfactory; the people, inflexible in their demands, insisted that no British soldier should be left within the town; their requisition was reluctantly complied with, and within four days the whole army decamped."*

---

53. *Destruction of Tea in Boston.*

The British ministry still persisting in their right to tax the colonies, had, for this purpose, given permission to the East India Company to ship a large quantity of teas to America, charged with duty. The Americans, fixed in their opposition to the principle of taxation in any shape, opposed the landing of the tea. In New York, and in Philadelphia, the cargoes sent out were returned without being entered at the custom house. In

---

* The circumstances and probable consequences of the tragical affair just related, sunk deep into the minds of the people, and were turned to the advantage of their cause. Its anniversary for many years was observed with great solemnity, and the most eloquent orators were successively employed to deliver an annual oration to preserve the remembrance of it fresh in their minds. On these occasions, the blessings of liberty, the horrors of slavery, the dangers of a standing army, the rights of the colonies, and a variety of such topics, were represented to the public view, under their most pleasing and alarming forms. These annual orations administered fuel to the fire of liberty, and kept it burning with an incessant flame.—*Morse's Revolution.*

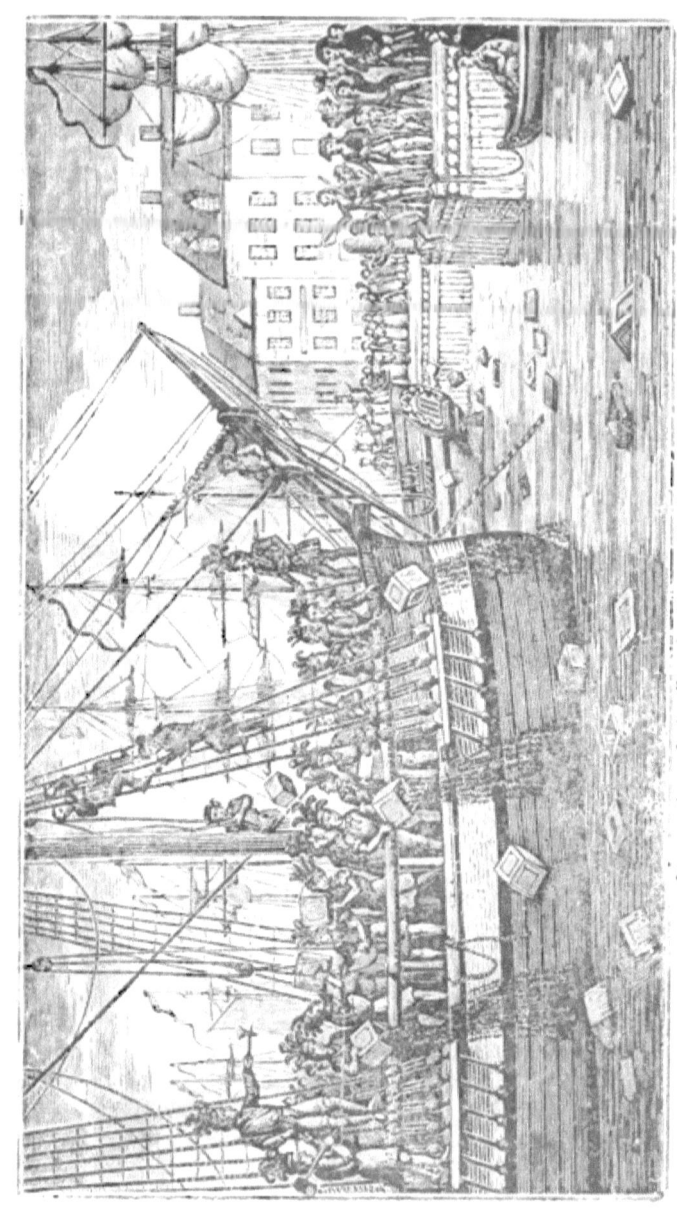

Destruction of the Tea in Boston Harbor. — Page 110.

Boston, the tea being consigned to the royal governor, (Hutchinson,) the populace, "clad like the aborigines of the wilderness, with tomahawks in their hands and clubs on their shoulders, without the least molestation, marched through the streets with silent solemnity, amidst innumerable spectators, and proceeded to the wharves, boarded the ships, demanded the keys, and without much deliberation, knocked open the chests, and emptied several thousand weight of the finest teas into the ocean. No opposition was made, though surrounded by the king's ships; all was silence and dismay. This done, the procession returned through the town, in the same order and solemnity as observed in the outset of their attempt. No other disorder took place; and it was observed, the stillest night ensued that Boston had enjoyed for several months." Intelligence of this transaction reached the British ministry, and in 1774, they passed an act to restrain all intercourse by water with the town of Boston, by closing the port. They also removed the government and public offices to Salem.

54. *First Continental Congress.*

The first general congress met at Philadelphia, in the beginning of September, 1774. It consisted of fifty-one delegates from twelve colonies. They chose Peyton Randolph president, and Charles Thompson secretary. The delegates were appointed by the colonial legislatures, or, where none existed, the appointments were made by select meetings and associations of citizens. "The novelty and importance of the meeting of this congress excited universal attention, and their transactions were such as could not but tend to render them respectable.

"The first act of congress was an approbation of the conduct of Massachusetts Bay, and an exhortation to continue in the same spirit which they had begun. Supplies for the suffering inhabitants, whom the operation of the port-bill had reduced to great distress, were strongly recommended; and it was declared, that in case of attempts to enforce the obnoxious acts by arms, all America should join to assist the town of Boston; and, should the inhabitants be obliged, during the course of hostilities, to remove farther up the country, the losses they might sustain should be repaired at the public expense.

"Congress next addressed a letter to General Gage; in which, having stated the grievances of the people of Massachusetts, they informed him of the fixed and unalterable determination of all the other provinces to support their brethren, and to oppose the British acts of parliament; that they themselves were appointed to watch over the liberties of America; and entreated him to desist from military operations, lest such hostilities might be brought on as would frustrate all hopes of reconciliation with the parent state.

"Their next step was to publish a declaration of rights. These they summed up in the rights belonging to Englishmen; and particularly insisted, that as their distance rendered it impossible for them to be represented in the British parliament, their provincial assemblies, with a governor appointed by the king, constituted the only legislative power within each province. They would, however, consent to such acts of parliament as were evidently calculated merely for the regulation of commerce, and for securing to the parent state the benefits of the American trade; but would never allow that they could impose any tax on the colonies, for the purpose of revenue, without their consent.

"They proceeded to reprobate the intention of each of the new acts of parliament, and insisted on all the rights they had enumerated as being unalienable, and what no power could deprive them of. The Canada act they pointed out as being extremely inimical to the colonies, by whose assistance it had been conquered; and they termed it, ' An act for establishing the Roman Catholic religion in Canada, abolishing the equitable system of English laws, and establishing a tyranny there.'

" They farther declared in favour of a non-importation and non-consumption of British goods, until the acts were repealed by which duties were imposed upon tea, coffee, wine, sugar, and molasses, imported into America, as well as the Boston port act, and the three others passed at the preceding session of parliament.

" The new regulations against the importation and consumption of British commodities, were then drawn up with great solemnity; and they concluded with returning the warmest thanks to those members of parliament who had with so much zeal, though without any success, opposed the obnoxious acts of parliament.

" The next proceedings of Congress were to frame a petition to the king, an address to the British nation, and another to the colonies; all of which were in the usual strain of American language at that time, and drawn up in such a masterly manner, as ought to have impressed the people of England with a more favourable opinion of the Americans, than they could at that time be induced to entertain."*

After a session of eight weeks, congress dissolved themselves, after recommending another congress to be convened on the 10th of May ensuing, unless the grievances should be previously redressed. Although the power of this congress was merely advisory, their resolutions received the general sanction of the provincial congresses, and of the colonial assemblies; " and their recommendations were more generally and more effectually carried into execution than the laws of the best regulated state."

55. *Battle of Lexington.*

Determined to reduce the rebellious colonies to submission, the British ministry transported a force of 10,000 men, who were stationed at Boston.

The Americans having deposited a considerable quan-

* Williams' History of the Revolution.

tity of military stores at Concord, an inland town, about eighteen miles from Boston, Gen. Gage determined to destroy them. For this purpose, he, on the night preceding the 19th of April, detached Lieutenant Colonel Smith and Major Pitcairn, with 800 grenadiers and light infantry; who, at 11 o'clock, commenced a silent and expeditious march for Concord. Although a number of British officers, who had dined at Cambridge the preceding day, had taken the precaution to disperse themselves along the road leading to Concord, to stop any expresses that might be sent from Boston to alarm the country, yet such was the vigilance of the Americans, that the expedition was discovered, and the alarm rapidly spread by church bells, signal guns, and volleys. When the British troops arrived at Lexington, about five in the morning, they found about seventy men, belonging to the minute company of the town, under arms. Major Pitcairn, who led the van, galloping up to them, called out, "*Disperse, disperse, you rebels; throw down your arms and disperse.*" Not being obeyed, he advanced nearer; fired his pistol; flourished his sword, and ordered his troops to fire. A discharge of arms from the British soldiers, with a huzza, immediately succeeded; several of the Americans fell, and the rest dispersed. The firing continued after the dispersion, and the fugitives stopped and returned the fire: eight of the Americans were killed, three or four of them by the first fire of the British; the others after they had left the parade. A number also were wounded.

The British now proceeded to Concord, disabled two twenty-four pounders; threw 500 pounds of ball into the river, and destroyed about sixty barrels of flour. The Americans being reinforced, a skirmish ensued between them and the regulars. The whole detachment was soon obliged to retreat with precipitancy, closely followed by the people of the adjacent country, who were by this time all aroused, and in arms. Some fired from behind stone walls and other coverts; others pressed on their rear; and thus harassed, the British retreated six miles back to Lexington. Here they were joined by Lord Percy, who, most fortunately for them, had arrived with a detachment of nine hundred men, and two pieces of cannon.*

The enemy having halted an hour or two at Lexington, re-commenced their march; the provincials continuing to harass them by firing from stone walls, &c. A little after sunset, the British reached Bunker Hill, where, being exhausted by excessive fatigue, they remained during the night, under the protection of the Somerset man of war; and the next morning went into Boston. During this excursion 65 of their number had been killed, 180 wounded, and 28 made prisoners; total 273. The Americans had 50 killed, and 38 wounded and missing.

56. *Taking of Ticonderoga by Col. Allen.*

The seizure of the important fortress of Ticonderoga, by Col. Ethan Allen, on the 10th of May, 1775, is thus related by himself:—

"The first systematical and bloody attempt at Lexington, to enslave America, thoroughly electrified my mind, and fully determined me to take a part with my country. And while I was wishing for an opportunity to signalize myself in its behalf, directions were privately sent to me from the then colony, now state of Connecticut, to raise the Green Mountain Boys, and, if possible, with them to surprise and take the fortress of Ticonderoga. This enterprise I cheerfully undertook; and after first guarding all the several passes that led thither, to cut off all intelligence between the garrison and the country, made a forced march from Bennington, and arrived at the lake opposite Ticonderoga, on the evening of the ninth day of May, 1775, with two hundred and thirty valiant Green Mountain Boys; and it was with

---

* Lord Percy formed his detachment into a square, in which he inclosed Col. Smith's party, "who were so much exhausted with fatigue, that they were obliged to lie down for rest on the ground, their tongues hanging out of their mouths, like those of dogs, after a chase."
Stedman.

the utmost difficulty that I procured boats to cross the lake. However, I landed eighty-three men near the garrison, and sent the boats back for the rear guard, commanded by Col. Seth Warner; but the day began to dawn, and I found myself necessitated to attack the fort before the rear could cross the lake; and as it was hazardous, I harangued the officers and soldiers in the manner following: 'Friends and fellow soldiers,—You have for a number of years past, been a scourge and terror to arbitrary powers. Your valour has been famed abroad, and acknowledged, as appears by the advice and orders to me from the general assembly of Connecticut, to surprise and take the garrison now before us. I now propose to advance before you, and in person conduct you through the wicket gate; for we must this morning either quit our pretensions to valour, or possess ourselves of this fortress in a few minutes; and inasmuch as it is a desperate attempt, which none but the bravest of men dare undertake, I do not urge it on any contrary to his will. You that will undertake voluntarily, poise your firelocks.' The men being at this time drawn up in three ranks, each poised his firelock. I ordered them to face to the right; and at the head of the centre file, marched them immediately to the wicket gate aforesaid, where I found a sentry posted, who instantly snapped his fusee at me. I ran immediately towards him, and he retreated through the covered way into the parade within the garrison, gave a halloo, and ran under bomb proof. My party, who followed me into the fort, I formed on the parade in such a manner as to face the barracks which faced each other. The garrison being asleep, except the sentries, we gave three huzzas, which greatly surprised them. One of the sentries made a pass at one of my officers with a charged bayonet, and slightly wounded him. My first thought was to kill him with my sword, but in an instant I altered the design and fury of the blow, to a slight cut on the side of the head; upon which he dropped his gun and asked quarters, which I readily granted him; and demanded the place where the commanding officer kept. He showed me a pair of stairs in the front, which led up to a second story in said barracks, to which I immediately repaired, and orde.ed the commander, Capt. Delaplace, to come forth instantly, or I would sacrifice the whole garrison; at which time the captain came immediately to the door with his breeches in his hand, when I ordered him to deliver to me the fort instantly; he asked me by what authority I demanded it. I answered him, '*In the name of the Great Jehovah and the continental congress.*' The authority of congress being very little known at that time, he began to speak again, but I interrupted him, and with my drawn sword near my head, again demanded an immediate surrender of the garrison; with which he then complied, and ordered his men to be forthwith paraded without arms, as he had given up the garrison. In the mean time some of my officers had given orders, and in consequence thereof, sundry of the barrack doors were beat down, and about one third of the garrison imprisoned, which consisted of said commander, a lieutenant Feltham, a conductor of artillery, a gunner, two sergeants, and forty-four rank and file; about one hundred pieces of cannon, one thirteen inch mortar, and a number of swivels. This surprise was carried into execution in the gray of the morning of the tenth of May, 1775. The sun seemed to rise that morning with a superior lustre; and Ticonderoga and its dependencies smiled on its conquerors, who tossed about the flowing bowl, and wished success to congress, and the liberty and freedom of America. Happy it was for me at that time, that the future pages of the book of fate, which afterwards unfolded a miserable scene of two years and eight months imprisonment, were hid from my view."

---

57. *Battle of Bunker Hill.*

The following "*full and correct account*" of the battle of Bunker Hill, is taken from a pamphlet published in Boston, June 17, 1825.

After the affair of Lexington and Concord, on the 19th of April, 1775, the people, animated by one common impulse, flew to arms in every direction. The husbandman changed his plough-share for a musket; and about 15,000 men, 10,000 from Massachusetts, and the remainder from New Hampshire, Rhode Island, and Connecticut, assembled under General Ward in the environs of Boston, then occupied by 10,000 highly disciplined and well equipped British troops, under the command of Generals Gage, Howe, Clinton, Burgoyne, Pigot, and others.

Fearing an intention, on the part of the British, to occupy the important heights at Charlestown and Dorchester, which would enable them to command the surrounding country, Colonel Prescott was detached, by his own desire, from the American camp at Cambridge, on the evening of the 16th of June, 1775, with about 1000 militia, mostly of Massachusetts, including 120 men of Putnam's regiment from Connecticut, and one artillery company, to Bunker Hill, with a view to occupy and fortify that post. At this hill the detachment made a short halt, but concluded to advance still nearer the British, and accordingly took possession of Breed's Hill, a position which commanded the whole inner harbour of Boston. Here, about midnight, they commenced throwing up a redoubt, which they completed, notwithstanding every possible effort from the British ships and batteries to prevent them, about noon the next day.

So silently had the operations been conducted through the night, that the British had not the most distant notice of the design of the Americans, until day-break presented to their view the half-formed battery and daring stand made against them. A dreadful cannonade, accompanied with shells, was immediately commenced from the British battery at Copps' Hill, and the ships of war and floating batteries stationed in Charles River.

The break of day, on the 17th of June, 1775, presented a scene, which for daring and firmness could never be surpassed; 1000 unexperienced militia, in the attire of their various avocations, without discipline, almost without artillery and bayonets, scantily supplied with ammunition, and wholly destitute of provisions, defying the power of the formidable British fleet and army, determined to maintain the liberty of their soil, or moisten that soil with their blood.

Without aid, however, from the main body of the army, it seemed impossible to maintain their position; the men having been without sleep, toiling through the night, and destitute of the necessary food required by nature, had become nearly exhausted. Representations were repeatedly made, through the morning, to head quarters, of the necessity of re-enforcements and supplies. Major Brooks, the late revered governor of Massachusetts, who commanded a battalion of minute-men at Concord, set out for Cambridge about nine o'clock, on foot, (it being impossible to procure a horse,) soliciting succour: but as there were two other points exposed to the British, Roxbury and Cambridge, then the head quarters, at which place all the little stores of the army were collected, and the loss of which would be incalculable at that moment, great fears were entertained lest they should march over the neck to Roxbury, and attack the camp there, or pass over the bay in boats, (there being at that time no artificial avenue to connect Boston with the adjacent country,) attack the head quarters, and destroy the stores: it was therefore deemed impossible to afford any re-enforcement to Charlestown heights, till the movements of the British rendered evidence of their intention certain.

The fire from the Glasgow frigate and two floating batteries in Charles River, were wholly directed with a view to prevent any communication across the isthmus that connects Charlestown with the main land, which kept up a continued shower of missiles, and rendered the communication truly dangerous to those who should attempt it. When the intention of the British to attack the heights of Charlestown became apparent, the remainder of Putnam's regiment, Col. Gardiner's regiment, (both of which, as to numbers, were very imperfect,) and some New Hampshire militia, marched, notwithstanding the heavy fire, across the neck, for Charlestown heights, where they arrived, much fatigued, just after the British had moved to the first attack.

The British commenced crossing the troops from Boston about 12 o'clock, and landed at Morton's Point, S. E. from Breed's Hill. At 2 o'clock, from the best accounts that can be obtained, they landed between 3 and 4,000 men, under the immediate command of Gen. Howe, and formed, in apparently invincible order, at the base of the hill.

The position of the Americans, at this time, was a redoubt on the summit of the height, of about eight rods square, and a breast-work extending on the left of it, about seventy feet down the eastern declivity of the hill. This redoubt and breast-work was commanded by Prescott in person, who had superintended its construction, and who occupied it with the Massachusetts militia of his detachment, and a part of Little's regiment, which had arrived about one o'clock. They were dreadfully deficient in equipments and ammunition, had been toiling incessantly for many hours, and it is said by some accounts, even then were destitute of provisions. A little to the eastward of the redoubt, and northerly to the rear of it, was a rail fence, extending almost to Mystick river; to this fence another had been added during the night and forenoon, and some newly mown grass thrown against them, to afford something like a cover to the troops. At this fence the 120 Connecticut militia were posted.

The movements of the British made it evident their intention was to march a strong column along the margin of the Mystick, and turn the redoubt on the north, while another column attacked it in front; accordingly, to prevent this design, a large force became necessary at the breast-work and rail fence. The whole of the re-enforcements that arrived, amounting in all to 800 or 1000 men, were ordered to this point by General Putnam, who had been extremely active throughout the night and morning, and had accompanied the expedition.

At this moment thousands of persons of both sexes

had collected on the church-steeples, Beacon Hill, house tops, and every place in Boston and its neighbourhood where a view of the battle ground could be obtained, viewing, with painful anxiety, the movements of the combatants; wondering, yet admiring the bold stand of the Americans, and trembling at the thoughts of the formidable army marshalled in array against them.

Before 3 o'clock the British formed, in two columns, for the attack; one column, as had been anticipated, moved along the Mystick river, with the intention of taking the redoubt in the rear, while the other advanced up the ascent directly in front of the redoubt, where Prescott was ready to receive them. General Warren, president of the provincial congress and of the committee of safety, who had been appointed but a few days before a major-general of the Massachusetts troops, had volunteered on the occasion as a private soldier, and was in the redoubt with a musket, animating the men by his influence and example to the most daring determination.

Orders were given to the Americans to reserve their fire till the enemy advanced sufficiently near to make their aim certain. Several volleys were fired by the British with but little success; and so long a time had elapsed, and the British allowed to advance so near the Americans without their fire being returned, that a doubt arose whether or not the latter intended to give battle; but the fatal moment soon arrived: when the British had advanced to within about eight rods, a sheet of fire was poured upon them and continued a short time with such deadly effect that hundreds of the assailants lay weltering in their blood, and the remainder retreated in dismay to the point where they had first landed.

From daylight to the time of the British advancing on the works, an incessant fire had been kept up on the Americans from the ships and batteries—this fire was now renewed with increased vigour.

After a short time, the British officers had succeeded in rallying their men, and again advanced, in the same order as before, to the attack. Thinking to divert the attention of the Americans, the town of Charlestown, consisting of 500 wooden buildings, was now set on fire by the British; the roar of the flames, the crashing of falling timber, the awful appearance of desolation presented, the dreadful shrieks of the dying and wounded in the last attack, added to the knowledge of the formidable force advancing against them, combined to form a scene apparently too much for men bred in the quiet retirement of domestic life to sustain. But the stillness o death reigned within the American works, and nought could be seen but the deadly presented weapon, ready to hurl fresh destruction on the assailants. The fire of the Americans was again reserved till the British came still nearer than before, when the same unerring aim was taken, and the British shrunk, terrified, from before its fatal effects, flying, completely routed, a second time to the banks of the river, and leaving, as before, the field strewed with their wounded and their dead.

Again the ships and batteries renewed their fire, and kept a continual shower of balls on the works. Notwithstanding every exertion, the British officers found it impossible to rally the men for a third attack; one third of their comrades had fallen; and finally it was not till a re-enforcement of more than 1000 fresh troops, with a strong park of artillery, had joined them from Boston, that they could be induced to form anew.

In the mean time every effort was made on the part of the Americans, to resist a third attack; Gen. Putnam rode, notwithstanding the heavy fire of the ships and batteries, several times across the neck, to induce the militia to advance; but it was only a few of the resolute and brave who would encounter the storm. The British receiving re-enforcements from their formidable main body—the town of Charlestown presenting one wide scene of destruction—the probability the Americans must shortly retreat—the shower of balls pouring over the neck—presented obstacles too appalling for raw troops to sustain, and embodied too much danger to allow them to encounter. Yet, notwithstanding all this, the Americans on the heights were elated with their suc ress, and waited with coolness and determination the now formidable advance of the enemy.

Once more the British, aided by their re-enforcements, advanced to the attack, but with great skill and caution; their artillery was planted on the eastern declivity of the hill, between the rail fence and the breast-work, where it was directed along the line of the Americans, stationed at the latter place, and against the gateway on the north-eastern corner of the redoubt; at the same time they attacked the redoubt on the south-eastern and south-western sides, and entered it with fixed bayonets. The slaughter on their advancing was great; but the Americans, not having bayonets to meet them on equal terms, and their powder being exhausted, now slowly retreated, opposing and extricating themselves from the British with the butts of their pieces.

The column that advanced against the rail fence was received in the most dauntless manner. The Americans fought with spirit and heroism that could not be surpassed, and had their ammunition held out, would have secured to themselves a third time the palm of victory; as it was, they effectually prevented the enemy from accomplishing his purpose, which was to turn their flank, and cut the whole of the Americans off; but having become perfectly exhausted, this body of the Americans also slowly retired, retreating in much better order than could possibly have been expected from undisciplined troops, and those in the redoubt having extricated themselves from the host of bayonets by which they had been surrounded.

The British followed the Americans to Bunker Hill, but some fresh militia at this moment coming up to the aid of the latter, covered their retreat. The Americans crossed Charlestown Neck about 7 o'clock, having in the last twenty hours performed deeds which seemed almost impossible. Some of them proceeded to Cambridge, and others posted themselves quietly on Winter and Prospect Hills.

From the most accurate statements that can be found, it appears the British must have had nearly 5,000 sol diers in the battle; between 3 and 4,000 having first landed, and the re-enforcement amounting to over 1,000. The Americans, throughout the whole day, did not have 2,000 men on the field.

The slaughter on the side of the British was immense, having had nearly 1,500 killed and wounded, 1,200 of whom were either killed or mortally wounded; the Americans about 400.

Had the commanders at Charlestown Heights become terrified on being cut off from the main body and supplies, and surrendered their army, or ever retreated before they did, from the terrific force that opposed them, where would now have been that ornament and example to the world, the Independence of the United States? When it was found that no re-enforcements were to be allowed them, the most sanguine man on that field could not have even indulged a hope of success, but all determined to deserve it; and although they did not obtain a victory, their example was the cause of a great many. The first attempt on the commencement of a war, is held up, by one party or the other, as an example to those that succeed it, and a victory or defeat, though not, perhaps, of any great magnitude in itself, is most powerful and important in its effects. Had such conduct as was here exhibited, been in any degree imitated by the immediate commander in the first military onset in the last war, how truly different a result would have been effected, from the fatal one that terminated that unfortunate expedition.

From the immense superiority of the British, at this stage of the war, having a large army of highly disciplined and well equipped troops, and the Americans possessing but few other munitions or weapons of war, and but little more discipline, than what each man possessed when he threw aside his plough and took the gun that he had kept for pastime or for profit, but now to be employed for a different purpose, from off the hooks that held it,— perhaps it would have been in their power, by pursuing the Americans to Cambridge, and destroying the few stores that had been collected there, to inflict a blow which could never have been recovered from: but they were completely terrified. The awful lesson they had just received, filled them with horror; and the blood of 1,500 of their companions, who fell on that day, presented to them a warning which they could never forget. From the battle of Bunker Hill, sprung the protection and the vigour that nurtured the tree of liberty, and to it, in all probability, may be ascribed our independence and glory.

The name of the first martyr that gave his life for the good of his country on that day, in the importance of the moment was lost; else a monument, in connexion with the gallant Warren, should be raised to his memory. The manner of his death was thus related by Col. Prescott.

"The first man who fell in the battle of Bunker Hill was killed by a cannon ball which struck his head. He was so near me that my clothes were besmeared with his blood and brains, which I wiped off, in some degree, with a handful of fresh earth. The sight was so shocking to many of the men, that they left their posts and ran to view him. I ordered them back, but in vain. I then ordered him to be buried instantly. A subaltern officer expressed surprise that I should allow him to be buried without having prayers said; I replied, this is the first man that has been killed, and the only one that will be buried to day. I put him out of sight that the men may be kept in their places. God only knows who, or how many of us, will fall before it is over. To your post, my good fellow, and let each man do his duty."

The name of the patriot who thus fell is supposed to have been POLLARD, a young man belonging to Billerica. He was struck by a cannon ball, thrown from the line-of-battle ship Somerset.

---

58. *Arnold's March through the Wilderness.*

About the same time that Canada was invaded by the usual route from New York, a considerable detachment of the American army was brought thither by a new and unexpected passage. Arnold, who conducted this bold undertaking, acquired thereby the name of the American Hannibal. He was sent, by General Washington, with a thousand men, from Cambridge, with orders to penetrate into that province, by ascending the Kennebec, and then, after crossing the mountains which divide Canada from Maine, by descending the Chaudiere to the St. Lawrence. Great were the difficulties, and severe the privations, they had to encounter, in marching three hundred miles, by an unexplored way, through an uninhabited country. In ascending the Kennebec, they were constantly obliged to struggle against an impetuous current; and were often compelled, by cataracts, to land, and haul their batteaux up rapid streams, and over falls of rivers. They had to contend with swamps, woods, and craggy mountains. At some places, they had to cut their way, for miles together, through forests so embarrassed, that their progress was only four or five miles a day. One third of their number were, from sickness and want of food, obliged to return. Provisions grew at length so scarce, that some of the men ate their dogs, cartouch boxes, leather small clothes, and shoes. Still they proceeded with unabated fortitude. They gloried in the hope of completing a march which would rival the greatest exploits of antiquity; and on the third of November, after thirty-one days spent in traversing a hideous desert, they reached the inhabited parts of Canada, where the people were struck with amazement and admiration when they saw this armed force emerging from the wilderness.*

---

59. *Death of General Montgomery.*

Richard Montgomery, a major general in the army of the United States, was born in the north of Ireland, in the year 1737. He possessed an excellent genius,

* Grimshaw's Hist. U. S.

which was matured by a fine education. Entering the army of Great Britain, he successfully fought her battles with Wolfe, at Quebec, in 1759, on the very spot where he was doomed to fall, when fighting against her, under the banners of freedom. After his return to England, he quitted his regiment, in 1772, though in a fair way of preferment. He had imbibed an attachment to America, viewing it as the rising seat of arts and freedom. After his arrival in this country, he purchased an estate in New York, about a hundred miles from the city, and married a daughter of Judge Livingston. He now considered himself as an American. When the struggle with Great Britain commenced, as he was known to have an ardent attachment to liberty, and had expressed his readiness to draw his sword on the side of the colonies, the command of the continental forces, in the northern department, was intrusted to him and Gen. Schuyler, in the fall of 1775.

By the indisposition of Schuyler, the chief command devolved upon him in October. He reduced fort Chamblee, and on the third of November captured St. Johns. On the 12th, he took Montreal. In December he joined Col. Arnold, and marched to Quebec. The city was besieged, and on the last day of the year it was determined to make an assault. The several divisions were accordingly put in motion, in the midst of a heavy fall of snow, which concealed them from the enemy. Montgomery advanced at the head of the New York troops along the St. Lawrence, and having assisted with his own hands in pulling up the pickets, which obstructed his approach to one of the barriers he was determined to force, he was pushing forward, when one of the guns from the battery was discharged, and he was killed with his two aids. This was the only gun fired, for the enemy had been struck with consternation, and all but one or two had fled. But this event probably prevented the capture of Quebec. When he fell, Montgomery was in a narrow passage, and his body rolled upon the ice, which formed by the side of the river. After it was found the next morning among the slain, it was buried by a few soldiers, without any marks of distinction. He was thirty-eight years of age. He was a man of great military talents, whose measures were taken with judgment, and executed with vigour. With undisciplined troops, who were jealous of him in the extreme, he yet inspired them with his own enthusiasm. He shared with them in all their hardships, and thus prevented their complaints. His industry could not be wearied, his vigilance imposed upon, nor his courage intimidated.

To express the high sense entertained by his country of his services, congress directed that a monument of white marble, to his memory, should be placed in front of St. Paul's church, New York.

The remains of Gen. Montgomery, after resting forty-two years at Quebec, by a resolve of the state of New York, were brought to the city of New York, on the 8th of July, 1817, and deposited, with ample form and grateful ceremonies, near the aforesaid monument in St Paul's Church.*

---

60. *Washington, Commander in Chief of the American Army.*

In May, 1775, congress met pursuant to adjournment. Hostilities having commenced, it was a point of vital importance to the American cause, to select a proper person for commander in chief of the American forces.

George Washington,† a delegate from Virginia, was, by the unanimous voice of congress, appointed, to fill

---

* Morse's Revolution.
† For three years subsequent to the defeat of Braddock, Washington superintended the troops of Virginia; in which highly dangerous service he continued, until peace was given to the frontier of his native colony, by the reduction of fort Duquesne; an enterprise undertaken in conformity with his repeated solicitations, and accompanied by himself, at the head of his own regiment. The arduous duties of his situation, rendered irksome by the invidious treatment experienced from the governor, and by the unmanageable disposition of the officers and privates under his command, were related by himself, in a highly interesting narrative, and fully acknowledged by the assembly of Virginia. Soon afterwards he retired to his estate at Mount Vernon, and pursued the arts of peaceful life, with great industry

his important station, on the 15th of June, 1775. "To Washington's experience in military affairs are united sound judgment, extensive knowledge of men, perfect probity, pure morals, a grave deportment, indefatigable industry, easy manners, strict politeness, a commanding person, cool bravery, unshaken fortitude, and a prudence that baffled and confounded his enemies."

Soon after his appointment, General Washington repaired to the army, who were besieging Boston; he was received with profound respect and joyful acclamations by the American army.

The Americans having so closely invested Boston, the British commander judged it prudent to evacuate the town, which they did on the 17th of March, 1776, taking with them 1500 of the inhabitants, who dared not stay on account of their attachment to the British cause.

General Washington immediately entered the town, to the great joy of the inhabitants.

and success. When the proceedings of the British parliament had alarmed the colonists with apprehensions that a blow was levelled at their liberties, he again came forward to serve the public: was appointed a delegate to congress; and in that body was chairman of every committee selected to make arrangements for defence. He was now in his forty-fourth year, possessed a large share of common sense, and was directed by a sound judgment. Engaged in the busy scenes of life, he knew human nature, and the most proper method of accomplishing his plans. His passions were subdued, and held in subjection to reason. His mind was superior to prejudice and party spirit; his soul too generous to burden his country with expense; his principles too just to allow his placing military glory in competition with the public good.

On the president of congress announcing his commission, he replied: "Though I am truly sensible of the high honour done me in this appointment, yet I feel deep distress, from a consciousness that my abilities and military experience may not be equal to the extensive and important trust. However, as the congress desire it, I will enter on the momentous duty, and exert every power I possess in their service, for the support of the glorious cause. I beg they will accept my most cordial thanks for this distinguished testimony of their approbation. But, lest some unlucky event should happen, unfavourable to my reputation, I beg it may be remembered by every gentleman in the room, that I this day declare, with the utmost sincerity, I do not think myself equal to the command I am honoured with. As to pay, sir, I beg leave to assure the congress, that, as no pecuniary consideration could have tempted me to accept this arduous employment, at the expense of my domestic ease and happiness, I do not wish to make any profit from it. I will keep an exact account of my disbursements; those, I doubt not, they will discharge, and that is all I desire." *Grimshaw's Hist. U. S.*

61. *Attack on Sullivan's Island.*

In the months of June and July, 1776, the British commanders, Gen. Clinton and Sir Peter Parker, attempted to destroy the fort on Sullivan's island, near Charleston, S. C. Their force consisted of two fifty gun ships, and four frigates of twenty-eight guns each, besides several smaller vessels, with 3000 troops on board. The fort was commanded by Col. Moultrie, with a garrison of but 375 regulars, and a few militia. This fort, though not entirely finished, was very strong.

"However, the British generals resolved, without hesitation to attack it; but though an attack was easy from the sea, it was very difficult to obtain a co-operation of the land forces. This was attempted by landing them on Long Island, adjacent to Sullivan's Island on the east, from which it is separated by a very narrow creek, said to be not above two feet deep at low water.

" Opposite to this ford, the Americans had posted a strong body of troops, with cannon and intrenchments, while Gen. Lee was posted on the main land, with a bridge of boats betwixt that and Sullivan's Island, so that he could at pleasure send re-enforcements to the troops in the fort on Sullivan's Island.

" On the part of the British, so many delays occurred, that it was the 24th of June before matters were in readiness for an attack; and by this time, the Americans had abundantly provided for their reception. On the morning of that day, the bomb-ketch began to throw shells into Fort Sullivan, and about mid-day, the two fifty gun ships, and thirty gun frigates, came up, and began a severe fire.

" Three other frigates were ordered to take their station between Charleston and the fort, in order to enfilade the batteries, and cut off the communication with the main land; but, through the ignorance of the pilots, they all stuck fast; and though two of them were disentangled, they were found to be totally unfit for service. The third was burnt, that she might not fall into the hands of the Americans.

"The attack was therefore confined to the five armed ships and bomb-ketch, between whom and the fort a dreadful fire ensued. The Bristol suffered excessively; the springs on her cable being shot away, she was for some time entirely exposed to the enemy's fire. As the Americans poured in great quantities of red hot balls, she was twice in flames. Her captain, Mr. Morris, after receiving five wounds, was obliged to go below deck, in order to have his arm amputated. After undergoing this operation, he returned to his place, where he received another wound, but still refused to quit his station. At last, he received a red hot ball in his belly, which instantly put an end to his life.

"Of all the officers and seamen who stood on the quarter deck of the Bristol, not one escaped without a wound, excepting Sir Peter Parker alone; whose intrepidity and presence of mind on this occasion, were very remarkable. The engagement lasted till darkness put an end to it. Little damage was done by the British, as the works of the Americans lay so low, that many of the shot flew over; and the fortifications, being composed of palm trees mixed with earth, were extremely well calculated to resist the impression of cannon.

"During the height of the attack, the American batteries remained for some time silent, so that it was concluded that they had been abandoned; but this was found to proceed only from want of powder; for, as soon as a supply of this necessary article was obtained, the firing was resumed as brisk as before. During the whole of this desperate engagement, it was found impossible for the land forces to give the least assistance to the fleet; the American works were found to be much stronger than they had been imagined, and the depth of the water effectually prevented them from making any attempt.

"In this unsuccessful attack, the killed and wounded on the part of the British amounted to about two hundred The Bristol and Experiment were so much damaged that it was thought they could not have been got over the bar; however, this was at last accomplished, by a very great exertion of naval skill, to the surprise of the Americans, who had expected to make them both prizes. On the American side, the loss was judged to have been considerable."*

---

62. *Declaration of Independence.*

The American people, exasperated by the proceedings of the British government, which placed them out of their protection, and engaging foreign mercenaries to assist in subduing them, began to broach the subject of independence from the British crown.

Accordingly, the subject was brought before congress; but some of the members of that body being absent, they adjourned its consideration to the first of July.

They accordingly met, and appointed Thomas Jefferson, John Adams, Benjamin Franklin, Roger Sherman, and Philip Livingston, to frame the Declaration of Independence. They agreed that each of their number should draft a declaration, and read it next day, in rotation, to the rest. They accordingly met, and Mr. Jefferson was fixed upon to "read first;" his gave such satisfaction that none other was read. Their report was accepted, and congress declared "the thirteen United States *Free and Independent*," July 4, 1776.

"This declaration was received by the people with transports of joy. Public rejoicings took place in various parts of the Union. In New York, the statue of George III. was taken down, and the lead of which it was composed, was converted into musket balls."

The Declaration of Independence was, by **order of congress**, engrossed, and signed by the following members:

* Williams' Revolution.

JOHN HANCOCK, *President*

New Hampshire.
Josiah Bartlett,
William Whipple,
Matthew Thornton.

Massachusetts Bay.
Samuel Adams,
John Adams,
Robert Treat Paine,
Elbridge Gerry.

Rhode Island, &c.
Stephen Hopkins,
William Ellery.

Connecticut.
Roger Sherman,
Samuel Huntington,
William Williams,
Oliver Wolcott.

New York.
William Floyd,
Philip Livingston,
Francis Lewis,
Lewis Morris.

New Jersey.
Richard Stockton,
John Witherspoon,
Francis Hopkinson,
John Hart,
Abraham Clark.

Pennsylvania.
Robert Morris,
Benjamin Rush,
Benjamin Franklin,
John Morton,
George Clymer,
James Smith,
George Taylor,
James Wilson,
George Ross,
Thomas M'Kean.

Delaware.
Cæsar Rodney,
George Read.

Maryland.
Samuel Chase,
William Paca,
Thomas Stone,
Chas. Carroll, of Carrollton.*

Virginia.
George Wythe,
Richard Henry Lee,
Thomas Jefferson,
Benjamin Harrison,
Thomas Nelson, Jr.
Francis Lightfoot Lee,
Carter Braxton.

North Carolina.
William Hooper,
Joseph Hews,
John Penn.

South Carolina.
Edward Rutledge,
Thomas Heyward, Jr.
Thomas Lynch, Jr.
Arthur Middleton.

Georgia.
Button Gwinnett,
Lyman Hall,
George Walton.

* The name of Carroll is the only one on the declaration to which the *residence* of the signer is appended. The reason why it was done in this case, is understood to be as follows. The patriots who signed that document, did it, almost literally, with ropes about their necks, it being generally supposed that they would, if unsuccessful, be hung as rebels. When Carroll had signed his name, some one at his elbow remarked, "You'll get clear—there are several of that

63. *Battle on Long Island.*

The command of the British force, destined to operate against New York, was given to Admiral Lord Howe and his brother Sir William, who, in addition to their military powers, were appointed commissioners for restoring peace to the colonies. Gen. Howe, after waiting two months at Halifax for his brother, and the expected re-enforcements from England, sailed with the force which he had previously commanded in Boston; and directing his course towards New York, arrived, in the latter end of June, off Sandy Hook. Admiral Lord Howe, with part of the re-enforcement from England, arrived at Halifax, soon after his brother's departure; and, without dropping anchor, followed and joined him near Staten Island. These two royal commissioners, before they commenced military operations, attempted to effect a re-union between the colonies and Great Britain; but both the substance and form of their communications for that purpose, were too exceptionable to be for a moment seriously regarded.

The British forces waited so long to receive accessions from Halifax, South Carolina, Florida, the West Indies, and Europe, that the month of August was far advanced before they were in a condition to open the campaign. Their commanders, having resolved to make their first attempt on Long Island, landed their troops, estimated at about twenty-four thousand men, at Gravesend Bay, to the right of the Narrows. The Americans, to the amount of fifteen thousand, under Major-General Sullivan, were posted on a peninsula between Mill Creek, a little above Red Hook and an elbow of East River, called Whaaleboght Bay. Here they had erected strong fortifications, which were separated from New York by East River, at the distance of a mile. A line of entrenchments from the Mill Creek enclosed a large space of ground, on which stood the American camp, near the village of Brooklyn. This line was secured by abattis, and flanked

name—they will not know which to take." "Not so," replied he, and immediately added, "of Carrollton."

by strong redoubts. The armies were separated by a range of hills, covered with a thick wood, which intersects the country from west to east, terminating on the east near Jamaica. Through these hills there were three roads; one near the Narrows, a second on the Flatbush road, and a third on the Bedford road; and these were the only passes from the south side of the hills to the American lines, excepting a road which leads to Jamaica, round the easterly end of the hills. General Putnam, agreeably to the instructions of General Washington, had detached a considerable part of his men to occupy the woody hills and passes: but in the performance of this service, there appears to have been a deficiency, either of skill or vigilance.

When the whole British army was landed, the Hessians, under General De Heister, composed the centre at Flatbush: Major-General Grant commanded the left wing, which extended to the coast; and the principal army, under the command of General Clinton, Earl Percy, and Lord Cornwallis, turned short to the right, and approached the opposite coast at Flatland. The position of the Americans having been reconnoitred, Sir William Howe, from the intelligence given him, determined to attempt to turn their left flank. The right wing of his army, consisting of a strong advanced corps, commanded by General Clinton, and supported by the brigades under Lord Percy, began, at nine o'clock at night, on the 26th of August, to move from Flatland; and, passing through the New Lots, arrived on the road that crosses the hills from Bedford to Jamaica. Having taken a patrol, they seized the pass without alarming the Americans. At half after eight in the morning, the British troops, having passed the heights and reached Bedford, began an attack on the left of the American army. In the centre, Gen. De Heister, soon after daylight, had begun to cannonade the troops, which occupied the direct road to Brooklyn, and which were commanded by General Sullivan in person. As soon as the firing towards Bedford was heard, De Heister advanced, and attacked the centre of the Americans, who, after a warm engagement, were routed, and driven into the woods. The firing towards Bedford giving them the alarming notice, that the British had turned their left flank, and were getting completely in their rear; they endeavoured to escape to the camp. The sudden rout of this party, enabled De Heister to detach a part of his force against those who were engaged near Bedford. There, also, the Americans were broken and driven into the woods; and the front of the British column, led by General Clinton, continuing to move forward, intercepted and engaged those whom De Heister had routed, and drove them back into the woods. They again met the Hessians, who drove them back on the British. Thus alternately chased and intercepted, some forced their way through the enemy to the lines of Brooklyn; several saved themselves in the coverts of the woods; but a great part of the detachment were killed or taken.

The left column, led by General Grant, advancing from the Narrows along the coast, to divert the attention of the Americans from the principal attack on the right, had, about midnight, fallen in with Lord Sterling's advanced guard, stationed at a strong pass, and compelled them to relinquish it. As they were slowly retiring, they were met on the summit of the hills, about break of day, by Lord Sterling, who had been directed, with the two nearest regiments, to meet the British on the road leading from the Narrows. Lord Sterling having posted his men advantageously, a furious cannonade commenced on both sides, which continued several hours. The firing towards Brooklyn, where the fugitives were pursued by the British, giving notice to Lord Sterling that the enemy had gained his rear, he instantly gave orders to retreat across a creek, near the Yellow Mills. The more effectually to secure the retreat of the main body of the detachment, he determined to attack, in person, a British corps under Lord Cornwallis, stationed at a house somewhat above the place where he proposed crossing the creek. With about four hundred men, drawn out of Smallwood's regiment for that purpose, he made a very spirited attack, and brought up this small corps several times to the charge, with confident expectations of disodging Lord Cornwallis from his post; but the force in his front increasing, and General Grant now advancing on his rear, he was compelled to surrender himself and his brave men prisoners of war. This bold attempt, however, gave an opportunity to a large part of the detachment to cross the creek, and effect an escape.*

"After this severe defeat, Gen. Washington, with the advice of a council of officers, ordered a retreat from Long Island. On the night of the 29th, this was effected with a success that was deemed a merciful interposition of heaven. Within a single night, an army of 9,000 men, with their artillery, tents, and baggage, was transported to New York, over a difficult ferry, a mile in width, while the British army was encamped within 600 yards, and did not discover the retreat till too late to annoy the Americans."

---

64. *Death of Captain Hale.*

After General Washington, by his retreat, had left the British in complete possession of Long Island, and not knowing what would be their future operations, he applied to General Knowlton, commander of a regiment of light infantry, to devise some means for gaining necessary information of the design of the British in their future movements. Captain Hale nobly offered himself for this hazardous and important service. His amiable, pious, intelligent, and patriotic character, and the sacrifice of his life in the manner in which he made the sacrifice, entitle him to a distinguished rank among the first patriots of the revolution. The particulars of this tragical event, sanctioned by General Hull, who knew them at the time,

---

* Holmes' Annals.
The loss of the British and Hessians is stated by American historians at about 450; Stedman says, "it did not exceed 300 killed and wounded." The loss of the Americans was not admitted by General Washington to exceed 1000 men: "but in this estimate, he could only have included the regular troops." Gen. Howe states the prisoners to have been 1097; among whom were Major-General Sullivan, and Brigadiers Lord Sterling and Woodhull.

are related by Miss H. Adams, in her History of New England.

"The retreat of Gen. Washington left the British in complete possession of Long Island. What would be their future operations remained uncertain. To obtain information of their situation, their strength, and future movements, was of high importance. For this purpose, General Washington applied to Colonel Knowlton, who commanded a regiment of light infantry, which formed the van of the American army, and desired him to adopt some mode of gaining the necessary information. Col. Knowlton communicated this request to Nathan Hale, of Connecticut, who was then a captain in his regiment. This young officer, animated by a sense of duty, and considering that an opportunity presented itself by which he might be useful to his country, at once offered himself a volunteer for this hazardous service. He passed in disguise to Long Island, examined every part of the British army, and obtained the best possible information respecting their situation and future operations.

"In his attempt to return, he was apprehended, carried before Sir William Howe, and the proof of his object was so clear, that he frankly acknowledged who he was, and what were his views.

"Sir William Howe at once gave an order to the provost marshal to execute him the next morning.

"The order was accordingly executed in the most unfeeling manner, and by as great a savage as ever disgraced humanity. A clergyman, whose attendance he desired, was refused him; a Bible, for a moment's devotion, was not procured, though he requested it. Letters, which, on the morning of his execution, he wrote to his mother and other friends, were destroyed; and this very extraordinary reason was given by the provost marshal, 'that the rebels should not know that they had a man in their army, who could die with so much firmness.'

"Unknown to all around him, without a single friend to offer him the least consolation, thus fell as amiable and as worthy a young man as America could boast.

with this as his dying observation, 'that he only lamented he had but one life to lose for his country.'"

---

65. *Battle of Trenton.*

The summer and fall of 1776 was the most gloomy period of the American revolution. Gen. Washington had been obliged to retreat from Long Island to New York, thence over the Hudson to New Jersey, and through New Jersey to Pennsylvania, vigorously pursued by an enemy flushed with a series of success. The retreat through New Jersey was attended with circumstances of a painful and trying nature. Washington's army, which had consisted of 30,000 men, was now diminished to scarcely 3,000, and these were without supplies, without pay, and many of them without shoes or comfortable clothing. Their footsteps were stained with blood as they fled before the enemy. The affairs of the Americans seemed in such a desperate condition, that those who had been most confident of success, began despairingly to give up all for lost. Many Americans joined the British, and took protections from them. In this season of general despondency, the American congress recommended to each of the states to observe "a day of solemn fasting and humiliation before God."

Gen. Washington saw the necessity of making a desperate effort for the salvation of his country. On the night of the 25th of December, 1776, the American army recrossed the Delaware, which was filled with pieces of floating ice, and marched to attack a division of Hessians, who had advanced to Trenton. The sun had just risen, as the tents of the enemy appeared in sight. No time was to be lost—Washington, rising on his stirrups, waved his sword towards the hostile army, and exclaimed, "*There, my brave friends, are the enemies of your country! and now all I have to ask of you is, to remember what you are about to fight for! March!*"

The troops, animated by their commander, pressed on

to the charge; the Hessians were taken by surprise, and the contest was soon decided; about 1000 were taken prisoners, and 40 killed, among whom was their commander, (a German officer,) Col. Rahl.

"In this important expedition, Washington divided his troops into three parts, which were to assemble on the banks of the Delaware, on the night of the 25th of December. One of these divisions, led by Gen. Irvine, was directed to cross the Delaware at the Trenton ferry, and secure the bridge below the town, so as to prevent the escape of any part of the enemy by that road. Another division, led by General Cadwallader, was to cross over at Bristol, and carry the post at Burlington. The third, which was the principal division, and consisted of about two thousand four hundred continental troops, commanded by General Washington in person, was to cross at M'Konkey's ferry, about nine miles above Trenton, and to march against the enemy posted at that town. The night fixed on for the enterprise, was severely cold. A storm of snow, mingled with hail and rain, fell in great quantities; and so much ice was made in the river, that the artillery could not be got over until three o'clock; and before the troops could take up their line of march it was nearly four. The general, who had hoped to throw them all over by twelve o'clock, now despaired of surprising the town; but knowing that he could not repass the river without being discovered and harassed, he determined, at all events, to push forward. He accordingly formed his detachment into two divisions, one of which was to march by the lower or river road, the other, by the upper or Pennington road. As the distance to Trenton by these two roads was nearly the same, the general, supposing that his two divisions would arrive at the place of destination about the same time, ordered each of them, immediately on forcing the outguards, to push directly into the town, that they might charge the enemy before they had time to form. The upper division, accompanied by the general himself, arrived at the enemy's advanced post exactly at eight o'clock, and immediately drove in the outguards. In three minutes, a firing from the division that had taken the river road, gave notice to the general of its arrival. Colonel Rahl, a very gallant Hessian officer, who commanded in Trenton, soon formed his main body, to meet the assailants; but at the commencement of the action he received a mortal wound. His troops, at once confused and hard pressed, and having already lost their artillery, attempted to file off by a road on the right, leading to Princeton; but General Washington perceiving their intention, threw a body of troops in their front, which intercepted and assailed them. Finding themselves surrounded, they laid down their arms. About twenty of the enemy were killed; and nine hundred and nine, including officers, surrendered themselves prisoners of war. The number of prisoners was soon increased to about one thousand, by the additional capture of those who had concealed themselves in houses. Six field pieces, and a thousand stand of small arms, were also taken. Of the Americans, two privates only were killed; two were frozen to death; one officer and three or four privates were wounded. General Irvine being prevented by the ice from crossing the Delaware, the lower road toward Bordentown remained open; and about five hundred of the enemy, stationed in the lower end of Trenton, crossing over the bridge in the commencement of the action, marched down the river to Bordentown. General Cadwallader was prevented by the same cause from attacking the post at Burlington. This well-judged and successful enterprise, revived the depressed spirits of the colonists, and produced an immediate and happy effect in recruiting the American army."[*]

---

66. *Battle of Princeton.*

On the 2d of January, 1777, Lord Cornwallis appeared near Trenton with a strong body of troops. Skirmishing took place, and impeded the march of the British army, until the Americans had secured their artillery and

[*] Holmes' Annals.

baggage; when they retired to the southward of the creek, and repulsed the enemy in their attempt to pass the bridge. As General Washington's force was not sufficient to meet the enemy, and his situation was critical, he determined, with the advice of a council of war, to attempt a stratagem. He gave orders for the troops to light fires in their camp, (which were intended to deceive the enemy,) and be prepared to march. Accordingly, at twelve o'clock at night, the troops left the ground, and, by a circuitous march, eluded the vigilance of the enemy, and, early in the morning, appeared at Princeton. A smart action ensued, but the British troops gave way. A party took refuge in the college, a building with strong stone walls, but were forced to surrender. The enemy lost, in killed, wounded, and prisoners, about five hundred men.* The Americans lost but few men; among them was a most valuable officer, General Mercer, who, while gallantly exerting himself in rallying the militia, (who were thrown into confusion at the commencement of the action,) received three bayonet wounds, which proved mortal. It is said he was stabbed after he had surrendered. Washington displayed the utmost coolness and presence of mind, with heroic valour; and was remarkably preserved, though, in this battle, his person was exposed to the fire of both armies.

67. *Battle of Brandywine.*

The British General Howe, with a force of 16,000 men, on the 15th of August, landed at the head of Elk river. It being obvious that his design was the occupation of Philadelphia, General Washington immediately put the American army in motion towards that place, to prevent its falling into the hands of the enemy. The two armies met at Brandywine, in Delaware.

"At day break, on the morning of the 11th, the royal army advanced in two columns; the one commanded by

* Webster.

Lieutenant General Knyphausen, and the other by Lord Cornwallis. While the first column took the direct road to Chadd's Ford, and made a show of passing it in front of the main body of the Americans, the other moved up on the west side of the Brandywine, to its fork, crossed both its branches about two in the afternoon, and marched down on its eastern side, with the view of turning the right wing of their adversaries. General Washington, on receiving intelligence of their approach, made the proper disposition to receive them. The division commanded by Sullivan, Sterling, and Stephen, advanced a little farther up the Brandywine, and fronted the column of the approaching enemy; Wayne's division, with Maxwell's light infantry, remained at Chadd's Ford, to keep Knyphausen in check; Greene's division, accompanied by General Washington, formed a reserve, and took a central position between the right and left wings. The division detached against Cornwallis, took possession of the heights above Birmingham church, their left reaching towards the Brandywine: the artillery was judiciously placed, and their flanks were covered by woods. About four o'clock, Lord Cornwallis formed the line of battle, and began the attack. The Americans sustained it for some time with intrepidity; but the right at length giving way, the remaining divisions, exposed to a galling fire on the flank, continued to break on the right, and the whole line was soon completely routed. As soon as Cornwallis had commenced the attack, Knyphausen crossed the ford, and attacked the troops posted for its defence; who, after a severe conflict, were compelled to give way. The retreat of the Americans, which soon became general, was continued that night to Chester, and the next day to Philadelphia. The loss sustained by the Americans in this action, is estimated at three hundred killed and six hundred wounded. Between three and four hundred, principally the wounded, were made prisoners. The loss of the British was stated to be rather less than one hundred killed, and four hundred wounded.

Among the wounded were two general officers; the

Marquis de La Fayette, and General Woodford. The first of these was a French nobleman, who, at the age of 19 years only, left France, and offered his services to congress, who gave him the rank of major-general in their army. Count Pulaski, a Polish nobleman, fought also with the Americans, in this battle.*

---

68. *Battle of Germantown, and the attack on Red Bank.*

After General Howe had taken possession of Philadelphia, it became necessary for him to take the forts on the Delaware, in order to open a communication with the Atlantic. Accordingly, a part of the royal army were detached for that purpose. General Washington seized this opportunity to attack the remainder at Germantown. On the morning of the 4th of October, Washington attacked the enemy with such judgment and fury, that they gave way in every quarter. "*The tumult, disorder, and despair in the British army,*" says Washington, "*were unparalleled.*" Lieutenant Col. Musgrave, in the retreat, in order to avoid the bayonets of his pursuers, threw himself, with six companies of the 40th regiment, into a stone house. The Americans, in full pursuit, attracted by this manœuvre, halted before the house and attempted to dislodge him. This circumstance appears to have led to an unfortunate issue of the action. Besides this, an uncommonly thick fog occasioned many mistakes in the American army; and after a severe action they were obliged to retreat, with the loss of about 1000 men in killed and wounded; among them was Gen. Nash, and his aid, Major Witherspoon. The British had 800 in killed and wounded, and among the former were Gen. Agnew and Col. Bird.

The detachment of the British army sent to attack the fort at Red Bank, on the Jersey shore, was commanded by Count Donop, a brave and high spirited German offi-

* Holmes' Annals.

cer. The fort was defended by about 400 men, under Col. Greene. Count Donop, with undaunted firmness, led on his men to an assault. After a few well directed fires, Greene and his men artfully retired from the *outworks*. The enemy now supposing the *day their own*, rushed forward in great numbers, along a large opening in the fort, and within twenty paces of a masked battery of eighteen pounders, loaded with grape shot and spike nails. Immediately the garrison opened a tremendous fire upon their assailants, which swept them down in great numbers. Count Donop was mortally wounded and taken prisoner. In this expedition the enemy are supposed to have lost about 400 men.

---

69. *Murder of Miss McCrea.*

Previous to the American revolution, there resided near fort Edward, an accomplished young man, named Jones, and a young lady by the name of McCrea, between whom a strong attachment subsisted. Upon the breaking out of war, Mr. Jones, who favoured the royalists, fled into Canada. Thence he accompanied the expedition of Burgoyne into the states. When the British army were within about three miles of fort Edward, Mr. Jones found means secretly to inform Miss McCrea of his approach; he entreated her not to leave the place, and informed her that as soon as the fort had surrendered, he would seek an asylum where they might peaceably consummate the nuptial ceremony. Confiding in her lover, Miss McCrea heroically refused to follow the flying villagers. The tears and entreaties of her parents and friends availed nothing. Mr. Jones, anxious to possess his intended bride, despatched a party of Indians to convey her to the British army, and offered to reward them for their service with a barrel of rum. The Indians brought a letter from her lover, and also his horse to convey Miss McCrea; she scrupled not to place herself under their protection, and accordingly set out for the

British camp. When about half way, a second party of Indians, hearing of the captivating offer made by Mr. Jones, determined to avail themselves of the reward. A bloody strife ensued, in which some Indians were killed, when the chief of the first party, to decide the contest, with his tomahawk knocked the lady from her horse, tore off her scalp, and bore it as a trophy to her anxious and expectant lover! This atrocious and cruel murder roused the American people, and produced one general burst of horror and indignation throughout the states, against the British and their savage allies, and probably hastened the downfall of Burgoyne.

70. *Battle of Bennington and Capture of Burgoyne.*

In the spring of 1777, it was determined in England that an invasion of the states should be attempted from the north, and a communication formed between Canada and the city of New York, and thus cut off the communication between the New England and more southern states.

"The troops destined for this service were upwards of seven thousand; with a train of artillery, the finest and most efficiently supplied, that had ever been assigned to second the operations of an equal force. Arms and accoutrements were provided for the Canadians, and several nations of Indians induced to take up the hatchet under royal banners. The command was given to Gen. Burgoyne; an officer whose abilities were well known, and whose spirit of enterprise and thirst for military fame could not be excelled. The British had the exclusive navigation of Lake Champlain. Their marine force on that inland sea, with which, in the preceding campaign, they had destroyed the American flotilla, was not only entire, but unopposed.

"Having gained possession of Ticonderoga, as well as of the other defences which had served to prevent or to impede the advance of an enemy into the United

States on the side of Canada, and with a degree of alacrity and perseverance not to be excelled, reached fort Edward, on the Hudson, Burgoyne proceeded, in the beginning of August, to force his passage down towards Albany. In the mean time, every obstruction had been thrown in his way, by Schuyler, Arnold, St. Clair, and other vigilant commanders; who, at this period, owing to the evacuations of the northern forts, and the exertions of the leading patriots in New York and the contiguous provinces, had in that quarter an army of 13,000 men.

" In his advance to Albany, Burgoyne formed a plan to draw resources from the farms of Vermont. For this purpose, he detached 500 Hessians and 100 Indians, with two field-pieces, under the command of Col. Baum; a force deemed sufficient to seize a magazine of provisions, collected by the Americans at Bennington. But he proceeded with less caution than his perilous situation required. On the 16th of August, Col. Starke attacked him near that place, with about 800 New Hampshire militia, undisciplined, without bayonets, or a single piece of artillery; killed or captured the greater part of his detachment, and got possession of his cannon. This was a brilliant service. Another achievement, scarcely less conspicuous, immediately succeeded. Col. Breyman, who had been sent by Gen. Burgoyne to support that party, arrived on the same day, not, however, until the action was decided. Instead of meeting his friends, he found himself vigorously assailed. This attack was made by Col. Warner; who, with his continental regiment, had come up, also, to support his friends, and was well assisted by Starke's militia, which had just defeated the party of Col. Baum. Breyman's troops, though fatigued with the preceding march, behaved with great resolution; but were at length obliged to abandon their artillery, and retreat. In these two actions, the Americans took four brass field-pieces, four ammunition wagons, and seven hundred prisoners.

" The overthrow of these detachments was the first, in a grand series of events, that finally involved in ruin the whole royal army. It deranged every plan for continuing, or even holding, the advantages previously obtained; inspired the Americans with confidence, animated their exertions, and filled them with justly formed expectations of future victory.

"After the evacuation of Ticonderoga, the Americans had fallen back from one place to another, until they at last rested at Vanshaick's Island. Soon after this retreating system was adopted, congress removed their commanding officers, and placed Gen. Gates at the head of the northern army. His arrival on the 19th of August, gave fresh vigour to the inhabitants. Encouraged by a hope of capturing the whole British forces, a spirit of adventure burst forth from every quarter, and was carried into various directions. An enterprise was undertaken by Gen. Lincoln, to recover Ticonderoga and the other posts in the rear of the British army; and though the first object was not accomplished, yet with so much address did Col. Brown, who was despatched to the landing at Lake George, proceed, that, with five hundred men, he not only surprised all the out-posts between the landing at the north end of the lake and the body of that fortress, took Mount Defiance and Mount Hope, the old French lines, and a block-house, also two hundred batteaux, several gun-boats, besides two hundred and ninety prisoners, but at the same time released one hundred Americans.

"Burgoyne, after crossing the Hudson, advanced along its banks, and encamped about two miles from Gen. Gates, a short distance above Stillwater. The Americans thought no more of retreating; and on the 19th of September, engaged him with firmness and resolution. The conflict, though severe, was only partial for the first hour and a half; but after a short pause, it became general, and continued for three hours without intermission. A constant blaze of fire streamed forth, and both sides seemed determined on victory or death. The Americans and British were alternately driven by each other, until night ended the effusion of blood. The enemy lost five hundred men, including killed, wounded, and prisoners; the Americans, three hundred.

"Every moment made the situation of the British army more critical. Their provisions were lessening, and their Indian and provincial allies deserting; whilst the animation and numbers of the Americans increased. From the uncertainty of receiving farther supplies, Burgoyne curtailed the soldiers' rations. His opponents pressed him on every side. Much hard fighting ensued. The British were again defeated. One of Burgoyne's generals, together with his aid-de-camp, was killed, and he himself narrowly escaped; as a ball passed through his hat, and another through his waistcoat. The American generals, Arnold and Lincoln, were wounded. To avoid being surrounded, Gen. Burgoyne left his hospital to the humanity of Gates, and retreated to Saratoga. He was still followed and harassed; driven on one side and straitened on another. The situation of his army was truly distressing: abandoned by their allies, unsupported by their fellow soldiers in New York, worn down by a series of incessant efforts, and greatly reduced in number; without a possibility of retreat, or of replenishing their exhausted stock of provisions, a continual cannonade pervaded their camp, and grape-shot fell in many parts of their lines.

"The 12th of October arrived; the day until which hope had bidden the afflicted general wait for the promised assistance from New York. But expectation vanished with the departing sun. He took an account of his provisions. There was only a scanty subsistence for three days. A council of war declared that their present situation justified a capitulation on honourable terms; and a negotiation was commenced. After various messages passed between the hostile armies, it was stipulated, that on the 17th, the British were to march out of their camp with the customary honours of war; the arms to be piled by word of command from their own officers: and an undisturbed passage allowed them to Great Britain, on condition of their not serving again in North America during the war.

"By this convention, were surrendered five thousand seven hundred and ninety, of all ranks; which number added to the killed, wounded, and prisoners, lost by the royal army during the preceding part of the expedition, made altogether, upwards of ten thousand men; an advantage rendered still more important to the captors, by the acquisition of thirty-five brass field pieces, and nearly five thousand muskets. The regular troops in General Gates' army were nine thousand; the militia four thousand; but, of the former, two thousand were sick or on furlough; and of the latter, five hundred.

"The celebrated Polish patriot, Kosciusko, was chief engineer in the army of Gen. Gates.

"On learning the fate of Burgoyne, the British on the North river retired to New York. Those who had been left in his rear, destroyed their cannon, and, abandoning Ticonderoga, retreated to Canada; so that this whole country, after experiencing for several months the devastations of war, was now restored to perfect tranquillity."*

71. *Treaty with France.*

On the 16th of March, 1778, Lord North intimated to the house of commons, that a paper had been laid before the king, by the French ambassador, intimating the conclusion of an alliance between the court of France and the United States of America. The preliminaries of this treaty had been concluded in the end of the year 1777, and a copy of them sent to congress, in order to counteract any proposals that might be made in the mean time by the British ministry. On the 6th of February, 1778, the articles were formally signed, to the great satisfaction of the French nation. They were in substance as follows:

1. If Great Britain should, in consequence of this treaty, proceed to hostilities against France, the two nations should mutually assist each other.

2. The main end of the treaty was, in an effectual manner, to maintain the independence of America.

* Grimshaw's Hist. United States.

3. Should those places of North America, still subject to Britain, be reduced by the states, they should be confederated with them, or subjected to their jurisdiction.

4. Should any of the West India islands be reduced by France, they should be deemed its property.

5. No formal treaty with Great Britain should be concluded, either by France or America, without the consent of each other; and it was mutually agreed, that they should not lay down their arms till the independence of the states had been formally acknowledged.

6. The contracting parties mutually agreed to invite those powers who had received injuries from Great Britain, to join in the common cause.

7. The United States guarantied to France all the possessions in the West Indies which she could conquer; and France, in her turn, guarantied the absolute independence of the states, and their supreme authority over every country they possessed, or might acquire during the war.*

This treaty was signed on the part of France by M. Gerard; on the part of the United States by Benjamin Franklin, Silas Deane, and Arthur Lee. On the 20th of March, the American commissioners were received at the court of France, as the representatives of a sister nation; an event which was considered in Europe, at that time, as the most important which had occurred in the annals of America, since its first discovery by Columbus.

72. *Battle of Monmouth, or Freehold.*

At the opening of the campaign in 1778, General Howe went to England, and left the command to Sir Henry Clinton. In June, the British army left Philadelphia, and marched towards Staten Island. In their march they were annoyed by the Americans; and on the 28th of June, a division of the army, under General

---

* Williams' History of the Revolution.

Lee, was ordered, if possible, to bring them to an engagement. Soon after the British had left the heights of Freehold, General Lee was on the same ground, and followed them into the plain. Whilst he was advancing to reconnoitre the enemy in person, Sir Henry Clinton marched back his whole rear division to attack the Americans. While Lee made a feint of retreating, in order to draw the British after him, one of his officers, Gen. Scott, who had under him the greater part of General Lee's force, misunderstood his orders, and *actually retreated*. This obliged Lee to follow, until he could overtake him, the army hanging upon his rear. In this situation he was met by General Washington, who, riding up to General Lee, addressed him in terms that implied censure. Lee answered with warmth and disrespectful language. General Washington led the troops in person, and a smart action took place, in which both parties claimed the victory, but the advantage was clearly on the side of the Americans. The loss in killed and wounded amounted to three or four hundred, on each side; but the British left the field of battle in the night, and pursued their retreat. This battle lasted through the whole of one of the warmest days of summer, the mercury being above ninety degrees by Fahrenheit's scale. Many of the soldiers died on the spot, by heat, fatigue, or drinking cold water. General Lee was tried by a court martial for disobedience, and his command suspended for one year.

73. *Taking of Savannah and Charleston.*

In 1778, Lieutenant-Colonel Campbell, an officer of courage and ability, embarked on the 27th of November from New York for Savannah, with about two thousand men, under the convoy of some ships of war, commanded by Commodore Hyde Parker; and in about three weeks landed near the mouth of Savannah river. From the landing place, a narrow causeway of six hundred yards in length, with a ditch on each side, led through a swamp. At this causeway a small party was posted, under Captain Smith, to impede the passage of the British; but it was almost instantly dispersed. Gen. Howe, the American officer, to whom the defence of Georgia was committed, had taken his station on the main road, and posted his little army, consisting of about six hundred continentals and a few hundred militia, between the landing place and the town of Savannah, with the river on his left, and a morass in front. While Col. Campbell was making arrangements to dislodge his adversaries, he received intelligence from a negro, of a private path, on the right of the Americans, through which his troops might march unobserved; and Sir James Baird, with his light infantry, was directed to avail himself of this path in order to turn their right wing, and attack their rear. As soon as it was judged that he had cleared his passage, the British in front of the Americans, were directed to advance and engage. General Howe, finding himself attacked both in front and rear, ordered an immediate retreat. The British pursued, and their victory was entire. Upwards of one hundred of the Americans were killed; and thirty-eight officers, four hundred and fifteen privates, the town and fort of Savannah, forty-eight pieces of cannon, twenty-three mortars, the fort, with its ammunition and stores, the shipping in the river, and a large quantity of provisions, were in a few hours in possession of the conquerors. The whole loss of the British during the day, amounted to no more than seven killed and nineteen wounded.*

Sir Henry Clinton, finding it more easy to make an impression on the southern states, which were less populous than the northern, and being a level country, rendered the transportation of artillery less difficult, determined to make them the seat of war. Agreeable to this resolution, he sailed from New York with a large force, in the severe winter of 1779-80; and, after a tempestuous passage, in which he lost some of his transports,

* Holmes' Annals.

arrived at Savannah the latter part of January. From Savannah the army proceeded to Charleston, and in April laid siege to that city. The enemy made regular approaches, and finally, being prepared to storm the town, General Lincoln was compelled to capitulate. About two thousand five hundred men, besides the militia and inhabitants, became prisoners, and all the cannon and military stores. This happened on the 12th of May, 1780. General Clinton left Lord Cornwallis to command the troops in the southern army, and returned to New York. Great numbers of the people in South Carolina, being left defenceless, returned to their allegiance, and the British commander represented the state as subdued.*

---

74. *Paul Jones' Naval Battle.*

On the 22d of September, 1778, occurred on the coast of Scotland, "that unexampled sea-fight," which gave to the name of Paul Jones such terrific eclat. This man was a native of Scotland, but engaged in the service of the United States. His flotilla was composed of the Bonhomme Richard, of forty guns, the Alliance of thirty-six, (both American ships,) the Pallas, a French frigate of thirty-two, in the pay of Congress, and two other smaller vessels. He fell in with a British merchant fleet, on its return from the Baltic, convoyed by Captain Pearson, with the frigate Serapis, of forty-four guns, and the Countess of Scarborough, of twenty.

Pearson had no sooner perceived Jones, than he bore down to engage him, while the merchantmen endeavoured to gain the coast. The American flotilla formed to receive him. The two enemies joined battle about seven in the evening. The British having the advantage of cannon of a longer reach, Paul Jones resolved to fight them closer. He brought up his ships, until the muzzles of his guns came in contact with those of his enemy

* Webster.

Here the phrenzied combatants fought from seven till ten. Paul Jones now found that his vessel was so shattered, that only three effective guns remained. Trusting no longer to these, he assailed his enemy with grenades; which, falling into the Serapis, set her on fire in several places. At length her magazine blew up, and killed all near it. Pearson, enraged at his officers, who wished him to surrender, commanded them to board. Paul Jones, at the head of his crew, received them at the point of the pike; and they retreated. But the flames of the Serapis had communicated to her enemy, and the vessel of Jones was on fire. Amidst this tremendous night-scene, the American frigate Alliance came up mistaking her partner for her enemy, fired a broadside into the vessel of Jones. By the broad glare of the burning ships, she discovered her mistake, and turned her guns against her exhausted foe. Pearson's crew were killed or wounded, his artillery dismounted, and his vessel on fire, and he could no longer resist. The flames of the Serapis were, however, arrested; but the leaks of the Goodman Richard could not be stopped, and the hulk went down soon after the mangled remains of the crew had been removed. Of the 375 who were on board that renowned vessel, only 68 left it alive. The Pallas had captured the Countess of Scarborough; and Jones, after this horrible victory, wandered with his shattered, unmanageable vessels, for some time; and at length, on the 6th of October, had the good fortune to find his way to the waters of the Texel.*

---

75. *Gen. Putnam's escape at Horseneck.*

About the middle of the winter of 1778, General Putnam, a bold and veteran officer, was on a visit to his outpost at Horseneck, in West Greenwich, Conn., where he found Tryon, the British governor, advancing upon that place with a corps of fifteen hundred men. To oppose this

* Willard's Hist. United States.

force, Gen. Putnam had only a force of one hundred and fifty men, with two iron field pieces, without horses or drag-ropes. Having planted his cannon on an eminence, he fired until the enemy's horse (supported by infantry) were about to charge; he then ordered his men to shelter themselves in a neighbouring swamp, inaccessible to the enemy's cavalry, and putting spurs to his horse, he plunged down a steep precipice of about 100 rude stone steps or stairs which had been constructed for the accommodation of foot passengers. The British dragoons, who were but a sword's length from him, not daring to follow, stopped, and before they could gain the valley, Putnam was far beyond their reach.

General Putnam was much distinguished, both in the French and revolutionary wars, for his bravery, and a spirit of daring enterprise. He also rendered himself famous by a noted exploit in a wolf's den. When he removed to Pomfret, Conn., that part of the country was much infested with wolves. In his immediate vicinity, a she-wolf committed considerable depredations for several years. After many unsuccessful attempts were made to destroy this ferocious animal, Putnam and his neighbours tracked her to her den, and endeavoured by fire and smoke, dogs, &c., to expel her from her habitation. These means proving ineffectual, Putnam at length came to the hazardous resolution of attacking the wolf in her den. With a torch in one hand and his gun in the other, he crawled a considerable distance into a subterraneous cavity, and discovered the wolf by the glare of her eyeballs, evidently on the point of springing at him. Putnam fired: upon this he was drawn out of the cave by his neighbours, by means of a rope he had attached to one of his legs. Putnam again descended, and finding the wolf dead, took hold of her ears, and the people above, with much exultation, dragged them out together.

76. *Storming of Stony Point.*

The reduction of this place, July 15, 1779, was one of the boldest enterprises which occurred in the revolutionary war. Stony Point is 40 miles north of New York on the Hudson.

"At this time Stony Point was in the condition of a real fortress; it was furnished with a select garrison of more than 600 men, and had stores in abundance, and defensive preparations which were formidable. Fortified as it was, General Washington ventured an attempt to reduce it. The enterprise was committed to General Wayne, who, with a strong detachment of active infantry, set out towards the place at noon. His march of fourteen miles over high mountains, through deep morasses, and difficult defiles, was accomplished by eight o'clock in the evening.

"At a distance of a mile from the point, General Wayne halted, and formed his men into two columns, putting himself at the head of the right. Both columns were directed to march in order and silence, with unloaded muskets and fixed bayonets. At midnight they arrived under the walls of the fort."*

"An unexpected obstacle now presented itself: the deep morass which covered the works, was at this time overflowed by the tide. The English opened a tremendous fire of musketry, and cannon loaded with grape shot: but neither the inundated morass, nor a double palisade, nor the storm of fire that poured upon them, could arrest the impetuosity of the Americans; they opened their way with the bayonet, prostrated whatever opposed them, scaled the fort, and the two columns met in the centre of the works. The English lost upwards of six hundred men in killed and prisoners. The conquerors abstained from pillage, and from all disorder; a conduct the more worthy, as they had still present in mind the ravages and butcheries which their enemies had so recently committed, in Virginia and

* Goodrich.

Connecticut. Humanity imparted new effulgence to the victory which valour had obtained."*

77. *Battle of Camden.*

On the 16th of August, 1780, Earl Cornwallis, who commanded the British troops, obtained a signal victory over the Americans under General Gates, at Camden. " The action began at break of day, in a situation very advantageous for the British troops, but very unfavourable to the Americans. The latter were much more numerous; but the ground on which both armies stood was narrowed by swamps on the right and left, so that the Americans could not avail themselves properly of their superior numbers.

There seems to have been some want of generalship on the part of Gates, in suffering himself to be surprised in so disadvantageous a position. But this circumstance was the effect of accident; for both armies set out with a design of attacking each other, precisely at the same time, at ten o'clock the preceding evening, and met together before day light, at the place where the action happened.

The attack was made by the British troops, with great vigour, and in a few minutes the action was general along the whole line. It was at this time a dead calm, with a little haziness in the air, which prevented the smoke from rising and occasioned so thick a darkness, that it was difficult to see the effect of a heavy and well supported fire on both sides. The British troops either kept up a constant fire, or made use of bayonets, as opportunities offered; and after an obstinate resistance of three quarters of an hour, threw the Americans into total confusion, and forced them to give way in all quarters.

The continental troops behaved remarkably well, but the militia were soon broken, leaving the former to op-

* Botta's Revolution.

pose the whole force of the British troops. General Gates did all in his power to rally the militia, but without effect; the continentals retreated in some order; but the rout of the militia was so great, that the British cavalry continued the pursuit of them to the distance of twenty-two miles from the place of action.

The loss of the Americans, on this occasion, was very considerable; about one thousand prisoners were taken, and more than that number were said to have been killed and wounded, although the number was not very accurately ascertained. Seven pieces of brass cannon, various stands of colours, and all the ammunition wagons of the Americans, fell into the hands of the enemy. Among the prisoners taken was Major General the Baron de Kalb, a Prussian officer in the American service, who was mortally wounded, after exhibiting great gallantry in the course of the action, having received eleven wounds. Of the British troops, the number of killed and wounded amounted to two hundred and thirteen."*

78. *Murder of Mrs. and Mr. Caldwell.*

In the summer of 1780, the British troops made frequent incursions into New Jersey, ravaging and plundering the country, and committing numerous atrocities upon its inhabitants. In June, a large body of the enemy, commanded by Gen. Kniphausen, landed at Elizabethtown Point, and proceeded into the country. They were much harassed in their progress by Col. Dayton, and the troops under his command. When they arrived at Connecticut Farms, according to their usual but sacrilegious custom, they burnt the Presbyterian church, parsonage house, and a considerable part of the village. But the most cruel and wanton act that was perpetrated during this incursion, was the murder of Mrs. Caldwell, the wife of the Rev. Mr. Caldwell, of Elizabethtown.

* Williams' Revolution.

This amiable woman seeing the enemy advancing retired with her housekeeper, a child of three years old, an infant of eight months, and a little maid, to a room secured on all sides by stone walls, except at a window opposite the enemy. She prudently took this precaution to avoid the danger of transient shot, should the ground be disputed near that place, which happened not to be the case; neither was there any firing from either party near the house, until the fatal moment when Mrs. Caldwell, unsuspicious of any immediate danger, sitting on the bed with her little child by the hand, and her nurse, with her infant babe by her side, was instantly shot dead by an unfeeling British soldier, who had come round to an unguarded part of the house, with an evident design to perpetrate the horrid deed. Many circumstances attending this inhuman murder, evince not only that it was committed by the enemy with design, but also, that it was by the permission, if not by the command, of Gen. Kniphausen, in order to intimidate the populace to relinquish their cause. A circumstance which aggravated this piece of cruelty, was, that when the British officers were made acquainted with the murder, they did not interfere to prevent the corpse from being stripped and burnt, but left it half the day, stripped in part, to be tumbled about by the rude soldiery; and at last it was removed from the house, before it was burned, by the aid of those who were not of the army.

Mrs. Caldwell was an amiable woman, of a sweet and even temper, discreet, prudent, benevolent, soft and engaging in her manners, and beloved by all her acquaintance. She left nine promising children.

Mrs. Caldwell's death was soon followed by that o. her husband. In November, 1781, Mr. Caldwell, hearing of the arrival of a young lady at Elizabethtown Point, whose family in New York had been peculiarly kind to the American prisoners, rode down to escort her up to town. Having received her into his chair, the sentinel, observing a little bundle tied in the lady's handkerchief, said it must be seized for the state. Mr. Caldwell immediately left the chair, saying he would deliver it to the commanding officer, who was then present; and as he stepped forward with this view, another soldier impertinently told him to stop, which he immediately did; the soldier notwithstanding, without farther provocation, shot him dead on the spot. Such was the untimely fate of Mr. Caldwell. His public discourses were sensible, animated, and persuasive; his manner of delivery agreeable and pathetic. He was a very warm patriot, and greatly distinguished himself in supporting the cause of his suffering country. As a husband, he was kind; as a citizen, given to hospitality. The villain who murdered him was seized and executed.*

---

79. *Massacre at Wyoming.*

The following account of the devastation of the flourishing settlements of Wyoming, in July, 1778, and the massacre of its inhabitants by a party of tories and Indians, under the command of the infamous *Col. Butler*, and *Brandt*, a half-blooded Indian, is thus related by Mrs. Willard, in her history of the United States.

"The devastation of the flourishing settlement of Wyoming, by a band of Indians and tories, was marked by the most demoniac cruelties. This settlement consisted of eight towns on the banks of the Susquehannah, and was one of the most flourishing as well as delightful places in America. But even in this peaceful spot, the inhabitants were not exempt from the baneful influence of party spirit. Although the majority were devoted to the cause of their country, yet the loyalists were numerous. Several persons had been arrested as tories, and sent to the proper authorities for trial. This excited the indignation of their party, and they determined upon revenge. They united with the Indians, and resorting to artifice, pretended to desire to cultivate peace with the inhabitants of Wyoming, while they were making every preparation for their meditated vengeance. The youth of Wyoming were at this time with the army, and but 500 men capable of defending the settlement remained. The inhabitants had constructed four forts for their security, into which these men were distributed. In the month of July, 1600 Indians and tories, under the command of Butler and Brandt, appeared on the banks of the Susquehannah. Two of the forts nearest the frontier immediately surrendered to them. The savages spared the women and children, but butchered the rest of their prisoners without exception. They then surrounded Kingston, the principal fort, and to dismay the garrison, hurled into the place 200 scalps, still reeking with blood. Col. Denison, knowing it to be impossible to defend the fort, demanded of Butler what terms would be allowed to the garrison if they surrendered; he answered, "*the hatchet.*" They attempted farther resistance, but were soon compelled to surrender. Enclosing the men, women, and children, in houses and barracks, they set fire to these, and the miserable wretches were all consumed.

"The fort of Wilkesbarre still remained in the power of the republicans; but the garrison, learning the fate of the others, surrendered without resistance, hoping in this way to obtain mercy. But submission could not soften the hearts of these unfeeling monsters, and their atrocities were renewed. They then devastated the country, burnt their dwellings, and consigned their crops to the flames. The tories appeared to surpass even the savages in barbarity. The nearest ties of consanguinity were disregarded; and it is asserted, that a mother was murdered by the hand of her own son. None escaped but a few women and children; and these, dispersed and wandering in the forest, without food and without clothes, were not the least worthy of commiseration."

---

80. *Distress and Mutiny of the American Army.*

The situation of Gen. Washington was often, during the war, embarrassing, for want of proper supplies for the army. It was peculiarly so, while at Morristown, in 1780, where he had encamped during the winter. The cold was uncommonly severe, and the army suffered extremely. The following account of the state of the American army is taken from Grimshaw's History of the United States.

"The distress suffered by the American army did not arrive at its highest pitch until the present season. The officers of the Jersey line now addressed a memorial to their state legislature, complaining, that four months' pay for a private would not procure for his family a single bushel of wheat; that the pay of a colonel would not purchase oats for his horse; and that a common labourer received four times as much as an American officer. They urged, that unless an immediate remedy was provided, the total dissolution of their line was inevitable; and concluded by saying, that their pay should be realized, either by Mexican dollars, or something equivalent. Nor was the insufficiency of their support the only motive to complaint. Other causes of discontent prevailed. The original idea of a continental army, to be raised, paid, and regulated, upon an equal and uniform principle, had been, in a great measure, exchanged, for that of state establishments; a pernicious measure, partly originating from necessity, because state credit was not quite so much depreciated as continental. Some states, from their superior ability, furnished their troops, not only with clothing, but with many articles of convenience. Others supplied them with mere necessaries; whilst a few, from their particular situation, could give little or perhaps nothing. The officers and men, in a routine of duty, daily intermixed and made comparisons. Those who fared worse than others, were dissatisfied with a service that allowed such injurious distinctions. Mutiny began to spread, and at length broke out among the soldiers at Fort Schuyler. Thirty-one privates of the garrison went off in a body. They were overtaken, and thirteen of their number instantly killed. About the same time, two regiments of Connecticut troops mutinied, and got under arms, determined to return home, or gain subsistence by the bayonet. Their officers reasoned with them, and used every argument that could interest their passions or their pride. They at first answered—'Our sufferings are too great—we want present relief;' but military feelings were, in the end, triumphant; after much expostulation, they returned to the encampment.

"It is natural to suppose that the British commander would not lose so favourable an opportunity of severing the discontented from their companions, and attracting them to his own standard. He circulated a printed paper in the American camp; tending to heighten the disorders by exaggeration, and create desertion by promises of bounty and caresses. But, so great was the firmness of the soldiery, and so strong their attachment to their country, that on the arrival of only a scanty supply of meat, for their immediate subsistence, military duty was cheerfully performed, and the rolls were seldom dishonoured by desertion.

"The necessities of the American army grew so pressing, that Washington was constrained to call on the magistrates of the adjacent counties for specified quantities of provisions, to be supplied in a given number of days; and was compelled even to send out detachments, to collect subsistence at the point of the bayonet. Even this expedient at length failed; the country in the vicinity of the army being soon exhausted. His situation was painfully embarrassing. The army looked to him for provisions; the inhabitants for protection. To supply the one, and not offend the other, seemed impossible. To preserve order and subordination, in an army of republicans, even when well fed, regularly paid, and comfortably clothed, is not an easy task; but to retain them in service, and subject them to the rules of discipline, when wanting, not only the comforts, but often the necessaries of life, requires such address and abilities, as are rarely found in human nature. These were, however, combined in Washington. He not only kept his army in the field, but opposed those difficulties with so much discretion, as to command the approbation of both soldiers and people.

"To obviate these evils, congress sent a committee of its own members to the encampment of the main army. They confirmed the representations previously made, of the distresses and the disorders arising from commissarial mismanagement, which every where prevailed. In particular, they stated that the main army was unpaid for five months; that it seldom had more than six days' provision in advance; and was on different occasions, for several successive days, without meat; that the horses were destitute of forage; that the medical department had no sugar, tea, chocolate, wine, or spirituous liquors of any kind; that every department was without money, and without credit; and that the patience of the soldiers, worn down by the pressure of complicated sufferings, was on the point of being exhausted.

"Misfortunes, from every quarter, were, at this time, pouring in upon the United States. But they seemed to rise in the midst of their distresses, and gain strength from the pressure of calamities. When congress could obtain neither money nor credit for the subsistence of their army, the inhabitants of Philadelphia gave three hundred thousand dollars, to procure a supply of necessary provisions for the suffering troops; and the ladies of that city, at the same time, contributed largely to their immediate relief. Their example was generally followed. The patriotic flame which blazed forth in the beginning of the war, was rekindled. The different states were ardently excited; and it was arranged, that the regular army should be raised to thirty-five thousand effective men."

---

81. *Capture of Andre, and Treason of Arnold.*

In the year 1780, a plot fraught with much danger to the American cause was happily discovered. This plot originated with Arnold, a general in the American army, who by his extravagance and overbearing behaviour had brought upon himself a reprimand from the American congress. Of a temper too impetuous to bear reproof, Arnold, bent on revenge, entered into a negotiation through Major John Andre, adjutant general in the British army, to deliver up to the enemy the important post of West Point, of which Arnold had the command.

Andre proceeded in disguise to West Point, drew a plan of the fortress, concerted with Arnold, and agreed upon the manner and time of attack. Having obtained a passport, and assumed the name of Anderson, Andre set out on his return to New York by land. He passed the outposts of the American army without suspicion. Supposing himself now out of danger, he pressed forward, elated with the prospect of the speedy execution of a plot, which was to give the finishing blow to liberty in America.

When Andre had arrived within about thirty miles of New York, and as he was entering a village called Tarrytown, three militia men, who happened that way, JOHN PAULDING, DAVID WILLIAMS, and ISAAC VAN WART, seized the bridle of his horse, and accosted him with, "Where are you bound?" Andre, supposing that they were of the British, did not immediately show his passport, but waving their question, asked them, "*where they belonged to?*" they replied "*to below*," (referring to the course of the river, and implying that they were of the British party.) "*And so do I*," said Andre, (confirmed in his mistake by this stratagem,) and at the same time informed them that he was a British officer on urgent business, and must not be detained. "*You belong to our enemies*," exclaimed the militia men, "*and we arrest you.*" Andre, struck with astonishment, presented his passport; but this, after what had passed, only rendered his case the more suspicious. He then offered them a purse of gold, his horse and watch, besides a large reward from the British government, if they would but liberate him. But these soldiers, though poor and obscure, were not to be bribed. They searched him, and found concealed in his boot, papers which evidenced his guilt, and they immediately conducted him to Colone. Jameson, their commanding officer.

Andre was tried by a board of general officers of the American army, and executed as a spy, at Tappan, New York, October 2. He was a young officer, high minded, brave, accomplished, and humane. He suffered with fortitude, and his fate excited the universal sympahy of all parties.*

---

82. *Battle at King's Mountain.*

"It had been the policy of the British, since the general submission of the inhabitants of South Carolina, to increase the royal force by embodying the people of the country as British militia. In the district of Ninety-

---

* Major Andre had many friends in the American army, and even Washington would have spared him, had duty to his country permitted. Every possible effort was made by Sir Henry Clinton in his favour; but it was deemed important that the decision of the board of war should be carried into execution.

When Major Andre was apprised of the sentence of death, he made a last appeal in a letter to Washington, that he might be shot rather than die on a gibbet.

The letter of Andre roused the sympathies of Washington, and had he only been concerned, the prisoner would have been pardoned and released. But the interests of his country were at stake, and the sternness of justice demanded that private feelings should be sacrificed.

Upon consulting his officers on the propriety of listening to Major Andre's request, to receive the death of a soldier, (to be shot,) it was deemed necessary to deny it, and to make him an example.

As a reward to Paulding, Williams, and Van Wart, for their virtuous and patriotic conduct, congress voted to each of them an annuity of $200, and a silver medal, on one side of which was a shield with this inscription—"fidelity,"—and on the other, the following motto—"*vincit amor patriæ*,"—the love of country conquers.

Arnold, the miserable wretch, whose machinations led to the melancholy fate Andre experienced, escaped to New York, where, as the price of his dishonour, he received the commission of *brigadier general*, and the sum of *ten thousand pounds sterling!*

This last boon was the grand secret of Arnold's fall from virtue, his vanity and extravagance had led him into expenses which it was neither in the power nor will of congress to support. He had involved himself in debt, from which he saw no hope of extricating himself; and his honour was therefore bartered for British gold.— *Goodrich's Hist. U. S.*

six, Major Ferguson, a partisan of distinguished merit, had been employed to train the most loyal inhabitants, and to attach them to his own corps. That officer was now directed by Lord Cornwallis to enter the western part of North Carolina, near the mountains, and to embody the loyalists in that quarter, for co-operation with his army. Cornwallis, in the mean time, commenced his march with the main army from Camden, through the settlement of the Waxhaws, to Charlotteville, in North Carolina. About the same time, Colonel Clark, of Georgia, at the head of a small body of men, which he had collected in the frontiers of North and South Carolina, advanced against Augusta, and laid siege to that place. Colonel Brown, who with a few loyal provincials held that post for the British, made a vigorous defence; and, on the approach of Colonel Cruger, with a re-enforcement from Ninety-Six, Clark relinquished the enterprise, and made a rapid retreat through the country along which he had marched to the attack. Major Ferguson, receiving intelligence of his movements, prepared to intercept him. The hardy mountaineers of Virginia and North Carolina, collecting at this time from various quarters, constituted a formidable force, and advanced by a rapid movement towards Ferguson. At the same time, Colonel Williams, from the neighbourhood of Ninety-Six, and Colonels Tracy and Banan, also of South Carolina, conducted parties of men towards the same points. Ferguson, having notice of their approach, commenced his march for Charlotteville. The several corps of militia, amounting to near three thousand men, met at Gilberttown, lately occupied by Ferguson. About one thousand six hundred riflemen were immediately selected, and mounted on their fleetest horses, for the purpose of following the retreating army. They came up with the enemy at King's Mountain, October 7, 1780, where Ferguson, on finding he should be overtaken, had chosen his ground, and waited for an attack. The Americans formed themselves into three divisions, led by Colonels Campbell, Shelby, and Cleaveland, and began to ascend the mountain in three different and opposite directions.* Cleaveland, with his division, was the first to gain sight of the enemy's pickets, and halting his men, he addressed them in the following simple, affecting, and animating terms:—"My brave fellows, we *have* beat the *tories*, and we *can* beat them; they are all cowards. If they had the spirit of men they would join with their fellow-citizens in supporting the independence of their country. When engaged, you are not to wait for the word of command from me. *I will show you by my example how to fight.* I can undertake no more. Every man must consider himself as an officer, and act from his own judgment. Fire as quick as you can, and stand your ground as long as you can. When you can do no better, get behind trees, or retreat; but I beg of you not to run quite off. If we are repulsed, let us make a point to return, and renew the fight; perhaps we may have better luck in the second attempt than in the first. If any of you are afraid, such have leave to retire, and they are requested *immediately to take themselves off.*" This address, which would have done honour to the hero of Agincourt, being ended, the men rushed upon the enemy's pickets, and forced them to retire; but returning again to the charge with the bayonet, Cleveland's men gave way in their turn. In the mean time, Colonel Shelby advanced with his division, and was in like manner driven back by the bayonets of the enemy; but there was yet another body of assailants to be received: Colonel Campbell moved up at the moment of Shelby's repulse, but was equally unable to stand against the British bayonet; and Ferguson still kept possession of his mountain. The whole of the division being separately baffled, determined to make another effort in co-operation, and the conflict became terrible. Ferguson still depended upon the bayonet; but this brave and undaunted officer, after gallantly sustaining the attack for nearly an hour, was killed by a musket ball, and his troops soon after surrendered at discretion. The enemy's loss on this occasion was 300 killed and wounded, 800 prisoners, and

1,500 stand of arms. Our loss in killed was about 20, among whom was Colonel Williams, one of our most active and enterprising officers; our number of wounded was very considerable.*

---

83. *Battle of the Cowpens.*

In the autumn of 1780 Gen. Greene was appointed to the command of the forces in Carolina. He was accompanied by Col. Morgan, a brave and active officer, who commanded a body of riflemen.

On the entrance of Morgan into the district of Ninety-Six, Lord Cornwallis detached Lieut. Col. Tarleton to drive him from his station, and to "*push him to the utmost.*" Tarleton's force consisted of about 1000 choice infantry, and 250 horse, with two field-pieces. To oppose this force, Morgan had but 500 militia, 300 regulars, and 75 horse, under the command of Colonel Washington. The two detachments met on the 17th of Jan., 1781, at the Cowpens. The ground on which this memorable battle was fought, was an open pine barren. The militia were drawn up about 280 yards in front of the regulars, and the horse some small distance in the rear. Just after daybreak, the British came in sight; and halting within about a quarter of a mile of the militia, began to prepare for battle. The sun had just risen, as the enemy, with loud shouts, advanced to the charge. The militia, hardly waiting to give them a distant fire, broke, and fled for their horses, which were tied at some distance. Tarleton's cavalry pushed hard after them, and coming up just as they reached their horses, began to cut them down. On seeing this, Col. Washington, with his cavalry, dashed on to their rescue. As if certain of victory, Tarleton's men were all scattered in the chase. Washington's men, on the contrary, advanced closely and compactly, and gave the British cavalry such a fatal charge, that they fled in the utmost precipitation. The Bri-

* Allen's Revolution.

tish infantry now came up; and having crossed a little valley, just as they ascended the hill, they found themselves within twenty paces of the regular Americans, under Col. Howard, who at this moment poured upon them a general and deadly fire. This threw them into confusion. The militia, seeing this change in the battle, recovered their spirits and began to form on the right of the regulars. Morgan, waving his sword, instantly rode up, exclaiming with a loud voice, "*Hurrah! my brave fellows! form! form! old Morgan was never beat in his life!—one fire more, my heroes, and the day is our own!*" With answering shouts, both regulars and militia then advanced upon the enemy; and following their fire with the bayonet, instantly decided the conflict.

The British lost in this engagement upwards of 300 killed and wounded, and more than 500 prisoners. The loss of the Americans was but 12 killed and 60 wounded.

---

84. *Battle of Guilford.*

After the disaster at the Cowpens, Lord Cornwallis determined to intercept Colonel Morgan, and retake the prisoners; but a heavy rain in the night, swelled the rivers so as to prevent his design. To enable his troops to march with more celerity, he destroyed all his heavy baggage. At length General Greene joined Colonel Morgan, with additional forces, and Lord Cornwallis having collected his troops, the armies met near the court-house in Guilford. The action was fought on the 15th of March, 1781. The Americans amounted to between 4 and 5000 men, but mostly militia, or inexperienced soldiers. The British force consisted of about half that number of veterans.[*] The Americans were drawn up in three lines. The front was composed of North Carolina militia, commanded by Generals Butler and Eaton; the second of Virginia militia, commanded by Stephens and Lawson; the third, of continental

[*] Webster.

troops, commanded by Gen. Huger and Col. Williams. The British, after a brisk cannonade in front, advanced in three columns, the Hessians on the right, the guards in the centre, and Lieut. Col. Webster's brigade on the left; and attacked the front line. The militia composing this line, through the misconduct of an officer, in giving occasion to a false alarm, precipitately quitted the field. The Virginia militia stood their ground, and kept up their fire, until they were ordered to retreat.* The continental troops were last engaged, and maintained the conflict with great spirit an hour and a half; but were then forced to give way before their veteran adversaries. The British broke the second Maryland brigade; turned the American left flank; and got in the rear of the Virginia brigade. On their appearing to be gaining Greene's right, and thus threatening to encircle the whole of the continental troops, a retreat was ordered, which was well conducted.† The battle was fought with great bravery and effect; for although Lord Cornwallis remained master of the field, his losses in a country where he could not recruit his army, had the effect of a defeat. His loss was more than five hundred men. That of the Americans was about four hundred in killed and wounded, of which more than three fourths were continentals.

---

85. *Battle of Eutaw Springs.*

On the 9th of September, 1781, Gen. Greene, having assembled about two thousand men, proceeded to attack the British, who, under the command of Col. Stewart, were posted at Eutaw Springs. The American force was drawn up in two lines: the first, composed of Carolina militia, was commanded by Generals Marion and Pickens, and Col. De Malmedy. The second, which consisted of continental troops from North Carolina, Vir-

---

* Gen. Stephens, their heroic commander, had posted forty riflemen, at equal distances in the rear of this brigade, with orders to shoot every man who should leave his post.
† Holmes' American Annals.

ginia, and Maryland, was commanded by Gen. Sumpter Lieut. Col. Campbell, and Col. Williams. Lieut. Col. Lee, with his legion, covered the right flank; and Lieut. Col. Henderson, with the state troops, covered the left. A corps de reserve was formed of the cavalry, under Lieut. Col. Washington, and the Delaware troops, under Capt. Kirkwood. As the Americans came forward to the attack, they fell in with some advanced parties of the enemy at about two or three miles ahead of the main body. These being closely pursued, were driven back; and the action soon became general. The militia were at length forced to give way, but were bravely supported by the second line. In the hottest part of the engagement, Gen. Greene ordered the Maryland and Virginia continentals to charge with trailed arms. This decided the fate of the day. "Nothing," says Dr. Ramsey, "could surpass the intrepidity of both officers and men on this occasion. They rushed on, in good order, through a heavy cannonade, and a shower of musketry, with such unshaken resolution, that they bore down all before them." The British were broken, closely pursued, and upwards of five hundred of them taken prisoners. They, however, made a fresh stand, in a favourable position, in impenetrable shrubs, and a picketted garden. Lieut. Col. Washington, after having made every effort to dislodge them, was wounded and taken prisoner. Four six pounders were brought forward to play upon them, but they fell into their hands; and the endeavours to drive them from their station being found impracticable, the Americans retired, leaving a strong picket on the field of battle. Their loss was about five hundred; that of the British upwards of eleven hundred.

Gen. Greene was honoured by congress with a British standard, and a gold medal, emblematic of the engagement and its success, "for his wise, decisive, and magnanimous conduct in the action of Eutaw Springs, in which, with a force inferior in number to that of the enemy, he obtained a most signal victory."

In the evening of the succeeding day, Col. Stewart abandoned his post, and retreated towards Charleston, leaving behind upwards of seventy of his wounded, and a thousand stand of arms. He was pursued a considerable distance, but in vain.

The battle of Eutaw produced the most signal consequences in favour of America. The British, who had for such a length of time, lorded it absolutely in South Carolina, were, shortly after that event, obliged to confine themselves to Charleston.*

---

86. *Storming of Fort Griswold*

While the combined armies were advancing to the siege of Yorktown, General Arnold, the traitor, who had lately returned from Virginia, was appointed to conduct an expedition against New London. The troops employed in this service, were landed on each side of the harbour, in two detachments; the one commanded by Lieut. Col. Eyre, and the other by Gen. Arnold. New London is a seaport town, situated near the mouth of the Thames, on the west side of that river. For the defence of the place, there had been constructed, below the town, on the western side of the harbour, a fort, called Fort Trumbull, with a redoubt; and opposite to it, on Groton Hill, another fort, called Fort Griswold, a strong square fortification, insufficiently garrisoned. Fort Trumbull, the redoubt, and the town of New London, being totally untenable, were evacuated on the approach of Arnold, who took possession of them with inconsiderable loss. Fort Griswold was defended by Col. Ledyard, with a garrison of about one hundred and sixty men, some of whom had just evacuated the works on the opposite side of the river. On the rejection of a summons to surrender, the British marched up to the assault on three sides; and, though the ascent was steep, and a continued fire was directed against them, they at length made a lodgment on the ditch and fraized work, and entered the embrasures with charged bayonets. An officer of the

* Morse's Revolution.

conquering troops, on entering the fort, asked who commanded it, "I did," answered Col. Ledyard, "but you do now;" and presented him his sword, which was instantly plunged into his own bosom. Although resistance had now ceased, yet, to the indelible infamy of the conquerors, they commenced a merciless slaughter, which "was kept up until a greater part of the garrison was killed or wounded." The town of New London, and the stores contained in it, were reduced to ashes; and General Arnold, having completed the object of the expedition, returned in eight days to New York.*

---

87. *Siege of Yorktown, and surrender of Cornwallis.*

The 19th of October, 1781, was rendered memorable by the surrender of the British army, consisting of 7000 men, under Cornwallis, at Yorktown, Va. This joyful event decided the revolutionary contest, and laid the foundation for a general peace. About the last of August, Count de Grasse, with a French fleet, arrived in the Chesapeake, and blocked up the British troops who had fortified themselves at Yorktown.

Previous to this, the American and French troops, under Gen. Washington, had moved to the southward: and as soon as he heard of the arrival of a French fleet, made rapid marches to the head of Elk river, where embarking, the troops soon arrived at Yorktown.

On the 6th of October, the trenches were opened by the combined army, upon his lordship, at the distance of 600 yards. On the 9th, the Americans completed their batteries in the afternoon, and began to play upon the camp of his lordship, with their twenty-fours, eighteens, and ten inch mortars, which continued through the night, without intermission.

The next morning the French opened a terrible fire from their batteries, without intermission, for about eight hours, and on the succeeding night a tremendous fire

* Holmes' Annals.

was kept up through the whole line, without intermission, through the night. The horrors of this scene were greatly heightened by the conflagration of two British ships, which were set on fire by the shells, and consumed in the night, October 10th. The next morning another guard ship of the enemy was consumed by the shells of the besiegers, and at the same time they opened their second parallel, at the distance of 200 yards from the enemy's lines.

On the 14th Gen. Washington ordered two battalions to advance to the second parallel, and begin a large battery, upon the centre and in advance. During this operation the enemy kept up an incessant fire, which proved very destructive, and continued through the night.

Gen. Washington detached the Marquis La Fayette at the head of the American light infantry, to storm a redoubt on the left of the British, and about 200 yards in advance of their lines; with full powers to revenge upon the enemy the cruelties practised at New London, and put the captives to the sword. The redoubt was carried at the point of the bayonet; but such was the humanity of these sons of liberty, that the captives were spared, and treated with kindness.

The fire of the allies, and the sickness that prevailed in the British camp, weakened his lordship, and prevented his making such sorties as he otherwise would have done; but the besieged, on the morning of the 16th, made a sortie, with a detachment of about 400 men, under the command of Lieut. Colonel Abercrombie; carried two batteries, which were nearly ready to open their fire, and spiked the cannon. The French suffered severely in defending these batteries, but the British gained no considerable advantage. On the same day, at four in the afternoon, the allies opened their batteries, covered with about 100 pieces of heavy cannon, and such was the destructive fire, that the British works were soon demolished, and silenced. Alarmed for his safety, Lord Cornwallis now began to prepare to retire; his boats were collected, and a part of his army embarked across to Gloucester Point; but a violent storm arose suddenly, which defeated the plan, and his lordship was enabled, with the greatest difficulty, to recover his boats, and restore the division that had already been embarked.

His lordship now saw that all hopes of succour or escape had failed, and that the tremendous fire of the allies, with its overwhelming destruction, bore down, killed, and destroyed the British army, so as to compel him to request a parley on the 18th, for twenty-four hours, and that commissioners* might be appointed to draw up the terms of capitulation, to which Gen. Washington assented, and commissioners were appointed accordingly. On the 19th, the articles of capitulation were signed, and on the 20th, the whole army of Cornwallis marched out, *prisoners of war.*

The spectacle of the surrender was impressive and affecting. The road through which the captive army marched, was lined with spectators. On one side, Gen. Washington, with the American staff, took their station; on the opposite side, was the Count de Rochambeau with the French staff.

"The captive army approached, moving slowly in columns, with grace and precision. Universal silence was observed amidst the vast concourse, and the utmost decency prevailed; exhibiting in demeanour, an awful sense of the vicissitude of human life, mingled with commisseration for the unhappy."

Lord Cornwallis, unable to endure the humiliation of marching at the head of his troops, appointed General O'Hara his representative, who delivered up the sword of Cornwallis to the American commander-in-chief.

* The commissioners on the part of the allies, were the Viscount De Noaille and Lieut. Col. Laurens, whose father had been appointed by congress, minister to the court of Versailles, and who was captured by the British on his passage, and confined in the tower at London, where he remained in close confinement at that very time.

88. *Washington taking leave of the Army.*

The storm of the revolution having subsided, the definitive treaty was signed on the 30th of September, 1783, and the 3d of November was fixed on by congress, for disbanding the United States' army. On the day preceding, General Washington gave an affectionate farewell to the soldiers, who, during "*the time that tried men's souls,*" had fought by his side. "Being now," he said in his address to the army, "to conclude these, my last public orders, to take my ultimate leave in a short time of the military character, and to bid a final adieu to the armies I have so long had the honour to command, I can only again offer in your behalf, my recommendations to our grateful country, and my prayer to the God of armies. May ample justice be done you here, and may the choicest favours, both here and hereafter, attend those, who, under the divine auspices, have secured innumerable blessings for others! With these wishes and this benediction, the commander-in-chief is about to retire from service. The curtain of separation will soon be drawn, and the military scene will be closed for ever."

The officers of the army assembled at New York. Washington was there also, and at parting, thus addressed them:—"With a heart full of love and gratitude, I now take my leave of you. I most devoutly wish that your latter days may be as prosperous and happy as your former ones have been glorious and honourable." Taking each by the hand, he bade them farewell. They then accompanied him to the shores of the Hudson, where he was received in a barge magnificently decorated, and manned with thirteen sea captains—and waving his hat, while the tears started from his eyes, he bade a silent adieu to the companions of his glory.

---

89. *Continental Money.*

The expedient of supplying the deficiencies of specie, by emissions of paper bills, was adopted very early in the colonies. In many instances, these emissions produced good effects. These bills were generally a legal tender, in all colonial or private contracts, and the sums issued did not generally exceed the granted requisite for a medium of trade; they retained their full nominal value in the purchase of commodities. But as they were not received by the British merchants, in payment for their goods, there was a great demand for specie and bills, which occasioned the latter at various times to depreciate. Thus was introduced a difference between the English sterling money, and the currencies of the different states, which remains to this day.*

The advantages the colonies had derived from paper currency under the British government, suggested to congress, in 1775, the idea of issuing bills for the purpose of carrying on the war. And this, perhaps, was the only expedient. They could not raise money by taxation, and it could not be borrowed. The first emissions had no other effect upon the medium of commerce, than to drive the specie from circulation. But when the paper substituted for specie, had, by repeated emissions, augmented the sum in circulation, much beyond the usual sum in specie, the bills began to lose their value. The depreciation continued, in proportion to the sums emitted, until one hundred paper dollars were hardly an equivalent for one Spanish milled dollar. With this depreciated paper was the army paid; and from 1775 to 1781, this currency was almost the only medium of trade, until the sum in circulation amounted to two hundred millions of dollars. But about the year 1780, specie began to be plentiful, being introduced by the French army, a private trade with the Spanish islands, and an illicit intercourse with the British garrison in New York. This circumstance accelerated the depreciation of the paper bills, until their value had sunk to almost nothing. In

* A dollar in sterling money is 4s. 6d. But the price of a dollar rose in New England currency to 6s.; in New York, to 8s.; in New Jersey, Pennsylvania, and Maryland, to 7s. 6d.; in Virginia, to 6s.; in North Carolina, to 8s.; in South Carolina and Georgia, to 4s. 8d. This difference, originating between paper and specie, or bills, continued afterwards to exist in the nominal estimation of gold and silver. *Franklin's Miscellaneous Works.*

1781, the merchants and brokers of the southern states, apprehensive of the approaching fate of the currency, pushed immense quantities of it suddenly into New England; made vast purchases of goods in Boston, and instantly the bills vanished from circulation.

The whole history of this continental paper, is a history of public and private frauds. Old specie debts were often paid in a depreciated currency; and even new contracts for a few weeks or days, were often discharged with a small part of the value received. From this plenty, and the fluctuating state of the medium, sprang hosts of *speculators*, and itinerant traders, who left their honest occupations for the prospects of immense gains, in a fraudulent business, that depended on no fixed principles, and the profits of which could be reduced to no certain calculations.*

90. *Shay's Insurrection in Massachusetts.*

In the year 1786, an insurrection took place in Massachusetts. "A heavy debt lying on the state, and almost all the corporations within it; a relaxation of manners; a free use of foreign luxuries; a decay of trade; with a scarcity of money; and above all, the debts due from individuals to each other; were the primary causes of this sedition. Heavy taxes, necessarily imposed at this time, were the immediate excitement to discontent and insurgency."

The leader of the malcontents in Massachusetts, was Daniel Shays. At the head of three hundred men, he marched to Springfield, where the supreme judicial court was in session, and took possession of the court-house. He then appointed a committee, who waited on the court with an order couched in the humble form of a petition, requesting them not to proceed to business; and both parties retired. The number of insurgents increased: the posture of affairs became alarming: and an

* Morse's Geography, 1789.

army of 4000 men was at length ordered out for their dispersion. This force was placed under the command of General Lincoln. His first measure was to march to Worcester; and he afforded such protection to the court at that place, that it resumed and executed its judicial functions. Orders were given to General Shepard, to collect a sufficient force to secure the arsenal at Springfield. Accordingly, he raised about 900 men, who were re-enforced by 800 militia from the county of Hampshire. At the head of this force, he marched, as directed, to Springfield.

On the 25th of January, Shays approached, at the head of 1100 men. Shepard sent out one of his aids to know the intention of the insurgents, and to warn them of their danger. Their answer was, that they would have the barracks, and they proceeded to within a few hundred yards of the arsenal. They were then informed that the militia were posted there by order of the governor; and that they would be fired upon, if they approached nearer. They continued to advance, when General Shepard ordered his men to fire, but to direct their fire over their heads; even this did not intimidate them, or retard their movements. The artillery was then levelled against the centre column, and the whole body thrown into confusion. Shays attempted in vain to rally them. They made a precipitate retreat to Ludlow, about ten miles from Springfield. Three men were killed, and one wounded. They soon after retreated to Petersham; but General Lincoln pursuing their retreat, they finally dispersed.

Some of the fugitives retired to their homes; but many, and among them their principal officers, took refuge in the states of New Hampshire, Vermont, and New York.*

---

91. *Adoption of the Federal Constitution.*

In pursuance of the request of Virginia, most of the states appointed delegates, who assembled at Annapolis,

* Mrs. Willard's Hist. U. S.

September 14, 1786. But on examining their commissions, it was judged that their powers were too limited to enable them to accomplish any desirable purpose. They therefore adjourned, with instructions to advise the states to appoint agents with more ample powers, to meet at Philadelphia, the next year. Accordingly, delegates from the several states assembled in that city, in May, 1787, and appointed the venerable Washington for their president. That gentleman had retired to his farm in 1783, with a fixed determination never more to engage in public affairs; but he was selected by Virginia as one of the delegates on this important occasion, and pressed to accept the appointment. After four months' deliberation, the convention agreed to a frame of government for the United States, and recommended it to the severa. states for adoption.

The states referred the question of adopting the frame of government to conventions appointed for that express purpose. On that occasion, popular jealousy appeared in all its force. It was objected, that the plan of government proposed abridged the states of their sovereignty, and amounted to a consolidation. This was a fruitful theme of declamation, notwithstanding all the calamities that had arisen from the jealousies and clashing interests of the states, and a want of uniformity in public measures. Many other objections were urged, especially in the large states. At length, however, the proposed frame of federal government was accepted and ratified in 1788, by eleven states, and became the constitution of the United States. The first convention of North Carolina rejected it; as did the town meetings, to which it was referred, in Rhode Island. But North Carolina acceded to it in November, 1789, and Rhode Island in May, 1790. The ratification of the constitution was celebrated in the large cities, with great joy and splendid exhibitions. A ship, the emblem of commerce, and stages for mechanical labour, the emblems of manufactures, were mounted on wheels and drawn through the streets, attended by immense processions of citizens, arranged according to their professions; while bands of music, streaming flags, and the roar of the cannon, manifested the enthusiasm with which the people received the authority of the national government.*

---

92. *Inauguration of President Washington.*

On the 3d of March, 1789, the delegates from the eleven states, which at that time had ratified the constitution, assembled at New York, where a convenient and elegant building had been prepared for their accommodation. On opening and counting the votes for president, it was found that George Washington was unanimously elected to that dignified office, and that John Adams was chosen vice-president. The annunciation of the choice of the first and second magistrates of the United States, occasioned a general diffusion of joy among the friends of the Union, and fully evinced that these eminent characters were the choice of the people.

On the 30th of April, 1789, George Washington was inaugurated president of the United States of America, in the city of New York. The ceremony was performed in the open gallery of Federal Hall, in the view of many thousand spectators. The oath was administered by Chancellor Livingston. Several circumstances concurred to render the scene unusually solemn; the presence of the beloved father and deliverer of his country—the impressions of gratitude for past service—the vast concourse of spectators—the devout fervency with which he repeated the oath, and the reverential manner in which he bowed to kiss the sacred volume; these circumstances, together with that of his being chosen to the most dignified office in America, and perhaps in the world, by the unanimous voice of more than three millions of enlightened freemen, all conspired to place this among the most august and interesting scenes which have ever been exhibited on this globe.†

" It seemed from the number of witnesses," said a

* Webster. † Dr. Morse.

spectator of the scene, "to be a solemn appeal to heaven and earth at once. Upon the subject of this great and good man, I may perhaps be an enthusiast; but I confess I was under an awful and religious persuasion, that the gracious Ruler of the universe was looking down at that moment, with peculiar complacency, on an act, which, to a part of his creatures, was so very important. Under this impression, when the chancellor pronounced, in a very feeling manner, '*Long live George Washington,*' my sensibility was wound up to such a pitch, that I could do no more than wave my hat with the rest, without the power of joining in the repeated acclamations which rent the air."

---

93. *Whiskey Insurrection in Pennsylvania.*

The year 1794 was distinguished by an insurrection in Pennsylvania, commonly called the *Whiskey Insurrection.* "In 1791, congress had enacted laws laying duties upon spirits distilled in the United States, and upon stills. From the commencement of the operation of these laws, combinations were formed in the four western counties of Pennsylvania to defeat them; and violences were repeatedly committed. In July of the present year, (1794,) about one hundred persons, armed with guns and other weapons, attacked the house of an inspector of the revenue, and wounded some persons within it. They seized the marshal of the district of Pennsylvania, (who had been previously fired on while in the execution of his duty, by a party of armed men,) and compelled him to enter into stipulations to forbear the execution of his office. Both the inspector and the marshal were obliged to fly from that part of the country to the seat of government. These, and many other outrages, induced President Washington, on the 7th of August, to issue a proclamation, commanding the insurgents to disperse, and warning all persons against aiding, abetting, or comforting, the perpetrators of these treason-able acts, and requiring all officers, and other citizens, according to their respective duties and the laws of the land, to exert their utmost endeavours to prevent and suppress such dangerous proceedings.

"The president, having ordered out a suitable number of the militia, proceeded in October to Bedford, whence he gave out instructions to Governor Lee, of Maryland, whom he appointed to conduct the militia army for the suppression of the insurgents. Governor Lee marched his troops, amounting to fifteen hundred men, into the western counties of Pennsylvania; and, on the approach of this respectable force, the insurgents laid down their arms, solicited the clemency of government, and promised future submission to the laws."* Eighteen of the insurgents were tried for treason, but not convicted. During the scene of insurgency, no person was killed, excepting Major M'Farlane, who was killed in an attack on the inspector's house, at the commencement of the insurrection, and two men, who were killed by some of the army on their march.

94. *Yellow Fever in Philadelphia in* 1793.

The yellow fever, which has been the scourge of most of our principal southern cities, appears to have been in existence ever since the first settlement of our country. What the first cause of this disease is, or how it is propagated, are subjects upon which physicians have a variety of opinions. The most remarkable and fatal instance of the prevalence of the yellow fever in our country, is that which occurred in Philadelphia, in 1793.

The following description is taken from Dr. Rush's account of the yellow fever. This distinguished physician continued in the city during the whole of this calamitous period, and rendered himself conspicuous by his humanity and courage, amidst the appalling scenes of contagion, and his skill in combating this destructive

* Holmes' Annals.

disorder. It commenced early in August, and continued till about the 9th of November, during which time four thousand persons died out of a population of 60,000. Its greatest height was about the middle of October, when one hundred and nineteen persons died in one day.

"The disease (says Dr. Rush) appeared in many parts of the town, remote from the spot where it originated; although in every instance it was easily traced to it. This set the city in motion. The streets and roads leading from the city were crowded with families flying in every direction for safety, to the country. Business began to languish. Water street, between Market and Race streets, became a desert. The poor were the first victims of the fever. From the sudden interruption of business, they suffered for a while from poverty as well as disease. A large and airy house at Bush-hill, about a mile from the city, was opened for their reception. This house, after it became the charge of a committee appointed by the citizens on the 14th of September, was regulated and governed with the order and cleanliness of an old and established hospital. An American and French physician had the exclusive medical care of it after the 22d of September.

"The contagion, after the second week in September, spared no rank of citizens. Whole families were confined by it. There was a deficiency of nurses for the sick, and many of those who were employed were unqualified for their business. There was likewise a great deficiency of physicians, from the desertion of some, and the sickness and death of others. At one time there were only three physicians able to do business out of their houses, and at this time there were probably not less than 6,000 persons ill with the fever.

"During the first three or four weeks of the prevalence of the disorder, I seldom went into a house the first time, without meeting the parents or children of the sick in tears. Many wept aloud in my entry or parlour, who came to ask advice for their relations. Grief after a while descended below weeping, and I was much struck in observing that many persons submitted to the loss of

THE NEW YORK
PUBLIC LIBRARY

ASTOR, LENOX
TILDEN FOUNDATIONS

Wayne's Victory over the Indians, on the Banks of the Miami. — Page 185.

relations and friends without shedding a tear, or manifesting any other of the common signs of grief.

"A cheerful countenance was scarcely to be seen in the city for six weeks. I recollect once, in entering the house of a poor man, to have met a child of two years old that smiled in my face. I was strangely affected with this sight, (so discordant to my feelings and the state of the city,) before I recollected the age and ignorance of the child. I was confined the next day by an attack of the fever, and was sorry to hear, upon my recovery, that the father and mother of this little creature died a few days after my last visit to them.

"The streets every where discovered marks of the distress that pervaded the city. More than one half the houses were shut up, although not more than one third of the inhabitants had fled into the country. In walking, for many hundred yards, few persons were met, except such as were in quest of a physician, a nurse, a bleeder, or the men who buried the dead. The hearse alone kept up the remembrance of the noise of carriages or carts in the streets. Funeral processions were laid aside. A black man, leading or driving a horse, with a corpse on a pair of chair wheels, with now and then half a dozen relations or friends following at a distance from it, met the eye in most of the streets of the city, at every hour of the day; while the noise of the same wheels passing slowly over the pavements, kept alive anguish and fear in the sick and well, every hour of the night."

95. *St. Clair's Defeat, and Wayne's Victory.*

In 1790, an Indian war opened on the north-western frontier of the States. Pacific arrangements had been attempted by the president with the hostile tribes in Ohio, without effect. On their failure, Gen. Harmer was sent with about 1400 men to reduce them to terms. In this expedition, Harmer succeeded in destroying a few villages, and a quantity of grain belonging to the Indians;

but in an engagement with them near Chillicothe, he was defeated with considerable loss. Upon the failure of Harmer, Gen. St. Clair was appointed to succeed him. With an army of nearly 1500 men, St. Clair suffered himself to be surprised, with the loss of 630 men killed and missed, and 260 wounded.

"On the 3d of November, 1791, Gen. St. Clair had reached the vicinity of the Miami villages, with an army of about 1400 strong, regulars and militia, when he was joined by a small force under the command of General Hamtrank.

"In this position Gen. St. Clair concerted measures to advance against the Miami villages; first by constructing a breast-work to cover his baggage, and next by detaching a party of militia to occupy a position about one fourth of a mile in advance of the main army.

"Thus posted, the general contemplated to commence the work of destruction the next morning; but the enemy, alive to their safety, surprised the militia at break of day the next morning; put them to flight, and pursued them with such fury as to drive them back with great disorder upon the main body. Gen. St. Clair beat to arms, and put himself at the head of his troops to cover the flying militia, and repulse the enemy; but all in vain; the action continued, the enemy appeared upon all sides of the American army, and poured in a deadly fire from the surrounding thickets, that strewed the field with heaps of the wounded, the dead, and the dying.

"Such was the fury of the contest, that the savages rushed to the combat, and penetrated even to the mouths of the cannon, regardless of danger and fearless of death; the artillerists were slain, the guns taken, and the enemy penetrated the camp; where General Butler fell, mortally wounded. General St. Clair ordered the charge of the bayonet to be renewed; the order was promptly obeyed by Majors Butler, Clark, and Drake; the enemy were repulsed, the camp was cleared, and the cannon recovered; but such was the destruction by the enemy's fire from the thickets, that General St. Clair ordered Major Clark to charge the enemy in front, and clear the road, that the army might effect a retreat, and thus be saved from total ruin; this order was promptly obeyed, the road was cleared, and the army commenced a flight, which was closely pursued about four miles, when the savages returned to share the spoils of the camp, and left Gen. St. Clair at liberty to pursue his flight to Fort Jefferson, (about thirty miles.) Here he was rejoined by the regiment under Major Hamtrank, and he called a council of war to decide on their future operations; it was resolved to pursue their retreat to Fort Washington, which was accordingly accomplished."*

The Indians still continuing hostile, Gen. Wayne was appointed to succeed Gen. St. Clair. Failing to conclude a treaty, Wayne, with a force of 900 men, on the 20th of August, 1794, attacked a body of 2,000 Indians, on the banks of the Miami. The Indians were totally routed, a great number killed, and their whole country laid waste. "By means of this victory over the Miamis, a general war with the Six Nations, and all the tribes north-west of the Ohio, was prevented."

"In the year after, Wayne concluded, at Greenville, treaties with the hostile Indians north-west of the Ohio; by which peace was established, on terms mutually satisfactory and beneficial. A humane system now commenced for ameliorating their condition. They were, henceforth, protected by the United States from the impositions and incursions of lawless white people; taught the use of the loom; and encouraged in the pursuits of agriculture: measures reflecting high praise on Colonel Hawkins, who was amongst the first to execute the benevolent intentions, originally projected by the humane spirit of General Washington."

---

96. *Difficulties with the French.*

In 1797, France wished to involve America in her European wars; but finding her maintaining a steady

* Butler's Hist. U. S.

system of neutrality, she adopted measures highly injurious to the American commerce, and many vessels were taken and confiscated. The American government sent envoys to France, in order to settle the differences. Before the French government would acknowledge the envoys, money by way of *tribute* was demanded; this was refused. " These events were followed by depredations on American commerce, by the citizens of France; which excited general indignation throughout the United States. Civil discord appeared extinct; and this was the general motto:—'*Millions for defence, not a cent for tribute.*' The treaty of alliance with France was considered by congress as no longer in force; and farther measures were adopted by congress, for retaliation and defence. A regular provisional army was established, taxes were raised, and additional internal duties laid. General Washington, at the call of congress, left his peaceful abode to command the armies of the United States, while General Hamilton was made second in command. The navy was increased, and reprisals were made on the water. At sea, the French frigate L'Insurgente, of forty guns, was captured after a desperate action, by the frigate Constellation, of thirty-eight guns, commanded by Commodore Truxton. The same officer compelled another frigate of fifty guns to strike her colours; but she afterwards escaped in the night.

" On hearing of these vigorous preparations, the French government indirectly made overtures for a renewal of the negotiations. Mr. Adams promptly met these overtures, and appointed Oliver Ellsworth, chief justice of the United States, Patrick Henry, late governor of Virginia, and William Van Murray, minister at the Hague, envoys to Paris for concluding an honourable peace. They found the directory overthrown, and the government in the hands of Napoleon Bonaparte, who had not partaken in the transactions which had embroiled the two countries. With him negotiations were opened, which terminated in an amicable adjustment of all disputes. The provisional army was soon after disbanded by order of congress."*

* Willard.

97. Death of Washington.

On the 14th of December, 1799, General Washington expired, at his seat at Mount Vernon, in Virginia, leaving a nation to mourn his loss, and to embalm his memory with their tears.

The disorder of which General Washington died, was an inflammatory affection of the windpipe, occasioned by an exposure to a light rain, while attending, the day before, to some improvements on his estate.

The disease at its commencement was violent, and medical skill was applied in vain. Respiration became more contracted and imperfect, until half past eleven o'clock on Saturday night, when, retaining the full possession of his intellect, he expired without a groan.

"The equanimity which attended him through life, did not forsake him on his death-bed. He submitted to the inevitable stroke with the becoming firmness of a man, the calmness of a philosopher, the resignation and confidence of a Christian. When convinced that his dissolution was near, he requested leave to die without farther interruption; then, undressing himself, went tranquilly to bed, and having placed himself in a suitable attitude, soon after closed his eyes with his own hands, and yielded up his spirit without a struggle."

On the melancholy occasion, the senate addressed to the president a letter, in which they say: "Permit us sir, to mingle our tears with yours. On this occasion i is manly to weep. To lose such a man at such a crisis, is no common calamity to the world. Our country mourns a father. The Almighty Disposer of events has taken from us our greatest benefactor and ornament. It becomes us to submit with reverence to HIM who maketh darkness his pavilion.

"With patriotic pride we review the life of Washington, and compare him with those of other countries who have been pre-eminent in favour. Ancient and modern names are diminished before him. Greatness and guilt have too often been allied; but *his* fame is whiter than it is brilliant. The destroyers of nations stood abashed at the majesty of *his* virtues. It reproved the intemperance of their ambition, and darkened the splendour of victory.

"The scene is closed; and we are no longer anxious lest misfortune should sully his glory. He has travelled on to the end of his journey, and carried with him an increasing weight of honour. He has deposited it safely where misfortune cannot tarnish it; where malice cannot blast it. Favoured of heaven, he departed without exhibiting the weakness of humanity; magnanimous in death, the darkness of the grave could not obscure his brightness."

The committee appointed to devise some mode by which to express the national feelings, recommended that a marble monument be erected by the United States, at the city of Washington, to commemorate the great events of Washington's military and political life; that a funeral oration be delivered by a member of congress; that the president be requested to write a letter of condolence to Mrs. Washington; and that it be recommended to the citizens of the United States, to wear crape on the left arm for thirty days.

These resolutions passed both houses unanimously. The whole nation appeared in mourning. The funeral procession at the city of Washington was grand and solemn, and the eloquent oration delivered on the occasion by Gen. Henry Lee, was heard with profound attention, and with deep interest.

Throughout the United States, similar marks of affliction were exhibited. Funeral orations were delivered, and the best talents devoted to an expression of grief, at the loss of "the man, first in war, first in peace, and first in the hearts of his fellow citizens."*

* Goodrich.

98. *Invention of Steam Boats.*

The first successful application of *steam*, for the purpose of propelling boats, was accomplished by *Robert Fulton*, a native of the state of Pennsylvania.

Mr. Fulton's inventive genius displayed itself at an early age. It seems that as early as the year 1793, he had conceived the idea of propelling vessels by steam, and he speaks in some of his writings with great confidence of its practicability.

After a number of years residence in Europe, and making a variety of experiments both in that country and in this, his labours were finally crowned with success.

In the spring of 1807, the first steam boat built in this country was launched from a ship yard in New York, on the East River. The engine, which he procured from England, was put on board in August, and the boat was completed, and moved by her machinery to the Jersey shore. This boat, which was called the *Clermont*, soon after sailed for Albany, which voyage she accomplished, going at the rate of about five miles an hour; she afterwards became a regular passage boat between New York and Albany. The account of her first voyage to Albany is thus described: "She excited the astonishment of the inhabitants on the shores of the Hudson, many of whom had not heard even of an engine, much less of a steam boat. She was described by some who had indistinctly seen her passing in the night, as a monster moving on the waters, defying the tide, and breathing flames and smoke. Her volumes of smoke and fire by night, attracted the attention of the crews of other vessels. Notwithstanding the wind and tide were adverse to its progress, they saw with astonishment that it was rapidly approaching them; and when it came so near that the noise of the machinery and paddles was heard, the crews, in some instances, sunk beneath their decks, from the terrific sight, and left their vessels to go on shore, while others prostrated themselves, and besought Providence to protect them from the approaches of this horrible monster, which was marching on the ..ides, and lighting its path by the fires which it vomited."

From the time that this boat was put in motion, this noble invention has been rapidly extended; till it is now used in every part of the civilized world.

The following is from a discourse delivered by Judge Story, before the Boston Mechanics' Lyceum—" I myself have heard the illustrious inventor relate, in an animated and affectionate manner, the history of his labours and discouragements. When, said he, I was building my first steam boat at New York, the project was viewed by the public either with indifference, or with contempt, as a visionary scheme. My friends, indeed, were civil, but they were shy. They listened with patience to my explanations, but with a settled cast of incredulity on their countenances. I felt the force of the lamentation of the poet—

> Truths would you teach to save a sinking land,
> All shun, none aid you; and few understand.

"As I had occasion to pass daily to and from the building yard, while my boat was in progress, I have often loitered unknown near the idle groups of strangers, gathering in little circles, and heard various inquiries as to the object of this new vehicle. The language was uniformly that of scorn, or sneer, or ridicule. The loud laugh often rose at my expense; the dry jest; the wise calculation of losses and expenditures; the dull but endless repetition of the Fulton Folly. Never did a single encouraging remark, a bright hope, or a warm wish, cross my path. Silence itself was but politeness, veiling its doubts or hiding its reproaches. At length the day arrived when the experiment was to be put into operation. To me it was a most trying and interesting occasion. I invited my friends to go on board to witness the first successful trip. Many of them did me the favour to attend as a matter of personal respect; but it was manifest, that they did it with reluctance, fearing to be the partners of my mortification and not of my triumph. I was well aware that in my case there were many reasons to doubt of my own success. The machinery was new and ill made; many parts of it were constructed by mechanics unaccustomed to such work; and unexpected difficulties might reasonably be presumed to present themselves from other causes. The moment arrived in which the word was to be given for the vessel to move; my friends were in groups upon deck; they were silent, and sad, and weary. I read in their looks nothing but disaster, and almost repented of my efforts. The signal was given, and the boat moved a short distance, and then stopped and became immoveable. To the silence of the preceding moment now succeeded murmurs of discontent, and agitations, and whispers, and shrugs. I could hear distinctly repeated, 'I told you it would be so—it is a foolish scheme—I wish we were well out of it.' I elevated myself upon a platform, and addressing the assembly, stated that I knew not what was the matter; but if they would be quiet, and indulge me for a half an hour, I would either go on, or abandon the voyage for that time. This short respite was conceded to, without objection. I went below, examined the machinery, and discovered that the cause was a slight mal-adjustment of some of the works. The boat was put in motion. She continued to move on. All were still incredulous. None seemed willing to trust the evidence of their own senses. We left the fair city of New York; we passed through the romantic and ever-varying scenery of the high-lands; we descried the clustering houses of Albany; we reached its shores; and then, even then, when all seemed achieved, I was the victim of disappointment. Imagination superseded the influence of fact. It was then doubted, if it could be done again; or if done, it was doubted, if it could be made of any great value.

"Such was the history of the first experiment, as it fell, not in the very language which I have used, but in substance, from the lips of the inventor. He did not live, indeed, to enjoy the full glory of his invention. It is mournful to say that attempts were made to rob him in the first place of the merits of his invention, and next of its fruits. He fell a victim to his efforts to sustain his title to both. When already his invention had covered the waters of the Hudson, he seemed little satisfied with the results, and looked forward to far more extensive operations. My ultimate triumph, he used to say, my ultimate triumph will be on the Mississippi. I know, indeed, that even now it is deemed impossible by many, that the difficulties of its navigation can be overcome. But I am confident of success. I may not live to see it; but the Mississippi will yet be covered with steam boats; and thus an entire change be wrought in the course of the internal commerce and navigation of our country.

"And it has been wrought. And the steam boat, looking to its effects upon commerce and navigation; to the combined influences of facilities of travelling and the facility of trade; of rapid circulation of news and still more rapid circulation of pleasure and products; seems destined to be numbered among the noblest benefactions of the human race."

99. *Wars with the Barbary States.*

War with Tripoli.—In 1803, congress sent out a squadron under the command of Commodore Preble, to the Mediterranean, to protect the American commerce, and to bring the Tripolitans to submission. The Tripolitan cruisers had long annoyed our commerce; many merchantmen had been taken, and their crews imprisoned, and cruelly used.

After having taken a number of the enemy's vessels, Commodore Preble arrived before Tripoli, and blockaded the harbour; his force consisted of one frigate, three brigs, three schooners, and six gun boats. The number of men engaged in the service amounted to one thousand and sixty. With this force, Preble repeatedly attacked and bombarded the city, although it was defended by a castle and batteries, on which were mounted 115 pieces of cannon; besides this, they had armed vessels in the harbour. In addition to the ordinary Turkish garrison, and the crews of the armed vessels, estimated at 3,000, upwards of 20,000 Arabs had been assembled for the defence of that city. Such, however, was the effect of American bravery, that the haughty bashaw was chastised into a peace, which was negotiated by Col. Lear, the American Consul. The *pope* made a public declaration, that the "United States, though in their infancy, had in this affair done more to humble the anti-christian barbarians, on that coast, than all the European States had done for a long series of time."

Closely connected with the above, is the celebrated expedition of Gen. Eaton, across the desert of Barca. "It happened that some time before this, the then reigning bashaw of Tripoli, Jussuf third, son of the late bashaw, had murdered his father and eldest brother, and proposed to murder the second, in order to possess himself of the throne. But the latter, Hamet Caramelli, made his escape, and Jussuf, without farther opposition, usurped the government.

Hamet took refuge in Egypt, where he was kindly treated by the beys. Here he was on the arrival of an accredited agent of the United States, (Gen. Eaton,) who revived his almost expiring hopes of regaining his rightful kingdom.

Gen. Eaton had been consul for the United States up the Mediterranean, and was returning home when he heard of the situation of Hamet. Conceiving a plan of liberating the Americans in captivity at Tripoli, by means of the assistance of Hamet, and, at the same time, of restoring this exile to his throne, he advised with Hamet, who readily listened to the project, and gave his co-operation.

Eaton contrived to obtain from the viceroy of Egypt an amnesty for Hamet, and permission for him to pass the Turkish army unmolested. A rendezvous was appointed; they met near Alexandria, and formed a convention, in the eighth article of which it was stipulated, that Eaton should be recognised as general commander-in-chief of the land forces which were or might be called into service against the common enemy, the reigning bashaw of Tripoli. The forces consisted of 9 Americans, a company of 25 cannoniers, and a company of 38 Greeks, the bashaw's suite of about 90 men, and a party of Arab cavalry; which, including footmen and camel drivers, made the whole number about 400. Such was the land expedition against Tripoli. The march was pursued through the desert of Barca, with a great variety of adventure and suffering, and Bomba was reached April 15th, where the United States vessel, the Argus, Capt. Hull, and the Hornet, had arrived with provisions, to enable the almost famished army to proceed to Derne. April 25th, they encamped on an eminence which commands this place, and immediately reconnoitred. On the morning of the 26th, terms of amity were offered the bey, on condition of allegiance and fidelity. The flag of truce was sent back with this laconic answer, "My head or yours!" Derne was taken, after a furious assault, but its possession was not secure. An army of the reigning bashaw of Tripoli, consisting of several thousand troops, approached the town, and gave battle to the victors, May 13, but were repulsed with considerable loss. June 2, they returned to the assault, and met with no better fate. On the tenth an engagement took place, in which there were supposed to be not less than 5000 men on the field. The hopes of Eaton were, however, suddenly blasted by official intelligence, received on the 11th, that the American negotiators, in the squadron before Tripoli, had concluded a peace with the usurper. Eaton was required to evacuate the post of Derne, and, with his Greek and American garrison, to repair on board the ships. It was necessary for him to do this clandestinely, lest his Arabian auxiliaries should endeavour to prevent him. Hamet embarked at the same time; the Arabians fled to the mountains; and thus ended this gallant and romantic affair, which is stated in the official correspondence of the American commissioners who negotiated the peace, to have had the effect of bringing the Tripolitans to terms.

Eaton returned to the United States, in August, where he received the most flattering marks of public favour. The president, in his message to congress, made honourable mention of his merit and services. A resolution was moved in the house of representatives, at Washington, for presenting him with a medal; but the motion, after being warmly debated, was rejected by a small majority. The legislature of Massachusetts gave him a tract of land, 10,000 acres, in testimony of their sense of his "undaunted courage and brilliant service."

Algerine War.—Soon after the ratification of peace with Great Britain, in February, 1815, congress, in consequence of the hostile conduct of the regency of Algiers, declared war against that power. A squadron was immediately sent out under the command of Com. Decatur, (who had formerly highly distinguished himself in the Tripolitan war,) consisting of three frigates, two sloops of war, and four schooners. With this force Com. Decatur sailed from New York, May 20th, 1815, and arrived in the bay of Gibraltar in twenty-five days. On the 17th of June, off Cape de Gatt, he captured the Algerine frigate Mazouda, after a running fight of twenty-five minutes. After the second broadside, the Algerines ran below. In this affair, the famous Algerine admiral, or rais, *Hammida*, who had long been the terror of this sea, was cut in two by a cannon shot. On the 19th of June, off Cape Palos, the squadron captured an Algerine brig of twenty-two guns. From Cape Palos the American squadron proceeded to Algiers, where it arrived on the 28th of June. Decatur immediately despatched a letter from the President of the United States to the Dey, in order to afford him a fair opportunity for negotiation. The captain of the port was immediately sent to the squadron on receipt of this letter, accompanied by the Swedish consul; and Commodore Decatur, who, with Mr. Shaler, had been empowered to negotiate a treaty, proposed a basis, on which alone he would consent to enter into a treaty. This was the absolute and unqualified relinquishment of any *demand of tribute*, on the part of the regency. To this the captain demurred. But being informed of the capture of the frigate and brig, and the death of Hammida, he was unnerved, and agreed to negotiate on the proposed basis.

The model of the treaty was sent to the Dey, who signed it. The principal articles in this treaty were, that no tribute, under any circumstances whatever, should be required by Algiers from the United States of America; that all Americans in slavery should be given up without ransom; that compensation should be made for American vessels or property, seized or detained at Algiers; that the persons and property of Americans, found on board of an enemy's vessel, should be sacred; that vessels of either party putting into port should be supplied at market price; that if a vessel of either party should be cast on the shore, she should not be plundered, &c. The rights of American citizens on the ocean, and the land, were generally fully provided for, in every instance; and it was particularly stipulated, that all citizens of the United States, taken in war, should be treated as prisoners of war are treated by other nations; and held subject to an exchange without ransom. After concluding this treaty, so highly honourable and advantageous to our country, the commissioners gave up the frigate and brig, which had been captured, to their former owners.

After this, Com. Decatur visited Tunis and Tripoli, and demanded and obtained compensation for the injuries done American citizens by those powers.

101. *Burr's Conspiracy.*

In the autumn of 1806, a project was detected, at the head of which was Col. Burr, for revolutionizing the territory west of the Alleganies, and of establishing an independent empire there, of which New Orleans was to be the capital, and himself the chief. Towards the accomplishment of this scheme, which it afterwards appeared had been some time in contemplation, the skilful cunning and intrigue of Col. Burr were directed.

In addition to this project, Col. Burr had formed another, which, in case of failure in the first, might be carried on independently of it—this was an attack on Mexico and the establishment of an empire there. 'A third object was provided, merely ostensible, to wit, the settlement of the pretended purchase of a tract of country on the Washita, claimed by a Baron Bastrop. This was to serve as a pretext for all his preparations, an allurement for such followers as really wished to acquire settlements in that country, and a cover under which to retreat in the event of a final discomfiture of both branches of his real designs.

"He found at once that the attachment of the western country to the present union was not to be shaken; that its dissolution could not be effected with the consent of the inhabitants: and that his resources were inadequate, as yet, to effect it by force. He determined, therefore, to seize New Orleans, plunder the bank there, possess himself of the military and naval stores, and proceed on his expedition to Mexico.

"He collected, therefore, from all quarters, where himself or his agents possessed influence, all the ardent, restless, desperate, disaffected persons, who were for an enterprise analogous to their character. He also seduced good and well meaning citizens, some by assurances that he possessed the confidence of the government, and was acting under its secret patronage; and others by offers of land in Bastrop's claim on the Washita."*

Burr was apprehended, and conveyed a prisoner to Richmond, in Virginia; the state in which his adherents had first collected. He was brought to trial August 17th, 1807. Several days were consumed in the examination of witnesses; who proved an assembling of twenty or thirty persons on Blannerhassett's island, in the preceding December; but as it did not appear that the conspirators had used any force against the United States, or that Burr was present at the meeting, he was acquitted. Indictments had been found against Herman Blannerhassett, and five others, for a similar offence; but on the issue of Burr's trial, the attorney-general declined farther proceedings. The following is a part of Mr. Wirt's speech on this trial:

* President's Message to Congress, July 21, 1807.

"Who is Blannerhasset? A native of Ireland, a man of letters, who fled from the storms of his own country to find quiet in ours. Possessing himself of a beautiful island in the Ohio, he rears upon it a palace, and decorates it with every romantic embellishment of fancy. A shrubbery, that Shenstone might have envied, blooms around him; music, that might have charmed Calypso and her nymphs, is his; an extensive library spreads its treasures before him; a philosophical apparatus offers to him all the secrets and mysteries of nature; peace, tranquillity, and innocence, shed their mingled delights around him; and to crown the enchantment of the scene, a wife, who is said to be lovely even beyond her sex, and graced with every accomplishment that can render it irresistible, had blessed him with her love, and made him the father of her children. The evidence would convince you, sir, that this is only a faint picture of the real life. In the midst of all this peace, this innocence, and this tranquillity, this feast of the mind, this pure banquet of the heart,—the destroyer comes; he comes to turn this paradise into a hell. A stranger presents himself. It is Aaron Burr! Introduced to their civilities by the high rank which he had lately held in his country, he soon finds his way to their hearts by the dignity and elegance of his demeanour, the light and beauty of his conversation, and the seductive and fascinating power of his address. The conquest was not a difficult one. Innocence is ever simple and credulous; conscious of no designs of itself, it suspects none in others; it wears no guards before its breast; every door, and portal, and avenue of the heart is thrown open, and all who choose it enter. Such was the state of Eden, when the serpent entered its bowers. The prisoner, in a more engaging form, winding himself into the open and unpractised heart of the unfortunate Blannerhasset, found but little difficulty in changing the native character of that heart and the objects of its affection. By degrees he infuses into it the poison of his own ambition; he breathes into it the fire of his own courage; a daring and desperate hirst for glory; an ardour panting for all the storms, and bustle, and hurricane of life. In a short time the whole man is changed, and every object of his former delight relinquished. No more he enjoys the tranquil scene; it has become flat and insipid to his taste: his books are abandoned; his retort and crucible are thrown aside; his shrubbery blooms and breathes its fragrance upon the air in vain; he likes it not: his ear no longer drinks the rich melody of music: it longs for the trumpet's clangour and the cannon's roar; even the prattle of his babes, once so sweet, no longer affects him; and the angel smile of his wife, which hitherto touched his bosom with ecstacy so unspeakable, is now unseen and unfelt. Greater objects have taken possession of his soul: his imagination has been dazzled by visions of diadems, and stars, and garters, and titles of nobility. he has been taught to burn with restless emulation at the names of Cromwell, Cesar, and Bonaparte. His enchanted island is destined soon to relapse into a desert; and in a few months we find the tender and beautiful partner of his bosom, whom he lately 'permitted not the winds of summer to visit too roughly,'—we find her shivering, at midnight, on the winter banks of the Ohio, and mingling her tears with the torrents that froze as they fell. Yet this unfortunate man, thus deluded from his interest and his happiness; thus seduced from the paths of innocence and peace; thus confounded in the toils which were deliberately spread for him, and overwhelmed by the mastering spirit and genius of another; this man, thus ruined and undone, and made to play a subordinate part in this grand drama of guilt and treason; this man is to be called the principal offender; while he, by whom he was thus plunged and steeped in misery, is comparatively innocent—a mere accessory. Sir, neither the human heart nor the human understanding will bear a perversion so monstrous and absurd; so shocking to the soul; so revolting to reason."

102. *Expedition of Captains Lewis and Clark; to the Pacific Ocean.*

In the year 1803, the extensive territory of Louisiana was purchased from the French government, by President Jefferson, for fifteen millions of dollars. Upon the acquisition of the new territory, the attention of the government of the United States was directed towards exploring the country. Accordingly, Captains Lewis and Clarke, and a party of 25 men, who were enlisted for the purpose, were sent on this expedition. The party proceeded to the mouth of Wood River, near St. Louis, and on the 14th of May, 1804, with three boats, began the tedious and difficult expedition of exploring the vast wilderness before them. Following the course of the Missouri, they arrived in October at the Mandan villages, where they built a kind of fort and encamped for the winter. In April they left their encampment, and with two large boats and six small canoes proceeded on their expedition. On the 12th of August, 1805, they discovered the sources of the Missouri, the longest river in the known world, if we add the distance after it unites with the Mississippi to the ocean, it being almost 4,500 miles long. After following the course of the river, at the foot of a mountain, it became so diminished in width that one of the men in a fit of enthusiasm, with one foot on each side of the river, *thanked God that he had lived to bestride the Missouri.* After they went about four miles, they reached a small gap, formed by the high mountains, which recede on each side, leaving room for an Indian road. "From the foot of one of the lowest of these mountains, which rises with an ascent of about half a mile, issues the remotest water of the Missouri."

After they had quenched their thirst at the fountain, they sat down by the brink of the little rivulet, and felt themselves rewarded for their labour and difficulties, in thus attaining one of the grand objects of their expedition.

Leaving this interesting spot, they, pursuing the Indian path through the interval of the hills, arrived at the top of a ridge, from whence they saw high mountains, partially covered with snow, still to the west of them. The ridge on which they stood formed the dividing line between the waters of the Atlantic and Pacific oceans. They followed the descent of the ridge, and at the distance of three quarters of a mile, reached a bold creek of clear, cold water, running to the westward. They stopped to taste, for the first time, the waters of the Columbia.

Having proceeded as far as they could with canoes, they were obliged to leave them and purchase horses of the natives, with which they crossed the Rocky Mountains. In performing this journey they were reduced to great straits, being obliged to kill some of their horses for food. After passing several ranges of steep and rugged mountains, they descended the Columbia River, till it discharges itself into the Pacific Ocean, where they arrived November 14th, 1805. They encamped for the winter, and on the 23d of March, 1806, set out on their return to the United States. After encountering many dangers, hardships, and privations, they finally arrived at St. Louis, Missouri, on the 23d of September, 1806. The route which the party took from St. Louis to the Pacific Ocean, was a distance of 4,134 miles. In returning, they passed upon a better and more direct route, shortening the distance to 3,555 miles, from the Pacific to St. Louis.

---

103. *Burning of the Theatre, at Richmond, Va.*

The following account of this awful catastrophe is from the Richmond Standard of Dec. 27th, 1811.

Last night the Play House in this city was crowded with an unusual audience. There could not have been less than 600 persons in the house. Just before the conclusion of the play, the scenery caught fire; and in a few minutes the whole building was wrapt in flames. It is already ascertained that 61 persons were devoured by that most terrific element. The editor of this paper was in the house when the ever-to-be-remembered deplorable accident occurred. He is informed that the scenery took fire in the back part of the house, by raising a chandelier; that the boy who was ordered by some of the players to raise it, stated, that if he did so, the scenery would take fire, when he was commanded in a peremptory manner to hoist it. The boy obeyed, and the fire was instantly communicated to the scenery. He gave the alarm in the rear of the stage, and requested some of the attendants to cut the cords by which the combustible materials were suspended. The person whose duty it was to perform this business, became panic struck, and sought his own safety. This unfortunately happened at a time when one of the performers was playing near the orchestra, and the greatest part of the stage, with its horrid danger, was obscured from the audience by a curtain. The flames spread with almost the rapidity of lightning; and the fire falling from the ceiling upon the performer, was the first notice which the people had of their danger. Even then many supposed it to be part of the play, and were for a little time restrained from flight by a cry from the stage, that there was no danger. The performers and their attendants in vain endeavoured to tear down the scenery. The fire flashed in every part of the house with a rapidity horrible and astonishing. No person, who was not present, can form any idea of this unexampled scene of human distress. The editor being not far from the door, was among the first to escape. No words can express his horror, when, on turning round, he discovered the whole building to be in flames. There was but one door for the greatest part of the audience to pass. Men, women, and children, were pressing upon each other, while the flames were seizing upon those behind. The editor went to the different windows, which were very high, and implored his fellow-creatures to save their lives by jumping out of them. Those nearest the windows, ignorant of their danger, were afraid to leap down, whilst those behind them were seen catching on fire and writhing in the greatest agonies of pain and distress. At length, those behind, urged by the pressing flames, pushed those who were nearest to the windows, and people of every description began to fall one upon another; some with their clothes on fire, others half roasted.* * *

The editor, with the assistance of others, caught several of those whom he had begged to leap from the windows. Fathers and mothers were deploring the loss of their children; children the loss of their parents. Husbands were heard to lament their lost companions. The people were seen wringing their hands, and beating their breasts; and those that had secured themselves, seemed to suffer greater torments than those who were enveloped in flames.* * * *

A sad gloom pervades this place, and every countenance is cast down to the earth. * * * Imagine what cannot be described. The most distant and implacable enemy, and the most savage barbarians, will condole our unhappy lot. All those who were in the pit escaped, and had cleared themselves from the house, before those in the boxes could get down. Those from above were pushing each other down the steps, when the hindermost might have got out by leaping into the pit. A gentleman and lady, who otherwise would have perished, had their lives saved by being providentially thrown from the second boxes. There would not have been the least difficulty in descending from the first boxes into the pit. * * * * *

104. *Second War with Great Britain.*

Causes of the War.—*Embargo.*—*Declaration of War.*—The remote causes of the second war with Great Britain appear to have arisen from the war existing between that power and France. America endeavoured to maintain a strict neutrality, and peaceably to continue a commerce with them. Jealousies, however, arose between the contending powers, with respect to the conduct of America, and events occurred, calculated to injure her commerce, and to disturb her peace. The *Berlin Decree* of 1806, and that of *Milan*, in the succeeding year, (both issued by the French government, to prevent the American flag from trading with their enemy,) were followed by the *British Orders in Council*; no less extensive than the former in the design, and equally repugnant to the law of nations. In addition to these circumstances, a cause of irritation existed some time between the United States and Great Britain. This was the *right of search*, claimed by Great Britain, as one of her prerogatives. This was to take her native born subjects, wherever found, for her navy, and to search American vessels for that purpose. Notwithstanding the remonstrances of the American government, the officers of the British navy were not unfrequently seizing native born British subjects, who had voluntarily enlisted on board our vessels, and had also impressed into the British service some thousands of American seamen.

"On the 22d of June, 1807, the indignation of the country was aroused by the attack on the American frigate Chesapeake, off the Capes of Virginia, by the British frigate Leopard; four men were killed, and sixteen were wounded on board the Chesapeake, and four seamen impressed, three of whom were natives of America."

In consequence of the British and French decrees, a general capture of all American property on the seas seemed almost inevitable. Congress therefore, on the recommendation of the president, on the 22d of December, 1807, laid an *embargo* on all vessels within the jurisdiction of the United States. "In a moment, the commerce of the American Republic, from being, in point of extent, the second in the world, was reduced to a coasting trade between the individual States." The opposition to the act in several States was so great, that they declared against it; and individuals throughout the whole, seized every opportunity of infringement. In

1809, congress repealed the embargo law, and substituted a *non-intercourse* with France and England.

On the 18th of June, 1812, an act was passed declaring war against Great Britain. This act passed the house of representatives by a majority of 89 to 49; in the senate by a majority of 19 to 13. In the manifesto of the president, the reasons of the war were stated to be "the impressment of American seamen by the British; the blockade of her enemies' ports, supported by no adequate force, in consequence of which the American commerce had been plundered in every sea; and the British orders in council."

---

103. *Mob in Baltimore.*

" A few days after the declaration of war the town of Baltimore was seriously disturbed. Some harsh strictures on the conduct of government having appeared in a newspaper of that city, entitled the "Federal Republican," the resentment of the opposite party was shown by destroying the office and press of that establishment. The commotion excited by this outrage had, however, in a great measure subsided, and the transaction was brought before a criminal court for investigation. But events more alarming and tragical shortly afterwards succeeded. On the 26th of July, Mr. Hanson, the leading editor of the obnoxious journal, who had deemed it prudent to leave the disordered city, returned, accompanied by his political adherents; amongst whom was General Henry Lee, of Alexandria, an officer distinguished in the revolution, for his bravery in partisan warfare at the head of a legion of cavalry, afterwards governor of Virginia, and a representative from that State in the congress of the Federal Government. Determined to re-commence the paper, by first printing it in Georgetown, in the District of Columbia, and then transmitting it to Baltimore for distribution, a house was for this purpose occupied in Charles-street, secured against external violence, and guarded by a party well provided for defence. On the 28th, papers were accordingly issued. These contained severe animadversions against the mayor, police, and the people of Baltimore, for the depredations committed on the establishment in the preceding month, and were generally circulated throughout the city.

" In the course of the day it became known that Mr. Hanson was in the new office in Charles-street, and it was early whispered that the building would be assailed. A number of citizens who espoused his opinions, went, therefore, to the house, and joined in its protection. Towards the evening, a crowd of boys collected; who, after using opprobrious epithets to those within, began to throw stones at the windows; and about the same time, a person on the pavement, endeavouring to dissuade the youths from mischief, was severely wounded by something ponderous thrown from the house. They were cautioned from the windows to desist; but still continued to assail the place with stones. Two muskets were then fired from the upper story; charged, it was supposed, with blank cartridges to deter them from further violence; immediately the crowd in the street greatly increased; the boys were displaced by men; the sashes of the lower windows were broken, and attempts made to force the door. Muskets, in quick succession, were discharged from the house; some military arrived to disperse the crowd; several shots were fired in return; and at length a Dr. Gale was killed by a shot from the office door. The irritation of the mob was increased. They planted a cannon against the house, but were restrained from discharging it, by the timely arrival of an additional military force, and an agreement that the persons in the house would surrender to the civil authority. Accordingly, early in the following morning, having received assurances on which they thought themselves safe in relying, they surrendered, and were conducted to the county jail, contiguous to the city. The party consisted of about twenty persons; amongst whom were General Lee, General James Lingan, and Mr. Hanson.

"The mayor directed the sheriff to use every precaution to secure the doors of the prison, and the commander of the troops to employ a competent force to preserve the peace. In the evening every thing bore the appearance of tranquillity; and the soldiers, by the consent of the magistrate, were dismissed. But, shortly after dark, a great crowd of disorderly persons reassembled about the jail, and manifested an intention to force it open. On being apprised of this, the mayor hastened to the spot, and with the aid of a few other gentlemen, for a while prevented the execution of the design: but they were at length overpowered by the number and violence of the assailants. The mayor was carried away by force; and the turnkey compelled to open the doors. A tragedy ensued, which cannot be described: it can be imagined only by those who are familiar with scenes of blood. General Lingan was killed; eleven were beaten and mangled with weapons of every description, such as stones, bludgeons, and sledge-hammers, and then thrown as dead, into one pile, outside of the door. A few of the prisoners fortunately escaped through the crowd: Mr. Hanson, fainting from his repeated wounds, was carried by a gentleman, (of opposite political sentiments,) at the hazard of his own life, across the adjoining river, whence he with difficulty reached the dwelling of a friend.

"No effectual inquisition was ever made into this signal violation of the peace, nor punishment inflicted on the guilty. The leaders, on both sides, underwent trials; but, owing to the inflammation of public feeling, they were acquitted."*

---

106. *General Hull's Surrender.*

Soon after the declaration of war, on the 16th of August, General Hull, the governor of Michigan Territory, surrendered his whole army, and the fort at Detroit, without a single battle, to General Brock. "So entirely un-

* Grimshaw's Hist. U. S.

prepared was the public for this extraordinary event, that no one could have believed it to have taken place, until communicated from an official source." Hull had been sent at the head of about 2,500 men, to Detroit, with a view of putting an end to the Indian hostilities in that part of the country. At the time of the surrender of the fort, it is said that his force consisted of more than 1000 men, that of the British of 1900, of whom more than half were Indians. When the British column had arrived within 500 yards of the American lines, General Hull ordered his men, who were placed in a favourable situation to annoy the enemy, to retreat into the fort, and that the cannon should not be fired. "Immediately there was heard a universal burst of indignation." The order, however, could not be disobeyed. The men were ordered to stack their arms; a white flag was hung out upon the walls, and a communication passed between the two generals, which was shortly followed by a capitulation. Not only the American force at Detroit, but various detachments from the fort, the volunteers, and all the provisions at Raisin, the fortified posts and garrisons, and the whole territory and inhabitants of Michigan, were delivered over to the commanding general of the British forces. Two thousand five hundred stand of arms, forty barrels of powder, and twenty-five iron and eight brass pieces of ordnance, the greater part of which had been captured from the British in the revolutionary war, were surrendered with them. The American volunteers and militia were sent home, on condition of not serving again during the war, unless exchanged. The general, and the regular troops were sent to Quebec as prisoners of war.

Being exchanged, General Hull was prosecuted by the government of the United States, and arraigned before a military tribunal, who acquitted him of the charge of treason, but sentenced him to death, for cowardice and unofficerlike conduct. But in consequence of his age and revolutionary services, the president remitted the punishment of death, but deprived him of all military command.

107. *Capture of the Guerriere.*

The Constitution, Captain Hull, had sailed from Annapolis on the 5th of July. On the 17th, he was chased by a ship of the line and four frigates; when by an exertion of able seamanship, than which, the victory itself, though more beneficial, could not be more worthy of applause, he escaped from the unequal combat. On the 19th of August, he had an opportunity of trying his frigate against a single vessel of the enemy. This was the Guerriere; one of the best of the same class in the British navy, and in no way averse to the rencounter, as she promptly awaited her antagonist's arrival. She had, for some time, been searching for an American frigate; having given a formal challenge to every vessel of the same description. At one of her mast heads was a flag, on which her name was inscribed in conspicuous letters; and on another, the words, "Not the Little Belt;" alluding to the broadsides which the President had fired into that sloop, before the war. The Constitution being ready for action, now approached, her crew giving three cheers. Both continued manœuvring for three quarters of an hour; the Guerriere attempted to take a raking position, and failing in this, soon afterwards began to pour out her broadsides, with a view of crippling her antagonist. From the Constitution not a gun had been fired. Already had an officer twice come on the quarter-deck, with information that several of the men had fallen at the guns. Though burning with impatience, the crew silent awaited the orders of their commander. The long expected moment at length arrived. The vessel being brought exactly to the designed position, directions were given to fire broadside after broadside in quick succession. Never was any scene more dreadful. For fifteen minutes, the lightning of the Constitution's guns is a continual blaze, and their thunder roars without intermission. The enemy's mizzen mast lies over her side, and she stands exposed to a fire that sweeps her decks. She becomes unmanageable; her hull is shattered, her sails and rigging cut to pieces. Her mainmast and foremast fall overboard, taking with them every spar except the bowsprit. The firing now ceased, and the Guerriere surrendered. Her loss was fifteen killed, and sixty-three wounded; the Constitution had seven men killed, and seven wounded. The Guerriere was so much damaged, as to render it impossible to bring her into port; she was, therefore, on the following day, blown up. The Constitution received so little injury, that she was in a few hours ready for another action.*

---

108. *Battle at Queenstown.*

Early in the morning of the 13th October, 1812, a detachment of about 1000 men, from the army of the Centre, crossed the river Niagara, and attacked the British on Queenstown heights. This detachment, under the command of Colonel Solomon Van Rensselaer, succeeded in dislodging the enemy; but not being re-enforced by the militia from the American side, as was expected, they were ultimately repulsed, and obliged to surrender. The British General, Brock, was killed during the engagement.

The forces designed to storm the heights, were divided into two columns; one of 300 militia, under Colonel Van Rensselaer, the other, 300 regulars, under Colonel Christie. These were to be followed by Colonel Fenwick's artillery, and then the other troops in order.

Much embarrassment was experienced by the boats, from the eddies, as well as by the shot of the enemy, in crossing the river. Colonel Van Rensselaer led the van, and landed first with 100 men. Scarcely had he leaped from the boat, when he received four severe wounds. Being, however, able to stand, he ordered his officers to move with rapidity and storm the fort. This service was gallantly performed, and the enemy were driven down the hill in every direction.

* Grimshaw.

Both parties were now re-enforced; the Americans by regulars and militia, the British by the 49th regiment, consisting of 600 regulars, under General Brock. Upon this the conflict was renewed, in which General Brock, and his aid, Captain M'Donald, fell almost in the same moment. After a desperate engagement, the enemy were repulsed, and the victory was thought complete.

Colonel Van Rensselaer now crossed over, for the purpose of fortifying the heights, preparatory to another attack, should the enemy be re-enforced. This duty he assigned to Lieutenant Totten, an able engineer.

But the fortune of the day was not yet decided. At 3 o'clock in the afternoon, the enemy, being re-enforced by several hundred Chippewa Indians, rallied, and again advanced, but were a third time repulsed. At this moment, General Van Rensselaer, perceiving the militia on the opposite side embarking but slowly, hastily recrossed the river, to accelerate their movements. But what was his chagrin, on reaching the American side, to hear more than 1200 men (militia) positively refuse to embark. The sight of the engagement had cooled that ardour, which, previously to the attack, the commander-in-chief could scarcely restrain. While their countrymen were nobly struggling for victory, they could remain idle spectators of the scene. All that a brave, resolute, and benevolent commander could do, General Van Rensselaer did—he urged, entreated, commanded, but it was all in vain. Eight hundred British soldiers, from Fort George, now hove in sight, and pressed on to renew the attack. The Americans, for a time, continued to struggle against this force, but were finally obliged to surrender themselves prisoners of war.

The number of American troops killed, amounted to about 60, and about 100 were wounded. Those who surrendered themselves prisoners of war, including the wounded, were about 700. The loss of the British is unknown, but must have been severe.*

* Goodrich.

109. *Massacre at Fort Mimms.*

In 1812, Tecumseh, the celebrated Shawnee chief and British ally, appeared among the Indians of the south, and by his arts of persuasion, induced a large majority of the Creek nation, and a considerable portion of the other tribes, to take up arms against the United States. Being supplied with implements of war from the British, through the channel of the Floridas, they accordingly commenced hostilities.

" Alarm and consternation prevailed among the white inhabitants; those of Tensaw district, a considerable settlement of the Alabama, fled for safety to Fort Mimms, on that river, sixteen miles above Fort Stoddard. The place was garrisoned by one hundred and fifty volunteers, of the Mississippi territory, under Major Beasly. The inhabitants collected at the fort amounted to about three hundred.

" At eleven o'clock in the forenoon of the 30th of August, a body of Indians, to the amount of six or seven hundred warriors, issued from the adjoining wood, and approached the fort; they advanced within a few rods of it before the alarm was given. As the sentinel cried out, "Indians," they immediately gave a war-whoop, and rushed in at the gate, before the garrison had time to shut it. This decided their fate. Major Beasly was mortally wounded at the commencement of the assault; he ordered his men to secure the ammunition, and retreat into the house; he was himself carried into the kitchen, and afterwards consumed in the flames.

" The fort was originally square, but Major Beasly had enlarged it by extending the lines upon two sides about fifty feet, and putting up a new side, into which the gate was removed; the old line of pickets were standing, and the Indians, on rushing in at the gate, obtained possession of the outer part, and through the port-holes of the old line of pickets, fired on the people who held the interior. On the opposite side of the fort was an offset, or bastion, made round the back gate, which, being open on the outside, was occupied by the Indians, who, with the axes that lay scattered about, cut down the gate. The people in the fort kept possession of the port-holes on the other lines, and fired on the Indians who remained on the outside. Some of the Indians ascended the block house at one of the corners, and fired on the garrison below, but were soon dislodged; they succeeded however, in setting fire to a house near the pickets, which communicated to the kitchen, and from thence to the main dwelling-house. When the people in the fort saw the Indians in full possession of the outer court, the gate open, men fast falling, and their houses in flames, they gave up all for lost, and a scene of the most distressing horror ensued. The women and children sought refuge in the upper story of the dwelling-house, and were consumed in the flames, the Indians dancing and yelling round them with the most savage delight. Those who were without the buildings, were murdered and scalped without distinction of age or sex; seventeen only escaped. The battle and massacre lasted from eleven in the forenoon until six in the afternoon, by which time the work of destruction was fully completed, the fort and buildings entirely demolished, and upwards of four hundred men, women, and children, massacred."*

---

110. *Capture of York, U. C.*

"On the 23d of April, Gen. Dearborn embarked at Sackett's Harbour, with sixteen hundred men, on an expedition against York, at the head of the lake, leaving the defence of the harbour, with all the stores, public property, and a new ship on the stocks, to a handful of regulars, under Colonel Backus, and the neighbouring militia, not then arrived. It seemed to have escaped the observation of the commanding general, that the enemy would probably, in his absence, strike at an important post thus left uncovered. On the 27th, General Dear-

* Perkin's Late War.

born, with the fleet, arrived before the town of York, and immediately commenced a disembarkation. The commanding general intrusted the further prosecution of the expedition to General Pike, and remained on board the fleet. To oppose their landing, a corps of British grenadiers, the Glengary fencibles, and several bodies of Indians, appeared at different points on the shore. At eight o'clock the troops commenced their landing, three miles westward of the town, and a mile and a half distant from the British works. The place first designed for their landing, was a cleared field near the site of the old French fort Tarento; but the wind was high, and prevented the first division from landing at that place, and also prevented the ships from covering their disembarkation. The riflemen, under Major Forsythe, first landed, under a heavy fire from the enemy. Major General Sheaffe had collected his whole force, consisting of about seven or eight hundred regulars and militia, with a hundred Indians, to oppose their landing, and commanded in person. Major Forsythe, although supported by the troops as promptly as possible, was obliged to sustain alone a sharp conflict with the whole British force, for nearly half an hour. As soon as General Pike had effected his landing, with about eight hundred men, the British retreated to their works. The main body of the Americans landed and formed at old fort Tarento, and quickly advanced through a thick wood to an open ground near the British works. The first battery was carried by assault, and the columns moved on towards the main works: when the head of the column had arrived within about sixty rods, a tremendous explosion took place, from a magazine prepared for that purpose, and killed and wounded one hundred men. General Pike was mortally wounded by a stone which was thrown up by the explosion, and struck him on the breast. He was immediately conveyed on board the commodore's ship, and soon expired. After the confusion which these events necessarily occasioned, the American troops proceeded to the town, and agreed to a capitulation with the commanding officers of the Canadian militia, by which t was stipulated, that all the public property should be delivered to the Americans, the militia surrendered prisoners of war, and private property protected. Immediately after the explosion, Gen. Sheaffe, with the regulars, retreated out of the reach of the American arms. Two hundred and fifty militia, and fifty marines and regulars, were included in the capitulation. The American loss was fourteen killed in battle, and fifty-two by the explosion; twenty-three wounded in battle, and one hundred and eight by the explosion. One large vessel on the stocks, and a quantity of naval stores, were set fire to by the British, and consumed; but more naval stores were taken by the Americans than could be carried away. The public buildings for military use, and the military stores which could not be removed, were destroyed. York was the seat of government for Upper Canada, and the principal depot for the Niagara frontier, and Detroit. General Sheaffe's baggage and papers were taken. In the government hall, a human scalp was found suspended over the speaker's chair, with the mace and other emblems of power. This building was burned, contrary to the orders of the American general."*

111. *Battle on Lake Erie.*

The American fleet consisted of nine vessels, carrying fifty-four guns, commanded by Commodore Perry, a young officer. The British fleet, of six vessels and sixty-three guns, under Commodore Barclay, an old and experienced officer, who had served under Nelson. The line of battle was formed at 11 o'clock, September 10, 1813. At fifteen minutes before twelve, the enemy's flag-ship, " Queen Charlotte," opened a furious fire upon the " Lawrence," the flag-ship of Commodore Perry. The wind being light, the rest of the squadron were unable to come to his assistance, and he was compelled for two hours to sustain the fire of two of the enemy's ships,

* Perkins.

each of equal force. By this time the Lawrence had become unmanageable, every gun was dismounted, and her crew, except four or five, were all killed or wounded.

In this desperate condition, Commodore Perry, with great presence of mind, formed the bold design to shift his flag, and leaping into an open boat, waving his sword, he passed unhurt through a shower of balls, to the Niagara, of twenty guns. At this critical moment the wind increased, and Perry bore down upon the enemy, passing the "Detroit," "Queen Charlotte," and "Lady Provost," on one side, and the "Chippewa" and "Little Belt" on the other, into each of which, while passing, he poured a broadside. He then engaged the "Lady Provost," which received so heavy a fire that the men ran below. The remainder of the American squadron, one after another, now came up. After a contest of three hours, the American fleet gained a complete victory, and captured every vessel of the enemy. Commodore Perry announced this victory in the following laconic style:—"*We have met the enemy, and they are ours!*"

The Americans lost in this action twenty-seven killed and ninety-six wounded. The British had about two hundred killed and wounded—the Americans took six hundred prisoners, which exceeded the whole number of Americans engaged in the action.

112. *Death of Tecumseh.*

On the 5th of October, a battle was fought between the American army under Gen. Harrison, and the British under Gen. Proctor, in which the British were defeated, and Detroit fell into the hands of the Americans.

The British were assisted by a body of 1200 or 1500 Indian warriors, led on by Tecumseh, a celebrated Indian chieftain. Upon the left, the onset was begun by Tecumseh, with great fury. He was opposed by Col. Johnson, of Kentucky. The Indians seemed determined to

Death of Tecumseh. — Page 230.

conquer or die. The terrible voice of Tecumseh was heard encouraging his warriors; although beset on every side, they fought with determined courage. Col. Johnson now rushed towards the spot, where the savage warriors were gathering around their undaunted chieftain. In a moment a hundred rifles were aimed at the American, the balls pierced his dress and accoutrements, and himself and his horse received a number of wounds. At the instant his horse was about to fall under him, he was discovered by Tecumseh; having discharged his rifle, he sprang forward with his tomahawk; but, struck with the appearance of the brave man before him, he hesitated for a moment, and that moment was his last. Col. Johnson levelled a pistol at his breast, and they both, almost at the same instant, fell to the ground. Col. Johnson's men now rushed forward to his rescue, and the Indians, hearing no longer the voice of their chief, soon fled.

"Thus fell Tecumseh, and with him fell the last hope of our Indian enemies." Since the year 1790, he had been in almost every engagement with the whites; he was a determined enemy to the attempts to civilize the Indians, and had for years endeavoured to unite the tribes in opposing the progress of the settlements of the whites, any farther to the westward. On the opening of the last war he visited many tribes, and by his uncommon eloquence and address, roused his countrymen to arms against the United States. "Tecumseh had received the stamp of greatness from the hand of nature, and had his lot been cast in a different state of society, he would have shone as one of the most distinguished of men. He was endowed with a powerful mind, and with the soul of a hero. There was an uncommon dignity in his countenance and manners, and by the former he could be easily distinguished, even after death, among the slain, for he wore no insignia of distinction."

113. *Barbarities of the British at Hampton, Va., in* 1813

The troops under Sir Sidney Beckwith, and the sailors under Admiral Cockburn, no sooner found themselves in possession of the town of Hampton, than they indulged in a system of pillage not less indiscriminate than that which had attended the visit of most of the same men to Havre de Grace. To these acts of cruelty and oppression upon the unresisting and innocent inhabitants, they added others of the most atrocious and lawless nature, the occurrence of which has been proved by the solemn affirmation of the most respectable people of that country. Age, innocence, nor sex, could protect the inhabitants whose inability to escape obliged them to throw themselves upon the mercy of the conquerors. The persons of the women were indiscriminately violated. The brutal desires of an abandoned and profligate soldiery, were gratified, within the view of those who alone possessed the power and authority to restrain them; and many of the unfortunate females, who had extricated themselves from one party, were pursued, overtaken, and possessed by another. Wives torn from the sides of their wounded husbands; mothers and daughters stripped of their clothing in the presence of each other; and, those who had fled to the river side, and as a last refuge had plunged into the water, with their infant children in their arms, were driven again at the point of the bayonet, upon the shore, where neither their own entreaties and exertions, nor the cries of their offspring, could restrain the remorseless cruelty of the insatiable enemy, who paraded the victim of his lust through the public streets of that town. An old man, whose infirmities had drawn him to the very brink of the grave, was murdered in the arms of his wife, almost as infirm as himself, and her remonstrance was followed by the discharge of a pistol into her breast. The wounded militia who had crawled from the field of battle to the military hospital, were treated with no kind of tenderness, even by the enemy's officers, and the common wants of nature were rigorously denied to them. To these transcendent enormities, were added the wanton and profligate destruction not only of the medical stores, but of the physician's drug rooms and laboratories; from which only those who had been wounded in battle, and those upon whose persons these outrages had been committed, could obtain that assistance, without which, they must inevitably suffer the severest privations. Two days and nights were thus consumed by the British soldiers, sailors, and marines; and, their separate commanders, were all that time quartered in the only house the furniture of which escaped destruction. On the morning of the 27th, at sunrise, apprehensions being entertained of an attack from the neighbouring militia, whom, it was reasonably conjectured, the recital of these transactions would arouse into immediate action, the British forces were ordered to embark; and in the course of that morning, they departed from the devoted town, which will immemorially testify to the unprovoked and unrelenting cruelty of the British troops. They had previously carried off the ordnance which had been employed in the defence of the town, as trophies of their victory; but, when they determined on withdrawing from the place, they moved away with such precipitation, that several hundred weight of provisions, a quantity of muskets and ammunition, and some of their men, were left behind, and captured on the following day by Captain Cooper's Cavalry. Having abandoned their intentions of proceeding to another attempt on the defences of Norfolk, the whole fleet stood down to a position at New-Point Comfort, where they proposed watering, previously to their departure from the bay, on an expedition against a town in one of the eastern States.

Such was the agitation of the public mind throughout Virginia, which succeeded the circulation of the account of the assault on Hampton, that representations were made to General Robert R. Taylor, the commandant of the district, of the necessity of learning from the commanders of the British fleet and army, whether the outrage would be avowed, or the perpetrators punished.— That able officer immediately despatched his aid to Admiral Warren, with a cartel for the exchange of prisoners, and a protest against the proceedings of the British troops, in which he stated, that "the world would suppose those acts to have been approved, if not excited, which should be passed over with impunity;" that he "thought it no less due to his own personal honour, than to that of his country, to repress and punish every excess;" that "it would depend on him (Warren) whether the evils inseparable from a state of war, should, in future operations, be tempered by the mildness of civilized life, or, under the admiral's authority, be aggravated by all the fiendlike passions which could be instilled into them." To this protest, Admiral Warren replied, that he would refer it to Sir Sidney Beckwith, to whose discretion he submitted the necessity of an answer. Sir Sidney not only freely avowed, but justified, the commission of the excesses complained of; and induced the American commander to believe the report of deserters, that a promise had been made to the fleet, of individual bounty, of the plunder of the town, and of permission to commit the same acts, if they succeeded in the capture of Norfolk. Sir Sidney stated, that "*the excesses at Hampton*, of which General Taylor complained, *were occasioned by a proceeding at Crany Island. That at the recent attack on* that place, the troops, in a barge which had been sunk by the fire of the American guns, had been fired on by a party of Americans, who waded out and shot these poor fellows, while clinging to the wreck of the boat; and *that with a feeling natural to such a proceeding, the men of that corps landed at Hampton.*" The British general expressed also a wish that such scenes should not occur again, and that the subject might be entirely at rest. The American general, however, alive to the reputation of the arms of his country, refused to let it rest, and immediately instituted a court of inquiry, composed of old and unprejudiced officers. The result of a long and careful investigation, which was forwarded to Sir Sidney Beckwith, was, that none of the enemy had been fired on, after the wreck of the barge, except a soldier, who had attempted to escape to that division of the British troops which had landed, that he was not killed, and that so far from shooting either of those unfortunate men, the American troops had waded out to their assistance. To this report Sir Sidney never deemed it necessary to reply, and the outrages at Hampton are still unatoned. Many of the unhappy victims died, of wounds and bruises, inflicted on them in their struggles to escape, which baffled the medical skill of the surrounding country.*

114. *Battle of Niagara.*

On the 25th of July, 1814, Gen. Scott arrived at the Niagara cataract, and learned that the British were in force directly in his front, separated only by a narrow piece of wood. Having despatched this intelligence to General Brown, he advanced upon the enemy, and the action commenced at six o'clock in the afternoon. Although General Ripley, with the second brigade, Major Hendman, with a corps of artillery, and General Porter, with the volunteers, pressed forward with ardour; it was an hour before they could be brought up to his support; —during this time his brigade alone sustained the conflict. General Scott had pressed through the wood, and engaged the British on the Queenston road, with the 9th, 11th, and 12th regiments, the 25th having been thrown on the right. The fresh troops under General Ripley, having arrived, now advanced to relieve General Scott, whose exhausted brigade formed a reserve in the rear. The British artillery had taken post on a commanding eminence, at the head of Lundy's Lane, supported by a line of infantry, out of reach of the American batteries. This was the key of the whole position; from hence they poured a most deadly fire on the American ranks. It became necessary either to leave the ground, or to carry this post and seize the height. The latter desperate task was assigned to Colonel Miller. On receiving the order from General Brown, he calmly surveyed the

* Thompson's Late **War.**

position, and answered, "*I will try, sir!*" which expression was afterwards the motto of his regiment. The first regiment, under the command of Colonel Nicholas, were ordered to menace the British infantry, and support Colonel Miller in the attack. This corps, after a discharge or two, gave way, and left him without support. Without regarding this occurrence, Colonel Miller advanced coolly and steadily to his object, amid a tremendous fire, and at the point of the bayonet, carried the artillery and the height. The guns were immediately turned upon the enemy; General Ripley now brought up the 23d regiment to the support of Colonel Miller; and the first regiment was rallied and brought into line, and the British were driven from the hill. At this time, Major Jessup, with the 25th regiment, was engaged in a most obstinate conflict, with all the British that remained on the field. He had succeeded in turning the British left flank. Captain Ketchum, with a detachment of this regiment, succeeded in gaining the rear of the British lines at the point where Generals Drummond and Riall, with their suites, had taken their stations, and made them all prisoners. The British officers, mistaking this detachment for a company of their own men, were ordering them to press on to the combat, when Capt. Ketchum stepped forward, and coolly observed, that he had the honour to command at that time, and immediately conducted the officers and their suites, into the rear of the American lines; General Drummond, in the confusion of the scene, made his escape. The British rallied under the hill, and made a desperate attempt to regain their artillery, and drive the Americans from their position, but without success; a second and third attempt was made with the like result. Gen. Scott was engaged in repelling these attacks, and though with his shoulder fractured, and a severe wound in the side, continued at the head of his column, endeavouring to turn the enemy's right flank. The volunteers under Gen. Porter, during the last charge of the British, precipitated themselves upon the lines, broke them, and took a large number of prisoners. General Brown, during the whole action was at the most exposed points, directing and animating his troops. He received a severe wound on the thigh, and in the side, and would have given the command to Gen. Scott, but on inquiring, found that he was severely wounded. He continued at the head of his troops until the last effort of the British was repulsed, when loss of blood obliged him to retire; he then consigned the command to Gen. Ripley. At twelve o'clock, both parties retired from the field to their respective encampments, fatigued and satiated with slaughter. The battle continued, with little intermission, from six in the afternoon until twelve at night. After Col. Miller had taken the battery, and driven the British from the heights, and Gen. Riall and suite had been taken, there was a short cessation, and the enemy appeared to be about yielding the ground, when re-enforcements arrived to their aid, and the battle was renewed with redoubled fury for another space of two hours; much of this time the combatants were within a few yards of each other, and several times officers were found commanding the enemy's platoons. Capt. Spencer, aid to Gen. Brown, was despatched with orders to one of the regiments; when about to deliver them, he suddenly found himself in contact with a British corps; with great coolness and a firm air, he inquired, what regiment is this? On being answered, *the Royal Scots*, he immediately replied, "*Royal Scots, remain as you are!*" The commandant of the corps, supposing the orders came from his commanding general, immediately halted his regiment, and Capt. Spencer rode off. Col. Miller's achievement, in storming the battery, was of the most brilliant and hazardous nature; it was decisive of the events of the battle, and entitled him and his corps to the highest applause; most of the officers engaged in that enterprise were killed or wounded. The battle was fought to the west of, and within half a mile of the Niagara cataract. The thunder of the cannon, the roaring of the falls, the incessant discharge of musketry, the groans of the dying and wounded, during the six hours in which the parties were engaged in close combat, heightened by the circumstance of its being night, affo ded such a scene, as is rarely to be met with in the history of human slaughter. The evening was calm, and the moon shone with lustre, when not enveloped in clouds of smoke from the firing of the contending armies. Considering the numbers engaged, few contests have ever been more sanguinary.*

This was one of the most severe and bloody battles which was fought during the war. The British force engaged, amounted to 5,000 men: many of their troops were selected from the flower of Lord Wellington's army. The American force consisted of 4,000 men. The loss of Americans in killed, wounded, and missing, was 860 men; that of the British was 878 men.

115. *Burning of Washington City.*

In August, 1814, a body of about 6,000 British troops, commanded by Gen. Ross, landed at Benedict, on the Patuxent, 47 miles from Washington; on the 21st of August, he marched to Nottingham. He met with little opposition on his march, until within about six miles of Washington, at Bladensburgh. Here Gen. Winder, with the American forces, composed mostly of militia, hastily collected, opposed them. The Americans, however, fled at the beginning of the contest. Com. Barney, with about 400 men, made a brave resistance; but the enemy, superior in numbers, compelled him to surrender.

Leaving Bladensburgh, Gen. Ross went to Washington, where he arrived in the evening of the 23d of August, about 8 o'clock, with 700 men, having left the main body about a mile and a half from the capital.† There being neither civil nor military authorities to whom any

---

* Perkins' late War.
† According to the account of the British officer, who was in this expedition, the sole object of the disembarkation was the destruction of the American flotilla. When that flotilla retreated to Nottingham, Admiral Cockburn urged the necessity of a pursuit, and finally prevailed on Gen. Ross to proceed on to attack Washington. When he arrived near the city, Gen. Ross sent in a flag of truce, with terms. Scarcely had the party with he flag entered the city, when they were

proposition could be made, the work of conflagration commenced. The capitol, the President's house, the offices of the treasury, war, and navy departments, and their furniture, with several private buildings, were destroyed. The party sent to burn the president's house, entered it, and found in readiness the entertainment which had been ordered for the American officers. In the dining hall the table was spread for forty guests, the sideboard furnished with the richest liquors, and in the kitchen the dishes all prepared. These uninvited guests devoured the feast with little ceremony, ungratefully set fire to the building where they had been so liberally fed, and returned to their comrades.—One house from which Gen. Ross apprehended himself to have been shot at, was burned, and all the people found in it slain. The most important public papers had been previously removed. The navy yard, with its contents, and apparatus, one frigate of the largest class on the stocks, and nearly ready to launch, and several smaller vessels, were destroyed by Commodore Tingey, under the direction of the secretary of the navy, after the capture of the city.

The loss to the United States, as estimated by a committee of the senate, was, in the capitol and other public buildings, - - - - - $460,000
At the navy yard, in moveable property, - 417,745
In buildings and fixtures, - - - 91,425

$969,170

To this estimate is to be added the loss of the public library, furniture, and other articles not included in the foregoing; making the whole public loss somewhat to exceed a million of dollars

The British, having accomplished the object of their

---

fired upon from the windows of one of the houses. Two corporals of the 31st, and the horse of the general himself, who accompanied them, were killed. This outrage roused the indignation of every individual of the army. All thoughts of accommodation were instantly laid aside; the troops advanced forthwith into the city, and having first put to the sword all who were found in the house from whence the shots were fired, and reduced it to ashes, they proceeded without delay to burn and destroy every thing in the most distant degree connected with the government.

visit, left the city on the 25th, and passed through Bladensburgh at midnight, on the route to Benedict. They left their dead unburied; such of their wounded as could ride were placed on horseback; others in carts and wagons, and upwards of ninety left behind. The wounded British prisoners were intrusted to the humanity of Commodore Barney, who provided every thing for their comfort; and such as recovered, were exchanged, and returned to the British. Two hundred pieces of artillery at the arsenal and navy yard fell into their hands, which they were unable to remove: these they spiked, knocked off the trunions, and left. Their retreat, though unmolested, was precipitate, and conducted under evident apprehensions of an attack. They reached Benedict on the 29th, and embarked on the 30th.*

Their whole loss during this expedition was 400 in killed and wounded, besides five hundred more, who were made prisoners or deserted.

---

116. *Battle of Plattsburgh.*

About the 1st of Sept. 1814, Sir George Provost, Governor General of Canada, with 14,000 men, entered the village of Champlain, and issued addresses and proclamations inviting the citizens to his standard, and promising them the protection of his majesty's government. From Champlain he continued to make gradual approaches towards Plattsburg, until the 6th. Early on the morning of that day, he made a rapid advance in two columns, one coming down the Beckmantown road, and the other along the Lake road. At a bridge crossing Dead creek, intersecting the latter, General Macomb had stationed a detachment of 200 men, under Captain Sproul of the 13th, to abbattis the woods, and to place obstructions in the road; after which he was to fortify himself with two field pieces, sent with him for that purpose, and to receive orders from Lieutenant Colonel Appling, who,

* Perkin's Late War.

with 100 riflemen, was reconnoitring the enemy's movements, some distance in advance of this position. The brigade of General Brisbane, which approached through the Beekmantown road, with more rapidity than the other, was met by about 700 militia, under Gen. Mooers, who, after a slight skirmish with the enemy's light parties, with the exception of one or two companies, fled in the greatest disorder. Those who were intrepid enough to remain, were immediately formed with a corps of 250 regulars, under Major Wool, of the 29th, and disputed the passage of the road for some time. But their fears also getting at length the better of their judgment, notwithstanding the enemy fired only from his flankers and patrolling parties, they followed the example of their comrades, and precipitately retired to the village. Major Wool's regulars remained firm however, and being joined by Captain L. Leonard's party of flying artillery, and the 6th, and a detachment of the 34th regiment, continued to annoy the advanced parties of the British column, and killed Lieutenant Colonel Wellington, of the 3d, or buffs, who was at its head. General Macomb, at this moment, personally directing the movements in the town, soon saw that the enemy's object, in making so much more rapid a march on its west than on the north, was to cut off Lieutenant Colonel Appling's and Captain Sproul's detachments, despatched his aid, Lieutenant Root, with orders to those officers to withdraw their forces from Dead creek, to join the detachment of Major Wool, and to fall upon the enemy's right flank. Whilst Lieutenant Colonel Appling was proceeding in obedience to this order, he was encountered on the north side of the town, by the light divisions of the enemy's 1st brigade, sent for the purpose of cutting him off, and which had that moment emerged from the woods. Their numbers were superior, and had he been delayed an instant longer on the Lake road, he must inevitably have yielded. Here he engaged, but after a short contest retired before them. In the centre of the town he re-engaged them, and being joined by Major Wool, was ordered to retire to the American works on the south of the Saranac.

The retreat was effected in good order, and covered by a guard of 120 men, under Captain M'Glossin, of the 15th infantry; the detachment alternately retreating and keeping up a brisk and effectual fire upon the British columns. Having reached the works with a trifling loss, General Macomb ordered Lieutenant Harrison, of the 13th, under the direction of Major Wool, and protected by Captain Leonard's artillery, to destroy the bridge over the Saranac.

This order was not executed without some difficulty. The British having occupied the houses near the bridge, with their light troops, kept up a constant fire from the windows, and wounded Lieuts. Harrison and Turner, of the 13th, and Taylor of the 34th. These troops were, however, soon after dislodged by a discharge of hot shot from the American works, and in conjunction with the right column, were engaged the remainder of the day in various attempts to drive the guards from the several bridges. But the planks had all been taken up, and being placed in the form of breastworks, served to cover the American light parties stationed for the defence of the passages. The obstructions which had been thrown in the way of the column advancing by the Lake road, and by the destruction of the bridge over Dead creek, greatly impeded its approaches, and, in attempting to ford the creek, it received a severe and destructive fire from the gun-boats, and galleys anchored in front of the town. But not all the galleys, aided by the armament of the whole flotilla, which then lay opposite Plattsburgh, under Commodore Macdonough, could have prevented the capture of Macomb's army, after its passage of the Saranac, had Sir George Provost pushed his whole force upon the margin of that stream. Like General Drummond, at Erie, he made a pause, in full view of the unfinished works of the Americans, and consumed five days in erecting batteries, and throwing up breastworks, for the protection of approaches. Of this interval the American general did not fail to avail himself, and kept his troops constantly employed in finishing his line of redoubts. Whilst both parties were thus engaged in providing for the protection of their forces, the main body of the British army came up with the advance; and General Macomb was also re-enforced by the militia of New York, and the volunteers from the mountains of Vermont. Skirmishes between light detachments, sallies from the different works, and frequent attempts to restore the bridges, served to amuse the besiegers and the besieged, while the former were getting up a train of battering cannon, and the latter strengthening their lines, and preparing to repel the attack.

On the morning of the 11th, the motives of the British general, in delaying his assault upon the American works, became apparent. Being assured of his ability, at any time, to destroy them by a single effort, he was regardless of the manner in which they might be gradually strengthened, and awaited the arrival of the British squadron from Lake Champlain, in co-operation with which he contemplated a general attack, and the easy capture of the American fleet and army. On that day his fleet, consisting of a large frigate, the Confiance, of 39 guns; the brig Linnet, of 16; the sloops Chub and Finch, (formerly the United States' sloops Growler and Eagle,) of 11 guns each; and 13 gun-boats and row-galleys, mounting in all 95 guns, and having a complement of 1,050 men, made its appearance, under Captain Downie, round Cumberland Head, and immediately engaged the American squadron, under Commodore Macdonough, then moored in Plattsburgh bay, and consisting of the ship Saratoga, the brig Eagle, the schooner Ticonderoga, the sloop Preble and 10 gun boats mounting altogether 86 guns, (the largest vessels carrying 26,) and being manned with 820 men. The first gun from the Confiance was the signal for a general action, and Sir George Provost instantly opened his batteries upon the works on the opposite bank of the Saranac. A tremendous cannonade ensued; bomb shells and Congreve rockets were thrown into the American lines during the whole day; and frequent but ineffectual attempts made to ford the river.

At a bridge about a mile up the river, an attempt to throw over a division of the enemy's army, was handsomely repulsed by a detachment of regulars; and an ef fort to force the passage of the bridge in the town, was effectually checked by a party of riflemen, under Captain Grosvenor.

But the principal slaughter took place at a ford three miles from the works. There the enemy succeeded in crossing over three companies of the 76th regiment, before his advance was impeded. A body of volunteers and militia stationed in a contiguous wood, opened a heavy fire upon them, and after a spirited contest, in which one of these companies was entirely destroyed, its captain killed, and three lieutenants and 27 men made prisoners, those who had attained the shore fell back in disorder upon an approaching column, then in the middle of the river. The receding and advancing columns mingled with each other, and being closely pressed by the volunteers, the whole body was thrown into a state of confusion, from which the officers could not recover them; numbers were killed in the stream, and the dead and wounded being swept along by the force of the current, sunk into one common grave.

But the result of the engagement between the two naval armaments, which continued upwards of two hours, in presence of the contending armies, soon determined the action upon land. Its effects were sensibly felt by the British general, whose plans were completely frustrated by its issue. After getting round Cumberland Head, Captain Downie anchored his fleet within 300 yards of the line formed by Commodore Macdonough, placing the Confiance frigate in opposition to the Saratoga, the Linnet to the Eagle, Captain Henley; one of his sloops and all his galleys, to the schooner Ticonderoga, Lieutenant-commandant Cassin, and the sloop Preble. His other sloop, alternately assailing the Saratoga and Eagle. The latter vessel was so situated, shortly after the commencement of the action, that her guns could not be brought to bear, and Captain Henley cut her cable, and placed her between the commodore's ship and the Ticonderoga, from which situation, though she exposed the Saratoga to a galling fire, she annoyed the enemy's squadron with much effect. Some minutes after ten o'clock, nearly all the guns on the starboard side of the Saratoga being either dismounted or entirely unmanageable, Commodore Macdonough was obliged to put out a stern anchor, and to cut the bower cable, by which means the Saratoga winded on the enemy's frigate with a fresh broadside, which being promptly delivered, the Confiance immediately after surrendered, with 105 round shot in her hull, and her captain and 49 men killed, and 60 wounded.

The Saratoga had 55 round shot in her hull, and had been twice set on fire by hot shot from the Confiance, but she sustained a loss of only 28 in killed and 29 wounded, notwithstanding she mounted 13 guns less than her antagonist. The Confiance had no sooner surrendered, than the Saratoga's broadside was sprung to bear on the brig, whose flag struck fifteen minutes after. Captain Henley, in the Eagle, had already captured one of the enemy's sloops; and the Ticonderoga, after having sustained a galling fire, caused the surrender of the remaining vessel. The principal vessels of the British fleet being now all captured, and three of their row galleys sunk, the remaining ten escaped from the bay in a shattered condition. The total loss of Commodore Macdonough's squadron, amounted to 52 men killed, and 58 wounded. The enemy's loss was, 84 men killed, 110 wounded, and 856 prisoners, who alone amounted to a greater number than those by whom they were taken. The capture of his fleet being announced to Sir George Provost, he immediately, withdrew his forces from the assault of the American works. From his batteries, however, he kept up a constant fire until the dusk of the evening, when, being silenced by the guns of fort Monroe, under Colonel M. Smith, and of forts Brown and Scott, he retired within the town, and at 9 at night sent off his artillery, and all the baggage for which he could obtain transport. About midnight he made a disgraceful and precipitated retreat, leaving behind him all his sick and wounded, with a request that they might be generously treated by General Macomb.*

* Thompson's His. Sketches of the Late War.

117. *Hartford Convention.*

During the second war with Great Britain, the people of the United States were divided into two political parties; one condemning the war as unwise and unnecessary, the other contending that it was just, and necessary for the maintenance of national honour. The opposition to the war was the greatest in the New England states, and during its continuance this opposition was confirmed. Enlistments of troops were in some instances discouraged, and dissensions arose between the general and state governments, respecting the command of the militia, called out by order of the former, to defend the sea-board. In October, 1814, the legislature of Massachusetts appointed delegates to meet and confer with the delegates from the other states of New England, or any of them, upon the subjects of their public grievances and concerns. The delegates met at Hartford, Conn., Dec. 15, 1815, and sat nearly three weeks with closed doors. This convention consisted of delegates from the states of Massachusetts, Connecticut, and Rhode Island; two members from New Hampshire, and one from Vermont; these last were appointed at county meetings. After their adjournment, the convention published an address, charging the national government with pursuing measures hostile to the interests of New England, and recommending amendments to the federal constitution.

"These alterations consisted of seven articles; *first*, that representatives and direct taxes shall be apportioned to the number of free persons; *secondly*, that no new state shall be admitted into the Union without the concurrence of two thirds of both houses; *thirdly*, that congress shall not have power to lay an embargo for more than sixty days; *fourthly*, that congress shall not interdict commercial intercourse, without the concurrence of two thirds of both houses; *fifthly*, that war shall not be declared without the concurrence of a similar majority; *sixthly*, that no person who shall be hereafter naturalized, shall be eligible as a member of the senate or house

THE NEW YORK
PUBLIC LIBRARY

ASTOR, LENOX
TILDEN FOUNDATIONS

Battle of New Orleans. The British troops storming the Redoubt on the right of the American Lines. — Page 237.

of representatives, or hold any civil office under the authority of the United States; and, *seventhly*, that no person shall be elected twice to the presidency, nor the president be elected from the same state two terms in succession.

"The report of the convention concluded with a resolution, providing for the calling of another convention, should the United States 'refuse their consent to some arrangement whereby the New England states, separately, or in concert, might be empowered to assume upon themselves the defence of their territory against the enemy,' appropriating a reasonable proportion of the public taxes for this purpose; or 'should peace not be concluded, and the defence of the New England states be neglected as it has been since the commencement of the war.'"*

The committee appointed to communicate these resolutions to congress, met at Washington the news of peace: and owing to this event another convention was not called. The proposed amendments of the constitution were submitted to the several states, and rejected by all except Massachusetts, Rhode Island, and Connecticut.

118. *Gen. Jackson's Victory at New Orleans.*

In the month of December, 1814, fifteen thousand British troops, under Sir Edward Packenham, were landed for the attack of New Orleans. The defence of this place was intrusted to Gen. Andrew Jackson, whose force was about 6000 men, chiefly raw militia. Several slight skirmishes occurred before the enemy arrived before the city: during this time, Gen. Jackson was employed in making preparation for his defence. His front was a straight line of 1000 yards, defended by upwards of three thousand infantry and artillerists. The ditch contained five feet of water, and his front, from having been flooded by opening the levees, and by frequent rains, was rendered slippery and muddy. Eight distinct batteries were judiciously disposed, mounting in all

* Goodrich.

12 guns of different calibres. On the opposite side o the river was a strong battery of 15 guns.

"At daylight, on the morning of the 8th of January the main body of the British, under their commander-in-chief, General Packenham, were seen advancing from their encampment to storm the American lines. On the preceding evening they had erected a battery within eight hundred yards, which now opened a brisk fire to protect their advance. The British came on in two columns, the left along the levee on the bank of the river, directed against the American right, while their right advanced to the swamp, with a view to turn General Jackson's left. The country being a perfect level, and the view unobstructed, their march was observed from its commencement. They were suffered to approach in silence, and unmolested, until within three hundred yards of the lines. This period of suspense and expectation was employed by General Jackson and his officers, in stationing every man at his post, and arranging every thing for the decisive event. When the British columns had advanced within three hundred yards of the lines, the whole artillery at once opened upon them a most deadly fire. Forty pieces of cannon, deeply charged with grape, canister, and musket balls, mowed them down by hundreds, at the same time the batteries on the west bank opened their fire, while the riflemen, in perfect security behind their works, as the British advanced, took deliberate aim, and nearly every shot took effect. Through this destructive fire, the British left column, under the immediate orders of the commander-in-chief, rushed on with their fascines and scaling ladders, to the advance bastion on the American right, and succeeded in mounting the parapet; here, after a close conflict with the bayonet, they succeeded in obtaining possession of the bastion; when the battery, planted in the rear for its protection, opened its fire, and drove the British from the ground. On the American left, the British attempted to pass the swamp, and gain the rear, but the works had been extended as far into the swamp as the ground would permit. Some who attempted it, sunk in the mire and disappeared; those behind, seeing the fate of their companions, seasonably retreated, and gained the hard ground. The assault continued an hour and a quarter; during the whole time, the British were exposed to the deliberate and destructive fire of the American artillery and musketry, which lay in perfect security behind their breastworks of cotton bales, which no balls could penetrate. At eight o'clock, the British columns drew off in confusion, and retreated behind their works. Flushed with success, the militia were eager to pursue the British troops to their intrenchments, and drive them immediately from the island. A less prudent and accomplished general might have been induced to yield to the indiscreet ardour of his troops; but General Jackson understood too well the nature of his own and his enemy's force, to hazard such an attempt. Defeat must inevitably have attended an assault made by raw militia, upon an intrenched camp of British regulars. The defence of New Orleans was the object; nothing was to be hazarded which would jeopardize the city. The British were suffered to retire behind their works without molestation. The result was such as might have been expected from the different positions of the two armies. General Packenham, near the crest of the glacis, received a ball in his knee. Still continuing to lead on his men, another shot pierced his body, and he was carried off the field. Nearly at this time, Major General Gibbs, the second in command, within a few yards of the lines, received a mortal wound, and was removed. The third in command, Major General Keane, at the head of his troops near the glacis, was severely wounded. The three commanding generals, on marshalling their troops at five o'clock in the morning, promised them a plentiful dinner in New Orleans, and gave them *booty and beauty* as the parole and countersign of the day.* Before eight o'clock, the three generals were carried off the field, two in the agonies of death, and

* The giving of this countersign has been denied by Gen. Lambert, and four other superior officers of the British army, who were engaged in this expedition, in a published communication signed by them, and sent to this country during the present year, (1833.)

the third entirely disabled; leaving upwards of 2000 of their men dead, dying, and wounded, on the field of battle. Colonel Raynor, who commanded the forlorn hope which stormed the American bastion on the right, as he was leading his men up, had the calf of his leg carried away by a cannon shot. Disabled as he was, he was the first to mount the parapet, and receive the American bayonet; 700 were killed on the field, 1400 hundred wounded, and 500 made prisoners, making a total on that day of twenty-six hundred. But six Americans were killed, and seven wounded."*

On the 9th, General Lambert and Admiral Cochrane, with the surviving officers of the army, held a council of war, and determined to abandon the expedition. To withdraw the troops in the face of a victorious enemy, would have been difficult and hazardous. To withdraw in safety, every appearance of a renewal of the assault was kept up, till the night of the 18th, when the whole army moved off in one body, over a road which had been previously constructed through a miry slough, in which a number of the troops perished by sinking into the mire. On the 27th, the whole land and naval forces which remained of this disastrous expedition, found themselves on board of their ships, with their ranks thinned, their chiefs and many of their companions slain, their bodies emaciated by hunger, fatigue, and sickness.

119. *Bank of the United States.*

The Bank of the United States was established by an act of congress of April 10th, 1816, and continues to March 3d, 1836. Its stock consists of three hundred and fifty thousand shares, of one hundred dollars each, constituting a capital of thirty-five millions of dollars. Seventy thousand shares, or seven millions of the stock, was taken by the United States, and the remaining two hundred and eighty thousand shares, amounting to twenty-eight millions of dollars, by individuals, companies,

* Perkins.

&c. Of this twenty-eight millions of dollars, seven was required by the charter to be paid in gold or silver coin, and twenty-one millions in gold or silver coin, or funded debt of the United States. The property of the bank, including its whole capital, is not to exceed in value fifty-five millions of dollars.

The bank is located in Philadelphia, governed by twenty-five directors, chosen annually; five of whom, being stockholders, are appointed by the president of the United States, by and with the advice and consent of the senate; and twenty are annually elected at the banking-house, in Philadelphia, by the qualified stockholders of the capital, (other than the United States,) on the first Monday of January. No person can be a director in the bank of the United States at the same time that he is a director in any other bank. At the first meeting after their election, the directors choose a president. The president is selected from the directors.

The number of votes to which stockholders are entitled, are, for one share and not more than two, one vote; for every two shares above two, and not exceeding ten, one vote; for every four shares above ten, and not exceeding thirty, one vote; for every six shares above thirty, and not exceeding sixty, one vote; and for every ten shares above one hundred, one vote; but no person, co-partnership, or body politic, is entitled to more than thirty votes. No share or shares confer the right of voting, that shall not have been held three calendar months previous to the day of election. No stockholders, but those actually resident within the United States, can vote by proxy.

By the act of March 3d, 1819, it is provided that any person offering more than thirty votes, including those offered in his own right, and those offered by him as attorney, &c., the judges of the election are required to administer an oath to the person so offering more than thirty votes, to the following effect: "That he has no interest, directly or indirectly, in the shares upon which he offers to vote as an attorney; and that the shares are, to the best of his knowledge and belief, truly, and in good faith, owned by the persons in whose name they stand at that time." No person is allowed to vote as proxy, &c. without a power, witnessed with an oath, endorsed and filed in the bank, that the giver of the proxy is the real and only owner of the shares specified in the power of attorney; that he owns no other shares; that no other person has any interest in the said shares; and that no other power, now in force, has been given to any other person to vote at any election of directors of the said bank. Judges of elections permitting any person to give more than thirty votes at one election, without taking the oath prescribed by law, are subject to a fine not exceeding two thousand dollars, or to imprisonment not exceeding one year; and persons swearing falsely, are liable to the pains and penalties for the punishment of wilful and corrupt perjury.

Persons giving money, or any thing as a bribe, to procure the interest, &c., of the president or any director of the bank, or the president or director receiving such bribe, are for ever disqualified from holding any office of honour, trust, or profit, under the corporation, or under the United States.

Not more than three fourths of the directors elected by the stockholders, nor more than four fifths of those appointed by the United States, shall serve two successive years; no director shall hold his office more than three years out of four in succession; but the director who is President may serve without limitation.

None but a stockholder, resident citizen of the United States, shall be a director, nor shall be entitled to any emolument.

Seven directors may constitute a board, of whom the president shall always be one, unless unavoidably prevented, in which case his place may be supplied by any other director whom he, by writing under his hand, may depute for that purpose.

A number of stockholders not less than sixty, if proprietors of one thousand shares, have power to call a general meeting of the stockholders, giving ten weeks notice in two newspapers of the place where the bank is seated, and specifying the object of the meeting.

The cashier is required to give bond, with two or more sureties, in a sum not less than fifty thousand dollars, as a security for the faithful performance of his duties.

The lands, &c., lawful for the bank to hold, are only for its immediate accommodation in business, or mortgaged to it as security or satisfaction for debts previously contracted, or purchased at sales upon judgments for such debts.

The total amount of debts, of every description, which the bank shall at any time owe, must not exceed thirty-five millions of dollars, unless authorized by law to exceed that amount. In case of excess, the directors under whose administration it takes place, are liable in their private capacities. This provision, however, does not exempt the property of the bank from being also liable. Directors who may dissent, or be absent, when such excess is created, on giving notice thereof to the president of the United States, and to the stockholders, are exonerated from such liability.

The bank is prohibited from dealing or trading in any thing, except bills of exchange, gold and silver bullion, or sales of goods pledged for money lent by the bank. It cannot become the purchaser of any public debt, nor take more than six per centum per annum for or upon its loans or discounts.

The bank cannot loan more than five hundred thousand dollars to the United States; or to any particular State an amount exceeding fifty thousand dollars; or to any foreign Prince or State, unless previously authorized by a law of the United States.

The stock is assignable and transferable, according to rules established by the bank.

Bills obligatory and of credit, under the seal of the bank, made to any person, are assignable by the endorsement of such person. But the bank is prohibited from making any bill obligatory, &c., under its seal, for a less sum than five thousand dollars. All bills issued by order of the bank, and signed by the president and cashier, are binding as if made by private persons. All bills or notes so issued, are payable on demand, except such as are for the payment of a sum not less than one hundred dollars which may be made payable to order, at any time not exceeding sixty days from date.

Half-yearly dividends of the profits may be made. And once in three years the directors must lay before the stockholders an exact and particular statement of the situation of the bank.

The directors of the bank are authorized to establish offices of discount and deposit wheresoever they shall think fit, within the United States or the territories thereof. Or, instead of establishing such offices, it is lawful for the directors to employ any other bank or banks, to be first approved by the secretary of the treasury of the United States, to transact business other than discounting. Not more than thirteen, nor less than seven directors of every office of discount and deposit, shall be annually appointed by the directors of the bank, to serve for one year; each shall be a citizen of the United States, and a resident of the State or Territory where the office is established; not more than three fourths of those in office shall be appointed for the next succeeding year; and no director can hold his office more than three years out of four in succession; but the president may be always re-appointed.

The secretary of the treasury of the United States must be furnished, as often as he may require, not exceeding once a week, with full statements of the concerns of the bank, and he has a right to examine such of the books of the bank as relate to said statement.

No stockholder, unless he be a citizen of the United States, has a vote in the choice of directors.

No note can be issued of less amount than five dollars.

If the bank, or any person on its account, shall deal or trade in any respect contrary to its charter, every person concerned as agent or party therein, shall forfeit treble the value of the goods, &c., in which such dealing shall have been; one half thereof to the informer, the other to the United States; to be recovered in an action of law with costs of suit.

The bills or notes of the bank are receivable in all

payments to the United States, until otherwise directed by act of congress.

The banks must, whenever required by the secretary of the treasury, give the necessary facilities for transferring the public funds from place to place, within the United States, for the payment of public creditors, without charging commissions; and also perform the duties of commissioners of loans.

The deposites of moneys of the United States, in places in which the bank or its branches are established, must be made in the bank or its branches, unless the secretary of the treasury shall otherwise direct; in which case he must immediately lay before congress, if in session, and if not, immediately after the commencement of the next session, the reason of such direction.

The bank is prohibited from suspending payments in specie. In case of suspension, the holder of any bill, &c., can recover the amount thereof, and until it is paid, is entitled to interest at the rate of twelve per centum per annum.

Forging, counterfeiting, &c., the notes, &c., of the bank, is felony, and punishable by imprisonment and hard labour, or imprisonment and fine.

If any person shall engrave, or have in his possession, any metallic plate, similar to the plates from which the notes, &c., of the bank are printed, or shall cause or suffer the same to be used, &c., he shall, upon conviction, be sentenced to imprisonment at hard labour not exceeding five years, or imprisoned not exceeding five years, and fined in a sum not exceeding one thousand dollars.

No other bank shall be chartered by congress during the continuance of the charter of the bank of the United States, except within the district of Columbia. And the corporation of the bank shall exist for two years after the expiration of its charter, for the close of its concerns.

Committees of either houses of congress have power to inspect the books of the bank, and to examine into its proceedings, &c., and whenever there is reason to believe the charter has been violated, a scire facias may be sued out of the circuit court for the district of Pennsylvania, in the name of the United States, and the bank compelled to show cause why the charter should not be declared forfeited; and it is lawful for the said court to examine into the truth of the alleged violation, and if such violation be made to appear, then to pronounce the charter forfeited. The final judgment of the court aforesaid is examinable in the supreme court of the United States.*

After the United States bank went into operation, its stock was made an object of speculation, and at one time stood as high as $156 per 100. The dividends varied from 5 to 6 per cent. The branches of the bank were at Portland, Portsmouth, Boston, Providence, Hartford, New York, Baltimore, Washington, Richmond, Norfolk, Fayetteville, Charleston, Savannah, Mobile, New Orleans, Nashville, Louisville, Lexington, Cincinnati, Chilicothe, and Pittsburg. "The bank commenced operations under the presidency of Captain William Jones, in January, 1817. In 1820, the distinguished Langdon Cheves, of South Carolina, took charge of it, and restored it from a languishing condition to one of great prosperity. Nicholas Biddle, Esq., succeeded him in 1823. About the year 1828-9, the subject of the renewal of its charter began to be agitated. The bank was drawn into the vortex of politics, and a fierce war was waged between its partizans and opponents. In October, 1833, the deposits of the government, which had hitherto been made exclusively with this bank, were removed by order of President Jackson. A bill to recharter the bank had been vetoed by him the preceding year. The charter expired, according to limitation, in 1836, and the same year the 'United States bank of Pennsylvania,' was chartered by the legislature of that state, with the same capital of $35,000,000; and, purchasing the assets and assuming the liabilities of the former United States bank, continued the business under the same roof."

"In 1837, a reaction commenced. All the banks, with very rare exceptions, suspended specie payments throughout the union. A resumption was attempted in 1839, but was only persevered in by the banks in New England

* Force's National Calendar, 1823.

and New York. This new suspension, however, was not generally followed by contraction of the currency of Pennsylvania, until early in 1811, when another attempt was made to resume, but it proved fatal to the United States bank of Pennsylvania, and the Girard bank, which were obliged to go into liquidation."—*Day's Hist. Coll., of Pennsylvania.*

Owing to its national character, the operations of the United States bank were very extensive. Its notes circulated all over the Union, and, for mercantile purposes, were oftentimes better than gold or silver. About the time of the expiration of its charter, there arose an opposition to its renewal. It was argued that such an institution, so powerful and extensive in its operations, would eventually become uncontrollable by the people, and thus in some degree dangerous to their liberties. The failure of the bank caused great distress and suffering among those whose funds were invested in its stock under the belief of its being a safe and permanent institution.

---

121. *Conspiracy of the Blacks at Charleston, S. C. in* 1822.

The following account of an intended insurrection of the slaves in Charleston, S. C. and its most timely discovery, is extracted from a pamphlet published by the authority of the corporation of Charleston in 1822.

"On Thursday, the 30th of May last, about 3 o'clock in the afternoon, the Intendant of Charleston was informed by a gentleman of great respectability, (who, that morning, had returned from the country) that a favourite and confidential slave of his had communicated to him, on his arrival in town, a conversation which had taken place at the market on the Saturday preceding, between himself and a black man; which afforded strong reasons for believing that a revolt and insurrection were in contemplation among a proportion at least of our black population. The corporation was forthwith summoned to meet at 5 o'clock, for the purpose of hearing the narrative of the slave who had given this information to his master, to which meeting the attendance of his excellency the Governor was solicited; with which invitation he promptly complied. Between, however, the hours of 3 and 5 o'clock, the gentleman who had conveyed the information to the Intendant, having again examined his slave, was induced to believe, that the negro fellow who had communicated the intelligence of the intended revolt to the slave in question, belonged to Messrs. J. & D. Paul, Broad Street, and resided in their premises. Accordingly, with a promptitude worthy of all praise, without waiting for the interposition of the civil authority, he applied to the Messrs. Paul, and had the whole of their male servants committed to the guard house, until the individual who had accosted the slave of this gentleman, on the occasion previously mentioned, could be identified from among them.

"On the assembling of the Corporation at five, the slave of this gentleman was brought before them, having previously identified Mr. Paul's William as the man who had accosted him in the market; he then related the following circumstances:

"On Saturday afternoon last, (my master being out of town,) I went to market; after finishing my business, I strolled down the wharf below the fish market, from which I observed a small vessel in the stream with a singular flag; whilst looking at this object, a black man (Mr. Paul's William) came up to me, and remarking the subject which engaged my attention, said, I have often seen a flag with the number 76 on it, but never with 96 before. After some trifling conversation on this point, he remarked with considerable earnestness to me, Do you know that something serious is about to take place? To which I replied, no. Well, said he, there is, and many of us are determined to right ourselves! I asked him to explain himself—when he remarked, why we are determined to shake off our bondage, and for this purpose we stand on a good foundation, many have joined, and if you will go with me, I will show you the man who has the list of names, who will take yours down.—I was so much astonished and horror struck at this information, that it was a moment or two before I could collect myself sufficiently to tell him I would have nothing to do with this business, that I was satisfied with my condition, that I was grateful to my master for his kindness, and wished no change.—I left him instantly, lest, if this fellow afterwards got into trouble, and I had been seen conversing with him, in so public a place, I might be suspected and thrown into difficulty.—I did not, however, remain easy under the burden of such a secret, and consequently determined to consult a free man of colour, named ———, and to ask his advice. On conferring with this friend, he urged me with great earnestness to communicate what had passed between Mr. Paul's man and myself to my master, and not to lose a moment in so doing. I took his advice, and not waiting, even for the return of my master to town, I mentioned it to my mistress and young master.—On the arrival of my master, he examined me as to what had passed, and I stated to him what I have mentioned to yourselves.

"William, the man aforementioned, was then examined;—after much equivocation, he admitted all these facts. The Council being under the conviction that he was in the possession of more information than he had thought proper to disclose, kept him confined.

"Things remained in this state for six or seven days, until about the 8th of June, when William, who had been a week in solitary confinement, beginning to fear that he would soon be led forth to the scaffold, for summary execution, in an interview with Mr. Napier, (one of the committee appointed to examine him,) confessed, that he had for some time known of the plot, that it was very extensive, embracing an indiscriminate massacre of the whites, and that the blacks were to be headed by an individual, who carried about with him a charm which rendered him invulnerable. He stated, that the period fixed for the rising, was on the second Sunday in June. This information was without delay conveyed to his excellency the Governor, and a Council forthwith convened. Whatever faith we might have been disposed to place in the unsupported and equivocal testimony of William, it was not conceived to be a case in which our doubts should influence our efforts for preparation and defence. Measures were consequently promptly taken, to place the city guard in a state of the utmost efficiency. Sixteen hundred rounds of ball cartridges were provided, and the sentinels and patroles ordered on duty with loaded arms. Such had been our fancied security, that the guard had previously gone on duty without muskets, with sheathed bayonets and bludgeons.

"On the night of Friday the 14th, the information of William was amply confirmed by a gentleman who called on the Intendant, who stated that a faithful slave belonging to his family, in whom he had the utmost confidence, informed him that a contemplated insurrection of the blacks would occur on the succeeding Sunday, the 16th, at 12 o'clock at night, which, if not prevented, would inevitably take place at that hour. This slave also stated that one of his companions had informed him, that Rolla, belonging to Governor Bennet, had communicated to him the intelligence of the intended insurrection, and had asked him to join. That he remarked, in the event of their rising, they would not be without help, as the people from San Domingo and Africa would assist them in obtaining their liberty, if they only made the motion first themselves. That if A—— wished to know more, he had better attend their meetings, where all would be disclosed. After this, at another interview, Rolla informed A——, that the plan was matured, and that on Sunday night, the 16th June, a force would cross from James' Island and land on South Bay, march up and seize the Arsenal and guard house, that another body at the same time would seize the Arsenal on the Neck, and a third would rendezvous in the vicinity of his master's mills. They would then sweep the town with fire and sword, not permitting a single white soul to escape.

"The sum of this intelligence was laid before the Governor, who convening the officers of the militia, took such measures as were deemed the best adapted to the ap proaching exigency of Sunday night. On the 16th, at 10 o'clock at night, the military companies, which were placed under the command of Col. R. Y. Hayne, were ordered to rendezvous for guard.

"The conspirators finding the whole town encompassed at 10 o'clock, by the most vigilant patroles, did not dare to show themselves, whatever might have been their plans. In the progress of the subsequent investigation, it was distinctly in proof, that but for these military demonstrations, the effort would unquestionably have been made; that a meeting took place on Sunday afternoon, the 16th, at 4 o'clock, of several of the ringleaders, at Denmark Vesey's, for the purpose of making their preliminary arrangements, and that early in the morning of Sunday, Denmark despatched a courier, to order down some country negroes from Goose Creek, which courier had endeavoured in vain to get out of town.

"No development of the plot having been made on Sunday night, and the period having passed, which was fixed on for its explosion, it now became the duty of the civil authority to take immediate steps for the apprehension, commitment, and trial of those against whom they were in possession of information.

"The number of blacks arrested was one hundred and thirty-one; of these thirty-five were executed, fifty-one acquitted, the rest were sentenced to be transported.

"Among those executed, was one free black by the name of Denmark Vesey, who was considered the leader of the plot. In the revolutionary war, Captain Vesey of Charleston was engaged in supplying the French in St. Domingo with slaves from St. Thomas. In the year 1781 he purchased Denmark, a boy of about 14 years of age, and afterwards brought him to Charleston, where he proved for 20 years a faithful slave. In 1800, Denmark drew a prize of $1500 in the lottery, and purchased his freedom from his master for 600 dollars. From that period till the time of his apprehension he worked as a carpenter, distinguished for his great strength and activity. Among his colour he was always looked up to with awe and respect. His temper was impetuous and domineering in the extreme, qualifying him for the despotic rule of which he was ambitious. All his passions were ungovernable and savage, and to his numerous wives and children, he displayed the haughty and capricious cruelty of an eastern bashaw."

Among the most prominent of the other conspirators, was a slave by the name of Gullah Jack. "Born a conjuror and a physician, in his own country, (for in Angola they are matters of inheritance,) he practised these arts in this country for fifteen years, without its being generally known among the whites. Vesey, who left no engines of power unessayed, seems, in an early stage of his designs, to have turned his eye on this necromancer, aware of his influence with his own countrymen, who are distinguished both for their credulous superstition and clannish sympathies. Such was their belief in his invulnerability, that his charms and amulets were in request, and he was regarded as a man, who could *only* be harmed by the *treachery* of his fellows. Even those negroes who were born in this country seem to have spoken of his charmed invincibility with a confidence which looked much like belief."

Of the motives of Vesey in forming this conspiracy, "the belief is altogether justifiable, that his end would have been answered, if, after laying our city in ashes, and moistening its cinders with blood, he could have embarked with a part of the pillage of our banks for San Domingo; leaving a large proportion of his deluded followers to the exterminating desolation of that justice, which would have awaited, in the end, a transient success."

The following is extracted from the testimony of a black man on the trial of the conspirators:

" About the 1st of June, I saw in the public papers a statement that the white people were going to build missionary houses for the blacks, which I carried and showed to Peter, and said, see the good they are going to do for us; when, he said,—What of that?—Have you not heard, that on the 4th of July, the whites are going to create a false alarm of fire, and every black that comes out will be killed, in order to thin them? Do you think they would be so barbarous? (said I) Yes! (said he) I do!—I fear they have a knowledge of an army from San Domingo, and they would be right to do it, to prevent us joining that army, if it should march towards this land! I was then very much alarmed.

"Last Tuesday or Wednesday week, Peter said to me—You see, my lad, how the white people have got to windward of us? You won't, said I, be able to do any thing. O, yes! (he said) we will! By George, we are obliged to! He said, all down this way ought to meet, and have a collection to purchase powder. What, said I, is the use of powder?—the whites can fire three times to our once. He said, but *'twill be such a dead time of the night, they won't know what is the matter, and our horse companies will go about the streets and prevent the whites from assembling*. I asked him—Where will you get horses? Why, said he, there are many butcher boys with horses; and there are the livery stables, where we have several candidates; and the waiting men, belonging to the white people of the horse companies, will be told to take away their masters' horses. He asked me if my master was not a horseman? I said, Yes! Has he not got arms in his house? I answered, Yes! Can't they be got at? I said, Yes! Then (said he) it is good to have them. I asked what was the plan? Why, said he, after we have taken the arsenals and guard houses, then we will set the town on fire, in different places, and as the whites come out we will slay them. If we were to set fire to the town first, the man in the steeple would give the alarm too soon.—I am the Captain, said he, to take the lower guard house and arsenal. But, I replied, when you are coming up, the sentinel will give the alarm. He said, he would advance a little distance ahead, and if he could only get a grip at his throat, he was a gone man, for his sword was very sharp; he had sharpened it, and had made it so sharp, it had cut his finger, which he showed me. As to the arsenal on the Neck, he said, that it was gone as sure as fate, Ned Bennett would manage that with the people from the country, and the people between Hibbens' Ferry and Santee would land and take the upper guard house. I then said, then this thing seems true. My man, said he, God has a hand in it, *we have been meeting for four years, and are not yet betrayed.* I told him, I was afraid, after all, of the white people from the back country and Virginia, &c. He said that the blacks would collect so numerous from the country, we need not fear the whites from the other parts, for when we have once got the city we can keep them all out. He asked if I had told my boys. I said no. Then, said he, you should do it, for Ned Bennett has his people pretty well ranged. But, said he, take care and don't mention it to those waiting men who receive presents of old coats, &c. from their masters, or they'll betray us. I will speak to them. We then parted, and I have not since conversed with him. He said the rising was to take place last Sunday night, 16th June—*That any of the coloured people who said a word about this matter would be killed by the others. The little man, who can't be killed, shot, or taken, is named Jack, a Gullah Negro.* Peter said there was a French company in town, of three hundred men, fully armed—that he was to see Monday Gell, about expediting the rising."

122. *Western Antiquities.*

The numerous remains of ancient fortifications, mounds, &c. found in the Western States, are the admiration of the curious, and a matter of much speculation.

They are mostly of an oblong form, situated on well chosen ground, and near the water.

One of the fortifications or towns at Marietta, Ohio, contains forty acres, accompanied by a wall of earth from six to ten feet high. On each side are three openings at equal distances, resembling gateways. The works are undoubtedly very ancient, as there does not appear to be any difference in the age or size of the timber growing on or within the walls, and that which grows without; and the Indians have lost all tradition respecting them. Dr. Cutler, who accurately examined the trees on the works at Marietta, thinks from appearances, that they are on the second growth, and that the works must have been built upwards of one thousand years.

At a convenient distance from these works, always stands a mound of earth, thrown up in the form of a pyramid. Upon examination, some of these mounds are found to contain an immense number of human skeletons.

The ancient works on the western branches of the Muskingum river, extend nearly two miles, the ramparts of which are now in some places more than eighteen feet in perpendicular height.

In Pompey,* Onondaga County, New York, are vestiges of a town, the area of which included more than five hundred acres. It was protected by three circular or elliptical forts, eight miles distant from each other. They formed a triangle which enclosed the town. From certain indications, this town seems to have been stormed and taken on the line of the north side.

In Camillus, in the same county, are the remains of two forts, one covering about three acres, on a very high hill. It had one eastern gate, and a communication at west, towards a spring about ten rods from the fort. Its shape was elliptical. The ditch was deep, and the eastern wall ten feet high.

The other fort is almost half a mile distant, on lower ground, constructed like the other, and about half as large. Shells of testaceous animals, numerous fragments of pottery, pieces of brick, and other signs of an ancient settlement, were found by the first European settlers.

On the east bank of Seneca river, six miles south o. Cross and Salt lakes, the remains of an ancient Indian defence have been discovered, together with a delineation of ill shapen figures, supposed to have been hieroglyphical, and engraved as with a chisel, on a flat stone, five feet in length, three and a half in breadth, and six inches thick; evidently a sepulchral monument.

The principal fortification was two hundred and twenty

* Yates' and Moulton's History.

yards in length, and fifty-five yards in breadth. The bank and corresponding ditch were remarkably entire; as were two apertures, opposite each other in the middle of the parallelogram, one opening to the water, and the other facing the forest.

About half a mile south of the great work was a large half moon, supposed to have been an outwork, but attended with this singularity, that the extremities of the crescent were from the larger fort. The banks of the ditch, both of this and the first fortress, were covered with trees that exhibited extremity of age.

The flat stone above mentioned was found over a small elevation in the great fort. Upon removing it one of the visiting party dug up with his cane a piece of earthen vessel, which, from the convexity of the fragment, was supposed to contain two gallons. It was well burned, of a red colour, and had its upper end indented, as with the finger, in its impressionable state.

Eastward, these fortifications have been traced eighteen miles from Manlius Square; and in Oxford, Chenango county, on the east bank of Chenango river, are the remains of another fort, remarkable for its great antiquity. Northward, as far as Sandy Creek, about fourteen miles from Sacket's Harbour, near which, one covers fifty acres, and contains numerous fragments of pottery.

Westward, they are discovered in great number. There is a large one in the town of Onondaga, one in Scipio, two near Auburn, three near Canandaigua, and several between the Seneca and Cayuga lakes. A number of ancient fortifications and burial places have also been discovered in Ridgeway, Genesee county.

Near the Tonewande creek, at the *double fortified town*,* are some interesting antiquities, described by Dr. Kirkland. They are the remains of two forts. The first contained about four acres, and the other, distant about two miles, and situated on the other extremity of the ancient town, enclosed twice that quantity of ground.

The ditch around the former was about five or six feet

---

* This place is called by the Senecas, *Tegataineaaghque*, which imports a double fortified town, or a town with a fort at each end.

deep. A small stream of water, and a high bank, circumscribed nearly one third of the enclosed ground. There were traces of six gates or avenues round the ditch, and near the centre a way was dug to the water. A considerable number of large thrifty oaks had grown up within the enclosed ground, both in and upon the ditch; some of them appeared to be at least two hundred years old or more.

Near the northern fortification, which was situated on high ground, were found the remains of a funeral pile, probably the burying place of the slain, who had fallen in some sanguinary conflict. The earth was raised about six feet above the common surface, and betwixt twenty and thirty feet in diameter. The bones appeared on the whole surface of the raised earth, and stuck out in many places on the sides.

On the south side of Lake Erie, is a series of old fortifications, from Cattaraugus creek to the Pennsylvania line, a distance of fifty miles. Some are from two to four miles apart, others half a mile only. Some contain five acres. The walls, or breastworks, are of earth, and generally on ground where there are appearances of creeks having once flowed into the lake, or where there was a bay.

These vestiges of ancient fortified towns are widely scattered throughout the extensive territory of the Six Nations, and by Indian report, in various other parts. There is one on a branch of the Delaware river, which, from the size and age of some of the trees, that have grown on the banks, and in the ditches, appears to have existed nearly one thousand years, and perhaps for a still longer period.

These antiquities afford demonstrative evidence of the remote existence of a vast population, settled in towns, defended by forts, cultivating agriculture, and more advanced in civilization, than the nations which have inhabited the same countries since the European discovery.*

The most probable conjecture respecting these people

* Eastman's Hist. of N. Y.

is, that they were of Tartar origin, and came across to this continent near Beering's Straits, and going southward, followed the course of the great rivers—finding the soil fruitful on the Ohio and Mississippi, resided there for a while, till at length, following each other, they established themselves in the warm and fertile vales of Mexico.

123. *Erie Canal.*

This grand canal, the longest in the world, (if we except the Imperial Canal of China,) was commenced July 4th, 1817, and completed Oct. 26th, 1825, at the expense of about eight millions of dollars.

This canal is the property of the state of New York, and will probably afford a large revenue for public purposes.

The Erie Canal, extending from Albany to Buffalo, is 40 feet wide on the surface, 28 on the bottom, 4 feet deep, and 362 miles in length, exclusive of side cuts and navigable feeders. The locks, 83 in number, are 15 feet wide between the gates, and 90 feet in length, and constructed of the most imperishable stone, laid in water cement. The altitude of the water at the termination of the canal at Buffalo, is 565 feet above that of the Hudson at Albany. The total of ascent and depression overcome by means of lockage, throughout the whole extent, is 688 feet. A tow-path is constructed on the bank of the canal, which is elevated from 2 to 4 feet above the surface of the water.

The course of the Erie Canal, commencing at the *Albany Basin*, is along the bank of the Hudson to *Watervliet*, where it receives a navigable feeder from the *Mohawk*, constituting the communication with the *Northern* or *Champlain Canal*. Thence it proceeds along the bank of the Mohawk, and crosses that river above the *Cahoes Falls*, by an aqueduct 1188 feet in length, supported by 26 piers. It then continues about 12 miles on the north bank, after which it re-crosses the Mohawk, four miles below Schenectady, by an aqueduct 748 feet in length 25 feet above the water of the river, and supported by 16 piers. Thence it winds along the south bank of the river, through Schenectady and Utica, to Rome. At Little Falls, the Erie is connected with the old canal, by a stone aqueduct across the Mohawk, 170 feet in length, and supported by 3 arches. The Utica level, 69 1-2 miles in length, without a single lock, commences at Frankfort, 9 miles east of Utica, and proceeding through that village, Whitestown, Rome, Verona, Sullivan, and Manlius, terminates in the town of Salina, near the village of Syracuse. During this course, it passes the Sauquait, Oriscany, Oneida, Canastota, Chitteningo, and Limestone creeks, by aqueducts of various extent. It then proceeds through the village of Syracuse, and crosses the Skeneateles outlet, by a stone aqueduct, supported by 3 arches; and the Owasco creek, by an aqueduct of 4 arches, to Montezuma; thence through the Cayuga Marshes, the villages of Clyde and Lyons, and passing Mud Creek, by a stone aqueduct, 90 feet in length, continues through Palmyra, Pittsford, and Rochester, to Lockport. At Pittsford, it crosses the Irondequot creek, on a stupendous embankment, 72 feet in height. At Rochester it crosses the Genesee river, by a stone aqueduct, of superior architecture, 530 feet in length. Between Rochester and Lockport, the canal passes several deep ravines, by aqueducts and embankments. At Lockport is an ascent of 60 feet, overcome by five double combined locks, to the Mountain Ridge, through which the canal passes, by a deep excavation, to the Tonewande creek. It then enters the creek, and continues along its channel to its mouth, where a dam is erected 4 1-2 feet in height; and proceeds along the shore of the Niagara river and Lake Erie, to its termination at Buffalo.

Connected with the canal, a pier of great length has been constructed in the Niagara river, at Black Rock, for the purpose of forming a harbour at that place, and supplying water for the summit level. The water of Lake Erie continues in the canal to Montezuma. Thence there is an ascent to the Jordan summit, from which the canal descends to the level of Syracuse. It then ascends to the Utica summit, from which is a continuous descent to the Hudson.

The canal debt, in 1826, amounted to $7,602,000; the receipts of tolls on the canal the same year, to $750,000; and the revenue from salt, and auction duties, belonging to the canal fund, to $420,000. The tolls in 1827, amounted to $859,000. It is estimated, that the revenues arising from tolls and the canal fund, will, besides paying the interest, extinguish the canal debt in ten years, dating from 1826.*

When the canal was completed, October 26, a canal boat from Lake Erie entered the canal, which event was announced by the firing of cannon placed at suitable distances, from Lake Erie to the city of New York, and thence back again to Lake Erie.

On the 5th of November, when the canal-boat arrived at the city of New York, the day was celebrated by splendid processions, military parades, &c. &c.

In the aquatic procession, which accompanied the canal-boat, from New York to Sandy Hook, were 22 steam boats and barges. When they arrived at the Hook, Governor Clinton went through the ceremony of uniting the waters, by pouring that of Lake Erie into the Atlantic.

---

124. *Gen. Lafayette's Visit.*

Gilbert Mottier Lafayette, the *Marquis de Lafayette*, America's early and tried friend, was born on the 6th of September, 1757, in the province of Auvergne, now the department of Haute Loire, in France, about 400 miles from Paris.

He sprang from the ancient and illustrious family of Mottier, which for several centuries past has added the name of Lafayette. In 1774, at the age of seventeen, he was married to the Countess Anastasie de Noailles,

* Eastman's Hist. of N. Y.

daughter of the Duke de Noailles. The fortune of this lady, added to his own, increased his income to about 40,000 dollars annually; an immense revenue at that period.

The contest between Great Britain and her North American colonies, was a subject of much interest to the nations of Europe, especially to the French people. The Marquis Lafayette, fired with enthusiastic ardour in the cause of liberty, tore himself from an affectionate family and the honours of the court, and, notwithstanding the prohibition of the French court, embarked for America in January, 1777, and entered the American army as a volunteer, without compensation. The American congress, struck with his magnanimity, gave him the commission of major-general in the army of the United States.

His gallant conduct in the battle of Brandywine, (where he was wounded,) and at many other places, till the close of the war, proved him worthy of the confidence placed in him.

Lafayette likewise gave large sums for the purpose of clothing and arming the American troops.

After the close of the revolutionary war, Lafayette returned to France, where he was appointed commander of the French armies. During the furious and bloody storm of the French revolution, he was obliged to flee, and surrender himself to the Austrians, who imprisoned him in the castle of Olmutz.

Having suffered a rigorous imprisonment, for five years, he was, through the influence of Buonaparte, (afterwards emperor of France,) released, on the 25th of August, 1797.

After an absence of forty years, General Lafayette, determined once more to visit the country of his adoption. Congress hearing of his determination, offered a public ship for the conveyance of the "NATION'S GUEST;" but he politely declined their offer, and chose a private conveyance. He accordingly, with his son, George Washington Lafayette, embarked at Havre, on board the ship Cadmus, and arrived at New York, August 16, 1825.

He was received with enthusiastic demonstrations of

joy, by all classes of the American people. From New York he proceeded by land to Boston, passing through New Haven and Providence. From Boston he proceeded to Portsmouth, N. H., from whence he returned to Boston, and New York, passing through Worcester, Hartford, and Middletown. From New York he went up the Hudson, visiting Albany and other places on the river. Returning to New York, he proceeded on to Philadelphia, Baltimore, and Washington. Here he was received by the house of representatives and senate of the United States, who voted him two hundred thousand dollars and a township of land for the important services rendered by him during the revolutionary war.

General Lafayette commenced his tour from Washington, through the southern and western states, and returned to Albany by the way of Buffalo and the grand canal. From Albany he proceeded through Springfield to Boston, where he arrived on the 16th of June, and was received by the legislature of Massachusetts, then in session. On the 17th he was present at the ceremony of laying the foundation stone of the Bunker Hill monument. He then visited the states of New Hampshire, Maine, and Vermont, and returned to New York to participate in the celebration of the fiftieth anniversary of American independence.

He took his final leave of New York, July 14th, visited the ex-presidents in Virginia, and soon after embarked for France, on board the frigate Brandywine, followed with the grateful benedictions of the American people.

125. *Insurrection and Massacre in Southampton County, Va.*

In August, 1831, a body of sixty or seventy slaves in Southampton County, Virginia, rose upon the white inhabitants, and massacred fifty-five men, women, and children.

The leader of this insurrection and massacre was a

slave by the name of *Nat Turner*, about thirty-one years of age, born the slave of Mr. Benjamin Turner, of Southampton County. From a child, Nat appears to have been the victim of superstition and fanaticism. He stimulated his comrades to join him in the massacre, by declaring to them that he had been commissioned by Jesus Christ, and that he was acting under inspired direction in what he was going to accomplish.

In the confession which he voluntarily made to Mr Grey, while in prison, he says, "that in his childhoo a circumstance occurred which made an indelible impression on his mind, and laid the ground work of the enthusiasm which terminated so fatally to many. Being at play with other children, when three or four years old, I told them something, which my mother overhearing, said it happened before I was born—I stuck to my story, however, and related some things which went, in her opinion, to confirm it; others being called on were greatly astonished, knowing these things had happened, and caused them to say in my hearing, I surely would be a prophet, as the Lord had showed me things which happened before my birth." His parents strengthened him in this belief, and said in his presence, that he was intended for some great purpose, which they had always thought from certain marks on his head and breast. Nat, as he grew up, was fully persuaded he was destined to accomplish some great purpose; his powers of mind appeared much superior to his fellow slaves; they looked up to him as a person guided by divine inspiration, which belief he ever inculcated by his austerity of life and manners.

After a variety of revelations from the spiritual world, Nat says, in his confession, that, "on the 12th of May, 1828, I heard a loud noise in the heavens, and the Spirit instantly appeared to me and said the serpent was loosened, and Christ had laid down the yoke he had borne for the sins of men, and that I should take it on and fight against the serpent, for the time was fast approaching when the first should be last and the last should be first—and by signs in the heavens that it would make known to me when I should commence the great work—and until the first sign appeared, I should conceal it from the knowledge of men.—And on the appearance of the sign, (the eclipse of the sun last February, 1831,) I should arise and prepare myself, and slay my enemies with their own weapons. And immediately on the sign appearing in the heavens, the seal was removed from my lips, and I communicated the great work laid out for me to do, to four in whom I had the greatest confidence, (Henry, Hark, Nelson, and Sam.)—It was intended by us to have begun the work of death on the 4th July last.—Many were the plans formed and rejected by us, and it affected my mind to such a degree, that I fell sick, and the time passed without our coming to any determination how to commence—still forming new schemes and rejecting them, when the sign appeared again, which determined me not to wait longer."

Nat commenced the massacre by the murder of his master and family. He says, " Since the commencement of 1830, I had been living with Mr. Joseph Travis, who was to me a kind master, and placed the greatest confidence in me. In fact, I had no cause to complain of his treatment to me. On Saturday evening, the 20th of August, it was agreed between Henry, Hark, and myself, to prepare a dinner the next day for the men we expected, and then to concert a plan, as we had not yet determined on any. Hark, on the following morning, brought a pig, and Henry, brandy; and being joined by Sam, Nelson, Will, and Jack, they prepared in the woods a dinner, where about three o'clock I joined them. I saluted them on coming up, and asked Will how came he there; he answered, his life was worth no more than others, and his liberty as dear to him. I asked him if he thought to obtain it? He said he would, or lose his life. This was enough to put him in full confidence. Jack, I knew, was only a tool in the hands of Hark; it was quickly agreed we should commence at home (Mr. J. Travis') on that night, and until we had armed and equipped ourselves, and gathered sufficient force, neither age nor sex was to be spared, (which was invariably adhered to.)

We remained at the feast, until about two hours in the night, when we went to the house and found Austin; they all went to the cider press and drank, except myself. On returning to the house, Hark went to the door with an axe, for the purpose of breaking it open, as we knew we were strong enough to murder the family, if they were awaked by the noise; but reflecting that it might create an alarm in the neighbourhood, we determined to enter the house secretly, and murder them whilst sleeping. Hark got a ladder and set it against the chimney, on which I ascended, and hoisting a window, entered and came down stairs, unbarred the door, and removed the guns from their places. It was then observed that I must spill the first blood. On which, armed with a hatchet, and accompanied by Will, I entered my master's chamber; it being dark, I could not give a death blow, the hatchet glanced from his head, he sprang from the bed and called his wife, it was his last word. Will laid him dead with a blow of his axe, and Mrs. Travis shared the same fate as she lay in bed. The murder of this family, five in number, was the work of a moment, not one of them awoke; there was a little infant sleeping in a cradle, that was forgotten, until we had left the house and gone some distance, when Henry and Will returned and killed it; we got here four guns that would shoot, and several old muskets, with a pound or two of powder. We remained some time at the barn, where we paraded; I formed them in a line as soldiers, and after carrying them through all the manœuvres I was master of, marched them off to Mr. Salathiel Francis', about six hundred yards distant."

They proceeded in this manner from house to house, murdering all the whites they could find, their force augmenting as they proceeded, till they amounted to fifty or sixty in number, all mounted, armed with guns, axes, swords, and clubs. They then started for Jerusalem, and proceeded a few miles, when they were met by a party of white men who fired upon them, and forced them to retreat. "On my way back, (says Nat,) I called at Mrs. Thomas's, Mrs. Spencer's, and several other places, the white families having fled, we found no more victims to gratify our thirst for blood; we stopped at Major Ridley's quarter for the night, and being joined by four of his men, with the recruits made since my defeat, we mustered now about forty strong.

"After placing out sentinels, I laid down to sleep, but was quickly roused by a great racket; starting up, I found some mounted, and others in great confusion; one of the sentinels having given the alarm that we were about to be attacked, I ordered some to ride round and reconnoitre, and on their return the others being more alarmed, not knowing who they were, fled in different ways, so that I was reduced to about twenty again; with this I determined to attempt to recruit, and proceed on to rally in the neighbourhood I had left. Dr. Blunt's was the nearest house, which we reached just before day; on riding up the yard, Hark fired a gun. We expected Dr. Blunt and his family were at Major Ridley's, as I knew there was a company of men there; the gun was fired to ascertain if any of the family were at home, we were immediately fired upon and retreated, leaving several of my men. I do not know what became of them, as I never saw them afterwards. Pursuing our course back, and coming in sight of Captain Harris's, where we had been the day before, we discovered a party of white men at the house, on which all deserted me but two, (Jacob and Nat;) we concealed ourselves in the woods until near night, when I sent them in search of Henry, Sam, Nelson, and Hark, and directed them to rally all they could, at the place we had had our dinner the Sunday before, where they would find me, and I accordingly returned there as soon as it was dark and remained until Wednesday evening, when discovering white men riding around the place as though they were looking for some one, and none o. my men joining me, I concluded Jacob and Nat had been taken, and compelled to betray me. On this I gave up all hope for the present, and on Thursday night, after having supplied myself with provisions from Mr. Travis', I scratched a hole under a pile of fence rails in a field, where I concealed myself for six weeks, never leaving my hiding place but for a few minutes in the dead of the night to get water which was very near; thinking by this time I could venture out, I began to go about in the night, and evesdrop the houses in the neighbourhood; pursuing this course for about a fortnight, and gathering little or no intelligence, afraid of speaking to any human being, and returning every morning to my cave before the dawn of day. I know not how long I might have led this life, if accident had not betrayed me.—A dog in the neighbourhood, passing by my hiding place, one night while I was out, was attracted by some meat I had in my cave, and crawled in and stole it, and was coming out just as I returned. A few nights after, two negroes having started to go hunting with the same dog, and passed that way, the dog came again to the place, and having just gone out to walk about, discovered me and barked, on which, thinking myself discovered, I spoke to them to beg concealment. On making myself known they fled from me. Knowing then they would betray me, I immediately left my hiding place, and was pursued almost incessantly, until I was taken a fortnight afterwards, by Mr. Benjamin Phipps, in a little hole I had dug out with my sword, for the purpose of concealment, under the top of a fallen tree. On Mr. Phipps' discovering the place of my concealment, he cocked his gun and aimed at me. I requested him not to shoot and I would give up, upon which he demanded my sword. I delivered it to him and he brought me to prison."

Nat was executed according to his sentence at Jerusalem, Nov. 11th, 1831. The following is a list of the persons murdered in the insurrection, on the 21st and 22d of August, 1831.

Joseph Travis and wife and three children, Mrs. Elizabeth Turner, Hartwell Prebles, Sarah Newsome, Mrs. P. Reese and son William, Trajan Doyle, Henry Bryant and wife and child, and wife's mother, Mrs. Catharine Whitehead, son Richard and four daughters and grandchild, Salathiel Francis, Nathaniel Francis' overseer and two children, John T. Barrow, George Vaughan Mrs. Levi Waller and ten children, William Williams, wife and two boys, Mrs. Caswell Worrel and child, Mrs. Rebecca Vaughan, Ann Eliza Vaughan and son Arthur, Mrs. John K. Williams and child, Mrs. Jacob Williams and three children, and Edward Drury— amounting to fifty-five.

126. *Riot in Providence in Sept.* 1831.

The committee of citizens appointed at the town meeting in Providence on the 25th ult. to investigate and make a statement of facts, have made a report. It is stated that for several years there has been in Olney's lane, and in the part of Providence called 'Snow Town,' a number of houses inhabited chiefly by idle blacks, others by whites, and others by a mixture, constituting a continual nuisance, from their riots and affrays; that the town authorities had been remiss in not correcting the nuisance, as so hateful was it to those who lived within its sphere, that they made no efforts to discountenance the mob, whose proceedings on the night of the 22d ult. were scarcely interrupted in the presence of nearly 1000 satisfied and passive spectators. Yet those who thus countenanced the mob, are now convinced that of all the evils that can be inflicted upon civil society, that of a lawless and ferocious mob is the most capricious in its objects, the most savage in its means, and the most extensive in its consequences.

The first of the recent riots took place on Wednesday evening, Sept. 21. Five sailors, after supper, started from their boarding houses in the southerly part of the town to go 'on a cruise.' They arrived at the foot of Olney's lane about eight o'clock, where they met six or seven men, of one of the steamboats, with sticks or clubs in their hands, and without hats or jackets. They stated that they had been up and had a row with the 'darkies,' and asked the five sailors to go up and aid them. About a hundred persons were assembled, all of whom appeared ready for an affray. The five sailors admit that they proceeded up the lane with the multitude. A great noise was made, the crowd singing and shouting until they came near the elm tree, when a gun was discharged and stones thrown from the vicinity of the houses occupied by the blacks. Stones were also thrown by the crowd against the houses. The committee have received no satisfactory evidence whether the discharge of the gun and stones by the blacks preceded or succeeded the stones thrown by the crowd, or whether they were simultaneous. It is pretty certain that upon the firing of the gun, the main body of the crowd retreated to the foot of the lane. The five sailors, however, continued up the lane, and when nearly opposite the blacksmith's shop, another gun was discharged. William Henry, one of the five sailors, put his hand to his face, and said he was shot. George Erickson and William Hull proceeded to the house the farthest east but one, on the south side of Olney's lane, occupied by blacks. A black man standing on the steps presented a gun, and told them to keep their distance at their peril. Hull proposed taking the gun from him, but Erickson thought it best to leave him. They accordingly joined their three comrades, and proceeded up the lane about a hundred feet to a passage leading from the south side of the lane to a lot in the rear. They saw three or four men, one of whom Hull knew. The black whom they had seen on the steps with a gun, perceiving that they had stopped, ordered them again 'to clear out,' or he would fire upon them. He said, ' Is this the way the blacks are to live, to be obliged to defend themselves from stones ?' The sailors refused to go any farther. One of them, Hull thinks it was George, told the black to 'fire and be damned.' Two attempts to fire were made, a flash and a snap; upon the third, the gun went off.

George fell, mortally wounded, with a large shot in his breast. William Hull and John Phillips were wounded, but not dangerously. George died in about half an hour, during which time Hull states that he could obtain no assistance from the crowd below. Before he was removed, and within half an hour of his death, as Hull states, the crowd had increased to a large mob, and they proceeded up the lane, and demolished two of the houses occupied by blacks, and broke the windows and some of the furniture of others.

On the 22d, the knowledge that a white man had been shot by the blacks, made a great excitement, and the mob assembled at 7 o'clock, and the sheriff arrested seven and committed them to jail, but in three or four other instances the mob made a rescue. Twenty-five soldiers o. Capt. Shaw's company being ordered out, they were pelted by the mob with some injury, and it being perceived that nothing short of firing would have any other effect than to exasperate the mob, they marched off, and no further attempt was made that night to quell the mob. On Friday morning it was generally reported that an attempt would be made to break into the jail and rescue the prisoners. A meeting of the State Council was had, three infantry, one cavalry, and one artillery company ordered to be under arms. Four of the rioters were liberated for want of evidence, and three bound over for trial, that the mob might have no pretence to attack the jail. In the afternoon the following placard was posted.

NOTICE.

' All persons ho are in favor of Liberating those Men ho are confined within the walls of the Providence Jail are requested to make due preparation, and govern themselves accordingly'

' N B—No quarters Shone.'

Most of the evening from 30 to 50 collected in front of the jail, many threats were uttered, and it was with difficulty that the mob could be made to believe that all the prisoners had been discharged. Soon after, a man who had an instrument under his arm, apparently a sword, appeared and ordered the mob to Snow Town, whither they went, but did but little damage.

On Saturday evening, 6 o'clock, the same companies mustered about 130 men at their armories, and the sheriff repaired to Snow Town at half past eight. There was a great crowd, and stones were thrown at the houses: he waited on the Governor, who at his request ordered out the troops, who on their way to their post on the hill west of the buildings the mob were destroying, were sorely pelted, and in clearing the hill, one of the mob seized an infantry soldier's musket, and pulled him down the bank 20 feet. A skirmish ensued between two or three soldiers and some of the mob, in which an artillerist gave the man who had seized the soldier, a sabre cut. After the military had taken their position, the riot act was read audibly by W. S. Patten, Esq. a Justice of the Peace, the mob listening in silence, after which all persons were repeatedly warned to disperse peaceably, and told that all who remained would be considered rioters. The night was still, and the proclamation and statements were plainly heard at a great distance: but the multitude answered by huzzas, shouts, and threats. The sheriff then gained attention, and stated that all must disperse, or in five minutes they would be fired upon. The shouts and stones were redoubled, and exclamations of 'fire and be damned' were heard from all quarters. The civil officers were constantly employed in trying to induce the mob to depart. Soldiers being injured from an opposite hill, the sheriff directed the crowd to retire from that, or he would have to fire upon them; one party moved off towards Mr. Newell's residence, and another portion towards the houses near the bridge.

The mob then again attacked one of these houses, throwing stones and demolishing the windows. The sheriff, in a very loud voice, commanded them to desist, but no attention was paid to him. The violence of the attack increased, so that it was supposed they had begun to tear the building down. At this time the sheriff requested the Governor to detach a portion of the force to suppress the riot. The Light Dragoons and the first Light Infantry were accordingly ordered to march under the sheriff's directions. The Governor advised the sheriff not to fire unless in self-defence. As these two companies approached Mr. Newell's in order to gain the road, they found a portion of the tumultuous crowd still posted in that quarter, who threw stones upon them. The soldiers halted, and musketry was discharged into the air, with a view to intimidate the rioters, and thus cause them to disperse without injury, but this firing produced no other effect than a shower of missiles, accompanied with hootings and imprecations. The sheriff left this detachment, returned to the Governor, and said he did not deem it prudent to move down the hill, leaving this large body of the mob in the rear. The Governor then directed the company of Cadets to occupy a position to protect their rear, which they did accordingly. The sheriff with the two companies first detached, then marched down, the infantry in front, he constantly directing all persons to retire, and moving sufficiently slow to give them an opportunity to do so. As he approached the house, the mob desisted from their work.

During this march, the stones were continually heard rattling against the muskets, and fell thick among the soldiers. As the troops approached the bridge, part of the mob retired before them; some occupied the ground upon each flank, and the sides of the bridge were filled. They slowly crossed the bridge, the sheriff continually and earnestly repeating his request for the rioters to disperse, warning them of their danger. The crowd immediately closed in upon their rear with great clamour, throwing stones without cessation. After the detachment had gained the street east of the bridge, the assaults upon them increased to so great a degree of violence, that the Cavalry were forced against the Infantry, and the rear platoon of Infantry nearly upon the front. The Dragoons called out to the Infantry that they could not withstand the incessant shower of missiles; and unless the Infantry fired upon the rioters, it was impossible that they could remain. The Cavalry were without ammunition. The Infantry also exclaimed that they could no longer sustain these dangerous volleys of stones, and if they were not permitted to defend themselves, they felt they were sacrificed. The detachment halted in Smith-street, near its junction with North Main-street, at a distance of about forty rods from the residue of the military on the hill. The Infantry faced about to present a front to the assailants and the Light Dragoon; who had been compelled to advance partly along their flanks, filed past them, and formed upon the left.

After they halted, the stones were still hurled unremittingly. Many of the soldiers were seriously injured. The stocks of several of the muskets were split by the missiles. The air was filled with them. The sheriff, who was by the side of the Captain of the Infantry during the whole march, repeatedly commanded the mob to desist, but those orders were wholly unavailing. It having now become manifest that no other means existed by which the riot could be suppressed, or the lives of the men preserved, the sheriff directed the Captain to fire. The Captain then gave the word, 'ready.' Here a momentary pause took place. The stones were still thrown with the greatest violence, and exclamations were vociferated, 'Fire and be damned.' The Captain turned to the sheriff and asked, 'Shall I fire?' Perceiving that the crisis had at length arrived, and that the danger was imminent, he replied, 'Yes, you must fire.' The further orders were then given, 'Aim—Fire.' A discharge followed in a somewhat scattering manner.* After the order was thus executed, a second was immediately given to cease firing. The most perfect silence ensued, not a sound was heard, and all violence instantly ceased. In about five minutes, it being evident the mob was now quelled, the Infantry assumed a new position in the line on the east side of Main-street, facing westwardly with the Cavalry on their left.

At the moment these two companies passed the bridge on their march eastward, the shouts were so violent, and the attacks upon them appeared so alarming, that the Governor, apprehensive for their safety, ordered the company of Cadets to march double quick time to their support. The firing of the Infantry was heard immediately after. The Cadets were then moving down, but had not passed below the point where the Governor with the Artillery and volunteer companies remained. They however continued their march, crossed the bridge, and proceeded down Canal-street to Weybosset bridge, dispersing

* Four persons were killed.—*Ed.*

the mob before them. After the firing ceased, information was brought to the Governor, that the multitude was separating. Before leaving the hill, the Governor requested Dr. Parsons, who was with him, to attend upon the wounded, and render them every possible assistance.

Throughout this investigation, the committee have not been able to conceal from their view the disastrous consequences of a predominance of the mob over the Infantry, on the night of the 24th. The Dragoons had been driven upon the Infantry, and forced partly around their flank; the men could stand the pelting no longer. Surrounded as they were, no effectual use could be made of the bayonet. They were obliged to fire, or suffer their ranks to be broken. Had their ranks been broken, the lives of many if not all of the soldiers would have been sacrificed, and their arms fallen into the possession of the mob.

The Committee therefore are of unanimous opinion, that the necessity of a discharge by the Infantry was forced upon them by the mob, and that it was strictly in defense of their lives.

127. *Florida or Seminole War.*

As early as 1821, General Jackson, at that time governor of Florida, urged upon the national government the necessity of removing the Creeks, who, in the difficulties with the Indians in 1814 and 1818, had fled to Florida and incorporated themselves with the Seminoles. It was feared that the increase of the Indian population east of the Mississippi would, sooner or later, produce bad consequences.

These representations were so far disregarded, that a treaty was held with these and other Indians on the peninsula of Florida, in September, 1823, at Camp Moultrie, which stipulated for their continuance in the territory during twenty years. By this treaty, the Seminoles relinquished all their claim to lands in Florida, with the exception of a tract of about five millions of acres, on which they bound themselves to continue. A further treaty was made at Payne's Landing, in 1832, by which they gave up all their reservations, and conditionally agreed to remove. This last treaty was generally considered by the Seminoles as unfair and treacherous.

In 1834, General Thompson was sent to Florida to take measures for the emigration of the Indians. He soon found that the greater part of the Indians were unwilling to remove. In June, 1835, General Thompson, while holding a conference with the Indians, got into a personal dispute with *Osceola*, the favorite chief of the Indians, and being somewhat irritated with his manner, arrested and put him in irons, and confined him for a day in prison. Osceola was deeply exasperated and bent on revenge. He dissembled his feelings; seemed penitent; signed a treaty to remove, and was released.

As the Indians had difficulties among themselves with regard to the treaty, some being for, others against it, the Government ordered troops from the southern posts, to repair to Fort Brooke at Tampa Bay, in order to settle their differences. The command was given to General Clinch, who was at Camp King. On the 28th of December, 1835, while Major Dade, with 117 men, was marching from Fort Brooke to Camp King, about forty miles from the latter place, he was suddenly attacked by a large body of Indians lying in ambush. Major Dade and many of his men fell dead on the first fire. The command now devolved upon Captain Gardiner, who when the Indians were driven to some distance, directed a breastwork to be thrown up for the protection of his men. Owing to the little time they had for the purpose, they were not able to erect one more than about two and a half feet high. The Indians being reinforced, advanced upon the little breastwork and shot down every man who attempted to work the field-piece they had with them. These brave men, although obliged to lie down to load and fire their guns, continued the conflict to the last extremity. At length their ammunition gave out, and the Indians broke into the enclosure, and every man was either killed, or so badly wounded as to be unable to make resistance; only three men survived the action, one or two of whom subsequently died of their wounds.*

On the same day that Major Dade and his men were killed, General Thompson and some of his companions were waylaid and killed, in sight of Fort King, by a body of Indians headed by Osceola, who now fully glutted his revenge.

The next event of importance which occurred after these tragedies, was the action of *Withlacoochee*. General Clinch, previously to this event, was lying in garrison at Fort Drane, about thirty miles from Fort King.

* The spot where these brave men fell was passed by the army under General Gaines, on their route from Fort Brooke to the north, on the 20th of February, 1836. The following account is given by an officer of the army: "Resuming their march at daybreak on the 20th, they pursued the even tenor of their way until about nine o'clock, when the appearance of large vultures but too plainly foretold the approach of the army to the sad spot of slaughter. The advance-guard having passed the battle-ground without halting, the general and his staff came upon one of the most appalling and affecting scenes that the human eye ever beheld. A short distance in the rear of the little field-work lay a few broken cartridge-boxes, fragments of clothing, here and there a shoe, or an old straw hat, which perhaps had been exchanged for a military cap; then a cart partly burnt, with the oxen still yoked lying dead near it; a horse had fallen a little to the right; and here, also, a few bones of the hapless beings lay bleaching in the sun; while the scene within and beyond the triangular enclosure baffles all description. One would involuntarily turn aside from the horrible picture to shed a tear of sorrow, and 'wish that *he* had nothing known or nothing seen.' From the positions in which the bodies of this devoted little band were found, it was evident that they had been shot down in the faithful discharge of their duty; their bodies were stretched with striking regularity, nearly parallel with each other; and it is very doubtful whether the Indians touched them after the battle, except to take some few scalps, and to divest the officers of their coats. A short distance further, in the middle of the road, was the advance guard, about twenty eight in number; and immediately in the rear lay the remains of poor Dade, while a few feet to the right, in the rear, were those of the estimable Captain Frazer. To guard against surprise, our troops had been immediately formed into a quadrangular line, and soon after a detail of the regulars commenced the pleasing though mournful task of consigning the remains of their mutilated brethren in arms to whence they came. Within the enclosure two large graves were dug, into which the bodies of ninety-eight non-commissioned officers and privates were placed; and outside of the northeast angle of the work, another grave received the bodies of eight officers, at the head of which, the field-piece which had been spiked and concealed by the enemy, but recovered, was planted vertically. The regular troops, formed into two columns and led by the immediate friends of the deceased officers, then moved, with reversed arms, in an opposite direction, three times around the breastwork, while the bands played the Dead March."

Being joined by about 500 volunteers from the adjoining counties, he set out on an expedition against the Indian head-quarters. When the army in part had crossed the Withlacoochee river, they were attacked by Osceola and his warriors, who had concealed themselves at this spot for the purpose. The troops stood firm, and finally, after a conflict of an hour, succeeded in driving the Indians away. In this conflict 4 men were killed and 52 wounded, some of whom died of their wounds. The Indian loss is supposed to have been greater.

General Clinch was obliged to return to Fort Drane without effecting his object, and his position was rendered critical. General Scott sent troops to his relief. General Gaines, with a force of about 1,000 men from New Orleans, landed at Tampa Bay, February 4, 1836. Four days afterwards, General Scott arrived at St. Augustine. General Gaines marched for the Withlacoochee to attack the Seminoles; he was opposed by them at and near this place, and suffered some loss; Major Izard, of the United States Dragoons, was killed. Osceola contrived to deceive General Gaines by a parley, till the Indian women and children were removed South, among the everglades and hammocks.

After General Scott left Florida, Major General Jesup was appointed to the command. Having a large force under his orders, he was quite confident of bringing the war to a close in a short time; but his efforts were equally unsuccessful as those before, and a great deal of time was wasted by fruitless negotiations with the Indians.

A body of about 1,000 men under Colonel Taylor being directed against the enemy, on the 25th of December, 1837, a battle was fought at Okee-Chobee lake, at the edge of the everglades, about 70 or 80 miles from Tampa Bay. A small party of Indians being seen at this place, they were pursued till they reached a hammock, where the Indians were posted in great numbers. This position was chosen with great judgment; the everglades over which the whites were to pass were cut down to give effect to their fire. When the whites adranced, each Indian selected his victim, and the advancing column was mowed down by the first destructive volley. The enemy poured in their destructive fire from the ground, the bushes, and the tops of trees; but they were afterwards forced to retire. Twenty-eight of the whites were killed, and one hundred and eleven were wounded. Among the killed were Colonel Thompson, Captain Van Swearingen, and Colonel Gentry mortally wounded.

In Oct., 1837, Osceola, with about 70 warriors, under the protection of a flag, came into the camp of General Jesup, who, believing him to be treacherous, caused him to be forcibly detained. He was taken to St. Augustine, and thence he was sent into confinement at Fort Moultrie, on Sullivan's Island, in the harbor of Charleston, South Carolina, where he died of the throat distemper, on the 31st of January, 1838.

This harassing warfare was brought to a close by the exertions of Colonel Worth, and on the 14th of August, 1842, an official announcement was made that the war with the Indians in the territory of Florida had ceased. There is not in the history of the United States a war related so fatal and expensive, when the comparative and apparent insignificance of the enemy is considered. Millions of money were expended, and hundreds of valuable lives were sacrificed; great numbers perished by disease contracted by traversing swamps and morasses, among poisonous reptiles, and through the mud, mire, and waters of stagnant lakes.

128. *Revolution in Texas.*

Settlements were made in the limits of Texas as early as 1692, but the savages were so hostile in the vicinity that but little progress was effected. The Spanish Government, and afterwards that of the Mexican, in order to establish settlements in this territory, offered grants of lands and other inducements to settlers from the United

States. Early in 1821, Stephen B. Austin, from Connecticut, went to the Brassos river to secure a portion of territory which his father had bequeathed to him. He secured the grant, and liberal offers were made by the Government to others who would go and settle there.

Many settlers accepted these offers, and their increase and prosperity soon began to alarm the Mexican Government. When Iturbide was dethroned in Mexico, a confederation was formed; Coquila and Texas were united in one state; and a system of measures was adopted which finally led to the declaration of Texan independence. In 1825, the Mexican Congress passed a law prohibiting all traffic in slaves, and freeing all born in Texas at the age of 14; and soon a law was passed freeing all slaves in the limits of Texas. As most of the settlers were planters from the Southern States, who had brought their slaves with them, these laws were considered by them as unjust and oppressive.

The Texans, in vain, petitioned the Mexican Congress for relief; and Stephen Austin, when visiting the capital for this purpose, was seized and put in prison, where he was confined two years. Upon the abrogation of the State Governments, and the establishment of *Centralism* under Santa Anna, a convention of the citizens of Texas was called, and independence from Mexico was declared. General Coss having been sent by the Mexican Government to dissolve the Legislature and seize the members, the people of Texas flew to arms. On the 8th of October, 1835, they moved upon Goliad, a strong fortress, which they carried after a bloody engagement. A force of 1000 men, under the command of Austin, advanced upon San Antonio, where General Coss was entrenched with 1,500 men, and forced him to surrender on condition that the prisoners should be allowed to pass beyond the Rio Grande.

Santa Anna, the President of Mexico, with a force of 8,000 men, now moved forward, threatening to exterminate the Americans from the soil of Texas. The right of his army moved in the direction of Matamoras; the center and left, under Santa Anna himself, marched towards San Jacinto. It was his intention that the divisions should move in parallel lines and keep up a communication, and so sweep the province, and meet at Galveston.

In March, 1836, San Antonio de Bexar was besieged, and the Alamo was defended by a force of only 187 men, commanded by Colonel W. B. Travis. The garrison sustained the siege for two weeks, till they were all slain but seven, who surrendered; and it is stated they were afterwards put to death by the order of Santa Anna. Besides Colonel Travis, here fell Colonel David Crockett, and Colonel James Bowie, the inventor of the *Bowie knife*. The loss of the Mexicans in storming the place is stated in some accounts to have been 1,000 in killed and wounded.

While Santa Anna was engaged at San Antonio, General Urrea marched upon Goliad. Before he reached this place, he came up with Colonel Fanning's troops, with whom a bloody action was fought. On the 20th of March, Colonel Fanning, with 520 Texans, surrendered as prisoners of war; and nine days afterwards, all were shot down by the Mexicans, except six only, who escaped under cover of the smoke of their guns.

On the 21st of April, 1836, Santa Anna came up with a body of 783 Texans, commanded by General Houston, near the banks of the *San Jacinto*. After some considerable skirmishing, the Mexicans retired to their camp. Being masked by the timber, the Texans marched into a valley in front of the Mexican camp, and at once rushed upon their line. When within about 600 yards, the Mexicans opened their fire upon them. Nothing daunted by this, the Texans moved on till they were within about 70 yards of their foes, when they opened a terrible and destructive fire. As they were most of them armed with double-barrelled guns, and many with five or six pistols, besides knives and tomahawks, they did not stop to reload, but rushed on amid the smoke, and as soon as they could see the enemy, fired again, and thus swept over them like wind. The Mexican artillery was taken already loaded and primed, and turned and fired upon the Mexicans as they retreated in total rout and confusion. The Texan loss was only 2 killed and 23 wounded, 6 mortally. The Mexican loss was stated to be 630 killed, 208 wounded, and 730 prisoners, among whom were Santa Anna and his principal officers.

In May, 1836, a convention or agreement was signed at Velasco, between D. G. Burnet, President of Texas, and Santa Anna, by which it was stipulated that hostilities between the Mexican and Texan troops should cease, and that Santa Anna should be sent to Vera Cruz. The Mexicans made repeated demonstrations, apparently with the view of recovering Texas; but, owing to dissensions among themselves and other causes, nothing of importance was effected.

On the 1st of March, 1845, the joint resolutions for the annexation of Texas to the United States, which had previously passed both Houses of Congress, received the signature of President Tyler, and thus became a law. On the 18th of June following, joint resolutions passed both branches of the Texan Congress, by an unanimous vote, giving the consent of that body to the annexation of Texas to the United States.

---

129. *Difficulties on the Canadian Frontier.*

In October, 1837, a large number of Canadians assembled at St. Charles, in Lower Canada, and passed resolutions expressing their dissatisfaction with the manner in which Canada was governed. S. J. Papineau speaker of the House of Assembly, Dr. Nelson, and others, were at the head of this movement, which was brought about by a party in Canada, who had for years been desirous of independence. Many citizens of the United States on the northern frontier, regarding their cause as that of liberty and human rights, formed secret associations for the purpose of aiding the "*Canadian patriots*" (as they were called) across the line.

"About the middle of the month of December, 1837,

wenty-eight men, principally Canadians, with Rensselaer Van Rensselaer and William Lyon Mackenzie, went on Navy Island. They called to them the patriots of Canada, and all others the friends of that cause. In the space of three weeks, between three and four hundred responded to the call: some from the United States, and others from Canada. They brought with them arms and provisions. They staid on the island for one month, and then, at their own choice, left it, and not in fear of their opponents. Opposite to them, were assembled five thousand men, consisting of British regulars, incorporated militia, and a body of Indians and negroes. Batteries were erected, and balls and shells were, at intervals, cast upon the island. The islanders were incessantly in a state of danger and alarm; yet they would, at times, provokingly return the fire; still they remained unattacked. For a month, a raw, undisciplined band of men, in the severity of winter, with no shelter but such as they then constructed, and miserably clad, set at defiance and laughed at the overwhelming force, which lay so near to them that they frequently conversed together.

"The steamboat Caroline came from Buffalo, on the 29th of December, it was said, to ply as a ferry-boat between Schlosser and Navy Island. It passed, that day, forth and back several times, and before sundown was brought to at the wharf, at Schlosser, and moored for the night. At that place, there was but one house, and that a tavern. The warlike movements between the patriots and British, had drawn to the frontier, through motives of curiosity, a great number of persons. The tavern was crowded—lodgings could not be obtained—and several persons, observing the steamboat, sought for accommodations on board, and were received. In the middle of the night, the watch, for a watch on board steamboats is usually kept, saw something advancing on the water. He hailed, but before he could give the alarm, a body of armed men rushed on board, shot at the sentinel and all they met, crying—'*Cut them down!*' '*Give no quarter!*' No arms were on board the boat; no attack was expected, and no resistance was made. Some got on shore uninj jured; others were severely cut and dangerously wounded. One man was shot dead on the wharf, and twelve were missing, either killed, or burnt and sunk with the boat. They towed the boat out in the river, and set it on fire; the flames burst forth; it drifted slowly, and its blaze shone far and wide over the water and adjacent shores. On the Canada side, at a distance above Chippewa, was burning a large light, as a signal to those engaged in the expedition. In a short time, an astounding shout came booming over the water: it was for the success and return of those who had performed this deed. The beacon was extinguished. The Caroline still moved on, and cast its lurid light far and wide, clothing the scene in gloom and horror; and just below the point of Iris island, suddenly disappeared. Many of the wrecked and charred remains were, the next morning, floating in the current and eddies below the falls."*

The disturbances continued on the frontier till near the close of the year 1838. The battle of Prescott, U. C., opposite Ogdensburg, N. Y., on the 13th and 15th of Nov., effectually put down armed resistance to the regular authorities in Canada. The insurgents, about one hundred and fifty in number, withstood a force of upward of one thousand British troops. The patriots, with the exception of two or three who escaped, were all either killed or taken prisoners. The British loss was about 150 men killed, and 20 officers; among whom was Captain Drummond. The patriots were commanded by Van Schoultz, a native of Poland. He, with Colonels Abbey and Woodruff, and others of the prisoners, were sentenced to death and executed: twenty-three were sent to England, and from thence were transported to Van Diemen's Land.

---

130. *Account of the Mormons.*

Joseph Smith, the founder of Mormonism, was born in Royalton, Vermont, and removed to Manchester, Ontario county, New York, about the year 1820, at an early age,

* "De Veaux's Falls of Niagara."

with his parents, who were in quite humble circumstances. He was occasionally employed in Palmyra as a laborer, and bore the reputation of a lazy and ignorant young man. According to the testimony of respectable individuals in that place, Smith and his father were persons of doubtful moral character, addicted to disreputable habits, and moreover, extremely superstitious, believing in the existence of witchcraft. They at one time procured a mineral rod, and dug in various places for money. Smith testified that when digging he had seen the pot or chest containing the treasure, but never was fortunate enough to get it into his hands. He placed a singular looking stone in his hat, and pretended by the light of it to make many wonderful discoveries of gold, silver, and other treasures, deposited in the earth. He commenced his career as the founder of the new sect, when about the age of 18 or 19, and appointed a number of meetings in Palmyra, for the purpose of declaring the divine revelations which he said were made to him. He was, however, unable to produce any excitement in the village; but very few had curiosity sufficient to listen to him. Not having the means to print his revelations, he applied to Mr. Crane, of the society of Friends, declaring that he was moved by the Spirit to call upon him for assistance. This gentleman bid him to go to work, or the state-prison would end his career. Smith had better success with Martin Harris, an industrious and thrifty farmer of Palmyra, who was worth about $10,000, and who became one of his leading disciples. By his assistance, 5,000 copies of the Mormon bible (so called), were published at an expense of about $3,000. It is possible that Harris might have made the advances with the expectation of a profitable speculation, as a great sale was anticipated. This work is a duodecimo volume, containing 590 pages, and is perhaps one of the weakest productions ever attempted to be palmed off as a divine revelation. It is mostly a blind mass of words, interwoven with scriptural language and quotations without much of a leading plan or design. It is, in fact, such a production as might be expected from a person of Smith's abilities and turn of mind.

Soon after the publication of the Mormon Bible, one Parley B. Pratt, a resident of Lorrain county, Ohio, happening to pass through Palmyra, on the canal, and hearing of the new religion, called on the prophet, and was soon converted. Pratt was intimate with Sidney Rigdon, a very popular preacher of the denomination called "Reformers," or "Disciples." About the time of the arrival of Pratt at Manchester, the Smiths were fitting out an expedition for the western country, under the command of Cowdery, in order to convert the Indians, or Lamanites, as they termed them. In October, 1830, this mission, consisting of Cowdery, Pratt, Peterson, and Whitmer, arrived at Mentor, Ohio, the residence of Rigdon, well supplied with the new Bibles. Near this place, in Kirtland, there were a few families belonging to Rigdon's congregation, who, having become extremely fanatical, were daily looking for some wonderful event to take place in the world: 17 of these persons readily believed in Mormonism, and were all re-immersed in one night by Cowdery. By the conversion of Rigdon soon after, Mormonism received a powerful impetus, and more than 100 converts were speedily added. Rigdon visited Smith at Palmyra, where he tarried about two months, receiving revelations, preaching, &c. He then returned to Kirtland, Ohio, and was followed a few days after by the prophet Smith and his connexions. Thus, from a state of almost beggary, the family of Smith were furnished with the "fat of the land" by their disciples, many of whom were wealthy.

A Mormon temple was erected at Kirtland, at an expense of about $50,000. In this building there was a sacred apartment, a kind of holy of holies, in which none but the priests were allowed to enter. An unsuccessful application was made to the Legislature for the charter of a bank. Upon the refusal, they established an unchartered institution, commenced their banking operations, issued their notes, and made extensive loans. The society now rapidly increased in wealth and numbers, of whom many were doubtless drawn thither by mercenary motives. But the bubble at last burst. The bank being an unchartered institution, the debts due were not legally collectable. With the failure of this institution, the society rapidly declined, and Smith was obliged to leave the state to avoid the sheriff. Most of the sect, with their leader, removed to Missouri, where many outrages were perpetrated against them. The Mormons raised an armed force to "drive off the infidels," but were finally obliged to leave the state.

The last stand taken by the Mormons was at Nauvoo, Illinois, a beautiful location on the Mississippi river. Here they erected a splendid temple, 120 feet in length by 80 in width, around which they built their city, which at one time contained about 10,000 inhabitants. Being determined to have their own laws and regulations, the difficulties which attended their sojourn in other places followed them here, and there was constant collision between them and the surrounding inhabitants. By some process of law, Joseph Smith (the Prophet) and his brother Hyram were confined in the debtor's apartment in the jail at Carthage, in the vicinity of Nauvoo, and a guard of 8 or 10 men were stationed at the jail for their protection. While here, it appears that a mob of about 60 men, in disguise, broke through the guard, and firing into the prison, killed both Joseph Smith and his brother Hyram, June 27, 1844. Their difficulties still continued, and they determined to remove once more. At this time (November, 1846) nearly all the Mormons have left Nauvoo, and are now on their way to California.

131. *War with Black Hawk.*

In the spring of 1832, the Winnebagoes, Sacs, and Foxes, inhabiting the northwestern frontier, on the Upper Mississippi, commenced a warfare, by which many settlements were broken up and destroyed, and many of the defenceless inhabitants were killed. The war appears to have been occasioned by driving the Indians from the lands on the eastern side of the Mississippi These lands had been sold to the United States in 1830 by *Keokuk*, at that time the principal chief of the Sacs. A part of the tribe were dissatisfied with the treaty, which conveyed away the territory on which their village was situated, at the point of land formed by the confluence of Rock river with the Mississippi. This party, headed by a chief named *Black Hawk*, was determined not to remove. Difficulties having arisen, General Atkinson, about the 1st of April, 1832, set out for the Upper Mississippi, at the head of the sixth Regiment U. S. Infantry. On his approach, Black Hawk and his party abandoned their camp on the Mississippi and ascended Rock river.

Black Hawk, with a small party, having put to rout a party of 270 men under Major Stillman, created a great alarm in this region. Governor Reynolds, of Illinois, ordered out 2,000 militia, to drive the hostile Indians from that state. By the beginning of June, there were so many troops spread over the Indian country, that Black Hawk found but few opportunities to murder the inhabitants on the frontiers. And although there were about 3,000 men in arms to combat 500 Indians, yet Congress ordered 600 mounted Rangers to be raised for the defence of the frontiers.

General Scott was ordered from the seaboard with nine companies of artillery, and their cannon were to be drawn from the coast; nine companies of infantry were ordered from the lakes, and two companies from Baton Rouge, to put an end to the war. Such was the promptness with which these orders were executed, that all except one of the six companies of artillery ordered from Fort Monroe, on the Chesapeake, arrived in 18 days at Chicago, Illinois, 1,800 miles distant in the interior of the country. This detachment was attacked on the route by the Cholera, and the whole of them were rendered unfit to take the field before they arrived at the scene of action. Several companies were broken up. "Of a corps of 208 men under Colonel Twiggs, but 9 were left alive."

A correspondent from Detroit wrote on the 12th of July as follows:—

"I regret to add that the intelligence from the regular troops is disastrous. Of the three companies of artillery under Colonel Twiggs, and two or three more companies of infantry with them, but few remain. These troops landed from the steamboat Henry Clay below Fort Gratiot. A great number of them have been swept off by disease. Nearly all the others have deserted. Of the deserters scattered over the country, some have died in the woods, and their bodies have been devoured by the wolves; others have taken their flight to the world of spirits, without a companion to close their eyes. Their straggling survivors are occasionally seen marching, some of them know not whither, with their knapsacks on their backs, shunned by the terrified inhabitants as a source of a mortal pestilence . . . . . . One half of the command of General Scott, ordered to Chicago by the Lakes, will never reach him; a large portion of them dying, a still larger number deserting from an overwhelming dread of the disease, and the residue obliged to march back again."

Black Hawk, instead of crossing the country to escape beyond the Mississippi, as was expected, descended the Wisconsin to escape in that direction; by which means General Dodge came upon his trail and commenced a vigorous pursuit. The state of the Indians now became deplorable; many of them were found dead in the way—emaciated and starved to death! Many children were found in such a famished state that they could not be revived. On the 2d of August, a force of about 1,600 men, under General Atkinson, crossed over to the north side of the Wisconsin, and by a forced march came up with the main body of the Indians, and after a conflict of upward of three hours, succeeded in putting a finishing stroke to the war. About 150 of them were killed. Black Hawk managed to make his escape; but soon after, with a small party, he went to the Winnebagoe village at Prairie du Chien, and told the chief he desired to give himself up to the whites, and let them kill him if they wished to do so. The squaws at this place made him a dress of white deer-skins, preparatory to his departure for Prairie du Chien, to which it appears he went voluntarily with those who went out after him. Black Hawk and the *Prophet* were delivered by two Winnebagoes to General Street, at Prairie du Chien, on the 27th of August. The following are extracts from the speech of Black Hawk, which is said to have been delivered when he surrendered himself to the agent at this place:—

"You have taken me prisoner with all my warriors. * * * * The sun rose dim on us in the morning, and at night it sunk into a dark cloud, and looked like a ball of fire! It was the last sun that shone on Black Hawk. His heart is dead and no longer beats quick in his bosom. He is now a prisoner to the white men; they will do with him as they wish. But he can stand torture, and is not afraid of death. He is no coward. Black Hawk is an Indian. He has done nothing for which an Indian ought to be ashamed. He has fought for his countrymen, the squaws, and pappooses, against white men, who came year after year to cheat them and take away their lands. * * * * An Indian who is bad as the white man, could not live in our nation; he would be put to death, and eat up by the wolves. * * * * The spirit of our fathers arose and spoke to us to avenge our wrongs or die. * * * * We set up the war-whoop, and dug up the tomahawk; our knives were ready, and the heart of Black Hawk swelled high in his bosom, when he led his warriors to battle. He is satisfied; he will go to the world of spirits contented. He has done his duty. His father will meet him there and commend him. * * * * He can do no more. His sun is setting and will rise no more. Farewell to Black Hawk."

On the 22d of April, 1833, Black Hawk, his son, and the Prophet, with seven other captives, arrived in Washington, and the next day they had a long interview with President Jackson. The first words (it is said) with which he accosted the President, were: "*I am a man, and you are another.*" Accompanied with a conductor, they visited various places, where they attr̄ted great attention, and were conducted back to their coṉatry by way of New York.

132. *Cholera in the United States.*

The Asiatic or malignant cholera first manifested itself on this continent at Quebec, the capital of Canada, on the 8th of June, 1832, at a distance of 3,000 miles, across the ocean, to the nearest infected place in Europe. Out of a population of about 30,000, about 2,000 persons died. On the 10th of June it appeared in Montreal, where, out of a population of 28,000, there were upwards of 4,000 cases, nearly one half of which terminated fatally. "The course of the epidemic in Canada was along the St. Lawrence, affecting the villages which line its banks, and extending to the farms of the open country. From the St. Lawrence it spread along the shores of Ontario, skirted Lake Erie, arrived at Detroit, and penetrated by Lake Superior to the Mississippi."

This epidemic first invaded the United States at the city of New York, June 27, 1832, about 400 miles south of Montreal, without any apparent trace of its progress from that place. "The first subject of it was an old resident of the city. No place on the line of communication between New York and Canada was attacked with the disease previous to its appearance in that city." Even Albany, the half-way place between New York and Montreal, remained untouched until the 3d of July Out of a population of 25,000 in this place, upwards of 400 persons died.

The population of New York, during the prevalence of the cholera, is supposed to have been reduced by removals to 140,000; previous to the outbreak of the disease, it is estimated to have been 225,000. The number of deaths, from the 1st of July to the middle of October, when this pestilence ceased, has been estimated differently; but from the best sources of information, it appears that about 4,000 persons, during this period, died of the cholera. The ratio of deaths to cases was 1 to 2. This pestilence arrived at its height July 21st, on which day 311 new cases were reported.

"With the exception of a very limited number of cases at New Haven, Newport, Providence, Boston, Troy, and a few other places, all that part of the United States lying east of the Hudson river, has been entirely exempted from the ravages of this great destroyer."

The first case of cholera in Philadelphia appeared on the 5th of July, 1832, and the second case on the 9th; but its influence did not acquire its full sway until the 27th. The population of Philadelphia within the bills of mortality was 160,000: but it must be granted that many persons left the city. The number of cases in this city to September 13th was 2,314; the number of deaths 935; ratio of deaths to cases, one to two and a half. Many cases in private practice were not reported. The disease reached its climax on the 7th of August. At Arch-street prison it appeared with great violence; there were 86 cases and 46 deaths. It appears, from observations made in this city, New York, and elsewhere, that the period of life most liable to attack was from 50 to 60 years of age; and that most exempt, from 2 to 10 years. The proportion in regard to sexes in this city was $59\frac{30}{100}$ males, to $40\frac{70}{100}$ females. Ratio of cases to white population, 1 to 74; black population, 1 to 41. "The city of Philadelphia, previous to her waterworks being in operation, suffered severely by yellow fever; but unlike yellow fever, which always located itself in the most filthy parts of the city, the cholera diffused itself indiscriminately over every portion of her wide and beautiful domain."

In Baltimore, the number of deaths by cholera to September 29, 1832, was 710; in Norfolk, to September 11, 400; in Cincinnati, from May 1 to August 7, 1833, 307; in Nashville, from March 27 to July 12, 27 whites and 50 blacks. The disease appeared in New Orleans, October 27, 1832, and raged at different periods after that time with great severity, particularly among the black population. It is stated that the pecuniary loss to Louisiana by the death of slaves amounted to four millions of dollars.—*See Hayward's Statistical Register.*

---

133. *Great Fire in New York in* 1835.

The following is an account of the greatest fire ever known in the United States, which took place in New York, December 16th, 1835. It broke out about nine o'clock in the evening, in the richest part of the city, and extended in all directions. The night was exceedingly cold, and the wind high. It is estimated that upwards of *seventeen millions* worth of property was destroyed.

"One of the most alarming and destructive fires ever known in this hemisphere, broke out on Wednesday evening, December 16th, 1835, in the premises of Messrs. Crawford and Andrews, situate No. 25 Merchant street, which in a short time raged with such intensity as to defy the exertions of the firemen, and others, who with equal zeal and promptitude, were quickly on the spot for the purpose of stopping its ravages. The inutility of all aid was, however, soon perceptible, and all that could be done, was to remove what could in haste be got together, to such places as were deemed beyond the reach of the devouring element. With this impression, an immense quantity of goods were placed for safety, from buildings in the immediate vicinity of the fire, in the Merchants' Exchange and reformed Dutch church, where it was presumed they would remain free from danger: alas! the futility of human speculation; but a short time had elapsed from the time of such deposite, to the whole being enveloped in flames, and these splendid buildings were soon reduced to a heap of ashes. The power of man was fruitlessly employed in attempts to stay its impetuosity, which every minute increased in the most alarming manner, spreading in all directions, and causing the utmost dismay and consternation through the whole city. Any attempt to convey to the mind a faithful description of the awfully grand scene that presented itself to the view of those who were witnesses of this dreadful catastrophe, must of necessity be very feeble.

"The morning of the 17th of December, 1835, opened upon New York with a scene of devastation around, sufficient to dismay the stoutest heart. The fine range of buildings and splendid stores in Exchange place, Merchant street, and all the adjoining streets down to the river, lay literally levelled to the earth, with their contents consumed; the Merchant's Exchange and post-office entirely destroyed—the whole one heap of smoking ruins.

"A tolerably correct idea of the extent of the devastation may be formed from the following account, which appeared the next morning in the 'Courier and Enquirer.'

"'South street is burned down from Wall street to Coenties slip. Front street is burned down from Wall street to Coenties slip. Pearl street is burned down from Wall street to Coenties alley, and was there stopped by blowing up a building. Stone-street is burned down from William street to No. 32 on the one side, and No. 39 on the other. Beaver street is burned down halfway to Broad street. Exchange place is burned down from Hanover street to within three doors of Broad street; here the flames were stopped by blowing up a house. William street is burned down from Wall-street to South street, both sides of the way. Market house down. Wall street is burned down on the south side, from William street to South street, with the exception of 51, 53, 55, 57, 59, 61, opposite this office. All the streets and alleys within the above limits are destroyed.

"'The following will be found a tolerably accurate statement of the number of houses and stores now levelled with the ground: 26 on Wall street, 37 on South street, 80 on Front street, 62 on Exchange place, 44 on William street, 16 on Coenties slip, 3 on Hanover square, 20 on Gouverneur's lane, 20 on Cuyler's alley, 79 on Pearl street, 76 on Water street, 16 on Hanover street, 31 on Exchange street, 33 on Old slip, 40 on Stone street, 23 on Beaver street, 10 on Jones' lane, 38 on Mill street: total 674.

"'Six hundred and seventy-four tenements. By far

the greater part in the occupancy of our largest shipping and wholesale drygood merchants, and filled with the richest products of every portion of the globe. Of the Merchant's Exchange nothing but its marble walls remain standing.

"'Three or four vessels lying at the wharfs on South street, were slightly injured in their yards and rigging They were all hauled out into the river as soon as practicable.

"'A detachment of marines from the navy yard under Lieutenant Reynolds, and of sailors under Captain Mix of the navy, arrived on the spot at two o'clock in the morning. They rendered most valuable service. The gunpowder brought from the magazine at Red Hook was partly under their charge.

"'The cold during the whole time was excessive; the thermometer at zero. It may be easily supposed that this greatly paralyzed the exertion of the firemen. One sank under its effects, and was with difficulty resuscitated. Two companies with their engines arrived here from Newark, and rendered very material assistance.

"'The passengers in a steamboat coming down the river, saw the flames from the Highlands, forty-five miles distant, and such was the violence of the gale, during the prevalence of the fire, that burning embers were carried across the East river to Brooklyn and set fire to the roof of a house there, which was however speedily extinguished.

"'Strong bodies of cavalry and volunteer infantry were patrolling the streets near the fire, and preserved perfect order for the purpose of preventing depredations.'"

---

134. *Captain Wilkes' Exploring Expedition.*

The first expedition fitted out by the United States, at the national expense, for scientific objects, was that under the command of Lieutenant Charles Wilkes who was appointed to the command, March 20 1838. The ves sels appointed for this service were the sloops of war Vincennes and Peacock, the brig Porpoise, and the store-ship Relief. The tenders Sea-Gull and Flying Fish were subsequently added. The Expedition left Hampton Roads, near Norfolk, August 18, 1838. After an absence of nearly four years in various parts of the globe, Lieut. Wilkes arrived at New York, on board the Vincennes, on the 10th of June, 1842.

The following is an outline of the instructions given Lieut. Wilkes by the Navy Department, as to the places to be visited, viz.: First, he was to shape his course to Rio Janeiro, where he was directed to replenish his supplies; thence to make a particular examination of the Rio Negro, which falls into the South Atlantic; thence to a safe port in Terra del Fuego; here the larger vessels were to be left, while the Porpoise and tenders were directed to explore the southern Antarctic. On the rejoining of the vessels at Terra Del Fuego, the squadron was directed to stretch southward and westward to longitude 105° W., and return northward to Valparaiso, where a store-ship would meet them in March, 1839. From this port they were to shape their course to the Navigators' Group, and thence to the Feejee Islands, where they were to select a safe harbor for vessels of the United States. From these islands the squadron was directed to proceed to the port of Sidney (New Holland), and thence make a second attempt to penetrate within the Antarctic region, south of Van Dieman's Land. From this place they were to rendezvous at Kerguelen's Land, or the Isle of Desolation, from which they were to proceed to the Sandwich Islands, where a storeship from the United States with provisions would meet them in April, 1840. From the Sandwich Islands, the Expedition was to proceed to the northwest coast of America, where they were directed to make surveys along the territory of the United States, and afterwards along the coast of California. From this coast, they were directed to proceed to that of Japan, where they were to make an examination of the Sea of Sooloo, or Mindoro. After this examination they were to proceed to the Straits of Sunda, and examine those of Billiton, and thence to the port of Singapore. From this last-named place they were to return to the United States by the way of the Cape of Good Hope.

Although the primary object of the Expedition was the promotion of the great interests of commerce and navigation, yet, to extend the bounds of science, a corps of scientific gentlemen, nine in number, were appointed and accompanied the Expedition, viz: 3 Naturalists, 2 Artists or Draughtsmen, 1 Mineralogist, 1 Philologist, 1 instrument-maker, and 1 assistant Taxidermist.

On the 28th of April, 1839, when near Cape Horn, the tender Sea-Gull, having on board two officers, Passed Midshipmen James W. E. Reid and Frederick A. Bacon, with a crew of 15 persons, was supposed to have been lost in a severe gale, as nothing was ever heard of them afterwards. On the 16th of January, 1840, land was discovered to the south of New Holland, which may be considered as the *first discovery* of the *Antarctic continent*. The vessels engaged in this discovery were in an extremely perilous condition amid fields of ice and towering icebergs, particularly the Peacock, which was for a time wedged in between large masses of ice, from which impending destruction she was most providentially delivered.

On the 24th of July, 1840, Lieutenant Underwood and Midshipman Henry, while engaged in surveying some of the small islands in the Feejee group, being on shore for the purpose of trading, were both killed by the natives. Captain Wilkes, in order to strike terror into these savages, and prevent such murders for the future, determined to chastise them. He accordingly invaded the island, burned their two villages, and killed about fifty men. This brought them to terms; they sued in the most abject manner for mercy, and promised never to injure the white men more.

From the Feejee Islands the squadron proceeded to the Sandwich Islands. On the 2d of December, 1840, the Peacock and the Flying-Fish left Oahu under the command of Captain Hudson, who was directed by Captain Wilkes to steer for the Equator, so as to fall in with it in about 160° W.; thence he was directed to visit various groups of islands in many directions; and finally, he was to proceed towards the north to Columbia river, on the coast of Oregon, and there await the arrival of the rest of the squadron. On the 18th of July, 1841, in attempting to enter Columbia river, having no pilot on board, the Peacock struck in shoal water and became a total wreck, but, by the skilful management of Captain Hudson, no lives were lost.

The Vincennes having arrived at Columbia river, Captain Wilkes shifted his pennant to the Porpoise, and with that vessel, the Flying-Fish, and the boats of the Peacock, proceeded to make a survey of the Columbia to its extreme navigable point. The Vincennes, under Lieutenant Commandant Ringgold, was sent to San Francisco, California, to make a survey of the Sacramento river. These objects having been attended to, the squadron, reinforced by the addition of the Oregon, departed from San Francisco, and after visiting various islands, arrived at Singapore in January, 1842. Here the tender Flying-Fish was found to be so much injured by arduous service, that she was deemed unseaworthy, and accordingly sold for $3,700. From this place the squadron sailed for the United States, and the Vincennes arrived at New York on the 10th of June, 1842.

---

135. *Dorr Insurrection in Rhode Island.*

The original Constitution of Rhode Island was derived from a charter obtained from the British Crown in 1663. Many modifications of its provisions were made by the Legislature, from time to time, to the period of the insurrection; but that part which confined the right of suffrage principally to the landholders remained unchanged. As Rhode Island became a manufacturing State, this was considered a grievance; but all efforts to extend the right of suffrage were resisted by the Legislature.

In January, 1811, the Legislature, upon the petition of the Suffrage party, consented to have a Convention called, for the purpose of forming a new State Constitution, in the following November. This, however, did not satisfy the Suffrage party. They held a volunteer Convention, April 17, and another on the 5th of July, at Providence, and issued a call for a delegate Convention to meet there in October, the month previous to the assembling of the legal Convention authorised by the State authority.

These different Conventions met; each formed a Constitution, and submitted it to the people for ratification. The Suffrage party, deeming it necessary to procure the votes of the majority of all those in whom their Constitution declared the political power justly to reside, kept the polls open for six days, and received *proxies:* (votes sent in by persons who were not able or willing personally to attend the polls). By this means they obtained in all, 13,944 votes; whereupon, computing the whole number of adult citizens at 23,142, they declared their Constitution adopted and established as the paramount law of the State. Owing to a number of causes, the Constitution submitted to the people by the Government or Charter party was rejected by a majority of 677 votes. Both parties chose their State officers, and the rival Legislatures assembled, Governor King at the head of the Charter party, and Thomas W. Dorr at the head of the other.

On the 16th of May, 1842, Dorr entered Providence escorted by a party of his friends, about 1,300 in number, of whom 300 were in arms. When arrived at his quarters, he issued his proclamation defying the power of those opposed to him, and expressing his determination to maintain his claims to the last extremity. About 2 o'clock on the morning of the 18th May, Dorr, at the head of his adherents, made an attempt to obtain possession of the State arsenal. Having drawn up his troops on the plain, and planted his cannon, he sent a flag of truce to the arsenal. Colonel Blodget, who was in command, asked, "For whom, and in whose name?" The answer was: "For Governor Dorr, in the name of Col. Wheeler." He said he knew no such men, and if they attacked the arsenal it would be defended. When the flag returned, Dorr gave orders to fire; but his gun flashed three times. It is said that there was dissatisfaction in his ranks, and some of his men had dampened the powder. Whatever was the cause, it was a merciful dispensation, sparing probably the effusion of much human blood. Dorr then retired to his quarters, a house on a hill guarded by men armed with muskets and cannon. The military were now ordered out, with orders to arrest Dorr in the name of Governor King. The insurgents were intimidated, and after some persuasion the most of them dispersed. The house was searched, but Dorr could not be found. Most of the officers chosen by the Suffrage party resigning their situations, this difficulty ended without bloodshed.

On the 28th of June, 1842, another disturbance took place, caused by the disagreement between the Charter and Suffrage parties. The adherents of Dorr, about 700 in number, took possession of a hill in Chepachet, where they intrenched themselves with five pieces of cannon. Martial law was proclaimed throughout the State, and about 3,000 militia were ordered out to support the Government. The greater part of the insurgents left the camp in consequence of these preparations, and the hill was taken by the State troops without bloodshed. Dorr was eventually tried for treason, and sentenced to hard labor during life, June 25, 1844. By an act of amnesty from the Legislature, he was liberated from prison June 27, 1845.

---

136. *Riots in Philadelphia in* 1844.

On the afternoon of Friday, May 3, 1844, a political meeting of the "Native American party" was held in a vacant lot at the corner of Second and Master streets, Kensington, a quarter of the city where many Irish

Catholics resided. The meeting was soon interrupted by an assault of a large body of Irish, men and women, who rushed simultaneously towards the platform, which they speedily demolished, and compelled the whole body of Native Americans to flee under a shower of missiles, accompanied with shouts, hisses, and groans. This outrage produced much excitement throughout the city and county. On the following Monday, May 6, the Native American party reassembled at the same place in great numbers, for the avowed purpose of testing their right to meet, even in the midst of an Irish population, without molestation.

The American flag was raised over the platform, and two or three addresses delivered without interruption. A sudden shower of rain then dispersed the multitude, most of whom took refuge in a market-house in an adjoining street. Here the meeting was reorganized; but as soon as the speaker had taken the stand, a disturbance occurred, in which a pistol was fired, at the report of which the majority of the assembly dispersed. The Irish in the neighboring houses now rushed out to join in the fray. Fire-arms were discharged by them upon the assembly, and several were wounded, some mortally. The Native Americans were driven from the ground, but they soon rallied around the remnants of their flag, which had been torn in shreds by the Irish, and after a contest of about an hour, succeeded in driving them into their houses. The sheriff now appeared on the ground, and order was somewhat restored. In the evening, however, the rioting was renewed, and an attempt made to destroy a Catholic seminary in the vicinity; but the crowd was dispersed by a volley of musketry from the Irish. Five persons were shot, one of whom, a bystander, fell dead upon the spot.

On the next day, May 7, at 3 o'clock in the afternoon, a great meeting of Native Americans was held in Independence Square, about one and a half miles from the scene of these outrages. The addresses made by the speakers on this occasion were the most of them of a peaceable character; but a large portion of the assembly remembering the events of the preceding day, instead of quietly dispersing to their homes, resolved, in spite of the remonstrances of several prominent members of the party, to go in procession to Kensington. In order to arouse the spirit of the people against the Catholics, they bore aloft in the procession the tattered flag, by the side of which was a banner with the inscription in black letters, "*This is the flag which was trampled under foot by the Irish Papists.*"

On reaching the scene of the former outrages, an attempt was made to organize a meeting; but before it could be done, a shot was fired from a house opposite the market, and a young man in the assembly was instantly killed. This was followed by continued volleys from most of the surrounding houses. Several of the Native Americans hastened from the scene of action to procure muskets, and at length about 40 persons, thus armed, presented themselves in front of the market. They fought with desperation for nearly an hour, and their ranks were thinned by the fall of the killed and wounded. They were exposed in the open street, while their assailants were protected by the walls of their houses.

At length the Native Americans succeeded in setting fire to one of the buildings whence they had been fired on. The flames spread with great rapidity. In a short time between twenty and thirty dwellings were on fire, together with the market-house, which took fire by accident. Between 8 and 9 o'clock, a detachment of military, under the command of General Cadwallader, arrived on the ground, who acted with promptness and decision: field-pieces, loaded with grape and canister, were planted so as to sweep two of the most turbulent streets, and the mob were at once intimidated. Under the protection of the military, the firemen, who had been restrained by the mob, succeeded in extinguishing the flames about midnight. It is probable that some of the Irish people were consumed in their dwellings, and others shot down while attempting to escape. Many innocent families were driven from their flaming houses, they knew not whither, exposed to the insults of a mob. Here the Native Americans claim that their doings as a party ended, and utterly disclaim any participation in the outrages that followed.

Early in the morning, a gang of desperadoes, ripe for tumult and plunder, began to search the houses of the Irish, and wherever they found arms secreted, they either demolished the building, or set it on fire. The Irish offered little resistance, as they were completely overawed, and fled in terror to save themselves. The church of St. Michael, the priest's house adjoining, with the nunnery, were fired in open day and consumed. Late in the afternoon the mob began to move towards the city proper, and it was soon apparent that their fury would next be directed against St. Augustine's church. A large force was drawn out to protect it; and the Mayor of the city made several attempts to disperse the mob, but without effect, as nothing but *words* were used. He was himself injured by a stone thrown by some one in the crowd, and the police officers were driven from their station. Two or three boys were lifted over the railing in front of the church, who broke the windows, applied a match to the drapery, cut open the gas-pipes, and in a moment the building was all in flames. The firemen were prevented from making any attempt to extinguish the fire, and it was consumed to the bare walls.

The citizens now felt that a crisis had come, which demanded the most energetic efforts for the suppression of mob violence and disorder. On the following morning, Thursday, an immense number of citizens, both of the city and county, assembled in Independence Square to devise measures for the restoration of the public peace. The citizens were organized as patrols, and a proclamation was issued by the Mayor and sheriff declaring martial law, forbidding all persons to appear in any street or other place in occupation of the authorities, and authorizing the military to employ *force of arms* to compel obedience. This proclamation had the desired effect. A mob assembled in front of the principal cathedral was instantly dispersed by the announcement of General Cadwallader that he would comply with the letter of the proclamation.

On the afternoon of the same day, the Governor of the State arrived with several military companies, and the city was put under martial law. A renewal of violence was apprehended on the following Sunday; but the Catholic Bishop suspended public worship in all the churches under his care, although he was assured by Major General Patterson that sufficient protection should be afforded to all religious denominations in the exercise of their rights. Order was soon restored, and in a few days the Native American party held a meeting in Kensington without molestation.

---

137. *Mexican War.*

The principal and immediate cause of the movements which led to the war between the United States and Mexico, was the annexation of Texas (a territory which Mexico claimed to be within her own limits) to the United States. The terms of annexation were accepted by Texas, July 4, 1845. Immediately on intelligence of this event, General TAYLOR, in accordance with the orders of the Secretary of War, sailed from New Orleans for Western Texas, and arrived at St. Joseph's Island (Aransas Inlet) on the 25th of July. At the head of a considerable force, he soon after established his camp at Corpus Christi, on the west side of the Nueces, then the farthest point west to which the Texan population had extended.

The army of occupation remained at Corpus Christi for about six months unmolested. On the 13th of January, 1846, General Taylor received orders to march his force through the uninhabited region between the Nueces and the Rio Grande, and take possession of Point Isabel, Laredo, and points opposite Matamoros and Mier. On the 9th or 10th of March, he took up his line of advance for the Rio Grande. On his way he met several small bodies of Mexican troops; but neither offered nor received any molestation. As he was approaching Point Isabel, on the 24th, he was met by some 50 citizens, at the head of which was the prefect of the state of Tamaulipas, who protested against his occupying the country. General Taylor stated to them that he would give them an answer when he reached Matamoros. General Garcia, who was stationed at Point Isabel at the head of 280 Mexican troops, on receiving this reply, set fire to the custom-house and some other buildings, and immediately evacuated the place.

General Taylor caused Point Isabel to be surveyed with a view to its defence; a work was thrown up, and a small garrison was left under the command of Major Monroe. General Taylor then proceeding, reached a point opposite the town of Matamoros, a place containing about 10,000 inhabitants, and the capital of the State of Tamaulipas. Here, on the 28th, he commenced intrenching himself within short cannon-shot, and in sight of the bayonets and banners of the Mexican forces under General Mejia. The force of General Taylor at this time consisted of about 2,300 men; that of Gen. Mejia was 2,000. General Ampudia, who had succeeded General Arista in the command of the army of the North, was soon expected to arrive with about as many more.

Soon after the American flag was raised opposite Matamoros, General Worth and his staff were directed to cross the river with a communication to the commander-in-chief of the Mexican forces and the civil authorities. He did not succeed in obtaining an interview with Mejia, but communicated with General La Vega, the second in command; nothing, however, of importance, was accomplished in the conference.

On the 11th of April, General Ampudia arrived at Matamoros with 1,000 cavalry and 1,500 infantry. On the following day he sent a communication to General Taylor, ordering him to quit his position in twenty-four hours, and retire to the Nueces, there to await the settlement of this question by negotiation; in default of which, Mexico would look upon his attitude as a declaration of war. General Taylor, in reply, stated that he had been sent to the place he occupied by order of his Government, and intended to remain; and in the mean time he placed his troops in the best possible position to resist an attack. He also blockaded the river, thus cutting off the supplies of the Mexican army.

On the 10th of April, Colonel Cross, commissary-general of the army, rode out about two miles from the American camp, when he was killed, it is supposed, by a party of Mexican *rancheros*. General Taylor made a formal demand for the murderers, but they were never found. Lieutenant Porter (son of Commodore Porter), while out with a fatigue party of ten men near the camp, on the 19th, was fired upon, and himself and three of his men were killed. On the 24th, about 2,500 Mexican troops having crossed the river above General Taylor's camp, Captain Thornton, with a squadron of more than sixty dragoons, was despatched to observe their movements; but he was suddenly surprised, and all his party were either killed or taken prisoners. These events soon brought on open and avowed hostilities between the two nations.

138. *Battles of Palo Alto and Resaca de la Palma.*

While General Taylor's forces were engaged in fortifying the camp opposite Matamoros, the communication with Point Isabel, the *entrepôt* whence their supplies were received, was cut off by the Mexicans. On the 1st of May, General Taylor, finding his situation to be critical, left the fort under the charge of Major Brown, with less than 300 men, and marched with the main body of his army to Point Isabel, to reopen a communication with his stores, and bring back ammunition and guns for the fort. During the absence of the main army, some thousands of Mexicans surrounded the fort, and notwithstanding their severe cannonading for seven days, were unable to obtain possession. The American loss was only 2 killed and 13 wounded; one of the former was the brave Major Brown, who was mortally wounded by a shell thrown into the fort.

General Taylor arrived at Point Isabel without opposition. On the 7th of May he took up his line of march on his return to the fort. On the 8th, about noon, he came in sight of the enemy, 6,000 strong, drawn up in order of battle, extending a mile and a half across the plain, along the edge of a *chapporal* (a kind of thicket of thorn-bushes, interspersed with dwarfish trees). The American army, only about 2,000 in number, " was immediately formed in a column of attack, and, curtained by two squadrons in advance, moved steadily forward to within cannon range, when one of the enemy's batteries opened. The column was then deployed in line, except the 8th Infantry, which stood still in column, and the battle was set. Colonel Twiggs commanded the right, composed of the 3d, 4th, and 5th Infantry, and Ringgold's Artillery. Lieutenant Churchill commanded the two eighteen-pounders in the centre, while Lieutenant-Colonel Belknap was placed over the left wing, composed of Duncan's Artillery and the 8th Infantry: and the *Battle of Palo Alto* commenced."

The fire from Major Ringgold's guns told with fearful effect upon the enemy's cavalry, who were waiting for a favorable opportunity to bear down upon the American infantry. Unable to stand such a deadly fire, they wheeled off, and, by a circular sweep, threatened the American flank and train in the rear. In order to oppose this movement, the 5th Infantry were thrown into square, and with fixed bayonets awaited the shock. A deadly fire from one of the angles of the formation staggered the enemy; but they pressed on till they discovered the 3d Infantry advancing in column to the attack, when they wheeled and fled.

While the fire of Ringgold was so effective on the right, that of Captain Duncan was equally or more so on the left. These two commands, occupying both extremes of the American lines, sent hope and confidence through the army, as it saw with what superior skill and address their artillery was managed. About 4 o'clock, Duncan set the prairie on fire with smoke-balls, and the thick smoke, rolling along the lines, shut out both armies from the sight of each other, and stayed for a while the work of carnage. Taking advantage of the smoke, Duncan made a movement on the enemy's flank, and poured upon it a galling and destructive fire. The Mexicans changed their line of battle to escape the close and well-directed fire of Ringgold's battery, and the eighteen-pounders which had been pushed forward during the brief cessation of cannonading. The enemy made a desperate but unsuccessful attempt to silence these guns. During their furious fire, two brave American officers fell—Captain Page, who had the lower part of his face torn off by a cannon-shot, and Major Ringgold, who fell mortally wounded by having the flesh torn off from both legs upward from his knees. It was now sundown, and both armies, as by mutual consent, ceased their fire.

"This was a pure cannon fight, in which our infantry, though cool and steady throughout, and ready at any moment to pour themselves in a furious charge on the enemy, took scarcely any active part. Appointed simply to sustain batteries, they stood and saw the artillery contest the field .... The Mexican commanders saw that they could do nothing in an open field and fair fight, and so retreated to a still more formidable position."

The next day the army recommenced its march, and came up with the enemy, occupying a strong position on the farther side of a ravine, and resting his left on a pond so as to prevent the possibility of being outflanked on that side. Eight pieces of artillery defended this position, divided into three portions—one on the left side of the road, one on the right, and one in the centre. It was evident that the great struggle by this arrangement would be along the road where the batteries were placed, protected by a ditch and breastwork in front. The Mexicans during the night were reinforced by about 2,000 men; and here, within three miles of the fort, the *Battle of Resaca de la Palma* was fought.

Scarcely were the American troops formed in order

of battle, before the artillery of the enemy opened a heavy and rapid fire on the advancing ranks. The road was swept at every discharge with grape-shot and ball There was a fierce conflict on each side of the road between the American infantry and the enemy. From the outset, the Americans steadily advanced on every side except along the road, where the central Mexican battery kept up a destructive fire. General Taylor now ordered Captain May to charge this battery, "*and to take it.*" Captain May replied, " I will do it :" and turning to his men, he said, " Remember your regiment and follow your officers." The bugles sounded, and the attention of the whole army was directed to the desperate charge. The commanding form of May was seen in the advance, with his long hair streaming in the wind; one discharge from the enemy's battery stretched nearly one third of his men and half his horses on the ground ; but he pressed onward, leaped the breastwork, and rode down the artillery at their guns ; the American infantry followed, and the rout of the Mexicans became complete.

The Mexicans lost their whole artillery—2,000 stand of arms, and 600 mules. General Vega was taken prisoner by Captain May in his desperate charge on and over the battery. The American loss, in killed and wounded, was about 170 ; that of the Mexicans is unknown, but is supposed to have been about 1,000 men.

139. *Capture of Monterey.*

On the 19th of September, 1846, General Taylor with a force of 6,645 men, and 19 pieces of cannon, arrived before Monterey, and after reconnoitring the city, encamped at the Walnut Springs, three miles distant On the 20th, General Worth was ordered with his division to move by a circuitous route to gain the Saltillo road, beyond the west of the town, and to storm the heights above the Bishop's Palace, which vital point to the Mexicans appears to have been strangely neglected

Captain May, at the head of his Dragoons, charging the Mexican Battery. — Page 308.

On the morning of the 21st, after an encounter with a large body of the Mexican cavalry and infantry, supported by artillery from the heights, he repulsed them, and finally encamped, covering the passage of the Saltillo road. It was here discovered, that besides the fort at the Bishop's Palace, and the occupation of the heights above it, two forts on commanding eminences, on the opposite side of the San Juan river, were fortified. These also were then stormed and carried; and the guns of the last fort that was carried were immediately turned upon the Bishop's Palace.

General Taylor ordered the first division of regular troops and a division of volunteers under General Butler, to make a diversion to the left of the town, in order to favor the movements of General Worth. Lieut. Colonel Garland was ordered forward, and, if possible, to carry the advanced battery on the extreme left of the city. A heavy and destructive fire opened upon the advance of the Americans, but they soon turned it by entering and engaging with the enemy in the streets of the city, having passed through an incessant crossfire from the citadel, two batteries, and the thousand musketeers on the housetops, and from behind barricades. The rear of the first battery was soon turned, and the reverse fire of the troops, through the gorge of the works, killed or dislodged the artillery immediately in its rear. The first division was followed and supported by the Mississippi, Tennessee, and first Ohio regiments. The two former regiments were the first to scale and occupy the fort. The American loss in killed and wounded, during the operations of this day, was 394. Among the killed of the regular troops were Major Barbour, and Captains Morris, M'Kavett, and Field; of the volunteers, Colonel Watson, of the Baltimore battalion, and Captain Allen, of Tennessee. A large proportion of those who were wounded died.

On the 22d of May, at the dawn of day, the 2d division under General Worth, carried the height above the Bishop's Palace; and soon after meridian, the palace itself was taken and its guns turned upon the fugitive garrison

In the lower part of the city, during the day, the Mexicans continued their fire from the citadel and other works upon the American troops who came within the range of their guns. On the night of the 22d they evacuated nearly all their defences in the lower part of the city. On the morning of the 23d, General Taylor ordered General Quitman to advance into the city, he being assisted by Captain Bragg's battery, and the dismounted Texan volunteers under General Henderson. The troops advanced from house to house, and from square to square, until they reached a street, but one square in the rear of the principal *plaza*, in and near which the enemy's force was mainly concentrated. This advance was conducted vigorously, but with due caution; and although destructive to the enemy, was attended with but small loss on the part of the Americans.

On the morning of the 24th, General Ampudia, the Mexican commander, made an offer of capitulation. The terms finally accepted were, that the Mexican troops should march out of the city with their arms and accoutrements, and should be allowed seven days to evacuate the city. The American troops were not to occupy it till evacuated. The cathedral fort or citadel, however, was to be evacuated the next day (the 25th), and an American garrison to be marched in. It was also agreed that there should be an armistice of eight weeks.

The American loss in capturing the city was 12 officers and 108 men killed; 31 officers and 337 men wounded. The loss of the enemy is supposed to have been greater. The town and works of Monterey were armed with 42 pieces of cannon, well supplied with ammunition, and manned with a force of at least 7,000 troops of the line, and from 2,000 to 3,000 irregulars.

The Field of Buena Vista. — Page 311.

Santa Anna sent an officer with a flag of truce to inquire what General Taylor was waiting for — to which he replied, he was waiting for Santa Anna to surrender.

140. *Battle of Buena Vista.*

After the capture of Monterey, the American forces were employed in various military movements having for their object the occupation of several places in the vicinity. On the 31st of January, 1847, General Taylor left Monterey for Saltillo, a distance of 65 miles in the direction of San Luis de Potosi. He reached this place on February 2d, and proceeded thence about 20 miles farther to Agua Nueva, where he encamped. At this point, hearing of the advance of General Santa Anna, with a large force to attack him, General Taylor fell back to the hacienda of Buena Vista, a strong position in a mountainous pass, which could be defended against superior numbers.

On the morning of the 22d of February, the Mexican army, *twenty thousand* in number, of the finest troops of Mexico, were seen approaching the field of conflict in perfect order, presenting a most imposing scene of military splendor. The force under General Taylor consisted of about five thousand men; of which no more than 500 were regular troops, the others being volunteers. On the right wing of the American position, were numerous deep and almost impassable ravines; while on the left were the precipitous mountains of the " Sierra Madre," towering into the air upward of two thousand feet.

General Taylor having refused a summons to surrender at discretion, sent by General Santa Anna, the Mexican forces endeavored to outflank the American left, by ascending the mountain. The Kentucky and Arkansas troops being stationed at this point, clambered up the rugged ascent to counteract this movement, firing as they advanced. The firing continued till after dark, and the whole side of the mountain from its base to its summit, seemed at times a sheet of fire. The Americans, however, retired, lying on their arms during the night, leaving the enemy in possession of the heights.

Early next morning, a powerful body of the Mexicans advanced upon the American left flank near the mountain, and forced it back about 250 yards. They however rallied, and bravely contested the field with the enemy. The conflict continued with slight intermissions till night. For several hours, the fate of the day seemed doubtful, and it is said that General Taylor was urged by some of his officers to fall back and take up a new position, which however, he refused to do. The Americans retained their position, and repulsed the enemy by their superior skill in the management of their artillery.

The bloodiest part of the conflict, took place near the close of the day, in an attack made on the Mexican left, which was supposed to have been weakened by the events of the day. The Illinois and Kentucky regiments, came in contact with a column of the enemy 12,000 in number, who forced them into a ravine, where being disordered, they were shot down in great numbers by the overwhelming force of the Mexicans. Colonels Hardin, M'Kee, and Lieut. Col. Clay, son of the distinguished statesman of that name, who fell wounded at this fatal spot, were lanced to death, and stripped of their clothing. Night put a stop to the contest, and both armies occupied the same position which they did in the morning before the battle commenced. The Americans laid on their arms during the night, expecting the next day a renewal of the conflict, but when morning dawned it was found that the Mexicans had retired from the field leaving their dead and wounded, upward of *two thousand* in number, including several officers of high rank, to the mercy of the Americans.

The American loss was two hundred and sixty-seven killed; four hundred and fifty-six wounded; and 23 missing, and three guns captured by the enemy. Twenty-eight officers were killed on the field of battle. The retreat of the Mexicans is represented as peculiarly distressing. Previous to the battle they had suffered much from the want of food, water, and a shelter from the weather. After the action, their miseries were increased. In many instances they were obliged to abandon their sick and wounded companions on a desert steeped in their own blood, shivering with cold, parched with thirst, to be de voured by jackals and dogs; who often in sight, awaited their horrid banquet. The loss sustained by the Mexican army by sickness and desertion, in their return from Buena Vista to San Luis, exceeded 10,500 men.

---

141. *Expedition against New Mexico.*

The orders for the organization of a force, for the conquest and occupation of New Mexico and Upper California, were issued in May, 1846, and Colonel Kearney was appointed to command the expedition. A requisition was made on the governor of Missouri, for one thousand mounted volunteers, to follow on his route. Colonel Kearney was authorized to raise such a number of Mormons, who were preparing to emigrate to California, as he might think proper, provided this number did not exceed one third of his entire force.

By the last of July, "the army of the west," consisting of eighteen hundred men, was concentrated near Brent's Fort, on the Arkansas river. Before his entry into New Mexico, Col. Kearney issued a conciliatory proclamation to the inhabitants, stating that he entered the country "for the purpose of seeking union with, and ameliorating the condition of its inhabitants." The governor of the country, General Armijo, collected a few soldiers of the Mexican army, a body of militia, New Mexicans, and Indians; in all between three and four thousand men, with six pieces of artillery, and took post about fifteen miles from Santa Fé, to dispute the advance of the invaders. Upon the near approach of Kearney, Armijo called a council of war in which his principal officers advised a retreat. He adopted the advice, broke up his force, collected his property, all the merchandise he had in Santa Fé, and fled southward to the interior of Mexico.

General Kearney reached the town of Vegas, August 14th, and the next day, took the first step in establishing the civil authority of the United States, by assembling the people in the plaza of the village, and declaring them absolved from allegiance to the Mexican government. He caused the *alcalde*, and some other officers, to take the oath of allegiance. On August 18th, Gen. Kearney entered and took possession of Santa Fé, being courteously received by the lieutenant-governor, Vigil, who remained after Armijo's flight. The mass of the population professed to be satisfied with the change of government; and the chiefs of the Pueblos Indians, came in soon after to give in their adhesion, and express their satisfaction at the arrival of the Americans.

The civil government which General Kearney established in New Mexico, was successfully administered without opposition till the month of December; when the authorities received information of a contemplated insurrection. On the 14th of January, 1847, Governor Brent, who had been selected for that office was brutally murdered, with five other civil officers of the territory at San Fernado de Taos, a pueblo about fifty miles northward of Santa Fé. Throughout the northern part of the province, the Indians and New Mexicans murdered every American upon whom they could lay hands, and likewise all Mexicans who held office under the new government.

The rebellion now became truly formidable. On the 23d of January, Colonel Price with 350 men, marched for the valley of Taos. The next day he fell in with the enemy about 1500 in number, near Canada, a small village north of Santa Fé, and routed and dispersed them. He continued his march up the valley of the Rio del Norte, and was reinforced by Captain Burgwin, so that his whole command now amounted to 479 men. On the 3d of February, after a passage through a deep snow, Colonel Price arrived at Taos, the place where Governor Brent and his companions were massacred. The next day, the Americans made an attack on this place, which was obstinately defended by the Indians. They were, however, compelled to sue for peace, which was granted them on condition of delivering up the ringleaders of the insurrection, which they did; and of the five principal leaders, but one escaped death. By this action the rebellion was quelled; the loss of the insurgents was 150 killed, besides a large number wounded. The Americans had seven killed, and forty-six wounded, many of whom died, among the number was Captain Burgwin.

---

142. *Military Operations in California.*

In the autumn of 1845, Captain John C. Fremont, who had previously made two exploring expeditions to the west of the Rocky mountains, started again on a new expedition, one object of which was to discover, if possible, a new route to Oregon, south of the one usually travelled by emigrants. In the latter part of January, 1846, he arrived within one hundred miles of Monterey, in California. As his animals needed recruiting, he determined to halt for this purpose. Aware of the difficulties between the American and Mexican governments, Captain Fremont left his party, and in person applied to the commandant of the province, General De Castro, for permission to remain during the winter. This, after some hesitation, was granted. It soon, however, appeared that De Castro was endeavouring to raise the province against him; and Fremont bravely mached his small party of sixty-two backwoodsmen to within thirty miles of Monterey, took a position on the Sierra Nevada, hoisted the American flag, and prepared for resistance. He was not, however, molested, and in March he started for Oregon.

On the 9th of May, Fremont was overtaken by Lieutenant Gillespie of the marines, who had crossed the continent from Vera Cruz to Mazatlan, bearing a letter from Mr. Buchanan, and a private one from Senator Benton. From certain passages in these letters, Fremont felt himself authorized to return to the vicinity of the Sacramento. Upon his arrival at the bay of San Francisco, he found that, after his retreat from his position on the Sierra Nevada, De Castro had taken steps to expel all the American settlers from the territory. This determined Fremont to put a stop to his proceedings, by overthrowing the Mexican authority in California.

Being assisted by the American residents, Captain Fremont on the 15th of June surprised Sonoma, the rendezvous of the Mexican forces, captured General Vallejo and other officers, nine pieces of cannon, 250 stand of muskets, and other military stores. On the 4th of July, Fremont called the American settlers together at Sonoma, and advised them to declare themselves independent of Mexico, and to continue the war as the only means to insure their safety. His advice was followed, and the revolutionary flag was at once displayed.

During these events, Commodore Sloat, the commander of the Pacific squadron, having been apprised of the declaration of hostilities between the United States and Mexico (which fact was unknown to Fremont), commenced taking possession of the towns upon the coast. On the 7th of July, the commodore landed 250 seamen and marines at Monterey, and took possession of the place. On the 17th of August, Commodore Stockton, who had succeeded Commodore Sloat, being joined by a party under Fremont, entered Ciudad de los Angelos, the capital of California, and took possession of the government-house without opposition. Commodore Stockton, believing the American authority to be firmly established, commissioned Lieutenant-Colonel Fremont as military commander of California.

Official declarations of war between Mexico and the United States having reached California, an insurrection broke out at Ciudad de los Angelos. The Americans were forced to retire from that place, and were closely besieged in others. About this time, General Kearney, with about one hundred men, having penetrated through the Indian country, arrived in the vicinity of the settlements of California. Here he was attacked by the Mexicans under General Pico, who killed a number of his officers, and put his party in circumstances of extreme peril. He was, however, shortly after relieved by a reinforcement of 200 men, sent to his assistance by Commodore Stockton. On the 10th of January, 1847, the Americans having combined their forces, after some opposition again took possession of Ciudad de los Angelos, the capital; and on the 13th of January a convention was signed by Colonel Fremont, in the character of military commandant of California, and the Mexican authorities, by which an end was put to further hostilities.

143. *Taking of Vera Cruz.*

The attention of the American government was, at an early period of the Mexican war, directed to preparations for an expedition against Vera Cruz, a city of about 15,000 inhabitants, situated immediately on the shore of the gulf of Mexico. The city was strongly fortified, particularly by the castle of San Juan d'Ulloa, which stands on a reef of rocks about a thousand yards in front of the city. The capture of this place was deemed important, as by it a direct route would be opened toward the Mexican capital, about three hundred miles distant. The command of the expedition was intrusted to General Scott, who was fully supplied with all the munitions of war to accomplish this object. The American troops, upward of 13,000 strong, were landed by the squadron under Commodore Conner, near Vera Cruz, without the loss of a single man; and by the 13th of March, 1847, the investment of the city was effected.

The Mexican force in Vera Cruz at the time of its investment was 3,360 men, and in the castle 1,030. Both the castle and the city were scantily supplied with provisions. The governor of the state had endeavoured to procure a supply, but, owing to dissensions, &c., in the capital, his requests were but little heeded. Nevertheless, with what he had been able to collect, General Morales determined to defend the city, hoping, it is said, that the *vomito* or yellow fever would soon come to his aid by sweeping off the invaders; or perhaps he might be relieved by the approach of a Mexican army from the interior.

General Scott, having completed his preparations for bombardment, on the 22d demanded a surrender of the city. General Morales, who commanded both the city and castle, returned a peremptory refusal. Upon this, the bombardment was commenced and continued, with heavy artillery. The Americans were assisted in their work of destruction by the naval force, which was much greater than had ever before been sent into action by the United States government. For four days a shower of bomb-shells was poured into the devoted city, which, in many instances as they fell, crushed the roofs of houses, and, exploding within the Mexican dwellings, caused horrid destruction to their inmates, most of whom were women and children. Early on the 25th, the consuls of Great Britain, France, Spain, and Prussia, went to the American camp to ask permission for the neutrals—the old men, the women, and children—to leave the city. This was refused by General Scott, on the ground that he had, as soon as the investment was completed, given them an opportunity to retire. This they did not accept; they must therefore run the hazards attending the bombardment. The general also informed them that any further prayer must be addressed through the Mexican governor.

As soon as the consuls had returned to the city, the American batteries resumed their fire, which was continued with dreadful effect through the night and until the morning of the 26th, when the besieged sent a flag of truce, offering terms of capitulation. General Morales, it is stated, unable to endure the humiliation of this, feigned sickness, and turned over his command to General Landero, who agreed to terms of surrender. Vera Cruz, the castle, and all the munitions of war, were given up. The garrisons were permitted to retire, after laying down their arms; the officers giving their parole, for themselves and their men, not to serve during the war, until regularly exchanged. The Mexican troops were allowed to march out of the city with the honours of war, and the civil and religious rights of the inhabitants were guarantied.

Says the Mexican account: "All was over with Vera Cruz. In vain had four or five hundred of her inhabitants perished; in vain had six hundred soldiers shed their blood, and four hundred of them been killed. The graves of those brave men were to be dishonoured by the conqueror! .... In vain had the city suffered the ravages of 6,700 projectiles of the weight of 463,000 pounds, thrown into it by the enemy. ... Day dawned on the 29th. At eight in the morning the artillery saluted the national flag, which was displayed at Ulloa and on the land-batteries, with the last honours which the unfortunate but gallant garrison would be able to pay to their standard. ... The fatal hour arrived. The soldiers, in tears, divested themselves of their accoutrements; and while stacking their arms, some broke them in pieces to avoid surrendering them to the enemy. ... The sacrifice was consummated; but the soldiers of Vera Cruz received the honour due to their valour and misfortunes—the respect of the conqueror. ... The march having now been commenced by the road to Medellin (to avoid the insults of the volunteers, whom their chiefs could not restrain), the batteries of the square, where the arms had been surrendered, fired their salute, and, in the words of an eye-witness, 'the shores, as well as the trees and tops of the houses, became blue with people clothed in that colour, who appeared upon them, shouting, ' HURRAH!'"

---

144. *Battle of Cerro Gordo.*

After the fall of Vera Cruz, General Scott began his advance toward the Mexican capital. The Mexican forces, over 13,000 strong, in order to oppose the advance of the Americans, fortified themselves at Cerro Gordo, a mountain-pass on the road to Jalapa, about sixty miles from Vera Cruz. Many of the Mexican troops were new levies, raised by compulsion, and unaccustomed to the use of arms; but their commander, General Santa Anna, the president of the republic, appeared to be confident that the strength of his position and his powerful artillery would insure him success.

The Mexican fortifications were situated principally on three commanding elevations, the principal of which was *Cerro Gordo*, a conical hill or mountain, which towered above the heights and forests of the surrounding country. To attack these works in front seemed extremely hazardous, and would be attended with great loss of life. General Scott therefore determined to cut a passage through the thick undergrowth to the right, and operate upon the left flank of the enemy.

On the morning of the 18th of April, General Worth's division and General Pillow's brigade moved forward to attack the enemy, General Twiggs having been previously directed forward to take up a position to cut off the retreat of the Mexicans toward Jalapa. In order to cover the advance, General Twiggs was ordered to plant a battery on a steep elevation in front and near Cerro Gordo. This position was taken by Colonel Harney, who was detached for this purpose. On the following day, the battery was opened upon Cerro Gordo, and under its fire the American line commanded by Harney descended the slope into the valley with rapidity; and, although exposed to a severe fire, commenced at once the steep and rugged ascent, to storm the battery on the summit of the Cerro Gordo. The Mexicans in the fort, and in the intrenchments around and below it, poured down a continual stream of fire of musketry, which, aimed too high, passed mostly over the heads of the Americans, who at length entered the work on the summit. The struggle for its possession was of short duration. The Mexican troops tried to engage in close conflict; the commander, General Vasquez, was killed; other generals were captured, and the mass of the garrison fled down the hill for safety.

Besides the struggle at Cerro Gordo, there were other severe conflicts on the field of action. General Shields, in an attack upon a Mexican battery, received a grape-shot through his lungs. General Pillow, with a body of volunteers, commenced an attack upon one of the strong positions of the enemy, commanded by La Vega and other brave generals, and was obliged to withdraw from their heavy fire. As he was preparing for a second attack, the enemy, seeing the day was lost by the capture of Cerro Gordo, concluded to surrender. The victory was now complete. The Mexican army was dispersed, with an indefinite loss in killed and wounded; 3,000 in prisoners, including five generals; all its artillery (forty-three pieces of different caliber), and seven standards. The American forces present at the battle, including those in reserve as well as those in action, did not exceed 9,000 men. The loss in the two days' action was in all, killed and wounded, 431, of which number 33 were officers.

General Santa Anna, having witnessed the capture of Cerro Gordo, and seeing all was lost, effected his escape, though hotly pursued His carriage, which was riddled with shot, was taken, and in or near it was found his cork leg. It is said he made his escape on a mule attached to his carriage, the harness of which was cut in order to effect his escape. A wagon containing sixteen thousand dollars, received the day before for the payment of the troops, was also taken.

The defeat of the Mexicans at Cerro Gordo seemed for a time to have broken the spirit of resistance to the advance of the Americans. The city of Jalapa surrendered to General Twiggs without opposition. On the 22d of April, General Worth took possession of Peroté, a walled city, and the castle of the same name. This place was about midway between Vera Cruz and the city of Mexico. The castle of Peroté, one of the strongest places in Mexico, was given up without resistance. On the 15th of May, General Worth entered Puebla, a fine fortified city of about 60,000 inhabitants, with scarcely any opposition. Here the American army rested and recruited themselves for several weeks, before their advance upon the capital.

145. *Battle of Contreras.*

General Scott, having received a small reinforcement while remaining at Puebla, broke up his camp, and marched for the capital. About the tenth of August, 1847, he arrived in the vicinity of the Penuon, an isolated mound eight miles from Mexico, of great height, strongly fortified, and flooded around its base by trenches filled with water. This fortification commanded the principal eastern approach to the city. The Mexicans, believing that no other passage could or would be made by the Americans, had fortified it in the most formidable manner. With the small number of men under the command of General Scott, it was deemed too hazardous to attempt to take this place by assault. By a masterly movement, the whole American army passed south of Lake Chalco to San Augustine, about ten miles south of Mexico. This was accomplished by taking advantage of an old blind road, deemed impassable by the Mexicans, but was found to be otherwise by the close examination of Colonel Duncan of the American artillery.

On the 19th, about noon, the Americans came in contact with the enemy, under the command of General Valentia, at Contreras, a place where he had intrenched himself in a formidable manner. The firing continued on both sides till dark, the Americans maintaining their ground. A cold heavy rain now commenced, and the troops had to endure the peltings of the storm without tents or blankets. During the action, a large force under Santa Anna appeared in sight, apparently in a condition to repel the assault of the Americans. Instead of rendering any assistance to General Valentia, he ordered that officer to retire from his position. Valentia, confident of victory, refused to obey the order.

At three o'clock on the morning of the 20th, Colonel Riley was ordered to advance and drive the enemy from their battery. This was effected by overcoming great obstacles in a most rapid manner. Streams and deep ravines had to be crossed, and their passage was made over immense masses of lava thrown up in the roughest, sharpest manner possible, and covered in many places with dense brushwood. The Americans arrived at the intrenchments, and, having delivered their fire, rushed upon the Mexicans with loud shouts, and entered their works almost in a body.

The rout was complete. From the time the assault was commenced, the Mexicans were thrown into confusion. Their position being nearly surrounded by bodies of American troops, it was difficult to escape their terrible fire. Whole masses of soldiers, intermingled with mules, loose horses, wounded men who filled the air with their groans; shrieking women, who were seen running in every direction, pressed forward and filled the road toward Mexico. For more than a mile from the intrenched camp, the road, literally strewed with the dead and wounded, presented a shocking spectacle.

The division of Valentia was totally destroyed as a military body. The loss which it suffered in killed and wounded was extremely severe, and could not have been less than 2,000 men. About 1,000 rank and file, four general officers, four colonels, and thirty captains, were made prisoners. The whole train of artillery, consisting of twenty-two cannon, and large stores of ammunition, were captured. Among the cannon which were captured were two pieces which were taken at Buena Vista from the Americans, at General Taylor's last battle. The number of American rank and file engaged in this action amounted to about 4,500: their loss did not exceed sixty.

146. *Battle of Churubusco.*

After the rout of General Valentia at Contreras, August 20th, the victorious Americans pushed on toward the hamlet of Churubusco, the next point of opposition on their advance toward Mexico. In this village, about two leagues from Mexico, was a massive stone convent, which was prepared for defence, and was surrounded by a field-work. This point was occupied by General Rincon with 3,000 Mexican troops. The other fortifications were at the bridge over the Churubusco (a small stream), by which the causeway of San Antonio led into the capital. Such, however, was the confusion made by the defeat of General Valentia in the morning, that no part of the Mexican force appeared ready for battle except Rincon's command. But though some confusion prevailed, yet the Mexican troops were formidable from their overwhelming numbers and the strength of their position.

The Americans, in advancing against the convent, suffered much from the fire of the enemy, particularly from the convent, which was one sheet of flame and smoke. The Mexicans, from their elevation in the convent, could overlook the field, and observe the presence of the American troops, who became somewhat disordered in the high cornfields in the vicinity. While the conflict was raging near the convent and the bridge which stood near, General Scott ordered Generals Pierce and Shields, with a number of regiments, to move round in a circuit upon the rear of the Mexican position, to the causeway which led to the city. Upon this causeway was stationed the Mexican reserve, a strong body which had that morning left the capital. The reserve, on the approach of the Americans, placed themselves in a ditch, and opened a destructive fire, which swept down many brave men and officers. The New York and South Carolina regiments of volunteers advanced in line against the murderous discharges of the enemy. Colonel Butler, of the South Carolina troops, was killed, and Lieutenant-Colonel Dickinson severely wounded; Colonel Burnet, of the New York troops, besides many other officers, were wounded. This checked the advance for a while, but those unhurt struggled on, and finally the Mexican line wavered, broke, and fled a disordered multitude into the city.

After the battle had continued about two hours, the Mexican left wing gave way, and fled through the cornfields in their rear toward the city. The Americans now pressed forward, and rushing through the wet ditches waist-deep, and over the parapets into the works at the head of the bridge, carried it by storm.

The convent was now closely invested, and immediate preparations were made to storm it The garrison, being dispirited by the events of the day, and having expended their ammunition, surrendered just as the assaulting party had mounted the parapet. General Rincon, with the officers and soldiers who had not attempted to make their escape, 1,200 in number, surrendered themselves as prisoners of war. The American force engaged in the conflicts of the day amounted to about 6,000 men, their loss was about 1,100, among whom were 76 officers. The Mexican loss in the battle of Churubusco is estimated to have been about 7,000 men in killed, wounded, and missing.

In the action, sixty-nine of the battalion of *San Patricio*, deserters from the American army, were made prisoners. In a general court-martial held afterward, twenty-nine of them were found guilty, and sixteen were hung on the 10th of September. Some, who had deserted before the actual commencement of hostilities, were branded on the cheek with the letter D, and in addition were severely whipped; others were recommended to mercy, which was granted.

---

147. *Battle of Molina del Rey, and Storming of Chapultepec.*

After the battle of Churubusco, an armistice was agreed upon by General Scott and the Mexican authorities. The terms of this armistice having been violated by the Mexicans, and no satisfactory explanations having been given, it was terminated on the 7th of September. Preparations were immediately made for a final advance on the capital. At this time, the whole effective force under the command of General Scott, consisted of but 8,500 men.

At three o'clock in the morning of the 8th of September, General Worth's division moved to attack Molina del Rey, a range of strong stone buildings about 1,100 yards from the castle of Chepultepec. This place was ordered to be destroyed by General Scott, as he was informed that the Mexicans were within at work casting cannon, shot, &c. The American infantry advanced down the plain upon the enemy's works, and when they had approached within a short distance, the Mexicans opened a most deadly fire upon them, and of the fourteen American officers who went into the attack, eleven fell dead or wounded. As the Americans fell back, the Mexicans rushed forward and murdered nearly every wounded man left on the field. A large body of Mexican lancers, numbering it is said about four thousand men, seeing the effect of the deadly fire on the Americans rushed onward to charge and put them to rout. This was prevented by the spirited exertions of Colonel Duncan with his light battery, and a small number of dragoons and mounted riflemen.

The Americans rallied and pressed forward to the conflict. An attack was made on Casa Mata, a work on the Mexican right. When within about thirty yards, Colonel M'Intosh the commander, fell mortally wounded, and Lieutenant-Colonel Scott, the second in command, was shot dead by the fire poured upon them by the enemy, which swept off about one third of the attacking party. On the American right, the contest continued with fury; the Americans keeping up their fire on Molino del Rey, which was obstinately defended. The Americans at length broke into the building through the gates; when a sanguinary contest ensued; they finally succeeded in getting possession of the Mexican works. The American force engaged in this action was 3,117. Their loss in killed and wounded, amounted to 787, including 59 officers. The Mexican force engaged was estimated at 10,000. It is said their loss, including killed, wounded, and prisoners, amounted to 3,000. Among their killed, were Generals Leon and Balderas, both brave and valuable officers.

The principal obstacle now remaining to the approach of the city, was the fortress of Chapultepec, which was built upon a rocky elevation 150 feet in height. The fortifications around it, and the castle on its summit, made this place truly formidable. A military college, once the palace of a Spanish viceroy, and its dependent buildings, were within the fortifications. The only practicable ascent to the castle, was on the west and southwestern sides; and these were extremely rugged and precipitous. The Mexican defensive force in the castle and its dependencies, amounted to about 6,000 men, commanded by General Bravo, a distinguished officer.

On the 12th of September, it was determined to cannonade Chapultepec, previous to its being stormed. In order to divert the attention of the enemy, General Twiggs was ordered to make a demonstration near the southern part of the city; this stratagem was admirably executed. The batteries commenced their fire upon Chapultepec early in the morning, and continued it through the day, causing shocking destruction to its garrison. On the morning of the 13th, the storming parties advanced to the attack. General Pillow's division began the ascent of Chapultepec on the west side. The advance was necessarily slow, over rocks, chasms, mines, and over the works of the enemy, exposed to a heavy fire of cannon and musketry. The enemy were driven from shelter to shelter, so closely that they had no time to fire their mines. As the troops gained the summit of the hill, General Pillow was wounded, and Colonel Ransom was shot dead at the head of his regiment, the command of which fell on Major Seymour, who scaled the parapet, entered the citadel, and with his own hands struck the Mexican flag from its walls.

Although the conflict continued in other parts of the vicinity, yet the fall of Chapultepec may be considered as the finishing blow of this contest between Mexico and the United States. On the night of the 13th, General Santa Anna abandoned the city of Mexico. Early in the morning of the 14th of September, 1847, Generals Quitman and Smith entered the capital at the head of their commands. At eight o'clock, General Scott and staff entered the city amid the huzzas of the soldiery on all sides. As he entered escorted by the cavalry, the band of the dragoons struck up "Hail Columbia," and when the grand plaza and the national palace were reached, the American flag was descried waving triumphantly over the "*Halls of the Montezumas.*"

148. *California.*

On the 2d of February, 1848, a "treaty of peace, friendship, and settlement," was signed at Guadalupe Hidalgo, by Mr. Trist, in behalf of the United States, and the Mexican commissioners. By this treaty, Mexico relinquished all claim to Texas, and the country lying between the Nueces and the Rio Grande, and ceded to the United States the territories of New Mexico and Upper California. For this cession, the United States agreed to pay to Mexico fifteen millions of dollars.

The acquisition of this territory by the United States, is an important event in their history, also in the history of this continent, and indeed in the history of the world. The great point of interest just at present, in this newly-acquired territory, is its "*placers*" or deposites of gold. This precious metal is found near the banks and in the beds of streams which empty into the bay of San Francisco, one of the best harbors in the world.

It is probable that the existence of gold in these regions, has been known to individuals for a long period, but owing to a want of energy and enterprise on the part of the Spaniards and their descendants, together with the jealousies, and political troubles with which they have been afflicted, any attempt to collect the precious metal has been prevented. The discovery which first gave rise to the present "gold excitement," was made about forty or fifty miles up the river Sacramento, near a place known as "*Sutter's Fort.*" Captain Sutter, desirous of erecting a saw-mill, contracted with a Mr. Marshall for that purpose in September, 1847. In making the necessary excavations, he observed in the mud and dirt thrown up some glittering particles, which on examination proved to be gold. Further explorations soon followed, and at length satisfactory evidence was given that large portions of the valley abounded in the precious metal.

California by the treaty with Mexico, having become a part of the territory of the United States, numerous vessels were fitted out in various parts of the country, and in foreign countries; and thousands of adventurers sailed for the "gold region." The excitement still continues. A government has been established, towns and villages are rapidly springing up, and California now (1850), asks for admission into the American Union as a sovereign state.

---

149. *Gold-Digging in California.*

The following, relative to the California gold-mines is extracted from the official report of Colonel Mason, the military commandant of California, dated August 17, 1848:

"I started on the 12th of June last, to make a tour through the northern part of California. My principal purpose, however, was to visit the newly-discovered gold "*placer*" in the valley of the Sacramento. .... We reached San Francisco on the 20th, and found that all, or nearly all, its male inhabitants had gone to the mines. The town, which a few months before was so busy and thriving, was then almost deserted.

"On the evening of the 25th, the horses of the escort were crossed to Sousoleto in a launch, and on the following day we resumed the journey to Sutter's fort, where we arrived on the morning of the 2d of July. Along the whole route, mills were lying idle, fields of wheat were open to cattle and horses, and farms going to waste. At Sutter's, there was more life and business. Launches were discharging their cargoes at the river, and carts were hauling goods to the fort, where already were established several stores, a hotel, &c. Captain Sutter had only two mechanics in his employ (a wagon-maker and a blacksmith), whom he was paying ten dollars per day. Merchants pay him a monthly rent of $100 per room; and while I was there, a two-story house in the fort, was rented as a hotel for $500 a month.

"On the 5th, I resumed the journey, and proceeded twenty miles up the American fork to a point on it now known as the "lower mines," or "*Mormon diggings.*" The hillsides were thickly strewn with canvass tents and bush arbors; a store was erected, and several boarding shanties in operation. The day was intensely hot, yet about 200 men were at work in the full glare of the sun washing for gold—some with tin pans, some with close-woven Indian baskets, but the greater part had a rude machine, known as the cradle. This is on rockers, six or eight feet long, open at the foot, and at its head has a coarse grate or sieve; the bottom is rounded with small cleets nailed across. Four men are required to work this machine; one digs the ground in the bank close by the stream; another carries it to the cradle and empties it on the grate; a third gives a violent rocking motion to the machine; while a fourth dashes on water from the stream itself.

"The sieve keeps the coarse stones from entering the cradle, the current of water washes off the earthy matter, and the gravel is gradually carried to the foot of the machine, leaving the gold mixed with a heavy fine black sand above the first cleets. The sand and gold mixed together, are then drawn off through auger-holes in a pan below, and afterward separated by blowing off the sand. A party of men thus employed at the lower mines, averaged $100 a day. The gold in the lower mines is in fine bright scales.

"As we ascended the north branch of the American fork, the country became more broken and mountainous, and at the saw-mill, twenty-five miles above the lower washings, or fifty miles above Sutter's, the hills rise a thousand feet above the level of the Sacramento plain. Here a species of pine occurs which led to the discovery of the gold. Captain Sutter, feeling the great want of lumber, contracted in September last, with a Mr. Marshall to build a new saw-mill at that place. It was erected in the course of the past winter and spring—a dam and race were constructed, and a large bed of mud and gravel was carried to the foot of the race.

One day Mr. Marshall, as he was walking down the race to this deposite of mud, observed some glittering particles at its upper edge, he gathered a few, examined them, and became satisfied of their value. He then went to the fort, told Captain Sutter of his discovery, and they agreed to keep it secret, until a certain grist-mill of Sutter's was finished. It however got out, and spread like magic. Remarkable success attended the labors of the first explorers, and in a few weeks hundreds of men were drawn thither. At the time of my visit, but little over three months after its first discovery, it was estimated that upward of 4,000 people were employed. . . . .

"The discovery of the vast deposites of gold has entirely changed the character of Upper California. Its people, before engaged in cultivating their small patches of ground, and guarding their herds of cattle and horses, have all gone to the mines, or are on their way thither. Laborers of every trade have left their work-benches and tradesmen their shops. Sailors desert their ships as fast as they arrive on the coast, and several vessels have gone to sea with hardly enough hands to spread a sail. Two or three are now at anchor in San Francisco without a crew on board."

---

150. *First Steamer across the Atlantic.*

The first voyage across the Atlantic in a steam-vessel was performed by the steamship Savannah, commanded by Captain Moses Rogers, of New London, Connecticut, in 1819. This ship was built in New York in 1818, by "Fitchet and Crotchet," under the direction of Captain Rogers. The engine was made by Daniel Dodd, of

Elizabethtown, New Jersey, and Stephen Vail, of Morristown. On the 29th of March, 1819, this ship sailed from New York to Savannah, Ga. (where she was owned). After a short stay at the latter place, she proceeded to Charleston, South Carolina, to take the President, James Monroe, to Savannah, whence (after these successful experiments) she sailed on May 25th direct for Liverpool—a full-rigged ship of about three hundred and fifty tons burden, with a low-pressure engine of eighty or ninety horse-power. She proved a fast sailer, and, by the power of her engine alone, would make eight knots per hour.

After a most successful passage of twenty-two days, fourteen of which her engine was used, she arrived at Liverpool. The ship was first discovered from the telegraphic station at Cape Clear (the southern part of Ireland), and reported as "*a ship on fire.*" The admiral who lay at the cove of Cork despatched one of the king's cutters to her *relief;* but great was their wonder at their inability, with all sails set, and in a fast vessel, to come up with a ship moving *under bare poles.*

On approaching the city, the shipping, piers, and roofs of houses, were thronged with an excited populace, cheering the adventurous craft. During her stay at Liverpool, naval officers, noblemen, and merchants, from London, came down to visit her, and were singularly curious to ascertain her speed, destination, &c. After a stay of twenty-eight days in Liverpool, during which time the ship was visited by thousands of people of rank, and her officers the while treated with marked attention, she left for Copenhagen, Denmark. Here she excited similar manifestations of wonder and curiosity. Thence she proceeded to Stockholm, where she was visited by the royal family, foreign ministers, naval officers, nobility, and others, who, by the invitation of Mr. Hughes (the American minister), dined on board, and took an excursion among the neighbouring islands, with which they seemed much delighted.

Lord Lynedoch, of England, who was then on a tour through the north of Europe, by invitation of our minister took passage on board the Savannah for St. Petersburg, which place she reached in due time. Here she was visited by noblemen and military and naval officers, who also tested her superior sailing qualities by a trip to Cronstadt. In this city a valuable service of plate was presented to her officers. From St. Petersburg she sailed back to Copenhagen, and from there to Arendal, in Norway; and then returned to Savannah, where she safely arrived after a passage of twenty-five days. Shortly after his she sailed for Washington city, and was there laid up—being the *first steam-vessel that ever crossed the Atlantic.*

---

151. *Lynch's Expedition to the River Jordan and the Dead Sea.*

In May, 1847, Lieutenant W. F. Lynch, of the United States navy, made an application to the Hon. John Y. Mason, the head of the navy department, for permission to circumnavigate and thoroughly explore the lake Asphatites, or Dead sea. After some delay, a favourable decision was given to his application. The United States storeship "Supply" was placed under his command, and was laden with stores for the American squadron in the Mediterranean. She also carried two metallic boats, one of copper, the other of galvanized iron, for the use of the expedition. The members of the expedition were fourteen in number. The ten seamen shipped to serve as crews of the boats were of temperate habits, all of them having pledged themselves to abstain from all intoxicating drinks.

The expedition set out from New York, November 26, 1847. After stopping at Port Mahon, the "Supply" on February 16th anchored before Smyrna. Thence Lieutenant Lynch proceeded to Constantinople, where, by the influence of Mr. Carr, the United States resident minister, an audience of the sultan was granted, and a firman procured, giving permission to explore the Dead sea and the river Jordan. From Constantinople he returned to Smyrna, and thence proceeded to Beirut and Acre. On April 1, 1848, the party pitched their tents on the south bank of the Belus, having parted from the storeship "Supply," which now stood out to sea. The expedition directed its route toward the *sea of Galilee*, or *Tiberias*, as the first point in their tour of observation.

Lieutenant Lynch, in order to transport his baggage and boats to navigate the inland seas, made the nove. experiment of substituting camels for draught-horses which proved successful. Having mounted his boats on low-wheeled carriages or trucks, three of these huge animals were attached to each carriage, two abreast and one as leader. The first attempt to draw the trucks by camels was witnessed by an eager crowd of people. The successful result taught them the existence of an unknown accomplishment in that patient and powerful animal, which they had before thought fit only to plod along with its heavy load upon its back. On the 4th of April they took up their line of march, following the boats, with sixteen horses, eleven loaded camels, and a mule. The party numbered sixteen in all, including the dragoman and cook. They were accompanied by fifteen Bedouins, all well mounted. The metal boats, with flags flying, rattling and tumbling along, mounted on carriages drawn by huge camels, the officers and mounted sailors in single file, the loaded camels, the sheriff and sheikh with their tufted spears—all had the appearance of a triumphal march.

On the 6th of April the party reached the sea of Galilee. "Unable to restrain my impatience," says Lieutenant Lynch, "I now rode ahead with Mustafa, and soon saw below, far down the green sloping chasm, the sea of Galilee, basking in the sunlight! Like a mirror it lay embosomed in its rounded and beautiful but treeless hills. How dear to the Christian are the memories of that lake! the lake of the New Testament. . . . The roadside and the uncultivated slopes of the hills were full of flowers, and abounded with singing birds—there lay the holy lake, consecrated by the presence of the Redeemer! . . . Near by was the field where, according to tradition, the disciples plucked the ears of corn upon the sabbath; yet nearer was the spot where the Saviour fed the famishing multitudes, and to the left the mount of Beatitudes. . . . Not a tree! not a shrub! nothing but green grain, grass, and flowers, yet acres of bright verdure. . . . Beyond the lake and over the mountains, rise majestic in the clear sky the snowy peaks of Mount Hermon."

On the 8th of April, having arrived at Tiberias, the two boats, after some difficulty in getting them down the mountain, were launched into the sea of Galilee with their flags flying. "Since the time of Josephus and the Romans, no vessel of any size had sailed upon this sea, and for many, many years, but a solitary keel had furrowed its surface." In order to assist the transportation of his goods, Lieutenant Lynch purchased the only boat used by the misgoverned and listless inhabitants to navigate the beautiful lake of Tiberias, a lake which was filled with fish, and abounding with wild fowl. This boat was purchased for about twenty-one dollars, and was used by the inhabitants merely to bring wood from the opposite side of the lake.

On the 10th of April, the expedition started from the foot of the lake, and commenced the descent of the river Jordan. Notwithstanding the most diligent inquiry at Tiberias, they could not procure any reliable information respecting the river. They found, to their consternation, that the Jordan was interrupted in its course by frequent and fearful rapids. In some instances they had to clear out old channels, to make new ones, and sometimes plunged with headlong velocity down appalling descents. So great were the difficulties in passing down the river, that on the second evening they were but twelve miles in a direct line from Tiberias. So tortuous is the course of the Jordan, that in a space of sixty miles of latitude, and four or five of longitude, it traverses at least two hundred miles!

On the 18th of April they reached the *Dead sea*, and found its northern shore an extensive mud-flat, with a sandy plain beyond, and the very type of desolation. Branches and trunks of trees lay scattered in every direction; some charred and blackened by fire, others white with an incrustation of salt. The waters of the sea they found a nauseous compound of bitters and salt. As they passed on, they found scenes " where there was no vegetation whatever; barren mountains, fragments of rocks blackened by sulphurous deposites, and an unnatural sea, with low, dead trees upon its margin, all within the scope of vision bore a sad and sombre aspect."

Near the southern extremity of the Dead sea, the water became very shallow, from one to two fathoms deep. When near the salt mountain of *Usdum*, or *Sodom*, they were astonished at the appearance of a lofty round pillar, standing apparently detached from the general mass, at the head of a deep, narrow, and abrupt chasm. "We immediately pulled in for the shore," says Lieutenant Lynch, " and Dr. Anderson and I went up to examine it. The beach was a soft, slimy mud, encrusted with salt, and a short distance from the water covered with saline fragments and flakes of bitumen. We found the pillar to be of solid salt, capped with carbonate of lime, cylindrical in front and pyramidal behind. The upper or rounded part is about forty feet high, resting on a kind of oval pedestal, from forty to sixty feet above the level of the sea. It slightly decreases in size upward, crumbles at the top, and is one entire mass of crystallization." A similar pillar is mentioned by Josephus as having been seen by him, and he in his history expresses the belief of its being the identical one into which Lot's wife was transformed.

While passing over and encamping on the borders of this remarkable sea, the figures of each one of the expedition assumed a dropsical appearance. The lean had become stout, and the stout almost corpulent; the pale faces had become florid and ruddy; moreover, the slightest scratch festered, and the bodies of many of the party were covered with small pustules. The men complained bitterly of the irritation of their sores, whenever the acrid water of the sea touched them; still all had good appetites, and they hoped for the best.

On the 2d of May, the party made an excursion to *Kerak*, containing a population of about three hundred families, of whom three fourths professed Christianity. They found these Christians, though impoverished and oppressed, as kind and obliging as the Moslems were insolent. On the 10th of May they left the Dead sea, after spending twenty-two days in its exploration.

"We have," says Lieutenant Lynch, "carefully sounded this sea, determined its geographical position, taken the exact topography of its shores, ascertained the temperature, width, depth, and velocity, of its tributaries, collected specimens of every kind, and noted the winds, currents, changes of the weather, and all atmospheric phenomena. . . . The inference from the Bible, that this entire chasm was a plain sunk and '*overwhelmed*' by the wrath of God, seems to be sustained by the extraordinary character of our soundings . . . We entered upon this sea with conflicting opinions. One of the party was skeptical, and another, I think, a professed unbeliever of the Mosaic account. After twenty-two days' close investigation, if I am not mistaken we are unanimous in the conviction of the truth of the scriptural account of the destruction of the cities of the plain."

After leaving the Dead sea, the party proceeded toward Jerusalem, where they arrived on the 17th of May. After visiting various places of interest in and about the city, they proceeded to Jaffa. From Jaffa they went to Acre, in two parties—one under the command of Lieutenant Lynch, in an Arabian brig; the other by the land route, under the command of Lieutenant Dale. From Acre they went to Nazareth, Nain, Mount Tabor, Tiberias, Bethsaida, to the source of the Jordan, and thence to Damascus and Beirut. As they approached the latter place, many of the party sickened; and on the 24th o July, Lieutenant Dale died at a village in the vicinity of Beirut, at the house of the Rev. Mr. Smith, of the American Presbyterian mission. From Beirut they proceeded to Malta, where, on the 12th of September, the "Sup ply" being ready, the expedition re-embarked for the United States, and arrived there early in December.

---

152. *Death of Ex-President Adams*

On the evening of February 23d, 1848, John Quincy Adams expired in the capitol at Washington. Mr. Adams was born at Braintree, in Massachusetts, July 11th, 1767. In his eleventh year he accompanied his father (afterward president of the United States), to France, who was sent there as joint commissioner with Benjamin Franklin and Arthur Lee. In 1794, he was appointed by Washington as minister to the Netherlands. He afterward was appointed to important stations in most of the principal courts of Europe. In 1817, Mr. Adams was recalled from his mission in London, by President Monroe, to become secretary of state. In 1825, he was chosen by the house of representatives as president of the United States. In 1831, he was chosen to represent a congressional district in Massachusetts, and was continued in this service till his death.

On the 21st of February, Mr. Adams while in his seat in the house of representatives, was seized with paralysis. "At about twenty minutes past one o'clock, P. M.," writes a person present, "my attention was attracted by hearing Mr. Hubbard of Connecticut, calling upon Mr. Fisher of Ohio, who occupies a seat at Mr. Adams's right, to support the latter. Looking toward his seat I noticed Mr. Adams, apparently in the act of endeavouring to grasp the front of his desk, sinking back in his seat, dropping away to the left. He rallied, however, and as Mr. Fisher rose to assist him, he again fell back in the same position as before. His colleague, Mr. Grinnell, and others sitting near, flew to his side, when the occurrence becoming known, the members generally rushed toward the spot, but retired upon the exclamations, 'Keep back,' 'Give him air,' being uttered. The windows were raised, and Mr. Grinnell bathed his face with ice-water, when he rallied for an instant, and gave utterance in a feeble voice, to a sentence in keeping with the eloquence which ever distinguished his every-day conversation. He said, 'THIS IS THE LAST OF EARTH—I AM CONTENT,' and again relapsed into insensibility. Mr. Fries of Ohio, who is a regular physician, raised him in his arms and carried him to the speaker's room about fifty yards from Mr. Adams's seat in the house, the speaker and several of the Massachusetts delegation accompanying him."

Mr. Adams expired on Wednesday evening, on the sofa in the speaker's room in the capitol, where he lay in an apparently insensible state from the Monday previous. The funeral ceremonies were performed on February 26th. The remains were embalmed and lay in state, and were visited by thousands of persons the day previous.

At about twelve o'clock, the house was called to order by the speaker. The president of the United States, and heads of the departments entered the hall, the former taking his seat on the right of the speaker. The judges of the supreme court in their gowns; the officers of the army and navy, in full uniform; the foreign ministers and their suites, in splendid costume, followed, and took their seats upon the right and left of the area, in front of the speaker's chair. The senate then entered with the vice-president, the latter taking his seat on the speaker's left. After this the family of the deceased and the Massachusetts delegation preceding the coffin, entered as chief mourners. The chaplain, Mr. Gurley, pronounced an eloquent discourse from Job, xi. 17: "*And thine age shall be clearer than the noon-day: thou shalt be as the morning; and thou shalt be secure, because there is hope.*" The remains were subsequently placed in the receiving vault of the congressional cemetery, being carried in a funeral car drawn by six white horses, and led by grooms in white scarfs.

The speaker in conformity with the resolution of the house, appointed the following committee to accompany the remains of Mr. Adams to Quincy, viz:—

Mr. HUDSON, of Massachusetts, *Chairman.*

Mr. Williams, of Maine;	Mr. Brown, of Mississippi;
Wilson, of N. H.;	Morse, of Louisiana;
Marsh, of Vermont;	Vinton, of Ohio;
Smith, of Connecticut;	Duncan, of Kentucky;
White, of New York;	Cocke, of Tennessee;
Edsall, of New Jersey;	Lincoln, of Illinois;
Dickey, of Penn.;	Wick, of Indiana;
Houston, of Delaware;	Bowlin, of Missouri;
Roman, of Maryland;	Johnson, of Arkansas;
M'Dowell, of Virginia;	M'Clelland, of Mich.;
Barringer, of N. C.;	Cabell, of Florida;
Holmes, of S. C.;	Kaufman, of Texas;
Cobb, of Georgia;	Leffler, of Iowa;
Gayle, of Alabama;	Tweedy, of Wisconsin.

The arrival of the remains at New York, was announced by minute guns, and an immense procession which occupied an hour and a quarter in passing, began to move from the south ferry. About 2,000 troops composed the van, immediately behind whom was the hearse containing the body, drawn by eight horses, clad in black drapery, and led by eight mulatto grooms dressed in Turkish costume. Prominent to the eye was the memorable inscription, "*This is the last of earth,*" which were among the last words uttered by the expiring statesman.

On either side, the hearse was accompanied by the light-guards, preceded by the grand marshal and his aids. The pall-bearers, officers of the army and navy, the Hon. Henry Clay, General Gaines, and others, followed in carriages. The closing ceremonies consisting of a prayer by the Rev. Dr. Ferris, and a benediction by Rev. S. H. Cone, were performed on the esplanade of the city hall, and three volleys of musketry were fired by the national guards. The remains were then deposited in the governor's room, to be removed in the morning for Boston.

The remains of Mr. Adams were delivered in due form at Boston, March 10th, by the committee of Congress to the state authorities, through the committee of the legislature; thence taken to Faneuil Hall, which was dressed in mourning for the occasion, the rostrum being converted into a temporary mausoleum, and there transferred to the mayor and the authorities of the city. The ceremonies were attended by great crowds of both sexes, and on Saturday, the remains were deposited in the family burial-place at Quincy.

---

153. *Mob at the Opera-House, New York.*

One of the remote causes of this mob, appears to have been the publishing of some unfavorable strictures on the performances of Edwin Forrest, the American tragedian, in London. In 1849, Mr. Macready, a London actor (who was considered in some sort, a rival to Mr. Forrest), was announced to perform at the Astor Place opera house, New York. The friends of Mr. Forrest, connecting Mr. Macready with the authorship of the strictures in question, in order to show their indignation, and to redress his grievances, made inflammatory appeals through the press, so as to get up some public demonstration against Mr. Macready, who was in a certain sense, considered as a representative of the English stage or theatre.

A riotous disposition having been exhibited at the opera-house, on Mr. Macready's first appearance, Monday evening, May 7th, 1849, some prominent citizens who were in some way identified with the support of the drama, promised him protection against farther interference and induced him to appear again on Thursday evening. Early in the morning, placards were posted up through the city, stating (falsely no doubt, and for effect), that the crew of the British steamer then in port, had threatened violence to all who "dared to express their opinions at the English aristocratic opera-house," and calling on all working men to "stand by their lawful rights." In consequence of this, and similar threats, a large body of the police was ordered to attend at the opera-house. In addition to this, two bodies of the military were held in readiness, one stationed in the Park, the other at Centre market.

In anticipation of a riot, the rush for tickets was very great, and before night, none was to be had. For some time before the doors opened, people began to collect in Astor Place, and the police took their stations at the doors, and in the building. The crowd increased, and there was such a crush about the doors, that several of the entrances were obliged to be closed. The house was filled, but not crowded, and the amphitheatre was not more than half full. The first two scenes passed off without disturbance; but the appearance of Macready in the third act, was the signal for a perfect storm of cheers, groans, and hisses. The whole audience rose, and the nine tenths of it (who were friendly to Macready), cheered, waving their hats and handkerchiefs. A body in the parquette, with others in the second tier, and amphitheatre, hissed and groaned with equal zeal. The tumult lasted for ten or fifteen minutes, when an attempt was made to restore order, by a board being brought upon the stage, upon which was written, " The friends of order will remain quiet." This silenced all but the rioters. The leader of the disturbance was secured after a short, but violent struggle. One by one, of the rioters were taken and carried out, the greater part of the audience applauding as they disappeared.

Before the second act was over, something of the play could be heard. Mrs. Pope, as *Lady Macbeth*, first procured a little silence, which ended, however, immediately on Macready's reappearance. The obnoxious actor went through his part with perfect self-possession, and paid no regard to the tumultuous scene before him. As the parquette and gallery, were cleared of the noisiest rioters, the crowds without grew more violent, and stones and missiles were hurled against the windows (which had been previously boarded up), on the Astor-Place side. As one window cracked after another, and pieces of brick and paving-stones rattled in on the terraces and lobbies, the confusion increased till the opera-house resembled a fortress besieged by an invading army. Sometimes, heavy stones would dash in the boards, which had been nailed up as a protection, and a number of policemen were constantly occupied in nailing up and securing the **defences**

The attack was sometimes on one side, and sometimes on the other, but seemed to be most violent on Eighth street, where there was a continual volley of stones and other missiles. The retiring rooms were closed, and the lobbies so " raked" by the mob outside, that the only safe places were the boxes and the parquette. But in spite of the constant crashing and thumping of stones, and the terrible yells of the crowd in the street, the tragedy (too truly a tragedy to many), was played to an end ; the curtain fell, and Macready and the police were cheered. After the play was over, the noise being somewhat diminished, the audience were allowed to go out quietly by the door nearest Broadway.

The military under the command of Major-General Sandford, arrived at Astor Place about nine o'clock, where they were assailed by a shower of stones and brickbats, by which most of the horsemen in front, about forty in number, were more or less hurt, and their horses rendered almost unmanageable. Two or three times in succession the troops were ordered to charge. They did so, drove back the mob, but on falling back, were instantly again hemmed in, and pelted with stones. It is stated that several pistols were fired by the rioters at this time. Seeing that his men were falling around him, General Hall reported to the mayor, the condition of things, and stated that unless permission was given them to act on the defensive he would withdraw his troops. The recorder, Mr. Tallmadge, came forward, read the riot-act, and ordered the mob instantly to disperse. They did not obey, but continued their assault upon the troops, who were now ordered to fire. By this discharge one or two were killed, and several wounded.

The noise of the firing intensely excited the vast crowd in the streets, and all who had taken part in, or sympathized with the rioters, were exasperated to the highest pitch. Soon one or two wounded persons were carried on shutters through Broadway, which added fuel to the flame. Many of the rioters seized stones in Broadway, where the pavements had been torn up to make a sewer, and rushed through Astor Place, and presently another volley of musketry told of their reception. In about ten or fifteen minutes afterward, a third volley was fired, the mob now mainly left the streets, and gathered in separate crowds at different points in the vicinity. After the third discharge a company of light artillery arrived and posted their cannon so as to sweep every street in the neighbourhood.

After the firing had ceased, and the military had firmly occupied the ground, the rioters were scattered in squads through the streets, arming themselves with stones, and striving to arouse the indignation of the thousands who had assembled as spectators. They met, however, with but slight success. The crowd numbered it is supposed about twenty-five thousand persons; but it is supposed that but about *five hundred* took an active part in the riot; and of these *half* were boys. The whole number of the military engaged was about two hundred and ten. The number of persons killed, was nineteen.

154. *Colonel Fremont's Expeditions.*

The first expedition of John C. Fremont was made to the Rocky mountains in 1842, under the authority of the government of the United States. The object of this expedition was to explore the country lying between the Missouri river and the Rocky mountains, on the line of the Kansas and Great Platte rivers. Captain Fremont's party consisted of about twenty-five persons, mostly of French descent, principally creole and Canadian *voyageurs*, who had become familiar with prairie life in the service of the fur-companies in the Indian country. Christopher Carson (more familiarly known, for his exploits in the mountains, as *Kit Carson)* was the guide of the expedition. The company assembled at St. Louis, and thence they proceeded in a steamboat about four hundred miles near to Chouteau's trading-house, whence on the 10th of June they departed to explore the country. After an interesting journey, they on the 8th of

August came to the *South Pass*, and on the 15th Captain Fremont ascended the highest peak of the Rocky mountains, 13,570 feet above the gulf of Mexico.

Captain Fremont, in describing the ascent, says: "We rode on until we came almost immediately below the main peak, which I denominated the '*Snow-Peak*,' as it exhibited more snow to the eye than any of the neighbouring summits. Here were three small lakes of a green colour, each of perhaps a thousand yards in diameter, and apparently very deep. . . . We managed to get our mules up to a little bench about a hundred feet above the lakes, where there was a patch of good grass, and turned them loose to graze. . . . Having divested ourselves of every unnecessary encumbrance, we commenced the ascent. This time, like experienced travellers, we did not press ourselves, but climbed leisurely, sitting down so soon as we found breath beginning to fail. At intervals we reached places where a number of springs gushed from the rocks, and about eighteen hundred feet above the lakes came to the snow-line. From this point our progress was uninterrupted climbing. . . . Here I put on a light, thin pair of moccasins, as the use of our toes became necessary to a further advance. I availed myself of a sort of comb of the mountain, which stood against the wall as a buttress, and which the wind and the solar radiation, joined to the steepness of the smooth rock, had kept almost entirely from snow. Up this I made my way rapidly. In a few minutes we reached a point where the buttress was overhanging, and there was no other way of surmounting the difficulty than by passing around one side of it, which was the face of a vertical precipice of several hundred feet.

"Putting my hands and feet in the crevices between the blocks, I succeeded in getting over it, and when I reached the top, found my companions in a small valley below. Descending to them, we continued climbing, and in a short time reached the crest. I sprang upon the summit, and another step would have precipitated me into an immense field below. . . . As soon as I had gratified the first feelings of curiosity, I descended, and each man ascended in his turn; for I would only allow one at a time to mount the unstable and precarious slab, which it seemed a breath would hurl into the abyss below. We mounted the barometer in the snow of the summit, and, fixing a ramrod in a crevice, unfurled the national flag to wave in the breeze where never a flag waved before. . . . A stillness the most profound, and a terrible solitude, forced themselves constantly on the mind, as the great features of the place. . . . The day was sunny and bright, but a bright, shining mist hung over the lower plains, which interfered with our view of the surrounding country. On one side we overlooked innumerable lakes and streams, the spring of the Colorado of the gulf of California; and on the other was the Wind-river valley, where were the heads of the Yellowstone branch of the Missouri. Far to the north, we could just discover the snowy heads of the *Trois Tetons*, where were the sources of the Missouri and Columbia rivers; and at the southern extremity of the ridge the peaks were plainly visible, among which were some of the springs of the Nebraska or Platte river. Around us, the whole scene had one main striking feature, which was that of terrible convulsion. . . . We had accomplished an object of laudable ambition, and beyond the strict order of our instructions. We had climbed the loftiest peak of the Rocky mountains, and looked down upon the snow below; and, standing where never human foot had stood before, we felt the exultation of first explorers." After making some examination in the vicinity, the party returned to Missouri after an absence of four months.

Second Expedition.—The second expedition of Captain Fremont was made to Oregon and north California, in the years 1843–'44. The party amounted in all to thirty-nine men, consisting principally of creole and Canadian French, and Americans. The party set out from Kansas, a little town on the Missouri frontier, their route being up the valley of the Kansas river, to the head of the Arkansas, and to some pass in the mountains (if any could be found) at the sources of that river. On the

13th of August, they crossed the Rocky mountains at the South Pass, on the Oregon road, about fourteen hundred miles from the Columbia river, by the travelled route—being about half way between the Mississippi and the Pacific ocean.

As the party drew near to the Great Salt Lake, they descended Bear river, which at its entrance was spread out into several branches, covering the low grounds with water, where the miry nature of the bottom did not permit any further advance. The river was bordered with a fringe of willows and canes, among which were interspersed a few plants. The whole morass was animated with multitudes of sea-fowl, which appeared to be very wild—rising for the space of a mile around about at the sound of a gun, with a noise like distant thunder. . . . On the 6th of September they ascended an eminence, and immediately at their feet beheld the object of their anxious search—the waters of the *Inland sea* stretching in still and solitary grandeur far beyond the limit of their vision. "It was," says Captain Fremont, "one of the great points of the exploration; and as we looked eagerly over the lake in the first emotions of pleasure, I am doubtful if the followers of Balboa felt more enthusiasm when, from the heights of the Andes, they saw for the first time the great western ocean. It was certainly a magnificent object, and a noble *terminus* to this part of our expedition; and to travellers so long shut up in mountain-ranges, a sudden view over the expanse of the silent waters had in it something sublime."

After making some interesting explorations on the lake, the party resumed their route to the mouth of the Columbia. On the 4th of November, they came to the termination of their land journey westward. From this point they proceeded down the river in boats to *Fort Vancouver*, and were hospitably received by Dr. M'Laughlin, the executive officer of the Hudson Bay Company west of the Rocky mountains. On the 25th of November, the party, twenty-five in number, set out on their return by a southern route to the United States. Leaving the Columbia river, they passed to the southeastward of the

Cascade range of mountains, to the *Pass* in the Sierra Nevada, where the party encamped on the summit February 20, 1844, being one thousand miles south from the Dalles of the Columbia.

From this point they proceeded westward toward San Francisco. While passing this mountainous range, the party suffered severely. Some of the men became bewildered and deranged from extremity of suffering. Some of their horses perished; others of their horses and mules, ready to die of starvation, were killed for food: yet there was no murmuring or hesitation.

"On the 6th of March," says Captain Fremont, "we came unexpectedly into a large Indian village, where the people looked clean, and wore cotton shirts and various other articles of dress. They immediately crowded around us, and we had the inexpressible delight to find one who spoke a little indifferent Spanish, but who at first confounded us by saying there were no whites in the country; but just then a well-dressed Indian came up and made his salutations in very well-spoken Spanish. In answer to our inquiries, he informed us that we were upon the *Rio de los Americanos* (the river of the Americans), and that it joined the Sacramento about ten miles below. Never did a name sound more sweetly! We felt ourselves among our countrymen; for the name of *American* in these distant parts is applied to the citizens of the United States. To our eager inquiries, he answered, 'I am a *vaquero* (cowherd) in the service of Captain Sutter, and the people of this *rancheria* work for him.' Our evident satisfaction made him communicative; and he went on to say that Captain Sutter was a very rich man, and always glad to see his country-people. We asked for his house. He answered that it was just over the hill before us; and offered, if we would wait a moment, to take his horse and conduct us to it. We readily accepted his civil offer. In a short time we came in sight of the fort; and passing on the way the house of a settler on the opposite side (a Mr. Sinclair), we forded the river, and in a few miles were met a short distance from the fort by Captain Sutter himself. He gave us a most frank and cordial reception, conducted us immediately to his residence, and under his hospitable roof we had a night of rest, enjoyment, and refreshment, which none but ourselves could appreciate."

On the 24th of March, the route homeward was resumed. The party passed southward along the valley of the San Joaquin to its head-waters, where there was a pass through the mountains to the east. "When at this point," says Captain Fremont, "our cavalcade made a strange and grotesque appearance, and it was impossible to avoid reflecting upon our position and composition in this remote solitude. Within two degrees of the Pacific ocean; already far south of the latitude of Monterey, and still forced on south by a desert on one hand and a mountain-range on the other; guided by a civilized Indian, attended by two wild ones from the Sierra; a Chinook from the Columbia; and our own mixture of American, French, German—all armed; four or five languages heard at once; above a hundred horses and mules, half wild; American, Spanish, and Indian dresses and equipments intermingled—such was our composition. Our march was a sort of procession: scouts ahead, and on the flanks; a front and rear division; the pack-animals, baggage, and horned cattle, in the centre; and the whole stretching a quarter of a mile along our dreary path."

On the 18th of April the party struck the *Spanish trail*, the great object of their search. From the middle of December they had been forced south by mountains and deserts, and now would have to make six degrees of *nothing* to regain the latitude on which they wished to cross the Rocky mountains. After following the Spanish trail to New Mexico for 440 miles, they struck off in a northern direction toward *Utah* lake (the southern limb of the Great Salt lake), which they reached on the 25th of May, having completed in eight months' time the enormous circuit of 3,500 miles of travel! On the 13th of June, they ascended once more the summit of the Rocky mountains about two degrees south of the South Pass. Travelling eastward, they came to the head-waters of the Arkansas river, and on the 1st of July arrived a

Bent's fort; and on the last day of the same month they encamped again at Kansas, on the Missouri.

The Third Expedition of Captain Fremont was commenced in the autumn of 1845 (see page 315). The expedition which Colonel Fremont headed in December 1848, across the Rocky mountains, was attended with disastrous consequences. The party left the Upper Pueblo, near the head of the Arkansas, on the 25th of November, and had with them one hundred good mules and one hundred and thirty bushels of shelled corn, intended to support their animals over the deep snows of the mountains. to a fork of the Colorado of the gulf of California. They had for their guide an old trapper known as " Bill Williams," who had spent some twenty-five years in various parts of the Rocky mountains. The fatal error of this expedition was the employment of this man, who appears either to have never known or to have entirely forgotten the whole country through which they had to pass.

On the 11th of December, the party found themselves at the mouth of the Rio del Norte cañon, where that river issues from the Sierra San Juan, one of the highest and most rugged of all the Rocky-mountain ranges. Having confidence in their guide, the company pressed forward with fatal resolution. " We pressed up toward the summit," says Colonel Fremont, " the snow deepening as we rose, and in four or five days of this struggling and climbing, all on foot, we reached the naked ridges which lie above the line of the timbered region, and which form the dividing heights between the waters of the Atlantic and Pacific oceans. Along these naked heights it storms all winter, and the raging winds sweep across them with remorseless fury. On our first attempt to cross, we encountered a *pouderie* (dry snow driven thick through the air by violent wind, and in which objects are visible only at a short distance), and were driven back, having some ten or twelve men variously frozen—faces, hands, or feet. The guide came near being frozen to death here, and dead mules were lying about the camp-fires. Meantime, it snowed steadily. The next day we renewed the attempt to scale the summit, and were more fortunate, it then seemed. Making mauls, and beating down a road or trench through the deep snow, we forced the ascent in spite of the driving *pouderie*, crossed the crest, descended a little, and encamped immediately below in the edge of the timbered region. The trail showed as if a defeated party passed by—packs, pack-saddles, scattered articles of clothing, and dead mules, were strewed along. We were encamped about *twelve thousand feet* above the level of the sea. Westward the country was buried in snow. The storm continued. All movements were paralyzed. To advance with the expedition was impossible: to get back, impossible. Our fate stood revealed. We were overtaken by sudden and inevitable ruin! The poor animals were to go first. The only place where grass could be had were the extreme summits of the *sierra*, where the sweeping winds kept the rocky ground bare, and where the men could not live."

Colonel Fremont now determined to recross the mountain back to the valley of the Rio del Norte. With great labour the baggage was transported across the crest to the head-springs of a little stream leading to the river. Here he determined to send in a party to the Spanish settlements in New Mexico for relief. Five of the many who volunteered for this service were selected, and Mr. King, one of the number, was appointed their leader. This was on the 26th of December. Sixteen days having passed away without any tidings from the relief-party, Colonel Fremont became alarmed, and set off from the camp in search of relief, as their stock of provisions was reduced to a few meals only. On the sixth day after their departure from the camp they found three of the first relief-party—the most miserable objects they ever beheld. Mr. King had perished a few days before, having starved to death. On the tenth day after leaving the camp, Colonel Fremont reached the Spanish settlements. Supplies were soon obtained, and relief was sent to his suffering companions. The party, when they began their return from the summit of the mountains, was thirty in number; but, by the extremity of their sufferings, one third of this number perished.

---

155. *Reception of Father Mathew.*

The visit of THEOBALD MATHEW (the great Apostle of Temperance in Ireland) to the United States in 1849 is undoubtedly an event of vast importance to the happiness and well-being of many families and individuals. This philanthropist was born in the county of Tipperary, Ireland, October 10, 1790. He lost his parents when a child, and was taken under the care and patronage of General Mathew, brother to the earl of Landaff. He was educated for the ministry, and in 1814 was ordained in Dublin as a catholic clergyman. After he devoted his attention to the temperance reformation, the most astonishing results followed; and it is stated that, in about eighteen months, more than five millions of the Irish population gave the pledge of total abstinence, and entirely renounced the manufacture, sale, and use, of all intoxicating drinks.

After a detention of some years from his contemplated visit to America, Father Mathew arrived at New York in the packet-ship Ashburton, June 29, 1849, and was received with enthusiasm by the people. On Monday, July 2d, the general feeling was manifested during the morning by the flags floating from the public buildings and the shipping. At two o'clock, the steamer Sylph left Castle Garden with the common council, the committee of reception, committees of the temperance associations, &c., for the Quarantine, where the honoured guest was presented by Dr. Stewart, of the hospital, and cordially greeted in a brief speech by Alderman Haws, in behalf of the committee, surrounded by crowds. The response was modest and becoming. "He felt," he said, "wholly unworthy of such public honours, and could only accept them for the sake of the cause with which his humble name was identified." Being then introduced by the committee to the members of the common council on the boat, he was addressed by Alderman Kelly, president of the board of aldermen, and responded with a hearty expression of his sense of the honour done to the cause of temperance through his person. His whole aspect indicated simplicity and humility, his dress being a black frock-coat and breeches, with shoes and silk stockings, in the old-fashioned style.

Mr. William E. Dodge was then introduced, and welcomed Father Mathew in behalf of the friends of temperance in America. In the course of his address, he said: "You come among us, dear sir, not as a stranger; we all have long been familiar with your name and labours. There is not a town in the republic where your name is not familiar as a household word. Your triumphant career through your own afflicted country—your apostolic visits from city to city, from village to village, surrounded by thousands and tens of thousands, eagerly pressing to receive at your hands the potent pledge—animated us in the same noble cause here. We welcome you, not as a victorious general returning from a field of blood: you come a conqueror, not with the spoils of the battle-field, but crowned with the laurels of mightier victories—conquests of virtue over vice. You have conquered inveterate customs and habits, overthrown intemperance, and stayed the course of self-destruction. Proudly, then, do we welcome you, the benefactor of our race!"

After an excursion up the bay and East river, the steamer returned to Castle Garden, where Father Mathew was welcomed by the mayor, Mr. Woodhull, who in a speech reminded him that his victories were not made up of the dead and dying left behind in his path, but of living thousands whom he had rescued from a fate more remorseless than the conqueror's march: his trophies were seen in the smiling faces and happy homes of the countless multitudes whom he had won from the deepest abyss of wretchedness and despair. A procession was then formed from the Battery—the guest riding in an open carriage with the mayor, Rev. Dr. Pise, and Alderman Haws—and proceeded through Broadway, which wore the aspect of a gala-day, to the city-hall, where many ladies and citizens were introduced, and Father Mathew bowed his acknowledgments from the balcony to the multitude in the Park. Leaving the hall, the authorities escorted their guest to the Irving house. "Probably no private individual, unless La Fayette be so considered, was ever received with such public expressions of welcome and hospitality"

A CHRONOLOGICAL TABLE

OF THE

DISCOVERIES, SETTLEMENTS, WARS, AND REMARKABLE EVENTS,

IN THE

UNITED STATES.

DISCOVERIES AND SETTLEMENTS.

1492 AMERICA first discovered by Columbus.
1497 North America first discovered by Sebastian Cabot, a Venetian, in the service of England.
1512 John Ponce de Leon discovered and named *Florida*, from its being discovered on Easter day, or feast of flowers.
1528 P. de Narvaes, with 400 men, lands in Florida, and attempts the conquest of the country. He is defeated by the natives.
1535 Cartier, a Frenchman, first attempts a settlement in Canada.
1539 Ferdinand de Soto, a Spaniard, landed in Florida with 1200 men, in search of gold. He penetrated into the country, and discovered the Mississippi.
1562 Ribault, with a colony of French Protestants, began a settlement on the Edisto. It was abandoned.
1584 Sir Walter Raleigh obtains a patent for making discoveries. Amadas and Barlow, by order of Raleigh, landed on Woconan and Roanoke. On their return, Queen Elizabeth named the country *Virginia*.
1585 Sir R. Grenville sent with seven vessels to settle Virginia. A colony left at Roanoke under Governor Lane. The colony returned to England the next year.
1586 Grenville left a second colony at Roanoke, which was destroyed by the natives.
1587 A third colony, under Gov. White, left at Roanoke. Gov. White returned to England for supplies. He came back in 1590, but not finding the men he had left, he returned to England.
1602 Bartholomew Gosnold sailed to America, named Cape Cod, discovered Martha's Vineyard and the adjacent islands, built a fort and store-house, but returned to England the same year.
1607 Captain Newport arrived in Virginia, and began the first permanent British settlement in North America, at Jamestown, Virginia.
1608 Capt. Smith first explored the Chesapeake.
Canada settled by the French. Quebec founded July 3d.

1610 Capt. Henry Hudson, an Englishman, in the service of the Dutch, discovers the Manhattan, now Hudson river.
1611 *Champlain*, a Frenchman, discovered the lake which now bears his name.
1614 Capt. Smith made a fishing voyage to the northern part of America. Made a chart of the coast, which he presented to Prince Charles, who named the country *New England*.
Settlements commenced by the Dutch. at Manhattan, now New York, at Albany, and in New Jersey.
1616 Capt. Dermer, the first Englishman who sailed through Long Island sound.
1620 Plymouth settlers arrived at Plymouth, Dec. 22.
1623 First settlement of New Hampshire, at Dover, and at Little Harbour.
1627 Delaware and Pennsylvania settled by the Swedes and Fins.
1629 Salem settled by Gov. Endicott.
1630 Charlestown, Boston, Watertown, and Dorchester, settled by Gov. Winthrop and others.
1633 Maryland settled by Lord Baltimore and a colony of Roman Catholics.
The Dutch erect a fort on Connecticut river, in the present town of Hartford.
The Plymouth people erect a trading house in the present town of Windsor, Conn.
1634 Wethersfield, Conn., settled by people from Dorchester, Mass.
1635 Windsor settled by people from Dorchester.
Saybrook fort built by J. Winthrop's men.
1636 Hartford settled by Mr. Hooker and his congregation.
Providence, R. I., settled and named by Roger Williams.
1638 New Haven settled by Messrs. Davenport, Eaton, and others.
Exeter, New Hampshire, founded.
1639 Newport, Rhode Island, settled.
Milford, Guilford, Stratford, and Saybrook, in Connecticut, settled.
1640 Southampton, on Long Island, settled by people from Lynn, Massachusetts.
1642 T. Mayhew and others settle Martha's Vineyard.
1648 New London, Conn., settled.
1654 Col. Wood, of Virginia, sent a company of men to explore the country of the Ohio.
1658 Northampton and Hadley, Mass., settled by people from Connecticut.
1663 Carolina planted.
1664 Elizabethtown, New Jersey, settled.
1665 Sir J. Yeamans settled on the southern banks of Cape Fear river, with a colony from Barbadoes.
1677 Burlington, N. J., settled by a number of families from Yorkshire, England.
1680 Charleston, South Carolina, settled.
1682 Pennsylvania settled by William Penn and others. Philadelphia founded.
M. de la Salle descended the Mississippi to its mouth, took possession of the country in the name of Louis XIV. the French king, and named the country *Louisiana*.
1683 Germantown, Pa., settled by a number of Quakers from Germany.
1692 A fort built at Pemaquid by Sir William Phipps.
1702 The French send colonies into Louisiana.

1710 2706 Palatines, from Germany, arrived and settled in **New York** and Pennsylvania.
1717 New Orleans founded by the French.
1722 Gov. Burnet, of N. Y., erects a trading house at Oswego.
1723 First settlement in Vermont.
1724 Trenton, N. J., founded by William Trent.
1731 Fort at Crown Point built by the French.
1733 Georgia settled by Mr. Oglethorp and others.
A colony of Swiss came to Carolina.
1740 Tennessee explored by Col. Wood, Patton, Dr. Walker, and others.
1741 The Moravians, or *United Brethren*, began the settlement of Bethlehem, Pa.
1749 Halifax, Nova Scotia, settled by the British.
1756 Fort Loudon, on the Tennessee river, built.
1764 A large body of German settlers arrive in Carolina.
1765 The settlement of Tennessee commenced.
1771 Nootka Sound, the north-west coast of America, discovered by Capt. Cook.
1773 Kentucky settled by Col. Boon and others.
1773 Connecticut formed a township on the Susquehanna, forty miles square, called Westmoreland, and annexed it to the county of Litchfield.
1787-8 Twenty thousand settlers, men, women, and children, passed the Muskingum river, in Ohio.
1804 Capts. Lewis and Clark explored the Missouri to its source, crossed the Rocky Mountains, arrived at the Pacific ocean in November, 1805, returned to the United States in 1806.
1812 First house in Rochester, N. Y., built.

WARS, MILITARY EVENTS, &c.

1614 The Dutch built a fort at Manhattan, (near New York.)
1622 The Indians massacred 349 of the Virginia colonists, March 22.
Narragansett Indians threaten war.
1623 Massasoit discloses an Indian conspiracy.
1634 The Indians in Connecticut began hostilities.
1635 Fort built at Saybrook, Con.
1637 *War with the Pequots* in Connecticut: their fort taken by surprise and destroyed, May 26.
1638 Uncas, Sachem of the Mohegans, makes a treaty with the English.
1642 The Dutch fort at Hartford seized by the inhabitants of Connecticut.
Indian war in Maryland.
1643 War between the Mohegans and Narragansetts.
1645 Action between a New England ship and an Irish man of war.
Battle fought between the Dutch and Indians, near the confines of Connecticut; great numbers slain on both sides.
1651 Dutch trading house on the Delaware taken by the Swedes.
1654 The Iroquois Indians exterminate the Eries.
The Dutch extirpate the Swedes from the Delaware.
1664 New York and Albany taken from the Dutch.
1669 War between New York Indians and the Mohawks.

1673 New York and New Netherlands taken by the Dutch—they were restored to the English the next year.
1675 *King Philip's War* commenced; action at Swanzey, June: Brookfield burnt, Deerfield burnt, Sept. 1; Hadley assaulted; Springfield burnt; Capt. Lathrop, with 80 men, surprised by Indians—almost every man slain, Sept. 18.
   Gov. Winslow, with 1000 men, attacked the Narragansetts, (the allies of Philip,) in their fort: the fort destroyed, and their country ravaged, December.
1676 Lancaster burnt; Capt. Pierce and his company slain; Capt. Wadsworth and about fifty of his men killed; Falls fight—the Indians surprised in the night,—they lost 300 men, women, and children, May 18; Hatfield and Hadley attacked.—King Philip killed, Aug. 12—which ends the war.
   Bacon's insurrection in Virginia; Jamestown burnt.
1677 Insurrection in Carolina: the insurgents exercised authority for two years in that colony.
1678 Fort built at Pemaquid; treaty at Casco with the Indians.
1686 Port Royal, Carolina, broken up by the Spaniards from St. Augustine.
1687 The French under Denonville, make war upon the Seneca Indians.
1688 Gov. Andros' expedition against the eastern Indians.
1690 A body of French and Indians, from Montreal, burn Schenectady, and massacre the inhabitants, Feb. 8.
   Salmon Falls surprised by the French and Indians.
   Casco fort destroyed; fort at Pemaquid taken.
   Port Royal taken by Sir William Phipps—he makes an expedition against Quebec, but is unsuccessful.
1691 Major Schuyler, with a party of Mohawks, attacks the French settlements on Lake Champlain.
1692 The French and Indians attack York and Wells.
1593 Count Frontenac, Governor of Canada, makes an expedition against the Mohawks.
1694 Gov. Fletcher makes a treaty with the five Nations.
1696 The French destroy the fort at Pemaquid, and lay waste Nova Scotia.
1700 Carolina infested with pirates.
1702 Gov. Moore's expedition against the Spaniards, at St. Augustine—it proves abortive.
1703 Gov. Moore subdues the Apalachian Indians.
1704 Deerfield burnt and most of its inhabitants carried captive by the French and Indians, Feb. 28.
1705 The French ravage Newfoundland.
1706 The Spaniards and French invade Carolina—they are defeated.
1707 The New England troops make an unsuccessful expedition against Port Royal.
1708 Haverhill surprised by the French and Indians.
1710 Port Royal, in Nova Scotia, taken by general Nicholson, Oct. 2.
1711 Expedition against Quebec—failed by the loss of transports in the St. Lawrence, August.
1712 War with the Tuscaroras in North Carolina—they are defeated.
1715 A general conspiracy against the Carolinas, by the Yamasees, Cherokees, and other tribes.—Governor Craven attacks and defeats them in their camp.
1719 Pensacola taken by the French from the Spaniards.
1724 War with the eastern Indians in New England.

1730 The Natchez Indians extirpated by the French.
1736 The Chickasaw Indians defeat the French.
1740 General Oglethorp, with 2,000 men, makes an unsuccessful expedition against St. Augustine.
1741 Expedition against Cuba.
1742 Spanish expedition against Georgia—failed.
1745 Louisburg and Cape Breton taken by the New England troops, aided by a British squadron, June 17.
1746 French expedition under Duke D'Anville, which threatened New England, failed, by means of storms, sickness in the fleet, &c.
1747 Saratoga village destroyed, the inhabitants massacred by the French and Indians.
1753 The French erect forts on the back of the colonies.
1754 Colonel Washington, with 400 men, in fort Necessity, surrendered to the French, July 4.
1755 Expedition against Nova Scotia; the French are subdued, the inhabitants brought away and dispersed among the colonies. General Braddock defeated by the French and Indians, July 9. Battle of Lake George; the French under Baron Dieskau defeated, Dieskau wounded, Sept. 8.
1756 Oswego taken by the French under Montcalm.
1757 Fort William Henry capitulated to the French, many of the garrison massacred by the Indians.
1758 Louisburg taken by the British, July.
Gen. Abercrombie defeated at Ticonderoga with great loss; Lord Howe killed, July.
1758 Fort Frontenac taken from the French by Col. Bradstreet.
Fort du Quesne abandoned by the French and taken by the English and named Pittsburgh, Nov. 25.
1759 Ticonderoga and Crown Point taken by Gen. Amherst.
Niagara taken by the English, Gen. Prideaux killed.
English repulsed at Montmorency, near Quebec.
Battle of Quebec; Gen. Wolf, the English commander, and Montcalm, the French commander, killed; the French defeated and Quebec taken, September.
1760 M. de Levi attempts to recover Quebec; he is compelled to retire.
Montreal capitulated to the English, September, and Canada is subdued.
The Cherokees take fort Loudon, and treacherously massacre the garrison.
1761 The Cherokees defeated by Col. Grant and compelled to make peace.
1762 Havanna taken by the British and provincials.
1763 Treaty of peace signed at Paris between Great Britain and France; Canada, Nova Scotia, and Cape Breton confirmed to the British king.
1768 Two British regiments stationed at Boston, September.
1770 Massacre in Boston; the British troops fired upon the inhabitants, and killed three and wounded five, March 5.
1773 Tea thrown overboard at Boston, Dec. 16.
1775 *Battle of Lexington*, which began the revolutionary war, April 19.
Ticonderoga taken by Col. Ethan Allen, May 10.
George Washington appointed commander-in-chief of the American army, June 15; took command of the troops investing Boston, July 2.

1775 Generals Howe, Clinton, and Burgoyne, with a re-enforcement from England, arrived at Boston, May 25.
Battle of Bunker Hill, June 17.
General Montgomery penetrated into Canada, took fort hamblee, St. Johns and Montreal, Nov.
Col. Ethan Allen captured near Montreal, and sent in irons to England.
Col. Arnold, with 3,000 men, penetrates through the wilderness to Canada.
Assault upon Quebec: General Montgomery killed and the Americans defeated, Dec. 31.
1776 Norfolk, Va., burnt by the British, January 1.
Boston evacuated by the British, March 17.
Loyalists defeated in North Carolina by Gen. Moore, Feb. 27.
Blockade of Quebec raised by the Americans, May 5.
A body of the Americans at the Cedars surrendered, May.
The Americans evacuated Canada, June 18.
The British defeated in their attack on Sullivan's Island, July 28.
General Howe and Admiral Lord Howe, with 24,000 men. arrive at Sandy Hook, June.
Declaration of Independence, July 4.
Battle on Long Island, August 27.
American army withdrawn from Long Island, Aug. 30.
Captain Nathan Hale, of Connecticut, executed as a spy.
New York evacuated by the Americans, taken possession of by the British, Sept. 15.
Gen. Arnold defeated on Lake Champlain, Oct. 12.
Battle at the White Plains, Oct. 28.
Fort Washington taken, with about 2,000 prisoners, Nov. 16.
Fort Lee evacuated, Nov. 18.
Americans attack Fort Cumberland, Nova Scotia, but are repulsed, Nov. 20.
American army retreated through New Jersey, and crossed the Delaware, pursued by the British, November and December.
The British take possession of Rhode Island, Dec. 8.
Congress adjourn to Baltimore, Dec. 12.
Gen. Lee surprised and taken prisoner, Dec. 13.
Battle of Trenton, 1000 Hessians taken, Dec. 26.
77* Battle of Princeton, Gen. Mercer killed, Jan. 3.
Washington retires to Morristown.
More than 20,000 stands of arms and 1000 barrels of powder arrived from France.
Danbury, Con., burnt, Gen. Wooster killed, April 28.
Col. Meigs crosses over to Long Island from Connecticut, and captures 90 of the British without the loss of a man, May 23.
Gen. Prescott surprised and taken prisoner by Col. Barton, of Rhode Island.
Battle of Brandywine, Gen. Lafayette wounded, Sept. 11.
Gen. Wayne surprised and defeated with the loss of about 300 men, Sept. 28.
The British take possession of Philadelphia, Sept. 27.
Ticonderoga evacuated by the Americans, July 6.
Battle of Benington, August.
Battle of Germantown, Oct. 4.
Burgoyne encamps at Saratoga, Sept. 14.
Gen. Burgoyne surrendered to Gen. Gates, Oct. 17.

777 Assault on Red Bank; British defeated; Count Donop killed.
778 *Treaty of Alliance with France*, signed Feb. 6.
The British evacuate Philadelphia, June 18.
Battle of Monmouth; many soldiers died of the heat, June 28.
Count D'Estaing arrives with a French fleet off Newport, July.
Massacre at Wyoming, July.
Battle on Rhode Island, Aug. 29; Americans retreat from Rhode Island, Aug. 30.
Paul Jones' naval battle on the coast of Scotland, Sept. 22.
Colonel Baylor's regiment of cavalry surprised by Gen. Grey, Sept. 28.
Expedition of the Americans against East Florida, failed.
Savannah taken by the British under Col. Campbell, Dec. 29.
The American frigate Randolph, of 36 guns, and 300 men, blown up in an engagement; only four men saved.
1779 Gen. Ash surprised and defeated by the British at Brier Creek, with the loss of 300 men, March 3.
Engagement at Stono Ferry; Americans obliged to retreat, June 20.
Unsuccessful assault on Savannah; Count Pulaski, a Polish officer in the service of the Americans, mortally wounded, October 9.
The British make incursions into Virginia; property to an immense amount destroyed.
The British plunder New Jersey, June.
Gov. Tryon invades and plunders New Haven, July 5; Fairfield and Norwalk burnt.
Stony Point taken by General Wayne, July 15.
The Americans made an unsuccessful attempt against the British post at Penobscot.
Gen. Sullivan ravages the country of the Six Nations.
780 Gen. Lincoln capitulated, and Charleston, S. C. surrendered to Sir Henry Clinton, May 12.
Col. Buford defeated at the Wexhaws by the British under Col. Tarleton; the Americans lost about 300 men, in killed, wounded, and prisoners, May 28.
Col. Sumpter defeats a party of British at Williamson's plantation, July 12; and a body of Tories at Hanging Rock, August 6.
Gen. Rochambeau arrives at Newport, R. I. with a French fleet and army, July 10.
Battle of Camden; the Americans under Gen. Gates, defeated August 16; Baron de Kalb, a German officer, killed.
Gen. Sumpter surprised and defeated by Col. Tarleton, August 18.
Treason of Arnold; Major Andre taken and executed, Oct. 2.
Action at King's Mountain; the British and Tories, under Major Ferguson, defeated with the loss of 150 killed and 800 prisoners, October 7.
Incursion of the British Gen. Kniphausen, into New Jersey; action near Springfield, N. J. June 23.
781 Mutiny in the Pennsylvania line of troops, Jan. 1.
General Green takes command of the Southern American army.
Battle of the Cowpens; Gen. Morgan and Col. Tarleton, January 17.
Battle of Guilford, N. C. between Gen. Greene and Lord Cornwallis, March 15.

1781 Gen. Marion takes fort Watson, April 23.
Fort Cornwallis at Augusta, taken June 6.
Gen. Greene lays siege to Ninety-Six, but is repulsed, June 19.
The combined armies under Gen. Washington, decamp from the Hudson, and march for Virginia, August 19.
New London, Con. burnt, fort Griswold stormed and the garrison put to the sword by Arnold, September 8.
Battle of the Eutaw Springs; Gen. Greene defeats the British, with the loss of 1000 men, Sept. 8.
Lord Cornwallis pursues the Marquis de la Fayette, in Virginia.
Count de Grasse, with a French fleet, and 3,200 troops, enters the Chesapeake, September.
Yorktown invested, and batteries opened against it, Oct. 9.
The British army under Lord Cornwallis, surrendered at Yorktown, Va. to Gen. Washington, October 19; this event decided the revolutionary war.
1782 The British evacuated Savannah, July.
Provisional articles of peace signed, Independence of the United States acknowledged, Nov. 30.
1783 Definitive treaty signed, Sept. 3.
The army disbanded, Oct. 18.
Farewell address of Gen. Washington to the army, Nov. 2.
General Washington resigned his commission, Dec. 23.
1790 Gen. Harmer defeated by the Indians in Ohio.
1791 Gen. St. Clair defeated by the Indians.
1794 Gen. Wayne gains a decisive victory over the Indians on the Miami, August 20.
1797 Collision with the French republic.
1798 Gen. Washington appointed to command the armies of the United States, July 7.
1799 Capt. Truxtun, in the Constellation, took the French frigate Insurgent, Feb. 10.
1800 Treaty of Peace with France, September 30.
1803 War with Tripoli.
1804 Com. Preble makes an ineffectual attack on Tripoli.
1805 Gen. Eaton takes possession of Derne, a Tripolitan city, and a peace with Tripoli soon after ensues.
1807 The American frigate Chesapeake fired into by the British frigate Leopard, off the Capes of Virginia, 4 men killed and 16 wounded, June 22.
1809 Non-intercourse with Great Britain and France, established by congress, March 1.
1811 Engagement between the American frigate President, Captain Rogers, and the British sloop of war, Little Belt, Capt. Bingham, May.
Battle of Tippacanoe, between Gen. Harrison and the Indians, November 7.
1812 *Declaration of War* by the United States against Great Britain, June 18.
General Hull surrendered his army, and the fort of Detroit, to the British, August 16.
U. S. frigate Constitution, Capt. Hull, captured the British frigate Guerriere, Captain Dacres, Aug. 19.
400 men, women, and children, massacred at Fort Mimms, on the Alabama, by the Indians, Aug. 30.
U. S. frigate United States, Com. Decatur, captured the Macedonian, October 25.
Battle of Queenstown. U. C. Gen. Brock killed, Oct. 3.

812 U. S. frigate Constitution, Com. Bainbridge, captured the Java, Dec. 29.
1813 Bloody action at the river Raisin, between the Americans under Gen. Winchester, and the British and Indians under Gen. Proctor; Gen. Winchester killed, and the American prisoners massacred by the Indians, Jan. 22.
U. S. sloop of war Hornet, Captain Lawrence, captured the British sloop of war Peacock, Captain Peak, who was killed.
York, Upper Canada, taken by the Americans; Gen. Pike killed, April 27.
U. S. frigate Chesapeake, Capt. Lawrence, captured by the British frigate Shannon; Capt. Lawrence killed, June 1.
Gallant defence of fort Stephenson, by Major Croghan, August 1.
The American fleet on Lake Erie, under Com. Perry, capture the British fleet under Com. Barclay, Sept. 10.
Gen. Harrison defeats the British and Indians under Gen. Proctor; Tecumseh killed, Oct. 5.
Detroit fell into the hands of the Americans.
1813-14 War with the Creek Indians: March, 26, 1814, Gen. Jackson obtains a decisive victory over the Creeks; upwards of 500 warriors slain at the Great Bend of the Tallapoosa.
1814 U. S. frigate Essex, Capt. Porter, captured by a superior force, March 28.
Fort Erie taken by the Americans, July.
Battle of Chippewa, July 6.
Battle of Niagara, July 25.
Washington captured and burnt by the British under Gen. Ross, Aug. 24.
Attack on Baltimore; Gen. Ross killed, Sept. 12.
Unsuccessful attack by the British, under Gen. Drummond, on fort Erie, Aug. 14.
Castine taken by the British, Sept. 1.
Com. Macdonough captures the British fleet on Lake Champlain; retreat of Gen. Provost from Plattsburgh, Sept. 11.
1815 Memorable victory of General Jackson over the British before New Orleans, Jan. 8.
Treaty of Peace between the United States and Great Britain, signed at Ghent, Dec. 24, 1814, ratified by the president and senate, February 17, 1815.
Massacre of American prisoners at Dartmoor, Eng. April 6.
War declared against Algiers; Com. Decatur captures the Algerine frigate Mazouda, June 17; arrives with a squadron before Algiers, and compels the Dey to a treaty of peace.
1818 War with the Seminole Indians.
1823 Commodore Porter sent against the pirates in the West Indies.
1832 War with the Winnebagoes and other tribes. "Black Hawk," a famous Indian chief, captured, Aug. 27.

REMARKABLE EVENTS.

1587 Virginia Dare born—the first child of Christian parents born in the United States.
1608 John Laydon married to Ann Burras,—the first Christian marriage in Virginia, and in the United States.

1610 *Starving time* in Virginia; of nearly 500 colonists, all perished but 60, in the course of six months.
1613 Rolfe, an Englishman, married Pocahontas, daughter of Powhattan, the Indian king.
1616 Tobacco first cultivated by the English settlers in Virginia.
1617 Pocahontas died in England, aged 22.
1618 A great pestilence destroyed most of the Indians from Narraganset to Penobscot.
1619 20,000 pounds of tobacco exported from Virginia to England.
1620 African slaves first brought into Virginia by a Dutch ship and sold to the colonists.
Peregrine White, the first English child born in New England.
1621 Edward Winslow and Susannah White, married,—the first Christian marriage in New England.
1623 George Sandys, of Virginia, translated Ovid's Metamorphosis,—the first literary production of the English colonists in America.
1624 The first cattle brought into New England by Edward Winslow, agent for the Plymouth Colony.
1630 Gov. Winthrop first abolished the custom of drinking healths.
John Billington executed for murder,—the first execution in Plymouth colony.
1631 First vessel built in Massachusetts, called the *Blessing of Bay,* launched July 4.
1632 Magistrates of the colony of Massachusetts, first chosen by the freemen in the colony.
The magistrates of Massachusetts ordered that no tobacco should be used *publicly.*
The general court of Plymouth passed an act, that whoever should refuse the office of governor should pay a fine of 20l., unless he was chosen two years successively.
1633 Virginia enacted laws for the suppression of religious sectaries.
Messrs. Cotton, Hooker, and Stone, three eminent ministers, arrived at Boston, from England.
A specimen of *rye* first brought into the court of Massachusetts, as the first-fruits of English grains.
1634 Roger Williams, minister of Salem, banished on account of his religious tenets.
First merchant's shop in Boston opened.
1635 Great storm of wind and rain in New England; the tide rose twenty feet perpendicularly, August 15.
1636 The *Desire*, a ship of 120 tons, built at Marblehead, the first American ship that made a voyage to England.
The first court in Connecticut, held April 26.
1637 Ann Hutchinson holds lectures in Massachusetts for the propagation of her peculiar religious sentiments,—she gains many adherents.
A synod convened at Newtown, Mass., the first synod holden in America; they condemn 82 erroneous opinions which had been propagated in New England.
1638 Great earthquake in New England, June 1.
Two tremendous storms in August and December; the tide rose 14 feet above the spring tides, at Narraganset, and flowed twice in six hours.
Harvard College, Mass., founded; it was named after the Rev. John Harvard, one of its principal benefactors.
The ancient and honourable artillery company, formed at Boston.

1638 Three Englishmen executed by the government of Plymouth colony, for the murder of an Indian.
1639 First general election in Hartford, Conn.—John Haynes first Governor.
   First Baptist church in America formed at Providence, R. I.
   Severe tempest and rain, Connecticut river rose 20 feet above the meadows, March.
   First Printing in North America at Cambridge, Mass., by Samuel Green; the first thing printed was the Freemen's oath.
   House of Assembly established in Maryland.
1640 The general court of Massachusetts prohibited the use of tobacco.
1641 Severe winter; Boston and Chesapeake bays frozen; Boston bay passable for carts, horses, &c. for five weeks.
1642 The New England ministers invited to attend the Assembly of divines, at Westminster, England—but they declined.
   First commencement at Harvard College; 9 candidates took the degree of A. B.
1643 Union of the colonies of Plymouth, Massachusetts, Connecticut, and New Haven, for mutual defence.
1646 Mr. Elliott commenced his labours among the Indians.
   The Friends or Quakers first came to Massachusetts; laws passed against them; four executed in 1659.
1647 First influenza mentioned in the annals of America.
   Legislature of Massachusetts passed an act against the Jesuits.
   First general assembly of Rhode Island.
   Rev. Thomas Hooker, the first minister in Connecticut, died, aged 61 years.
1648 Laws of Massachusetts first printed.
   Margaret Jones of Charlestown, Mass., executed for witchcraft.
   The "Cambridge Platform" and the "Westminster Confession of Faith" received by most of the New England churches.
   The Congregational church and its pastor ordered to depart from Virginia by the governor of that colony.
1649 John Winthrop, governor of Massachusetts, and the Rev. Thomas Shepard died.
   The government of Massachusetts, with the assistants, signed a declaration against men's wearing long hair, as unscriptural.
1650 Indians of Martha's Vineyard christianized.
   Constitution of Maryland established.
1651 The legislature of Massachusetts passed laws against extravagance in dress.
1652 The province of Maine taken under the protection of Massachusetts.
   The first mint for coining money in New England erected.
   John Cotton, a celebrated minister in Boston, died, aged 68.
1654 College at New Haven projected by Mr. Davenport.
   Gov. Haynes of Connecticut died.
1656 Miles Standish, the hero of New England, died.
1657 Disputes concerning baptism in New England.
   Gov. Eaton, of New Haven, died.
1658 Earthquake in New England.
1660 At this time the colonies of Virginia, New England, and Maryland, were supposed to contain no more than 80,000 inhabitants.
   Goffe and Whalley, the regicides, arrived in Boston.

1661 Society for propagating the gospel among the Indians of New England, incorporated by Charles II.
1662 Charter of Connecticut granted by King Charles II.
The legislature of Massachusetts appointed two licensers of the press.
The assembly of Maryland established a mint in that colony.
1663 Great earthquake in Canada and New England.
1664 Elliott's *Indian Bible* printed at Cambridge, Mass., the first Bible printed in America.
A large comet seen in New England.
1665 New Haven and Connecticut united into one colony.
At this time, the Militia of Massachusetts consisted of 4,400 men.
The government of Rhode Island passed an order to outlaw Quakers, for refusing to bear arms.
1666 The buccaniers of America began their depredations in the West Indies.
1672 Laws of Connecticut printed; every family ordered to have a law book.
1673 New England contained at this time about 120,000 inhabitants.
1675 Virginia contained at this time about 50,000 inhabitants.
1680 New Hampshire separated from Massachusetts. The first assembly met at Portsmouth.
Great comet seen in New England; it occasioned much alarm.
1681 Thomas Mayhew died at Martha's Vineyard, aged 93.
1682 William Penn held a treaty with the Indians.
1683 The governor of Virginia ordered that no printing press should be used in that colony "on any occasion whatever."
1686 First Episcopal society formed in Boston.
1687 Charter of Connecticut hid from Andros, in a hollow oak, and saved.
M. de Salle, the discoverer of Louisiana, killed by his own men in a mutiny.
1688 New York and the Jersies added to the jurisdiction of New England.
Andros appointed captain-general and vice-admiral over the whole.
Opposition to Andros' administration in Massachusetts.
1689 William and Mary proclaimed in the colonies. Andros is seized and sent a prisoner to England.
Rev. J. Elliot, "apostle of the Indians," died.
1690 *Bills of credit* issued by the government of Massachusetts; the first ever issued in the American colonies.
The *whale fishery*, at Nantucket, commenced.
1691 The assembly of Virginia obtain of the crown the charter of William and Mary College, so named from the English sovereigns.
1692 Nineteen persons executed for witchcraft, in Massachusetts.
Edmund Andros, the tyrant of New England, made governor of Virginia.
Massachusetts and Plymouth colonies united.
Sir William Phipps arrived, as governor of Massachusetts, under the new charter.
1693 Episcopacy introduced into New York.
1694 Legislature of Massachusetts caused the names of drunkards, in the several towns, to be posted up in the public houses, and imposed a fine for giving them entertainment.
1695 Rice introduced into Carolina.

696 Thirty Indian churches in New England at this time.
697 Severe winter; the Delaware frozen.
1698 Seat of government in Virginia removed to Williamsburgh, the streets of which were laid out in the form of a W, in honour of the reigning King of England, William.
1699 Assembly of Maryland removed to Annapolis.
Yellow fever in Philadelphia.
1700 Legislature of New York made a law to hang every Popish priest who should come into the province.
262,000 inhabitants in the American colonies, at the beginning of this century.
1701 Yale College received its charter.
1702 First emission of paper currency in Carolina.
First Episcopal churches in New Jersey and Rhode Island.
1703 The church of England established by law in Carolina.
1704 *First newspaper* in America published in Boston, called the Boston News Letter.
1706 The legislature of Connecticut exempted the ministers of the gospel from taxation in that colony.
1707 Episcopal church formed at Stratford; the first formed in Connecticut.
1708 *Saybrook Platform* formed by a synod of ministers, under the authority of the state of Connecticut.
1709 First issuing of paper currency in New York, New Jersey, and Connecticut.
1717 Greatest snow storm ever known, February.
Yale College removed from Saybrook to New Haven.
Bellamy, a pirate, wrecked with his fleet on Cape Cod.
1718 Piracy suppressed in the West Indies.
William Penn, the founder of Pennsylvania, died in England, aged 74.
1719 Carolina throws off the proprietary government.
First Presbyterian church in New York founded.
Northern lights appeared in New England, Dec. 11th.
Lotteries suppressed by the legislature of Massachusetts.
1721 *First inoculation* for the small pox in America, at Boston.
Elihu Yale, the benefactor of Yale College, died in England.
1923 Twenty-six pirates executed at Newport, R. I.
Paper currency in Pennsylvania first issued.
1724 The sect of Dunkers took its rise in Pennsylvania.
1725 Synods abolished in New England.
First newspaper printed at New York, by William Bradford.
1727 Great earthquake in New England, Oct. 29.
1728 Drought and hurricane in Carolina; yellow fever in Charleston.
Rev. Cotton Mather, a distinguished writer, died, aged 65.
1731 Rev. Solomon Stoddard, a theological writer, died.
732 Corn and tobacco, made a legal tender in Maryland. Corn at 20 pence per bushel, and tobacco at 1 penny per pound.
George Washington born in Westmoreland county, Va., Feb. 22.
1733 First masonic lodge held in Boston.
737 Earthquake in New Jersey.
738 College at Princeton, N. J., founded.
740 George Whitefield, a celebrated preacher, first arrives in America. He died in Newburyport, Mass., Sept. 1770.
Hard winter; severe cold.
741 Four white persons executed, 13 negroes burnt, 18 hanged, and great numbers transported, for a conspiracy to burn the city of New York.

1745 Indigo plant discovered in South Carolina.
1746 First ordination among the *separate* ministers in New England. About 30 congregations of this order were formed from 1740 to 1750.
1749 Severe drought in New England; causes great distress; some of the inhabitants sent to England for hay.
1750 Massachusetts enacts a law against theatrical entertainments.
1752 *New Style* introduced into Britain and America; Sept. 2d reckoned 14th.
Charleston, S. C., laid under water by a tempest, Sept.
Dr. Franklin makes his electrical experiments.
1754 Convention at Albany, of delegates from seven of the colonies, agree on a plan of union—never carried into effect.
1755 Great earthquake in North America, Nov. 18.
1758 Jonathan Edwards, a celebrated theologian, died, aged 55.
1759 Lotteries granted by the legislature of Massachusetts for the benefit of public works.
1761 Violent whirlwind near Charleston, S. C.
1762 *Severest drought* known in America, no rain from May to Sept.
1764 Spanish *potatoe* introduced into New England.
Medical lectures first read in Philadelphia.
1768 or 9 First Methodist church in America built in New York.
1769 Dartmouth college, New Hampshire, received its charter. It was named from the Earl of Dartmouth, its benefactor.
American Philosophical Society, at Philadelphia, founded.
1771 R. Sandeman, founder of the Sandemanians, died, at Danbury Con.
1774 The Shakers first arrived from England; they settled near Albany.
First congress at Philadelphia.
1775 Peyton Randolph, first president of congress, died, aged 52.
The first line of post offices established; Dr. Franklin appointed postmaster.
1776 *Declaration of Independence,* July 4.
1777 Vermont declares herself an independent state.
1780 American Academy of Arts and Sciences incorporated.
Dark day in the northern states, 19th of May, candles necessary at noon.
1781 Massachusetts Medical Society incorporated.
1782 *First English Bible* printed in America, by Robert Aiken, of Philadelphia.
The American launched at Portsmouth, N. H., Nov. 5th, the first 74 ever built in America.
1783 Slavery abolished in Massachusetts.
1783—4 Severe winter, great floods in March.
1784 Empress of China, a ship of 360 tons, sailed from New York for Canton; the first voyage from the United States to China.
Anthony Benezet, a distinguished philanthropist, died.
The towns of Hartford, New Haven, Middletown, New London, and Norwich, in Connecticut, constituted cities by the legislature.
1785 First instance of instrumental music in the Congregational churches in Boston.
1786 Shay's insurrection in Massachusetts.
Universalist church founded in Boston.
1788 Federal constitution ratified, and became the constitution of the United States.
Cotton first planted in Georgia, by R. Leake.

1789 George Washington inaugurated first president, April 30th.
Convention of Episcopal clergy in Philadelphia; the first Episcopal convention in America.
Dr. Carrol, of Maryland, consecrated bishop of the Roman Catholic church; the first Catholic bishop in the U. States.
1790 Dr. Franklin died, aged 85.
1792 National mint established at Philadelphia.
1793 Yellow fever in Philadelphia, 4,000 persons died.
John Hancock, Henry Laurens, Arthur Lee, and Roger Sherman, died this year.
1794 Whiskey insurrection in Pennsylvania.
Destructive frost in New England, May 24th.
1796 Detroit given up by the British to the United States.
1797 John Adams elected president.
1798 Yellow fever in Philadelphia.
1799 Washington died, aged 68.
1800 Seat of government transferred from Philadelphia to Washington.
The inoculation of the kine pock introduced into America by Professor Waterhouse of Cambridge, Mass.
1801 Thomas Jefferson elected president of the United States.
1802 Merino sheep introduced into the United States by Mr. Livingston and Gen. Humphreys.
1803 Louisiana purchased of the French government for 15 millions of dollars.
1804 Gen. Hamilton killed in a duel by Col. Aaron Burr, vice-president of the United States.
1807 First steamboat built in this country.
Col. Aaron Burr arrested on a charge of treason.
Several meteoric stones fell in the county of Fairfield, Conn., one weighing 35 pounds, Dec. 4th.
1809 James Madison elected president.
1811 Richmond theatre burnt, Dec. 26; many persons lost their lives.
1814 Meeting of the Hartford Convention, Dec. 15.
1816 *American Bible Society* formed, May 8.
Colonization Society formed.
Cold summer.—Frost every month in the year in the northern states.
Bank of the United States, with a capital of 35 millions of dollars, incorporated in April.
1817 Grand canal in the state of New York commenced.
James Monroe elected president.
1820 First mariner's church erected at New York.
1821 Florida ceded to the United States.
1824 Gen. Lafayette arrived at New York.
1825 John Quincy Adams elected president.
1826 Thomas Jefferson and John Adams, two ex-presidents, died, July 4th, on the fiftieth anniversary of American independence.
American Temperance Society formed at Boston, Mass.
1828 Andrew Jackson elected president.
United States steam frigate Fulton blown up at New York; between 30 and 40 persons killed, June 4th.
1831 Insurrection of slaves in Southampton county, Virginia; about 60 men, women, and children, murdered, August.
Riot in Providence, R. I., several persons killed by the military, Sept. 24.
1832 The *cholera* appears in the city of New York, June 27.
Ordinance of S. Carolina "nullifying" the operation of the tariff laws in that state.

1833 The funds of the Government withdrawn from the U. S. bank.
1835 Major Dade, with upward of 100 men, killed by the Seminole Indians, in Florida. Dec. 28.
Arkansas admitted into the Union.
Great fire in New York—loss upward of *seventeen millions* of dolls
1836 Battle of San Jacinto, in Texas—Santa Anna taken prisoner. Texan independence established, April 21.
1837 Martin Van Buren president.
Great financial distress; banks suspend specie payments.
Riot at Alton, Ill.; E. P. Lovejoy killed, Nov. 7.
Steamboat Caroline burnt at Niagara, by the British, Dec. 30
Michigan admitted into the Union.
1838 U. S. exploring expedition sailed from Hampton Roads, Aug. 19
1841 Alexander McLeod, of Upper Canada, one of the party who burnt the steamboat Caroline, arrested Jan. 27.
U. S. Bank of Pennsylvania stopped payment, Feb. 5.
William H. Harrison president. He died April 4, and was succeeded by John Tyler.
1842 Dorr insurrection in Rhode Island, between the adherents of Thomas W. Dorr, of the suffrage, and those of the charter party. Dorr imprisoned.
Treaty settling the boundary of Maine ratified, Aug. 20.
Conspiracy detected on board U. S. brig Somers. Three executed, Dec. 1.
1844 Joseph Smith, the Mormon prophet, killed at Carthage, Ill., June 27.
Riots in Philadelphia commenced between the Catholics and the "Native American" party, May 3. Several persons killed.
Noah Webster, LL. D., author of the American Dictionary of the English Language, died at New Haven, Conn., aged 85.
Anti-rent disturbances in New York. Quelled in 1845.
1845 Texas annexed to the United States.
James K. Polk, president.
Mormon disturbances renewed in Illinois, Sept. 10.
Gen. Andrew Jackson died, near Nashville, Tenn., June 8.
1846 President Polk, by proclamation, declares war to exist between Mexico and the United States, May 13.
Mexicans defeated by Gen. Taylor, on the Rio Grande, May 8th and 9th, with the loss of 1,000 men; Gen. Vega taken prisoner. American loss 165 killed and wounded—Maj. Ringgold mortally
Oregon treaty ratified, June 18.
Santa Fe, New Mexico, taken by Gen. Kearney, June 18.
Monterey taken by Gen. Taylor, Sept. 25, after three days' fighting. American loss 500 killed and wounded; Col. Watson and Maj. Barbour killed.
Tampico taken, Nov. 14.
1847 Battle of Buena Vista. General Taylor forced Santa Anna to retreat with great loss. Colonels Hardin, M'Kee, and Clay, killed, Feb. 23. Vera Cruz surrendered to General Scott, March 26.
Battle of Cerro Gordo, Mexicans defeated with great loss, April 19.
Battles of Contreras and Churubusco, August 20.
Molina del Rey taken, Sept. 8. Chapultepec stormed, Sept. 13.
Mexico surrendered and entered by General Scott, Sept. 14.
1848 Treaty of peace between Mexico and the United States, signed Feb. 2.
1849 Zachary Taylor inaugurated President, March 5.

DECLARATION OF INDEPENDENCE

OF THE

UNITED STATES OF AMERICA,

Signed on the 4th of July, 1776, by a Congress of Delegates, assembled at Philadelphia, from the States of New Hampshire, Massachusetts, Rhode Island, Connecticut, New York, New Jersey, Pennsylvania, Delaware, Maryland, Virginia, North Carolina, South Carolina, and Georgia.

WHEN, in the course of human events, it becomes necessary for one people to dissolve the political bonds which have connected them with another, and to assume among the powers of the earth, the separate and equal station to which the laws of nature and of nature's God entitle them, a decent respect to the opinions of mankind, requires that they should declare the causes which impel them to the separation.

We hold these truths to be self evident—that all men are created equal; that they are endowed by their Creator with certain unalienable rights; that among these are life, liberty, and the pursuit of happiness. That to secure these rights, governments are instituted among men, deriving their just powers from the consent of the governed; that whenever any form of government becomes destructive of these ends, it is the right of the people to alter or to abolish it, and to institute a new government, laying its foundation on such principles, and organizing its powers in such form, as to them shall seem most likely to effect their safety and happiness. Prudence, indeed, will dictate, that governments long established, should not be changed for light and transient causes; and, accordingly, all experience hath shown, that mankind are most disposed to suffer, while evils are sufferable, than to right themselves by abolishing the forms to which they are accustomed. But when a long train of abuses and usurpations, pursuing invariably the same object, evinces a design to reduce them under absolute despotism, it is their right, it is their duty, to throw off such government, and to provide new guards for their future security. Such has been the patient sufferance of these colonies; and such is now the necessity which constrains them to alter their former system of government. The history of the present king of Great Britain, is a history of repeated injuries and usurpations, all having in direct object the establishment of an absolute tyranny over these States. To prove this, let facts be submitted to a candid world.

He has refused his assent to laws, the most wholesome and necessary for the public good.

He has forbidden his governors to pass laws of immediate and pressing importance, unless suspended in their operations till his assent should be obtained; and when so suspended; he has utterly neglected to attend to them.

He has refused to pass other laws, for the accommodation of large districts of people, unless those people would relinquish the right of representation in the legislature— a right inestimable to them, and formidable to tyrants only.

He has called together legislative bodies, at places unusual, uncomfortable, and distant from the depository of their public records, for the sole purpose of fatiguing them into compliance with his measures.

He has dissolved representative houses repeatedly, for opposing with manly firmness his invasions on the rights of the people.

He has refused, for a long time after such dissolutions, to cause others to be elected; whereby the legislative powers, incapable of annihilation, have returned to the people at large, for their exercise; the State remaining in the mean time, exposed to all the danger of invasion from without, and convulsions within.

He has endeavoured to prevent the population of these States; for that purpose obstructing the laws for the naturalization of foreigners; refusing to pass others to encourage their migration hither, and raising the condition of new appropriations of lands.

He has obstructed the administration of justice, by refusing his assent to laws for establishing Judiciary Powers.

He has made judges dependent on his will alone for the tenure of their offices, and the amount and payment of their salaries.

He has erected a multitude of new offices, and sent hither swarms of officers, to harass our people and eat out their substance.

He has kept among us, in time of peace, standing armies, without the consent of our legislature.

He has effected to render the military independent of, and superior to, the civil power.

He has combined with others to subject us to a jurisdiction, foreign to our constitution, and unacknowledged by our laws; giving his assent to their acts of pretended legislation.

For quartering large bodies of armed troops among us:

For protecting them, by a mock trial, from punishment for any murders which they should commit on the inhabitants of these States:

For cutting off our trade with all parts of the world:

For imposing taxes on us without our consent:

For depriving us, in many cases, of the benefits of trial by jury:

For transporting us beyond seas, to be tried for pretended offences:

For abolishing the free system of English laws in a neighbouring province, establishing therein an arbitrary government, and enlarging its boundaries, so as to render it at once an example and fit instrument for introducing the same absolute rule into these colonies:

For taking away our charters, abolishing our most

valuable laws, and altering fundamentally the forms of our governments:

For suspending our own legislatures, and declaring themselves invested with power to legislate for us in all cases whatsoever.

He has abdicated government here, by declaring us out of his protection, and waging war against us.

He has plundered our seas, ravaged our coasts, burnt our towns, and destroyed the lives of our people.

He is, at this time, transporting large armies of foreign mercenaries to complete the work of death, desolation, and tyranny, already begun, with circumstances of cruelty and perfidy, scarcely paralleled in the most barbarous ages, and totally unworthy the head of a civilized nation.

He has constrained our fellow citizens, taken captive on the high seas, to bear arms against their country, to become the executioners of their friends and brethren, or fall themselves by their hands.

He has excited domestic insurrection amongst us, and has endeavoured to bring on the inhabitants of our frontiers, the merciless Indian savages, whose known rule of warfare is an undistinguished destruction of all ages sexes, and conditions.

In every stage of these oppressions, we have petitioned for redress in the most humble terms; our repeated petitions have been answered only by repeated injury. A prince whose character is thus marked by every act which may define a tyrant, is unfit to be the ruler of a free people.

Nor have we been wanting in attention to our British brethren. We have warned them from time to time, of attempts made by their Legislature to extend an unwarrantable jurisdiction over us. We have reminded them of the circumstances of our emigration and settlement here. We have appealed to their native justice and magnanimity, and we have conjured them by the ties of our common kindred to disavow these usurpations, which would inevitably interrupt our connexion and correspondence. They, too, have been deaf to the voice of justice and consanguinity. We must, therefore, acquiesce in the necessity which denounces our separation, and hold them, as we hold the rest of mankind—enemies in war—in peace, friends.

We, therefore, the Representatives of the United States of America, in Congress assembled, appealing to the Supreme Judge of the world for the rectitude of our intentions, Do in the name, and by the authority of the good People of these Colonies, solemnly declare, that these United Colonies are, and of right ought to be, free and independent States.—That they are absolved from all allegiance to the British Crown, and that all political connexion between them and the State of Great Britain, is, and ought to be, totally dissolved; and that as free and independent States, they have full power to levy war, conclude peace, contract alliances, establish commerce, and to do all other acts and things which Independent States may of right do. And for the support of this Declaration, with a firm reliance on the protection of Divine Providence, we mutually pledge to each other our lives, our fortunes, and our sacred honour.

CONSTITUTION

OF THE

UNITED STATES OF AMERICA,

Framed during the year 1787, by a Convention of Delegates who met at Philadelphia, from the States of New Hampshire, Massachusetts, Connecticut, New York, New Jersey, Pennsylvania, Delaware, Maryland, Virginia, North Carolina, South Carolina, and Georgia.

WE, the people of the United States, in order to form a more perfect union, establish justice, insure domestic tranquillity, provide for the common defence, promote the general welfare, and secure the blessings of liberty

o ourselves and our posterity, do ordain and establish
this CONSTITUTION for the United States of America.

ARTICLE I.

SECTION 1

All legislative powers herein granted shall be vested in a Congress of the United States, which shall consist of a Senate and House of Representatives.

SECTION II.

I. The House of Representatives shall be composed of members chosen every second year by the people of the several States, and the electors in each state shall have the qualifications requisite for electors of the most numerous branch of the State Legislature.

II. No person shall be a Representative who shall not have attained the age of twenty-five years, and been seven years a citizen of the United States, and who shall not when elected, be an inhabitant of that State in which he shall be chosen.

III. Representative and direct taxes shall be apportioned among the several States which may be included within this Union, according to their respective numbers, which shall be determined by adding to the whole number of free persons, including those bound to service for a term of years, and excluding Indians not taxed, three fifths of all other persons. The actual enumeration shall be made within three years after the first meeting of the Congress of the United States, and within every subsequent term of ten years, in such manner as they shall by law direct. The number of representatives shall not exceed one for every thirty thousand, but each State shall have at least one representative; and until such enumeration shall be made, the State of New Hampshire shall be entitled to choose three, Massachusetts eight, Rhode Island and Providence Plantations one, Connecticut five, New York six, New Jersey four, Pennsylvania eight, Delaware one, Maryland six, Virginia ten, North Carolina five, South Carolina five, and Georgia three.

IV. When vacancies happen in the representation from any State, the executive authority thereof shall issue writs of election to fill such vacancies.

V. The House of Representatives shall choose their Speaker, and other officers; and shall have the sole power of impeachment.

SECTION III.

I. The Senate of the United States shall be composed of two senators from each State, chosen by the legislature thereof, for six years, and each senator shall have one vote.

II. Immediately after they shall be assembled in consequence of the first election, they shall be divided as equally as may be into three classes. The seats of the senators of the first class shall be vacated at the expiration of the second year, of the second class at the expiration of the fourth year, and of the third class at the expiration of the sixth year, so that one third may be chosen every second year; and if vacancies happen by resignation or otherwise, during the recess of the legislature of any State, the executive thereof may make temporary appointments until the next meeting of the legislature, which shall then fill such vacancies.

III. No person shall be a senator who shall not have attained the age of thirty years, and been nine years a citizen of the United States, and who shall not, when elected, be an inhabitant of that State for which he shall be chosen.

IV. The Vice President of the United States shall be President of the Senate, but shall have no vote unless they be equally divided.

V. The Senate shall choose their other officers, and also a President pro tempore in the absence of the Vice President, or when he shall exercise the office of President of the United States.

VI. The Senate shall have the sole power to try all impeachments. When sitting for that purpose, they shall be on oath or affirmation. When the President of the United States is tried, the chief justice shall preside;

and no person shall be convicted without the concurrence of two thirds of the members present.

VII. Judgment in cases of impeachment shall not extend further than to removal from office, and disqualification to hold and enjoy any office of honour, trust, or profit, under the United States; but the party convicted shall nevertheless be liable and subject to indictment, trial, judgment, and punishment, according to law.

SECTION IV.

I. The times, places and manner of holding elections for senators and representatives, shall be prescribed in each State by the legislature thereof; but the Congress may at any time by law make or alter such regulations, except as to the places of choosing senators.

II. The Congress shall assemble at least once in every year, and such meeting shall be on the first Monday in December, unless they shall by law appoint a different day

SECTION V

I. Each house shall be the judge of the elections, returns and qualifications of its own members, and a majority of each shall constitute a quorum to do business; but a smaller number may adjourn from day to day, and may be authorized to compel the attendance of absent members, in such manner, and under such penalties as each house may provide.

II. Each house may determine the rules of its proceedings, punish its members for disorderly behaviour, and, with the concurrence of two thirds, expel a member.

III. Each house shall keep a journal of its proceedings, and from time to time publish the same, excepting such parts as may in their judgment require secrecy; and the yeas and nays of the members of either house, on any question, shall, at the desire of one fifth of those present, be entered on the journal.

IV. Neither house, during the session of Congress, shall, without the consent of the other, adjourn for more than three days, nor to any other place than that in which the two houses shall be sitting.

SECTION VI.

I. The Senators and Representatives shall receive a compensation for their services, to be ascertained by law, and paid out of the treasury of the United States. They shall in all cases except treason, felony, and breach of the peace, be privileged from arrest during their attendance at the session of their respective houses, and in going to and returning from the same; and for any speech or debate in either house, they shall not be questioned in any other place.

II. No Senator or Representative shall, during the time for which he was elected, be appointed to any civil office under the authority of the United States, which shall have been created, or the emoluments whereof shall have been increased during such time; and no person holding any office under the United States, shall be a member of either house during his continuance in office.

SECTION VII.

I. All bills for raising revenue shall originate in the House of Representatives; but the Senate may propose or concur with amendments as on other bills.

II. Every bill which shall have passed the House of Representatives and the Senate, shall, before it becomes a law, be presented to the President of the United States; if he approve, he shall sign it; but if not, he shall return it, with his objections, to that house in which it shall have originated, who shall enter the objections at large on their journal, and proceed to reconsider it. If, after such reconsideration, two thirds of that house shall agree to pass the bill, it shall be sent, together with the objections, to the other house, by which it shall likewise be reconsidered, and if approved by two thirds of that house, it shall become a law. But in all such cases, the votes of both houses shall be determined by yeas and nays, and the names of the persons voting for and against the bill, shall be entered on the journal of each house respectively. If any bill shall not be returned by the President within ten days, (Sundays excepted,) after it shall have been presented to him, the same shall be a law, in the like manner as if he had signed it, unless the Congress by their adjournment prevent its return, in which case it shall not be a law.

III. Every order, resolution, or vote, to which the concurrence of the Senate and House of Representatives may be necessary, (except on a question of adjournment,) shall be presented to the President of the United States; and before the same shall take effect, shall be approved by him, or being disapproved by him, shall be re-passed by two thirds of the Senate and House of Representatives, according to the rules and limitations prescribed in the case of a bill.

SECTION VIII.

The Congress shall have power—

I. To lay and collect taxes, duties, imposts, and excises; to pay the debts, and provide for the common defence and general welfare of the United States; but all duties, imposts, and excises, shall be uniform throughout the United States.

II. To borrow money on the credit of the United States.

III. To regulate commerce with foreign nations, and among the several States, and with the Indian tribes.

IV. To establish a uniform rule of naturalization, and uniform laws on the subject of bankruptcies, throughout the United States.

V. To coin money, regulate the value thereof, and of foreign coin, and fix the standard of weights and measures.

VI. To provide for the punishment of counterfeiting the securities and current coin of the United States.

VII. To establish post offices and post roads.

VIII. To promote the progress of science and useful arts, by securing, for limited times, to authors and inventors, the exclusive right to their respective writings and discoveries.

IX. To constitute tribunals inferior to the supreme court.

X. To define and punish piracies and felonies committed on the high seas, and offences against the laws of nations

XI. To declare war, grant letters of marque and reprisal, and make rules concerning captures on land and water.

XII. To raise and support armies; but no appropriations of money for that use shall be for a longer term than two years.

XIII. To provide and maintain a navy.

XIV. To make rules for the government and regulation of the land and naval forces.

XV. To provide for calling forth the militia to execut the laws of the union, suppress insurrection, and repe invasions.

XVI. To provide for organizing, arming, and disciplining the militia, and for governing such parts of them as may be employed in the service of the United States, reserving to the States respectively the appointment of the officers, and the authority of training the militia, according to the discipline prescribed by Congress.

XVII. To exercise exclusive legislation, in all cases whatsoever, over such district (not exceeding ten miles square) as may by cession of particular States, and the acceptance of Congress, become the seat of the government of the United States, and to exercise like authority over all places purchased by the consent of the legislature of the State in which the same shall be, for the erection of forts, magazines, arsenals, dock-yards, and other needful buildings: and,

XVIII. To make all the laws which shall be necessary and proper for carrying into execution the foregoing powers, and all other powers vested by this constitution in the government of the United States, or in any department or office thereof.

SECTION IX.

I. The migration or importation of such persons as any of the States now existing shall think proper to admit, shall not be prohibited by the Congress prior to the year one thousand eight hundred and eight, but a tax or duty may be imposed on such importation, not exceeding ten dollars for each person.

II. The privilege of the writ of habeas corpus shall

not be suspended, unless when in cases of rebellion or invasion the public safety may require it.

III. No bill of attainder or ex post facto law shall be passed.

IV. No capitation, or other direct tax, shall be laid, unless in proportion to the census of enumeration, herein before directed to be taken.

V. No tax or duty shall be laid on articles exported from any State. No preference shall be given by any regulation of commerce or revenue to the ports of one State over those of another; nor shall vessels bound to or from one State, be obliged to enter, clear, or pay duties in another.

VI. No money shall be drawn from the treasury, but in consequence of appropriations made by law; and a regular statement and account of the receipts and expenditures of all public money shall be published from time to time.

VII. No title of nobility shall be granted by the United States; and no person holding any office of profit or trust under them, shall, without the consent of Congress, accept of any present, emolument, office, or title, of any kind whatever, from any king, prince, or foreign State.

SECTION X.

I. No State shall enter into any treaty, alliance, or confederation; grant letters of marque or reprisal; coin money; emit bills of credit; make any thing but gold and silver coin a tender in payment of debts; pass any bill of attainder, ex post facto law, or law impairing the obligation of contracts, or grant any title of nobility.

II. No State shall, without the consent of Congress, lay any imposts or duties on imports or exports, except what may be absolutely necessary for executing its inspection laws; and the net produce of all duties and imposts laid by any State on imports or exports, shall be for the use of the treasury of the United States, and all such laws shall be subject to the revision and control of Congress. No State shall, without the consent of Congress, lay any duty on tonnage, keep troops, or ships of war, in time of peace, enter into any agreement or compact with another State, or with a foreign power, or engage in war unless actually invaded, or in such imminent danger as will not admit of delay.

ARTICLE II.

SECTION I.

I. The executive power shall be vested in a President of the United States of America. He shall hold his office during the term of four years, and, together with the Vice President, chosen for the same term, be elected as follows:—

II. Each State shall appoint, in such manner as the legislature thereof may direct, a number of electors, equal to the whole number of senators and representatives to which the State may be entitled in the Congress; but no senator or representative, or person holding an office of trust or profit under the United States, shall be appointed an elector.

III. The electors shall meet in their respective States, and vote by ballot for two persons, of whom one at least, shall not be an inhabitant of the same State with themselves. And they shall make a list of all the persons voted for, and of the number of votes for each; which list they shall sign and certify, and transmit, sealed, to the seat of government of the United States, directed to the President of the Senate. The President of the Senate shall, in the presence of the Senate and House of Representatives, open all the certificates, and the votes shall then be counted. The person having the greatest number of votes shall be the President, if such number be a majority of the whole number of electors appointed: and if there be more than one who have such majority, and have an equal number of votes, then the House of Representatives shall immediately choose by ballot one of them for President; and if no person have a majority, then from the five highest on the list the said House shall in like manner choose the President. But in choosing the President, the votes shall be taken by States, the representation from each State having one vote; a quorum for this purpose shall consist of a member or members from two thirds of the States, and a majority of all the States shall be necessary for a choice. In every case after the choice of a President, the person having the greatest number of votes of the electors shall be the Vice President. But if there should remain two or more who have equal votes, the Senate shall choose from them by ballot, the Vice President.

IV. The Congress may determine the time of choosing the electors, and the day on which they shall give their votes; which day shall be the same throughout the United States.

V. No person except a natural born citizen, or a citizen of the United States at the time of the adoption of this constitution, shall be eligible to the office of President, neither shall any person be eligible to that office who shall not have attained the age of thirty-five years and been fourteen years a resident of the United States.

VI. In case of the removal of the President from office, or of his death, resignation, or inability to discharge the powers and duties of the said office, the same shall devolve on the Vice President, and the Congress may by law provide for the case of the removal, death, resignation, or inability, both of the President or Vice President, declaring what officer shall then act as President, and such officer shall act accordingly, until the disability be removed, or a President shall be elected.

VII. The President shall, at stated times, receive for his services a compensation, which shall neither be increased nor diminished during the period for which he shall have been elected, and he shall not receive within that period, any other emolument from the United States, or any of them.

VIII. Before he enter on the execution of his office, he shall take the following oath or affirmation:

"I do solemnly swear (or affirm) that I will faithfully execute the office of President of the United States, and will, to the best of my ability, preserve, protect, and defend the constitution of the United States."

SECTION II.

I. The President shall be commander-in-chief of the army and navy of the United States, and of the mi

litia of the several States, when called into the actual
service of the United States; he may require the opinion, in writing, of the principal officer in each of the
executive departments, upon any subject relating to the
duties of their respective offices; and he shall have the
power to grant reprieves and pardons for offences against
the United States, except in cases of impeachment.

II. He shall have power by and with the advice and
consent of the Senate, to make treaties, provided two
thirds of the Senators present concur; and he shall nominate, and, by and with the advice and consent of the
Senate, appoint ambassadors, other public ministers, and
consuls, judges of the supreme court, and all other officers of the United States, whose appointments are not
herein otherwise provided for, and which shall be established by law. But the Congress may by law vest the appointment of such inferior officers, as they think proper,
in the President alone, in the courts of law, or in the
heads of departments.

III. The President shall have power to fill up all vacancies that may happen during the recess of the Senate,
by granting commissions which shall expire at the end
of their next session.

SECTION III.

I. He shall, from time to time, give to the Congress
information of the state of the Union, and recommend to
their consideration such measures as he shall judge necessary and expedient; he may, on extraordinary occasions, convene both houses, or either of them, and, in
case of disagreement between them, with respect to the
time of adjournment, he may adjourn them to such time
as he shall think proper; he shall receive ambassadors
and other public ministers; he shall take care that the
laws be faithfully executed; and shall commission all
the officers of the United States.

SECTION IV.

I. The President, Vice President, and all civil officers
of the United States, shall be removed from office, on impeachment for, and conviction of, treason, bribery, or
other high crimes and misdemeanors.

ARTICLE III.

SECTION I.

I. The judicial power of the United States shall be vested in one supreme court, and in such inferior courts as the congress may from time to time order and establish. The judges, both of the supreme and inferior courts, shall, hold their offices during good behaviour; and shall at stated times, receive for their services a compensation which shall not be diminished during their continuance in office.

SECTION II.

I. The judicial power shall extend to all cases in law and equity, arising under this constitution, the laws of the United States, and treaties made, or which shall be made, under their authority; to all cases of admiralty and maritime jurisdiction; to controversies to which the United States shall be a party; to controversies between two or more States, between a State and citizens of another State, between citizens of different States, between citizens of the same State claiming lands under grants of different States, between a State, or the citizens thereof, and foreign States, citizens, or subjects.

II. In all cases affecting ambassadors, other public ministers, and consuls, and those in which a State shall be a party, the supreme court shall have original jurisdiction. In all other cases before mentioned, the supreme court shall have appellate jurisdiction, both as to law and fact, with such exceptions, and under such regulations, as the Congress shall make.

III. The trial of all crimes, except in cases of impeachment, shall be by jury; and such trials shall be held in the State where the said crimes shall have been committed; but when not committed within any State the trial shall be at such place or places as the Congress may by law have directed.

SECTION III.

I. Treason against the United States shall consist only in levying war against them, or in adhering to their enemies, giving them aid and comfort. No person shall be convicted of treason, unless on the testimony of two witnesses to the same overt act, or on confession in open court.

II. The Congress shall have power to declare the punishment of treason; but no attainder of treason shall work corruption of blood or forfeiture, except during the life of the person attainted.

ARTICLE IV.

SECTION I.

I. Full faith and credit shall be given in each State, to the public acts, records, and judicial proceedings of every other State. And the Congress may, by general laws, prescribe the manner in which such acts, records, and proceedings, shall be proved, and the effect thereof.

SECTION II.

I. The citizens of each State shall be entitled to all privileges and immunities of citizens in the several States.

II. A person charged, in any State, with treason, felony, or other crime, who shall flee from justice and be found in another State, shall, on demand of the executive authority of the State from which he is fled, be delivered up, to be removed to the State having jurisdiction of the crime.

III. No person held to service or labour in one State, under the laws thereof, escaping into another, shall, in consequence of any law or regulation therein, be discharged from such service or labour: but shall be delivered up on claim of the party to whom such service or labour may be due.

SECTION III.

I. New States may be admitted by the Congress into this Union; but no new State shall be formed or erected within the jurisdiction of any other State, nor any State be formed by the junction of two or more States, or parts of States, without the consent of the Legislatures of the States concerned, as well as of the Congress.

II. The Congress shall have power to dispose of and

make all needful rules and regulations respecting the territory or other property belonging to the United States; and nothing in this Constitution shall be so construed as to prejudice any claims of the United States, or of any particular State.

SECTION IV

I. The United States shall guaranty to every State in the Union, a republican form of government, and shall protect each of them against invasion; and on application of the Legislature, or of the Executive, (when the Legislature cannot be convened,) against domestic violence.

ARTICLE V.

I. The Congress, whenever two thirds of both houses shall deem it necessary, shall propose amendments to this Constitution, or on the application of the Legislatures of two thirds of the several States, shall call a Convention for proposing amendments, which, in either case, shall be valid to all intents and purposes, as a part of this Constitution, when ratified by the Legislatures of three fourths of the several States, or by Conventions in three fourths thereof, as the one or the other mode of ratification may be proposed by the Congress: Provided, that no amendment which may be made prior to the year one thousand eight hundred and eight shall in any manner affect the first and fourth clauses in the ninth section of the first article; and that no State, without its consent, shall be deprived of its equal suffrage in the Senate.

ARTICLE VI.

I. All debts contracted, and engagements entered into, before the adoption of this Constitution, shall be as valid against the United States under this Constitution, as under the confederation.

II. This Constitution, and the laws of the United States which shall be made in pursuance thereof; and all treaties made, or which shall be made, under the authority of the United States, shall be the supreme law of the land; and the judges in every State shall be bound thereby, any thing in the Constitution or laws of any State to the contrary notwithstanding.

III. The Senators and Representatives before mentioned, and the members of the several State Legislatures and all executive and judicial officers, both of the United States and of the several States, shall be bound by oath or affirmation, to support this Constitution; but no religious test shall ever be required as a qualification to any office or public trust under the United States.

ARTICLE VII.

I. The ratifications of the Conventions of nine States, shall be sufficient for the establishment of this Constitution between the States so ratifying the same.

Done in Convention by the unanimous consent of the States present, the seventeenth day of September, in the year of our Lord one thousand seven hundred and eighty-seven, and of the Independence of the United States of America, the twelfth. In witness whereof, we have hereunto subscribed our names.

NEW HAMPSHIRE.—John Langdon, Nicholas Gilman.
MASSACHUSETTS.—Nathaniel Gorham, Rufus King.
CONNECTICUT.—William S. Johnson, Roger Sherman.
NEW YORK.—Alexander Hamilton.
NEW JERSEY.—William Livingston, David Brearly, William Patterson, Jonathan Dayton.
PENNSYLVANIA.—Benjamin Franklin, Thomas Mifflin, Robert Morris, George Clymer, Thomas Fitzsimons, Jared Ingersol, James Wilson, Governeur Morris.
DELAWARE.—George Read, Gunning Bedford, Jun., John Dickinson, Richard Bassett, Jacob Broom.
MARYLAND.—James M'Henry, Daniel of St. Thomas Jenifer, Daniel Carroll.
VIRGINIA.—John Blair, James Madison, Junr.
NORTH CAROLINA.—William Blount, Richard Dobbs Spaight, Hugh Williamson.
SOUTH CAROLINA.—John Rutledge, Charles C. Pinckney, Pierce Butler.
GEORGIA.—William Few, Abraham Baldwin.
GEORGE WASHINGTON, President.
WILLIAM JACKSON, Secretary.

AMENDMENTS

TO THE

CONSTITUTION OF THE UNITED STATES.

Since the adoption of the foregoing Constitution, the following amendments have been made, and ratified by the Legislatures of three fourths of the several States in the Union.

ARTICLE I.

Congress shall make no law respecting the establishment of religion, or prohibiting the free exercise thereof; or abridging the freedom of speech, or of the press; or the right of the people peaceably to assemble, and to petition the government for a redress of grievances.

ARTICLE II.

A well regulated militia being necessary to the security of a free State, the right of the people to keep and bear arms shall not be infringed.

ARTICLE III.

No soldier shall, in time of peace, be quartered in any house, without the consent of the owner; nor in time of war, but in a manner to be prescribed by law.

ARTICLE IV.

The right of the people to be secure in their persons, houses, papers, and effects, against unreasonable searches and seizures, shall not be violated; and no warrants shall issue, but upon probable cause, supported by oath or affirmation, and particularly describing the place to be searched, and the persons or things to be seized.

ARTICLE V.

No person shall be held to answer for a capital or otherwise infamous crime, unless on a presentment or indictment of a grand jury, except in cases arising in the land and naval forces, or in the militia, when in actual service in time of war or public danger; nor shall any person be subject, for the same offence, to be twice put in jeopardy of life or limb; nor shall be compelled, in any criminal case, to be a witness against himself; nor be deprived of life, liberty, or property, without due process of law; nor shall private property be taken for public use, without due compensation.

ARTICLE VI.

In all criminal prosecutions, the accused shall enjoy the right to a speedy and public trial, by an impartial jury of the State and district wherein the crime shall have been committed, (which district shall have been previously ascertained by law,) and to be informed of the nature and cause of the accusation; and to be confronted with the witnesses against him; to have compulsory process for obtaining witnesses in his favour, and to have the assistance of counsel for his defence.

ARTICLE VII.

In suits at common law, where the value in controversy shall exceed twenty dollars, the right of trial by jury shall be preserved, and no fact tried by a jury, shall be otherwise re-examined in any court of the United States, than according to the rules of the common law.

ARTICLE VIII.

Excessive bail shall not be required, nor excessive fines imposed, nor cruel and unusual punishments inflicted.

ARTICLE IX.

The enumeration in the Constitution of certain rights, shall not be construed to deny or disparage others retained by the people.

ARTICLE X.

The powers not delegated to the United States by the Constitution, nor prohibited by it to the States, are reserved to the States respectively, or to the people.

ARTICLE XI.

The judicial power of the United States shall not be construed to extend to any suit in law or equity, commenced or prosecuted against one of the United States, by citizens of another State, or by citizens or subjects of any foreign State.

ARTICLE XII.

The electors shall meet in their respective States, and vote by ballot for President and Vice President, one of whom, at least, shall not be an inhabitant of the same State with themselves; they shall name in their ballots the persons voted for as President, and in distinct ballots of all persons voted for as Vice President; and they shall make distinct lists for all persons voted for as President, and for all persons voted for as Vice President, and of the number of votes for each, which lists they shall sign and certify, and transmit, sealed, to the seat of government of the United States, directed to the President of the Senate; the President of the Senate shall, in the presence of the Senate and House of Representatives, open all the certificates, and the votes shall then be counted: the person having the greatest number of votes for President shall be the President, if such number be a majority of the whole number of electors appointed; and if no person have such a majority, then from the persons having the highest numbers, not exceeding three, on the list of those voted for as President, the House of Representatives shall choose immediately, by ballot, the President. But in choosing the President, the votes shall be taken by States, the representatives from each State having one vote: a quorum for his purpose shall consist of a member or members from wo thirds of the States, and a majority of all the States shall be necessary to a choice; and if the House of Representatives shall not choose a President, whenever the right of choice shall devolve upon them, before the fourth day of March next following, then the Vice President shall act as President, as in case of death, or other constitutional disability of the President.

The person having the greatest number of votes as Vice President, shall be the Vice President, if such number be a majority of the whole number of electors appointed; and if no person have a majority, then from the two highest numbers on the list, the Senate shall choose the Vice President; a quorum for this purpose shall consist of two thirds of the whole number of senators, and a majority of he whole number shall be necessary to a choice.

But no person constitutionally ineligible to the office of President, shall be eligible to that of Vice President of the United States.

ARTICLE XIII.

If any citizen of the United States shall accept, claim, receive, or retain any title of nobility or honour, or shall, without the consent of Congress, accept and retain any present, pension, office, or emolument of any kind whatever, from any emperor, king, prince, or foreign power, such person shall cease to be a citizen of the United States, and shall be inca[pable] of holding any office of trust or profit under them, or either of them.

ARTICLE XIV.

After the first enumeration required by the first article of the Constitution, there shall be one representative for every thirty thousand, until the number shall amount to one hundred, after which the proportion shall be so regulated by Congress, that there shall be not less than one hundred representatives, or less than one representative for every forty thousand persons, until the number of representatives shall amount to two hundred, and after which the proportion shall be so regulated by Congress, that there shall not be less than two hundred representatives, nor more than one representative for every fifty thousand persons.

ARTICLE XV.

No law, varying the compensation for the services of the senators and representatives, shall take effect, until an election of representatives shall have intervened.

THE FAREWELL ADDRESS

OF

GEORGE WASHINGTON.

Friends and Fellow-Citizens,

The period for a new election of a citizen, to administer the executive government of the United States, being not far distant, and the time actually arrived, when your thoughts must be employed in designating the person who is to be clothed with that important trust, it appears to me proper, especially as it may conduce to a more distinct expression of the public voice, that I should now apprize you of the resolution I have formed, to decline being considered among the number of those out of whom a choice is to be made. I beg you, at the same time, to do me the justice to be assured, that this resolution has not been taken, without a strict regard to all the considerations appertaining to the relation which binds a dutiful citizen to his country; and that, in withdrawing the tender of service which silence in my situation might imply, I am influenced by no diminution of zeal for your future interest; no deficiency of grateful respect, for your past kindness; but am supported by a full conviction that the step is compatible with both.

2. The acceptance of, and continuance hitherto in, the office to which your suffrages have twice called me, have been a uniform sacrifice of inclination to the opinion of duty, and to a deference for what appeared to be your desire. I constantly hoped, that it would have been much earlier in my power, consistently with motives which I was not at liberty to disregard, to return to that retirement

from which I have been reluctantly drawn. The strength of my inclination to do this, previous to the last election, had even led to the preparation of an address to declare it to you; but mature reflection on the then perplexed and critical posture of our affairs with foreign nations, and the unanimous advice of persons entitled to my confidence, impelled me to abandon the idea.

3. I rejoice that the state of your concerns, external as well as internal, no longer renders the pursuit of inclination incompatible with the sentiment of duty, or propriety; and am persuaded, whatever partiality may be retained for my services, that in the present circumstances of our country, you will not disapprove my determination to retire.

4. The impressions with which I first undertook the arduous trust, were explained on the proper occasion. In the discharge of this trust, I will only say, that 1 have, with good intentions, contributed towards the organization and administration of the government, the best exertions of which a very fallible judgment was capable. Not unconscious, in the outset, of the inferiority of my qualifications, experience in my own eyes, perhaps still more in the eyes of others, has strengthened the motives to diffidence of myself; and, every day, the increasing weight of years admonishes me more and more that the shade of retirement is as necessary to me as it will be welcome. Satisfied that if any circumstances have given peculiar value to my services, they were temporary, I have the consolation to believe, that while choice and prudence invite me to quit the political scene, patriotism does not forbid it.

5. In looking forward to the moment, which is intended to terminate the career of my public life, my feelings do not permit me to suspend the deep acknowledgment of that debt of gratitude which I owe to my beloved country, for the many honours it has conferred upon me; still more for the steadfast confidence with which it has supported me; and for the opportunities I have thence enjoyed of manifesting my inviolable attachment, by services faithful and persevering, though in usefulness une-

qual to my zeal. If benefits have resulted to our country from these services, let it always be remembered to your praise, and as an instructive example in our annals, that under circumstances in which the passions, agitated in every direction, were liable to mislead, amidst appearances sometimes dubious—vicissitudes of fortune often discouraging—in situations in which not unfrequently want of success has countenanced the spirit of criticism —the constancy of your support was the essential prop of the efforts, and the guarantee of the plans by which they were effected.

6. Profoundly penetrated with this idea, I shall carry it with me to my grave, as a strong incitement to unceasing vows that Heaven may continue to you the choicest tokens of its benevolence—that your union and brotherly affection may be perpetual—that the free constitution, which is the work of your hands, may be sacredly maintained—that its administration in every department may be stamped with wisdom and virtue—that, in fine, the happiness of the people of these states, under the auspices of liberty, may be made complete, by so careful a preservation, and so prudent a use of this blessing, as will acquire to them the glory of recommending it to the applause, the affection, and the adoption of every nation which is yet a stranger to it.

7. Here, perhaps, I ought to stop. But a solicitude for your welfare, which cannot end but with my life, and the apprehension of danger, natural to that solicitude, urge me, on an occasion like the present, to offer to your solemn contemplation, and to recommend to your frequent review, some sentiments, which are the result of much reflection, of no inconsiderable observation, and which appear to me all important to the permanency of your felicity as a people. These will be offered to you with the more freedom, as you can only see in them the disinterested warnings of a parting friend, who can possibly have no personal motives to bias his counsel. Nor can I forget as an encouragement to it, your indulgent reception of my sentiments on a former and not dissimilar occasion. Interwoven as is the love of liberty with every ligament

of your hearts, no recommendation of mine is necessary to fortify or confirm the attachment.

8. The unity of government which constitutes you one people is also now dear to you. It is justly so; for it is a main pillar in the edifice of your real independence, the support of your tranquillity at home, your peace abroad; of your safety; of your prosperity; of that very liberty which you so highly prize. But as it is easy to foresee, that from different causes, and from different quarters, much pains will be taken, many artifices employed, to weaken in your minds the conviction of this truth; as this is the point in your political fortress against which the batteries of internal and external enemies will be most constantly and actively (though often covertly and insidiously) directed, it is of infinite moment, that you should properly estimate the immense value of your national union, to your collective and individual happiness; that you should cherish a cordial, habitual, and immoveable attachment to it; accustoming yourselves to think and speak of it as of the palladium of your political safety and prosperity; watching for its preservation with jealous anxiety; discountenancing whatever may suggest even a suspicion that it can in any event be abandoned; and indignantly frowning upon the first dawning of every attempt to alienate any portion of our country from the rest, or to enfeeble the sacred ties which now link together the various parts.

9. For this you have every inducement of sympathy and interest. Citizens by birth or choice, of a common country, that country has a right to concentrate your affections. The name of *America*, which belongs to you in your national capacity, must always exalt the just pride of patriotism, more than any appellation derived from local discriminations. With slight shades of difference, you have the same religion, manners, habits, and political principles. You have, in a common cause, fought and triumphed together; the independence and liberty you possess, are the work of joint councils, and joint efforts, of common dangers, sufferings, and successes. But these considerations, however powerfully they address

themselves to your sensibility, are greatly outweighed by those which apply more immediately to your interest—here every portion of our country finds the most commanding motives for carefully guarding and preserving the union of the whole.

10. The *North*, in an unrestrained intercourse with the *South*, protected by the equal laws of a common government, finds in the productions of the latter, great additional resources of maritime and commercial enterprise, and precious materials of manufacturing industry. The *South*, in the same intercourse, benefiting by the agency of the *North*, sees its agriculture grow and its commerce expand. Turning partly into its own channels the seamen of the *North*, it finds its particular navigation invigorated; and while it contributes, in different ways, to nourish and increase the general mass of the national navigation, it looks forward to the protection of a maritime strength, to which itself is unequally adapted. The *East*, in a like intercourse with the *West*, already finds, and in the progressive improvement of interior communications, by land and water, will more and more find, a valuable vent for the commodities which it brings from abroad, or manufactures at home. The *West* derives from the *East* supplies requisite to its growth and comfort; and what is perhaps of still greater consequence, it must of necessity owe the secure enjoyment of indispensable *outlets* for its own productions, to the weight, influence, and the future maritime strength of the Atlantic side of the Union, directed by an indissoluble community of interest as ONE NATION. Any other tenure by which the *West* can hold this essential advantage, whether derived from its own separate strength, or from an apostate and unnatural connexion with any foreign power, must be intrinsically precarious.

11. While, then, every part of our country thus feels an immediate and particular interest in union, all the parties combined cannot fail to find, in the united mass of means and efforts, greater strength, greater resources, proportionably greater security from external danger, a less frequent interruption of their peace by foreign nations;

and, what is of inestimable value! they must derive from union an exemption from those broils and wars between themselves, which so frequently afflict neighbouring countries, not tied together by the same government; which their own rivalships alone would be sufficient to produce, but which opposite foreign alliances, attachments, and intrigues, would stimulate and embitter. Hence, likewise, they will avoid the necessity of those overgrown military establishments, which, under any form of government, are inauspicious to liberty, and which are to be regarded as particularly hostile to republican liberty; in this sense it is, that your union ought to be considered as a main prop of your liberty, and that the love of the one ought to endear to you the preservation of the other.

12. These considerations speak a persuasive language to every reflecting and virtuous mind, and exhibit the continuance of the *Union* as a primary object of patriotic desire. Is there a doubt whether a common government can embrace so large a sphere? Let experience solve it. To listen to mere speculation in such a case were criminal. We are authorized to hope that a proper organization of the whole, with the auxiliary agency of government for the respective subdivisions, will afford a happy issue to the experiment. 'Tis well worth a fair and full experiment. With such powerful and obvious motives to union, affecting all parts of our country, while experience shall not have demonstrated its impracticability, there will always be reason to distrust the patriotism of those, who, in any quarter, may endeavour to weaken its bands.

13. In contemplating the causes which may disturb our Union, it occurs as a matter of serious concern, that any ground should have been furnished for characterizing parties by *geographical* discriminations—*northern* and *southern*—*Atlantic and western;* whence designing men may endeavour to excite a belief that there is a real difference of local interests and views. One of the expedients of party to acquire influence within particular districts, is to misrepresent the opinions and aims of other districts. You cannot shield yourselves too much against the jealousies and heart-burnings which spring from these

misrepresentations: they tend to render alien to each other those who ought to be bound together by fraternal affection. The inhabitants of our western country have lately had a useful lesson on this head: they have seen in the negotiation by the executive, and in the unanimous ratification by the senate, of the treaty with Spain, and in the universal satisfaction at that event throughout the United States, a decisive proof how unfounded were the suspicions propagated among them, of a policy in the general government and in the Atlantic States, unfriendly to their interests in regard to the *Mississippi:* they have been witnesses to the formation of two treaties, that with Great Britain and that with Spain, which secure to them every thing they could desire, in respect to our foreign relations, towards confirming their prosperity. Will it not be their wisdom to rely for the preservation of these advantages on the UNION by which they were procured? Will they not henceforth be deaf to those advisers, if such there are, who would sever them from their brethren, and connect them with aliens?

14. To the efficacy and permanency of your Union, a government for the whole is indispensable. No alliances, however strict, between the parts, can be an adequate substitute: they must inevitably experience the infractions and interruptions which all alliances in all times have experienced. Sensible of this momentous truth, you have improved upon your first essay, by the adoption of a constitution of government, better calculated than your former, for an intimate union, and for the efficacious management of your common concerns. This government, the offspring of our own choice, uninfluenced and unawed, adopted upon full investigation and mature deliberation, completely free in its principles, in the distribution of its powers uniting security with energy, and containing within itself a provision for its own amendment, has a just claim to your confidence and your support. Respect for its authority, compliance with its laws, acquiescence in its measures, are duties enjoined by the fundamental maxims of true liberty. The basis of our political system, is the right of the people to make and alter their constitutions of government.

But, the Constitution which at any time exists, till changed by an explicit and authentic act of the whole people, is sacredly obligatory upon all. The very idea of the power and the right of the people to establish government, presupposes the duty of every individual to obey the established government.

15. All obstructions to the execution of the Laws, all combinations and associations, under whatever plausible character, with the real design to direct, control, counteract, or awe the regular deliberation and action of the constituted authorities, are destructive of this fundamental principle, and of fatal tendency. They serve to organize faction, to give it an artificial and extraordinary force—to put in the place of the delegated will of the nation, the will of a party, often a small but artful and enterprising minority of the community; and, according to the alternate triumphs of different parties, to make the public administration the mirror of the ill-concerted and incongruous projects of faction, rather than the organ of consistent and wholesome plans, digested by common councils, and modified by mutual interests. However combinations or associations of the above description may now and then answer popular ends, they are likely in the course of time and things to become potent engines, by which cunning, ambitious, and unprincipled men, will be enabled to subvert the power of the people, and to usurp to themselves the reins of government; destroying afterwards the very engines which have lifted them to unjust dominion.

16. Towards the preservation of your government, and the permanency of your present happy state, it is requisite, not only that you speedily discountenance irregular oppositions to its acknowledged authority, but also that you resist with care the spirit of innovation upon its principles, however specious the pretexts. One method of assault may be to effect in the forms of the constitution, alterations which impair the energy of the system, and thus to undermine what cannot be directly overthrown. In all the changes o which you may be invited, remember that time and habit are at least as necessary to fix the true character o governments as of other human institutions;—that experi

ence is the surest standard by which to test the real tendency of the existing constitution of a country—that facility in changes upon the credit of mere hypothesis and opinion, exposes to perpetual change from the endless variety of hypothesis and opinion; and remember, especially, that for the efficient management of your common interests, in a country so extensive as ours, a government of as much vigour as is consistent with the perfect security of liberty, is indispensable. Liberty itself will find in such a government, with powers properly distributed and adjusted, its surest guardian. It is, indeed, little else than a name, where the government is too feeble to withstand the enterprises of faction, to confine each member of the society within the limits prescribed by the laws, and to maintain all in the secure and tranquil enjoyment of the rights of person and property.

17. I have already intimated to you, the danger of parties in the State, with particular reference to the founding of them on geographical discriminations. Let me now take a more comprehensive view, and warn you in the most solemn manner against the baneful effects of the spirit of party, generally. The spirit, unfortunately, is inseparable from our nature, having its root in the strongest passions of the human mind. It exists under different shapes in all governments, more or less stifled, controlled, or repressed; but in those of the popular form, it is seen in its greatest rankness, and is truly their worst enemy. The alternate domination of one faction over another, sharpened by the spirit of revenge, natural to party dissension, which, in different ages and countries, has perpetrated the most horrid enormities, is itself a frightful despotism. But this leads at length to a more formal and permanent despotism. The disorders and miseries which result, gradually incline the minds of men to seek security and repose in the absolute power of an individual: and sooner or later the chief of some prevailing faction, more able or more fortunate than his competitor, turns this disposition to the purposes of his own elevation, on the ruins of public liberty.

18. Without looking forward to an extremity of this kind, (which nevertheless ought not to be entirely out of

sight,) the common and continual mischiefs of the spirit of party, are sufficient to make it the interest and duty of a wise people to discourage and restrain it. It serves always to distract the public councils and enfeeble the public administration. It agitates the community with ill-founded jealousies and false alarms; kindles the animosity of one part against another; foments occasionally riot and insurrection. It opens the door to foreign influence and corruption, which find a facilitated access to the government itself through the channels of party passions. Thus the policy and the will of one country are subjected to the policy and will of another.

19. There is an opinion that parties in free countries are useful checks upon the administration of the government, and serve to keep alive the spirit of liberty. This within certain limits is probably true; and in governments of a monarchical cast, patriotism may look with indulgence, if not with favour, upon the spirit of party. But in those of a popular character, in governments purely elective, it is a spirit not to be encouraged. From their natural tendency, it is certain there will always be enough of that spirit for every salutary purpose. And there being constant danger of excess, the effort ought to be by force of public opinion, to mitigate and assuage it. A fire not to be quenched, it demands a uniform vigilance to prevent its bursting into a flame, lest instead of warming, it should consume.

20. It is important likewise, that the habits of thinking in a free country, should inspire caution, in those intrusted with its administration, to confine themselves within their respective constitutional spheres, avoiding, in the exercise of the powers of one department, to encroach upon another. The spirit of encroachment, tends to consolidate the powers of all the departments in one, and thus to create, whatever the form of government, a real despotism. A just estimate of that love of power, and proneness to abuse it, which predominates in the human heart, is sufficient to satisfy us of the truth of this position. The necessity of reciprocal checks in the exercise of political power, by dividing and distributing it into different depositaries, and

constituting each the guardian of public weal against invasions by the others, has been evinced by experiments ancient and modern: some of them in our country and under our own eyes. To preserve them must be as necessary as to constitute them. If, in the opinion of the people, the distribution or modification of the constitutional powers be in any particular wrong, let it be corrected by an amendment in the way which the constitution designates. But let there be no change by usurpation; for though this, in one instance may be the instrument of good, it is the customary weapon by which free governments are destroyed. The precedent must always greatly overbalance in permanent evil any partial or transient benefit which the use can at any time yield.

21. Of all the dispositions and habits which lead to political prosperity, religion and morality are indispensable supports. In vain would that man claim the tribute of patriotism, who should labour to subvert these great pillars of human happiness, these firmest props of the duties of men and citizens. The mere politician, equally with the pious man, ought to respect and to cherish them. A volume could not trace all their connexions with private and public felicity. Let it simply be asked, where is the security for property, for reputation, for life, if the sense of religious obligation DESERT the oaths, which are the instruments of investigation in courts of justice; and let us with caution indulge the supposition, that morality can be maintained without religion. Whatever may be conceded to the influence of refined education on minds of peculiar structure, reason and experience both forbid us to expect that national morality can prevail in exclusion of religious principle. 'Tis substantially true, that virtue or morality is a necessary spring of popular government. The rule indeed extends with more or less force to every species of free government. Who that is a sincere friend to it can look with indifference upon attempts to shake the foundation of the fabric?

22. Promote, then, as an object of primary importance, institutions for the general diffusion of knowledge. In

proportion as the structure of a government gives force to public opinion, it is essential that public opinion should be enlightened. As a very important source of strength and security, cherish public credit: one method of preserving it is to use it as sparingly as possible; avoiding occasions of expense, by cultivating peace; and remembering also that timely disbursements to prepare for danger frequently prevent much greater disbursements to repel it; avoiding likewise the accumulations of debt, not only by shunning occasions of expense, but by vigorous exertions in time of peace to discharge the debts which unavoidable wars may have occasioned, not ungenerously throwing upon posterity the burden which we ourselves ought to bear. The execution of these maxims belongs to your representatives, but it is necessary that public opinion should co-operate. To facilitate to them the performance of their duty, it is essential that you should practically bear in mind, that towards the payment of debts there must be revenue; to have revenue there must be taxes; that no taxes can be devised which are not more or less inconvenient and unpleasant; and the intrinsic embarrassment inseparable from the selection of the proper object, (which is always a choice of difficulties,) ought to be a decisive motive for a candid construction of the conduct of the government in making it, and for a spirit of acquiescence in the measures for obtaining revenue which the public exigencies may at any time dictate.

23. Observe good faith and justice towards all nations; cultivate peace and harmony with all. Religion and morality enjoin this conduct; and can it be that good policy does not equally enjoin it? It will be worthy of a free, enlightened, and at no distant period, a great nation, to give to mankind the magnanimous and too novel example of a people always guided by an exalted justice and benevolence. Who can doubt that in the course of time and things, the fruits of such a plan would richly repay any temporary advantages which might be lost by a steady adherence to it? Can it be, that providence has not connected the permanent felicity of a nation with its

virtue? The experiment, at least, is recommended by every sentiment which ennobles human nature. Alas! is it rendered impossible by its vices?

24. In the execution of such a plan, nothing is more essential, than that permanent inveterate antipathies against particular nations, and passionate attachments for others, should be excluded; and that in place of them just and amicable feelings towards all should be cultivated. The nation, which indulges towards another an habitual hatred, or an habitual fondness, is in some degree a slave It is a slave to its animosity or to its affection, either of which is sufficient to lead it astray from its duty and its interest. Antipathy in one nation against another, disposes each more readily to offer insult and injury, to lay hold of slight causes of umbrage, and to be haughty and intractable, when accidental or trifling occasions of dispute occur. Hence frequent collisions, obstinate, envenomed, and bloody contests. The nation, prompted by ill will and resentment, sometimes impels to war the government, contrary to the best calculations of policy. The government sometimes participates in the national propensity, and adopts through passion what reason would reject; at other times, it makes the animosity of the nation subservient to projects of hostility instigated by pride, ambition, and other sinister and pernicious motives. The peace often, sometimes perhaps the liberty, of nations, has been the victim.

25. So likewise a passionate attachment of one nation for another, produces a variety of evils. Sympathy for the favourite nation, facilitating the illusion of an imaginary common interest, in cases where no real common interest exists, and infusing into one the enmities of the other, betrays the former into a participation in the quarrels and wars of the latter, without adequate inducement or justification. It leads also to the concessions to the favourite nation of privileges denied to others, which is apt doubly to injure the nation making the concessions; by unnecessarily parting with what ought to have been retained, and by exciting jealousy, ill will, and a disposition to retaliate, in the parties from whom equal privi

'eges are withheld,—and it gives to ambitious, corrupted, or deluded citizens, (who devote themselves to the favourite nation,) facility to betray or sacrifice the interests of their own country without odium, sometimes even with popularity; gilding with the appearances of a virtuous sense of obligation, a commendable deference for public opinion, or a laudable zeal for public good, the base or foolish compliances of ambition, corruption, or infatuation.

26. As avenues to foreign influence in innumerable ways, such attachments are particularly alarming to the truly enlightened and independent patriot. How many opportunities do they afford to tamper with domestic factions, to practise the arts of seduction, to mislead public opinions, to influence or awe public councils! Such an attachment of small or weak, towards a great and powerful nation, dooms the former to be the satellites of the latter. Against the insidious wiles of foreign influence, (I conjure you to believe me, fellow citizens,) the jealousy of a free people ought to be CONSTANTLY awake; since history and experience prove that foreign influence is one of the most baneful foes of republican government. But that jealousy, to be useful, must be impartial: else it becomes the instrument of the very influence to be avoided, instead of a defence against it. Excessive partiality for one foreign nation, and excessive dislike of another, cause those whom they actuate, to see danger only on one side, and serve to veil and even second the arts of influence on the other. Real patriots, who may resist the intrigues of the favourite, are liable to become suspected and odious; while its tools and dupes usurp the applause and confidence of the people, to surrender heir interests. The great rule of conduct for us, in regard to foreign nations, is, in extending our commercial relations, to have with them as little political connexion as possible. So far as we have already formed engagements, let them be fulfilled with perfect good faith. Here let us stop.

27. Europe has a set of primary interests, which to us have none, or a very remote relation. Hence she must be engaged in frequent controversies, the causes of

which are essentially foreign to our concerns. Hence, therefore, it must be unwise in us to implicate ourselves by artificial ties, in the ordinary vicissitudes of her politics, or the ordinary combinations and collisions of her friendships or enmities. Our detached and distant situation invites and enables us to pursue a different course. If we remain one people, under an efficient government, the period is not far off, when we may defy material injury from external annoyance; when we may take such an attitude, as will cause the neutrality we may at any time resolve upon, to be scrupulously respected; when belligerent nations, under the impossibility of making acquisitions upon us, will not lightly hazard the giving us provocation; when we may choose peace or war, as our interest, guided by justice, shall counsel.

28. Why forego the advantages of so peculiar a situation? Why quit our own to stand upon foreign ground? Why, by interweaving our destiny with that of any part of Europe, entangle our peace and prosperity in the toils of European ambition, rivalship, interest, humour, or caprice? 'Tis our true policy to steer clear of permanent alliances with any portion of the foreign world; so far, I mean, as we are now at liberty to do it; for let me not be understood as patronising infidelity to existing engagements. I hold the maxim no less applicable to public than to private affairs, that honesty is always the best policy. I repeat it, therefore, let those engagements be observed in their genuine sense. But, in my opinion, it is unnecessary, and would be unwise, to extend them. Taking care always to keep ourselves, by suitable establishments, on a respectable defensive posture, we may safely trust to temporary alliances for extraordinary emergencies.

29. Harmony, liberal intercourse with all nations, are recommended by policy, humanity, and interest. But even our commercial policy should hold an equal and impartial hand: neither seeking nor granting exclusive favours or preferences; consulting the natural course of things; diffusing and diversifying, by gentle means, the streams of commerce, but forcing nothing; establishing

with powers so disposed, in order to give trade a stable
course, to define the rights of our merchants, and to enable the government to support them, conventional rules
of intercourse, the best that present circumstances and
mutual opinion will permit, but temporary, and liable to
be from time to time abandoned or varied, as experience
and circumstances shall dictate; constantly keeping in
view, that 'tis folly in one nation to look for disinterested
favours from another; that it must pay with a portion of
its independence whatever it may accept under that character; that by such acceptance, it may place itself in
the condition of having given equivalent for nominal favours, and yet of being reproached with ingratitude for
not giving more. There can be no greater error than to
expect or calculate upon real favours from nation to nation. 'Tis an illusion which experience must cure, which
a just pride ought to discard.

30. In offering to you, my countrymen, these counsels
of an old and affectionate friend, I dare not hope they
will make the strong and lasting impression I could wish;
that they will control the usual current of the passions,
or prevent our nation from running the course which has
hitherto marked the destiny of nations: but if I may
even flatter myself, that they may be productive of some
partial benefit, some occasional good; that they may now
and then recur to moderate the fury of party spirit, to
warn against the mischiefs of foreign intrigues, and
guard against the impostures of pretended patriotism,
this hope will be a full recompense for the solicitude for
your welfare, by which they have been dictated. How
far, in the discharge of my official duties, I have been
guided by the principles which have been delineated, the
public records, and other evidences of my conduct, must
witness to you and to the world. To myself, the assurance of my own conscience is, that I have at least believed myself to be guided by them.

31. In relation to the still subsisting war in Europe,
my proclamation of the 22d of April, 1793, is the index
to my plan. Sanctioned by your approving voice, and
by that of your representatives in both houses of con

gress, the spirit of that measure has continually governed me; uninfluenced by any attempt to deter or divert me from it. After deliberate examination, with the aid of the best lights I could obtain, I was well satisfied that our country, under all the circumstances of the case, had a right to take, and was bound in duty and interest to take, a neutral position. Having taken it, I determined, as far as should depend upon me, to maintain it with moderation, perseverance, and firmness.

32. The consideration which respects the right to hold the conduct, it is not necessary on this occasion to detail. I will only observe, that according to my understanding of the matter, that right, so far from being denied by any of the belligerent powers, has been virtually admitted by all. The duty of holding a neutral conduct may be inferred, without any thing more, from the obligation which justice and humanity impose upon every nation, in cases in which it is free to act, to maintain inviolate the relations of peace and amity towards other nations. The inducements of interest for observing that conduct, will be best referred to your own reflection and experience. With me, a predominant motive has been to endeavour to gain time to our country to settle and mature its yet recent institutions, and to progress, without interruption, to that degree of strength and consistency, which is necessary to give it, humanly speaking, the command of its own fortunes.

33. Though in reviewing the incidents of my administration, I am unconscious of intentional error, I am nevertheless too sensible of my defects not to think it probable that I may have committed many errors. Whatever they may be, I fervently beseech the Almighty to avert or mitigate the evils to which they may tend. I shall also carry with me the hope that my country will never cease to view them with indulgence; and that after forty-five years of my life dedicated to its service, with an upright zeal, the faults of incompetent abilities will be consigned to oblivion, as myself must soon be to the mansions of rest. Relying on its kindness in this as in other things, and actuated by that fervent love towards it,

which is so natural to a man, who views in it the native soil of himself and his progenitors for several generations; I anticipate with pleasing expectation that retreat, in which I promise myself to realize, without alloy, the sweet enjoyment of partaking, in the midst of my fellow citizens, the benign influence of good laws under a free government—the ever favourite object of my heart, and the happy reward, as I trust, of our mutual cares, labours, and dangers.

GEORGE WASHINGTON.

A CIRCULAR LETTER

From his Excellency George Washington, Commander-in-chief of the Armies of the United States of America, to the Governors of the several States.

Head-Quarters, Newburgh, June 18, 1783.

Sir,—The great object for which I had the honour to hold an appointment in the service of my country, being accomplished, I am now preparing to resign it into the hands of Congress, and return to that domestic retirement, which, it is well known, I left with the greatest reluctance, a retirement for which I have never ceased to sigh, through a long and painful absence, in which, (remote from the noise and trouble of the world,) I meditate to pass the remainder of life, in a state of undisturbed repose. But, before I carry this resolution into effect, I think it a duty incumbent on me to make this my last official communication, to congratulate you on the glorious events which Heaven has been pleased to produce in our favour, to offer my sentiments respecting some important subjects, which appear to me to be intimately connected with the tranquillity of the United States, to take my leave of your Excellency as a public character, and to give my final blessing to that country in whose service I have spent the prime of my life; for whose sake I have consumed so many anxious days and watchful nights; and whose happiness, being extremely dear to me, will always constitute no inconsiderable part of my own.

Impressed with the liveliest sensibility on this pleasing occasion, I will claim the indulgence of dilating the more copiously on the subject of our mutual felicitation. When we consider the magnitude of the prize we contended for, the doubtful nature of the contest, and the favourable manner in which it has terminated; we shall find the greatest possible reason for gratitude and rejoicing. This is a theme that will afford infinite delight to every benevolent and liberal mind, whether the event in contemplation be considered as a source of present enjoyment, or the parent of future happiness; and we shall have equal occasion to felicitate ourselves on the lot which Providence has assigned us, whether we view it in a natural, a political, or moral point of view.

The citizens of America, placed in the most enviable condition, as the sole lords and proprietors of a vast tract of continent, comprehending all the various soils and climates of the world, and abounding with all the necessaries and conveniences of life, are now, by the late satisfactory pacification, acknowledged to be possessed of absolute freedom and independency; they are from this period to be considered as the actors on a most conspicuous theatre, which seems to be peculiarly designed by Providence for the display of human greatness and felicity: here they are not only surrounded with every thing that can contribute to the completion of private and domestic enjoyment, but Heaven has crowned all its other blessings by giving a surer opportunity for political happiness than any other nation has ever been favoured with. Nothing can illustrate these observations more forcibly than the recollection of the happy conjuncture of times and circumstances, under which our republic assumed its rank among the nations. The foundation of our empire has not been laid in a gloomy age of ignorance and superstition, but at an epocha when the rights of mankind were better understood and more clearly defined, than at any former period. Researches of the human mind after social happiness have been carried to a great extent; the treasures of knowledge, acquired by the labours of philosophers, sages, and legislators, through a long succession of years, are laid open for use; and their collected wisdom may be happily applied in the establishment of our forms of government; the free cultivation of letters, the unbounded extension of commerce, the progressive refinement of manners, the growing liberality of sentiment, and, above all, the pure and benign light of revelation, have had a meliorating influence on mankind, and increased the blessings of society. At this auspicious period, the United States came into existence as a nation, and if their citizens should not be completely free and happy, the fault will be entirely their own.

Such is our situation, and such are our prospects; but notwithstanding the cup of blessing is thus reached out to us—notwithstanding happiness is ours, if we have a disposition to seize the occasion, and make it our own; yet it appears to me, there is an option still left to the United States of America, whether they will be respectable and prosperous, or contemptible and miserable as a nation. This is the time of their political probation; this is the moment, when the eyes of the whole world are turned upon them; this is the time to establish or ruin their national character for ever; this is the favourable moment to give such a tone to the Federal Government, as will enable it to answer the ends of its institution; or this may be the ill fated moment for relaxing the powers of the Union, annihilating the cement of the confederation, and exposing us to become the sport of European politics, which may play one State against another, to prevent their growing importance, and to serve their own interested purposes. For, according to the system of policy the States shall adopt at this moment, they will stand or fall; and, by their confirmation or lapse, it is yet to be decided, whether the revolution must ultimately be considered as a blessing or a curse; a blessing or a curse not to the present age alone, for with our fate will the destiny of unborn millions be involved.

With this conviction of the importance of the present crisis, silence in me would be a crime. I will therefore speak to your Excellency the language of freedom and sincerity, without disguise. I am aware, however, those who differ from me in political sentiments, may perhaps remark, I am stepping out of the proper line of my duty; and they may possibly ascribe to arrogance or ostentation, what I know is alone the result of the purest intention; but the rectitude of my own heart, which disdains such unworthy motives—the part I have hitherto acted in life—the determination I have formed of not taking any share in public business hereafter—the ardent desire I feel and shall continue to manifest, of quietly enjoying in private life, after all the toils of war, the benefits of a wise and liberal government,—will, I flatter myself, sooner or later, convince my countrymen, that I could have no sinister views in delivering, with so little reserve, the opinions contained in this Address.

There are four things which I humbly conceive are essential to the well-being, I may even venture to say, to the existence of the United States, as an independent power.

1st. An indissoluble union of the States under one federal head.

2dly. A sacred regard to public justice.

3dly. The adoption of a proper peace establishment; and,

4thly. The prevalence of that pacific and friendly disposition among the people of the United States, which will induce them to forget their local prejudices and politics, to make those mutual concessions which are requisite to the general prosperity, and, in some instances, to sacrifice their individual advantages to the interest of the community.

These are the pillars on which the glorious fabric of our independence and national character must be supported. Liberty is the basis, and whoever would dare to sap the foundation, or overturn the structure, under whatever specious pretext he may attempt it, will merit the bitterest execration and the severest punishment which can be inflicted by his injured country

On the three first articles I will make a few observations, leaving the last to the good sense and serious consideration of those immediately concerned.

Under the first head, although it may not be necessary or proper for me in this place to enter into a particular disquisition of the principles of the Union, and to take up the great question which has been frequently agitated, whether it be expedient and requisite for the States to delegate a large proportion of power to Congress or not: yet it will be a part of my duty, and that of every true patriot, to assert, without reserve, and to insist upon the following positions. That unless the States will suffer Congress to exercise those prerogatives they are undoubtedly invested with by the constitution, every thing must very rapidly tend to anarchy and confusion. That it is indispensable to the happiness of the individual States, that there should be lodged, somewhere, a supreme power, to regulate and govern the general concerns of the confederated republic, without which the union cannot be of long duration. There must be a faithful and pointed compliance on the part of every State, with the late proposals and demands of Congress, or the most fatal consequences will ensue. That whatever measures have a tendency to dissolve the Union, or contribute to violate or lessen the sovereign authority, ought to be considered as hostile to the liberty and independency of America, and the authors of them treated accordingly. And, lastly, that unless we can be enabled by the concurrence of the States, to participate in the fruits of the revolution, and enjoy the essential benefits of civil society, under a form of government so free and uncorrupted, so happily guarded against the danger of oppression, as has been devised and adopted by the articles of confederation, it will be the subject of regret, that so much blood and treasure have been lavished for no purpose; that so many sufferings have been counteracted without a compensation, and that so many sacrifices have been made in vain. Many other considerations might here be adduced to prove, that without an entire conformity to the spirit of the Union, we cannot exist as an independent power. It will be sufficient for my purpose to mention but one or two, which seem to me of the greatest importance. It is only in our united character, as an empire, that our independence is acknowledged, that our power can be regarded, or our credit supported among foreign nations. The treaties of the European powers with the United States of America, will have no validity on the dissolution of the Union. We shall be left nearly in a state of nature; or we may find, by our own unhappy experience, that there is a natural and necessary progression from the extreme of anarchy to the extreme of tyranny; and that arbitrary power is most easily established on the ruins of liberty abused to licentiousness.

As to the second article, which respects the performance of public justice, Congress have, in their late Address to the United States, almost exhausted the subject; they have explained their ideas so fully, and have enforced the obligations the States are under to render complete justice to all the public creditors, with so much dignity and energy, that in my opinion no real friend to the honour and independency of America can hesitate a single moment respecting the propriety of complying with the just and honourable measures proposed. If their arguments do not produce conviction, I know of nothing that will have a greater influence, especially when we reflect that the system referred to, being the result of the collected wisdom of the continent, must be esteemed, if not perfect, certainly the least objectionable of any that could be devised; and that, if it should not be carried into immediate execution, a national bankruptcy, with all its deplorable consequences, will take place, before any different plan can possibly be proposed or adopted; so pressing are the present circumstances, and such the alternative now offered to the States.

The ability of the country to discharge the debts which have been incurred in its defence, is not to be doubted.—An inclination, I flatter myself, will not be wanting; the path of our duty is plain before us; honesty will be found, on every experiment, to be the best and only true policy. Let us then, as a nation, be just; let us fulfil the public contracts which Congress had undoubtedly a right to make for the purpose of carrying on the war, with the same good faith we suppose ourselves bound to perform our private engagements. In the mean time, let an attention to the cheerful performance of their proper business as individuals, and as members of society, be earnestly inculcated on the citizens of America; then will they strengthen the bands of government, and be happy under its protection. Every one will reap the fruit of his labours; every one will enjoy his own acquisitions, without molestation and without danger.

In this state of absolute freedom and perfect security, who will grudge to yield a very little of his property to support the common interests of society, and ensure the protection of government? Who does not remember the frequent declarations at the commencement of the war, that we should be completely satisfied, if at the expense of one half, we could defend the remainder of our possessions? Where is the man to be found, who wishes to remain indebted for the defence of his own person and property, to the exertions, the bravery, and the blood of others, without making one generous effort to pay the debt of honour and of gratitude? In what part of the continent shall we find any man, or body of men, who would not blush to stand up, and propose measures purposely calculated to rob the soldier of his stipend, and the public creditor of his due? And were it possible that such a flagrant instance of injustice could ever happen, would it not excite the general indignation, and tend to bring down upon the authors of such measures, the aggravated vengeance of Heaven? If, after all, a spirit of disunion, or a temper of obstinacy and perverseness, should manifest itself in any of the States; if such an ungracious disposition should attempt to frustrate all the happy effects that might be expected to flow from the Union; if there should be a refusal to comply with the requisitions for funds to discharge the annual interest of the public debts, and if that refusal should revive all those jealousies, and produce all those evils which are now happily removed;—Congress, who have in all their transactions shown a great degree of magnanimity and justice, will stand justified in the sight of God and man! And that State alone, which puts itself in opposition to the aggregate wisdom of the continent, and follows such mistaken and pernicious councils, will be responsible for all the consequences.

For my own part, conscious of having acted, while a servant of the public, in the manner I conceived best suited to promote the real interests of my country; having in consequence of my fixed belief, in some measure, pledged myself to the army, that their country would finally do them complete and ample justice, and not willing to conceal any instance of my official conduct from the eyes of the world, I have thought proper to transmit to your excellency the enclosed collection of papers, relative to the half-pay and commutation granted by Congress to the officers of the army: from these communications, my decided sentiments will be clearly comprehended, together with the conclusive reasons, which induced me, at an early period, to recommend the adoption of this measure in the most earnest and serious manner. As the proceedings of Congress, the army, and myself, are open to all, and contain, in my opinion, sufficient information to remove the prejudice and errors which may have been entertained by any, I think it unnecessary to say any thing more, than just to observe, that the resolutions of Congress now alluded to, are as undoubtedly and absolutely binding on the United States, as the most solemn acts of confederation or legislation.

As to the idea, which I am informed, has in some instances prevailed, that the half-pay and commutation are to be regarded merely in the odious light of a pension, it ought to be exploded for ever: that provision should be viewed, as it really was, a reasonable compensation offered by Congress, at a time when they had nothing else to give to officers of the army, for services then to be performed: it was the only means to prevent a total dereliction of the service; it was a part of their hire. I may be allowed to say, it was the price of their blood, and of your independency; it is therefore more than a common debt, it is a debt of honour; it can never be considered as a pension or gratuity, nor cancelled until it is fairly discharged.

With regard to the distinction between officers and soldiers, it is sufficient that the uniform experience of every nation in the world, combined with our own, proves the utility and propriety of the discrimination. Rewards, in proportion to the aid the public draws from them, are unquestionably due to all its servants. In some h)ce, the soldiers have perhaps generally had as ample compensation for their services, by the large bounties which have been paid to them, as their officers will receive in the proposed commutation; in others, if, besides the donation of land, the payment of arrearages of clothing and wages, (in which articles all the component parts of the army must be put upon the same footing,) we take into the estimate, the bounties many of the soldiers have received, and the gratuity of one year's full pay, which is promised to all, possibly their situation (every circumstance being duly considered) will not be deemed less eligible than that of the officers. Should a farther reward, however, be judged equitable, I will venture to assert, no man will enjoy greater satisfaction than myself, in an exemption from taxes for a limited time, (which has been petitioned for in some instances) or any other adequate immunity or compensation granted to the brave defenders of their country's cause; but neither the adoption or rejection of this proposition will, in any manner, affect, much less militate against the act of Congress, by which they have offered five years' full pay, in lieu of the half-pay for life, which had been before promised to the officers of the army.

Before I conclude the subject on public justice, I cannot omit to mention the obligations this country is under to that meritorious class of veterans, the non-commissioned officers and privates who have been discharged for inability, in consequence of the resolution of congress, of the 23d of April, 1782, on an annual pension for life. Their peculiar sufferings, their singular merits and claims to that provision, need only to be known, to interest the feelings of humanity in their behalf. Nothing but a punctual payment of their annual allowance can rescue them from the most complicated misery; and nothing could be a more melancholy and distressing sight, than to behold those who have shed their blood, or lost their limbs in the service of their country, without a shelter, without a friend, and without the means of obtaining any of the comforts or necessaries of life, compelled to beg their daily bread from door to door. Suffer me to recommend those of this description, belonging to your State, to the warmest patronage of your excellency and your legislature.

It is necessary to say but a few words on the third topic which was proposed, and which regards particularly the defence of the republic; as there can be little doubt but Congress will recommend a proper peace establishment for the United States, in which a due attention will be paid to the importance of placing the militia of the Union upon a regular and respectable footing. If this should be the case, I should beg leave to urge the great advantage of it in the strongest terms.

The militia of this country must be considered as the palladium of our security, and the first effectual resort in case of hostility; it is essential, therefore, that the same system should pervade the whole; that the formation and discipline of the militia of the continent should be absolutely uniform; and that the same species of arms, accoutrements, and military apparatus, should be introduced in every part of the United States. No one, who has not learned it from experience, can conceive the difficulty, expense, and confusion, which result from a contrary system, or the vague arrangements which have hitherto prevailed.

If, in treating of political points, a greater latitude than usual has been taken in the course of the Address, the importance of the crisis, and magnitude of the objects in discussion, must be my apology: it is, however, neither my wish nor expectation, that the preceding observations should claim any regard, except so far as they shall appear to be dictated by a good intention; consonant to the immutable rules of justice; calculated to produce a liberal system of policy, and founded on whatever experience may have been acquired by a long and close attention to public business. Here I might speak with more confidence, from my actual observations; and if it would not swell this letter (already too prolix) beyond the bounds I had prescribed myself, I could demonstrate to every mind, open to conviction, that in less time, and with much less ex pense than has been incurred, the war might have been brought to the same happy conclusion, if the resources of the continent could have been properly called forth; that the distresses and disappointments which have very often occurred, have, in too many instances, resulted more from a want of energy in the continental government, than a deficiency of means in the particular States; that the inefficiency of the measures, arising from the want of an adequate authority in the supreme power, from a partial compliance with the requisitions of Congress in some of the States, and from a failure of punctuality in others, while they tended to damp the zeal of those who were more willing to exert themselves, served also to accumulate the expenses of the war, and to frustrate the best concerted plans; and that the discouragement occasioned by the complicated difficulties and embarrassments, in which our affairs were by this means involved, would have long ago produced the dissolution of any army, less patient, less virtuous, and less persevering than that which I have had the honour to command. But while I mention those things, which are notorious facts, as the defects of our Federal Constitution, particularly in the prosecution of a war, I beg it may be understood, that as I have ever taken a pleasure in gratefully acknowledging the assistance and support I have derived from every class of citizens, so shall I always be happy to do justice to the unparalleled exertions of the individual States, on many interesting occasions.

I have thus freely disclosed what I wished to make known before I surrendered up my public trust to those who committed it to me. The task is now accomplished. I now bid adieu to your excellency, as the chief magistrate of your State; at the same time I bid a last farewell to the cares of office, and all the employments of public life.

It remains, then, to be my final and only request, that your excellency will communicate these sentiments to your legislature, at their next meeting, and that they may be considered as the legacy of one who has ardently wished, on all occasions, to be useful to his country, and who, even in the shade of retirement, will not fail to implore the divine benediction upon it.

I now make it my earnest prayer that God would have you, and the State over which you preside, in his holy protection; that he would incline the hearts of the citizens to cultivate a spirit of subordination and obedience to government; to entertain a brotherly affection and love for one another, for their fellow-citizens of the United States at large, and particularly for their brethren who have served in the field; and finally, that he would most graciously be pleased to dispose us all to do justice, to love mercy, and to demean ourselves with that charity, humility, and pacific temper of the mind, which were the characteristics of the divine Author of our blessed religion; without an humble imitation of whose example, in these things, we can never hope to be a happy nation.

I have the honour to be, with much esteem and respect, sir, your excellency's most obedient and most humble servant, G. WASHINGTON.

FAREWELL ORDERS

Of Gen. Washington to the Armies of the United States

ROCKY HILL, near Princeton, Nov. 2, 1783.

THE United States in Congress assembled, after giving the most honourable testimony to the merits of the federal armies, and presenting them with the thanks of their country, for their long, eminent, and faithful service, having thought proper, by their proclamation bearing date the 16th of October last, to discharge such part of the troops as were engaged for the war, and to permit the officers on furlough to retire from service, from and after to-morrow; which proclamation having been communicated in the public papers for the information and government of all concerned; it only remains for the commander in-chief to address himself once more, and that for the last time, to the armies of the United States, (however widely dispersed individuals who compose them may be,) and to bid them an affectionate, a long farewell.

But before the commander-in-chief takes his final leave of those he holds most dear, he wishes to indulge himself a few moments in calling to mind a slight review of the past: he will then take the liberty of exploring, with his military friends, their future prospects; of advising the general line of conduct which, in his opinion, ought to be pursued; and he will conclude the address, by expressing the obligations he feels himself under for the spirited and able assistance he has experienced from them, in the performance of an arduous office.

A contemplation of the complete attainment, (at a period earlier than could have been expected,) of the object for which we contended against so formidable a power, cannot but inspire us with astonishment and gratitude. The disadvantageous circumstances on our part, under which the war was undertaken, can never be forgotten. The singular interpositions of Providence in our feeble condition, were such as could scarcely escape the attention of the most unobserving—while the unparalleled perseverance of the armies of the United States, through almost every possible suffering and discouragement, for the space of eight long years, was little short of a standing miracle.

It is not the meaning, nor within the compass of this address, to detail the hardships peculiarly incident to our service, or to describe the distresses which in several instances have resulted from the extremes of hunger and nakedness, combined with the rigours of an inclement season: nor is it necessary to dwell on the dark side of our past affairs. Every American officer and soldier must now console himself for any unpleasant circumstances which may have occurred, by a recollection of the uncommon scenes in which he has been called to act no inglorious part, and the astonishing events of which he has been a witness; events which have seldom, if ever before, taken place on the stage of human action, nor can they probably ever happen again. For who has before seen a disciplined army formed at once from such raw materials?

Who that was not a witness could imagine that the most violent local prejudices would cease so soon, and that men who came from different parts of the continent, strongly disposed by the habits of education to despise and quarrel with each other, would instantly become but one patriotic band of brothers? Or who that was not on the spot, can trace the steps by which such a wonderful revolution has been effected, and such a glorious period put to all our warlike toils?

It is universally acknowledged, that the enlarged prospects of happiness, opened by the confirmation of our independence and sovereignty, almost exceed the power of description; and shall not the brave men who have contributed so essentially to these inestimable acquisitions, retiring victorious from the field of war to the field of agriculture, participate in all the blessings which have been obtained? In such a republic, who will exclude them from the rights of citizens, and the fruits of their labours? In such a country, so happily circumstanced, the pursuits of commerce and the cultivation of the soil, will unfold to industry the certain road to competence. To those hardy soldiers who are actuated by the spirit of adventure, the fisheries will afford ample and profitable employment; and the extensive and fertile regions of the West will yield a most happy asylum for those who, fond of domestic enjoyment, are seeking personal independence. Nor is it possible to conceive that any one of the United States, will prefer a national bankruptcy, and dissolution of the Union, to a compliance with the requisitions of Congress, and the payment of its just debts; so that the officers and soldiers may expect considerable assistance, in re-commencing their civil operations, from the sums due to them from the public, which must and will most inevitably be paid.

In order to effect this desirable purpose, and to remove the prejudices which may have taken possession of the minds of any of the good people of the States, it is earnestly recommended to all the troops, that, with strong attachments to the Union, they should carry with them into civil society the most conciliating dispositions; and that they should prove themselves not less virtuous and useful as citizens, than they have been persevering and victorious as soldiers. What though there should be some envious individuals, who are unwilling to pay the debt the public has contracted, or to yield the tribute due to merit; yet let such unworthy treatment produce no invective, or any instance of intemperate conduct; let it be remembered that the unbiassed voice of the free citizens of the United States has promised the just reward, and given the merited applause; let it be known and remembered, that the reputation of the federal armies is established beyond the reach of malevolence; and let a consciousness of their achievements and fame, still excite the men who composed them, to honourable actions, under the persuasion, that the private virtues of economy, prudence, and industry, will not be less amiable in civil life, than the more splendid qualities of valour, perseverance, and enterprise, were in the field. Every one may rest assured that much, very much, of the future happiness of the officers and men, will depend upon the wise and manly conduct which shall be adopted by them, when they are mingled with the great body of the community. And although the General has so frequently given it as his opinion, in the most public and explicit manner, that unless the principles of the federal government were properly supported, and the powers of the Union increased, the honour, dignity, and justice of the nation, would be lost for ever; yet he cannot help repeating on this occasion so interesting a sentiment, and leaving it as his last injunction to every officer and every soldier who may view the subject in the same serious point of light, to add his best endeavours to those of his worthy fellow-citizens, towards effecting these great and valuable purposes, on which our very existence as a nation so materially depends.

The commander-in-chief conceives little is now wanting to enable the soldier to change the military character into that of a citizen, but that steady and decent tenor of behaviour, which has generally distinguished not only the army under his immediate command, but the different detachments and separate armies, through the course o the war. From their good sense and prudence he anticipates the happiest consequences: and while he congratulates them on the glorious occasion which renders their services in the field no longer necessary, he wishes to express the strong obligations he feels himself under for the assistance he has received from every class, and in every instance. He presents his thanks, in the most serious and affectionate manner, to the general officers, as well for their counsel on many interesting occasions, as for their ardour in promoting the success of the plans he had adopted; to the commandants of regiments and corps, and to the officers, for their zeal and attention in carrying his orders promptly into execution; to the staff, for their alacrity and exactness in performing the duties of their several departments; and to the non-commissioned officers and private soldiers, for their extraordinary patience in suffering, as well as their invincible fortitude in action. To various branches of the army the General takes this last and solemn opportunity of professing his inviolable attachment and friendship. He wishes more than bare profession were in his power, that he was really able to be useful to them all in future life. He flatters himself, however, they will do him the justice to believe, that whatever could with propriety be attempted by him, has been done. And being now to conclude these his last public orders, to take his ultimate leave, in a short time, of the military character, and to bid a final adieu to the armies he has so long had the honour to command, he can only again offer, in their behalf, his recommendations to their grateful country, and his prayers to the God of armies. May ample justice be done them here, and may the choicest of Heaven's favours, both here and hereafter, attend those who, under the divine auspices, have secured innumerable blessings for others! With these wishes, and this benediction, the commander-in-chief is about to retire from service. The curtain of separation will soon be drawn—and the military scene to him will be closed for ever.

INDIAN ELOQUENCE.

Speech of Logan, a Mingo Chief.

This celebrated chief was distinguished for magnanimity in war, and greatness of soul in peace. He was always acknowledged the friend of the white people, until the year 1774, when his brother and others of his family were murdered by the whites. This drew on a bloody war with the whites, and the Indians were obliged to sue for peace. The following speech was delivered at a treaty held by Governor Dunmore, of Virginia, with the Mingoes, Shawanese, and Delawares. Logan, though desirous of peace, remained in his cabin in silence, till a messenger was sent to him, to know whether he would accede to the proposals. Logan, after shedding many tears for the loss of his friends, answered as follows.

" I appeal to any white man to say, if ever he entered Logan's cabin hungry, and he gave him not meat: if ever he came cold and naked, and he clothed him not. During the course of the last long and bloody war, Logan remained idle in his cabin, an advocate for peace. Such was my love for the whites, that my countrymen pointed as they passed, and said, ' Logan is the friend of white men.' I had even thought to have lived with you, but for the injuries of one man. Colonel Cresap, the last spring, in cold blood, and unprovoked, murdered all the relations of Logan, not even sparing my women and children. There runs not a drop of my blood in the veins of any living creature. This called on me for revenge. I have sought it: I have killed many: I have fully glutted my vengeance. For my country, I rejoice at the beams of peace: but do not harbour a thought that mine is the joy of fear. Logan never felt fear. He will not turn on his heel to save his life. Who is there to mourn for Logan?—Not one."

Speech of the Chiefs of the Seneca Nation to the President of the United States—1790.

Father—The voice of the Seneca nation speaks to you—the great counsellor, in whose heart the wise men of all the thirteen fires have placed their wisdom; it may be very small in your ears, and we therefore entreat you to hearken with attention, for we are about to speak of things which are to us very great.

When your army entered the country of the Six Nations, we called you the town destroyer: and to this day, when your name is heard, our women look behind them and turn pale, and our children cling close to the necks of their mothers. Our counsellors and warriors are men, and cannot be afraid; but their hearts are grieved with the fears of our women and children, and desire that it may be buried so deep as to be heard no more.

When you gave us peace, we called you father; because you promised to secure us in the possession of our lands. Do this, and so long as the land shall remain, that beloved name will be in the heart of every Seneca.

Father—We mean to open our hearts before you, and we earnestly desire that you will let us clearly understand what you resolve to do.

When our chiefs returned from the treaty at Fort Stanwix, and laid before our council what had been done there, our nation was surprised to hear how great a country you had compelled them to give up to you, without your paying to us any thing for it. Every one said that your hearts were yet swelled with resentment against us, for what had happened during the war; but that one day you would consider it with more kindness. We asked each other, what have we done to deserve such severe chastisement?

Father—When you kindled your thirteen fires separately, the wise men assembled at them told us, that you were all brothers—the children of one great father—who regarded the red people as his children. They called us brothers, and invited us to his protection. They told us that he resided beyond the great water, where the sun first rises—that he was a king whose power no people could resist, and that his goodness was bright as the sun—what they said, went to our hearts. We accepted the invitation, and promised to obey him. What the Seneca nation promises, they faithfully perform; and when you refused obedience to that king, he commanded us to assist his beloved men in making you sober. In obeying him, we did no more than yourselves had led us to promise. The men who claimed this promise, told us that you were children and had no guns; that when they had shaken you, you would submit. We hearkened unto them, and were deceived until your army approached our towns. We were deceived; but your people teaching us to confide in that king, had helped to deceive us; and we now appeal to your heart—Is all the blame ours?

Father—When we saw that we had been deceived, and heard the invitation which you gave us to draw near to the fire which you have kindled, and talk with you concerning peace, we made haste towards it. You then told us you could crush us to nothing, and you demanded from us a great country, as the price of that peace which you had offered to us; as if our want of strength had destroyed our rights. Our chiefs had felt your power, and were unable to contend against you, and they therefore gave up that country. What they agreed to, has bound our nation; but your anger against us must, by this time, be cooled, and although our strength has not increased, nor your power become less, we ask you to consider calmly—were the terms dictated to us by your commissioners reasonable or just?

Father—Hear our case. Many nations inhabited this country; but they had no wisdom; therefore they warred together—the Six Nations were powerful, and compelled them to peace. The land, for a great extent, was given up to them, but the nations which were not destroyed, all continued on those lands, and claimed the protection of the Six Nations, as brothers of their fathers. They were men, and, when at peace, had a right to live upon the earth.

The French came among us, and built Niagara; they became our fathers, and took care of us. Sir William

Johnson came and took that fort from the French; he became our father, and promised to take care of us; and he did so, until you were too strong for his king. To him we gave four miles round Niagara, as a place of trade. We have already said how we came to join against you; we saw that we were wrong; we wished for peace; you demanded a great country to be given up to you; it was surrendered to you, as the price of peace; and we ought to have peace and possession of a little land which you left us.

Father—When that great country was given up to you, there were but few chiefs present; and they were compelled to give it up. And it is not the Six Nations only that reproach those chiefs with having given up that country. The Chipeways, and all the nations who lived on these lands westward, call to us, and ask us, brothers of our fathers, where is the place which you have reserved for us to lie down upon?

Father—You have compelled us to do that which makes us ashamed; we have nothing to answer to the children of the brothers of our fathers. When last spring they called upon us to go to war, to secure them a bed to lie down upon, the Senecas entreated them to be quiet, until we had spoken to you; but on our way down we heard that your army had gone towards the country which those nations inhabited, and if they meet together, the best blood on both sides will fall to the ground.

Father—We will not conceal from you, that the Great God, and not men, has preserved the Corn Plant from the hands of his own nation. For they ask continually, where is the land which our children, and their children after them, are to lie down upon? You told us, say they, that the line drawn from Pennsylvania to Lake Ontario would mark it for ever on the east, and the line running from Beaver creek to Pennsylvania, would mark it on the west; and we see that it is not so, for first one and then another come, and take it away, by order of that people which you tell us promised to secure it to us. He is silent, for he has nothing to answer.

When the sun goes down, he opens his heart before

God, and earlier than the sun appears again upon the hills, he gives thanks for his protection during the night: for he feels that among men become desperate by the injuries they sustain, it is God only that can preserve him. He loves peace; and all he had in store he has given to those who have been robbed by your people, lest they should plunder the innocent to repay themselves. The whole season which others have employed in providing for their families, he has spent in endeavours to preserve peace; and this moment his wife and children are lying on the ground, and in want of food; his heart is in pain for them; but he perceives that the Great Spirit will try his firmness in doing what is right.

Father—the game which the Great Spirit sent into our country for us to eat, is going from among us. We thought he intended we should till the ground with the plough, as the white people do; and we talked to one another about it. But before we speak to you concerning this, we must know from you, whether you mean to leave us and our children any land to till. Speak plainly to us, concerning this great business.

Speech of the Chiefs of the Seneca Nation, to the President of the United States—1790.

Father—Your speech, written on the great paper, is to us like the first light of the morning to a sick man, whose pulse beats too strongly in his temples, and prevents him from sleeping; he sees it, and rejoices, but is not cured.

You say you have spoken plainly on the great point, that you will protect us in our lands secured to us at Fort Stanwix, and that we have a right to sell or refuse to sell it. This is very good.

But our nation complain, that you compelled us, at that treaty, to give up too much of our lands. We confess that our nation was bound by what was done there, and acknowledge your power. We have now appealed to yourselves against that treaty, as made while you were too angry at us, and therefore unreasonable and unjust. To this you have given us no answer.

Father—Look at the land we gave you at the treaty, and then cast your eyes upon what we now ask you to restore to us; and you will see that what we ask is a very little piece. By giving it back again, you will satisfy the whole of our nation. The chiefs who signed that treaty will be in safety; and peace between your children and our children will continue so long as your lands continue to join ours. Every man of our nation will turn his eyes away from all the other lands which we then gave up to you, and forget that our fathers ever said that they belonged to them.

Father—You say you will appoint an agent to take care of us. Let him come and take care of our trade; but we desire he may not have any thing to do with our lands; for the agents who have come among us, and pretended to take care of us, have always deceived us, whenever we sold lands: both when the king, and when the separate States have bargained with us. They have, by this means, occasioned many wars; and we are unwilling to trust them again.

Father—The blood that was spilt near Pine creek is covered, and we shall never look where it lies. We know that Pennsylvania will satisfy us for that which we speak of to them, before we speak to you. The chain of friendship will now, we hope, be made strong, as you desire it to be—we will hold it fast, and our end of it shall never rust in our hands.

Father—We told you what advice we gave to the people you are now at war with; and we now tell you, they have promised to come again next spring to our towns. We shall not wait for their coming, but set out very early in the season, and show them what you have done for us, which must convince them, that you will do for them every thing that they ought to ask. We think they will hear us, and follow our advice.

Father—You gave us leave to speak our minds concerning tilling of the ground. We ask you to teach us to plough and grind corn, and supply us with broad-axes, saws, augers, and other tools, to assist us in building saw-mills, so that we may make our houses more comfortable and durable; that you will send smiths among us; and above all, that you will teach our children to read and write, and our women to spin and weave. The manner of doing these things for us, we leave to you who understand them; but we assure you, we will follow your advice as far as we are able.

Speech of the Chiefs of the Seneca Nation to the President of the United States—1790.

Father—No Seneca ever goes from the fire of his friend, until he has said to him, I am going. We therefore tell you that we are now setting out for our own country.

Father—We thank you from our hearts that we now know that there is a country that we may call our own, and on which we may lie down in peace. We see, that there will be peace between our children and your children; and our hearts are very glad. We will persuade the Wyandots, and other western nations, to open their eyes, and look towards the bed which you have made for us, and to ask of you a bed for themselves and their children, that will not slide from under them. We thank you for your presents to us, and rely on your promise to instruct us in raising corn as the white people do. The sooner you do this, the better for us; and we thank you for the care which you have taken to prevent bad people coming to trade among us. If any come without your license, we will turn them back; and we hope our nation will determine to spill all the rum that shall hereafter be brought to our towns.

Father—You have not asked of us any surety for peace on our part; but we have agreed to send nine Seneca boys, to be under your care for education. Tell us at what time you will receive them, and they shall be sent at that time. This will assure you that we are indeed at peace with you, and determined to continue so. If you can teach them to be wise and good men, we will take care that our nation shall be willing to be instructed by them.

Speech of Farmer's Brother.

[The following Speech was delivered in a Public Council, at Genesee River, Nov. 21, 1798, by *Ho-na-ya-wus*, commonly called Farmer's Brother, and after being written as interpreted, it was signed by the principal Chiefs present, and sent to the Legislature of the State of New York.]

The Sachems, Chiefs, and Warriors of the Seneca Nation, to the Sachems and Chiefs assembled about the great Council Fire of the State of New York.

"Brothers—As you are once more assembled in council for the purpose of doing honour to yourselves, and justice to your country; we, your brothers, the Sachems, Chiefs, and Warriors of the Seneca Nation, request you to open your ears, and give attention to our voice and wishes.

"Brothers—You will recollect the late contest between you and your father, the great king of England. This contest threw the inhabitants of this whole island into a great tumult and commotion, like a raging whirlwind, which tears up the trees, and tosses to and fro the leaves, so that no one knows from whence they come, or where they will fall.

"Brothers—This whirlwind was so directed by the Great Spirit above, as to throw into our arms two of your infant children, Jasper Parrish and Horatio Jones. We adopted them into our families, and made them our children. We loved them and nourished them. They lived with us many years. At length, the Great Spirit spoke to the whirlwind, and it was still. A clear and uninterrupted sky appeared. The path of peace was opened, and the chain of friendship was once more made bright. Then these our adopted children left us, to seek their relations. We wished them to remain among us, and promised, if they would return and live in our country, to give each of them a seat of land for them and their children to sit down upon.

"Brothers—They have returned, and have for several years past been serviceable to us as interpreters. We still feel our hearts beat with affection for them, and now wish to fulfil the promise we made them, and to reward them for their services. We have therefore made up our minds to give them a seat of two square miles of land lying on the outlet of Lake Erie, about three miles below Black Rock, beginning at the mouth of a creek known by the name of Scoy-gu-quoy-des Creek, running one mile from the river Niagara, up said creek, thence northwardly as the river runs two miles; thence westwardly one mile to the river; thence up the river as the river runs, two miles to the place of beginning; so as to contain two square miles.

"Brothers—We have now made known to you our minds. We expect and earnestly request that you will permit our friends to receive this our gift, and will make the same good to them, according to the laws and customs of your nation.

"Brothers—Why should you hesitate to make our minds easy with regard to this our request? To you it is but a little thing, and have you not complied with the request, and confirmed the gift of our brothers the Oneidas, the Onondagas, and Cayugas, to their interpreters? And shall we ask and not be heard?

"Brothers—We send you this our speech, to which we expect your answer before the breaking up of your great council fire"

Speech of Red Jacket, called by the Indians, Sa-gu-yu-wha-hah, or Keeper Awake,

In answer to a Speech of the Rev. Mr. Alexander, a missionary from the Missionary Society in New York, to the *Seneca Nation* of Indians, delivered at a Council held at Buffalo Creek, in May, 1811.

"Brother—We listened to the talk you delivered to us from the council of black coats* in New York. We

* The appellation given to the clergymen by the Indians.

have fully considered your talk, and the offers you have made us; we perfectly understand them, and we return an answer, which we wish you also to understand. In making up our minds, we have looked back, and remembered what has been done in our days, and what our fathers have told us was done in old times.

"Brother—Great numbers of black coats have been amongst the Indians, and with sweet voices and smiling faces, have offered to teach them the religion of the white people. Our brethren in the East listened to the black coats—turned from the religion of their fathers, and took up the religion of the white people. What good has it done them? Are they more happy and more friendly one to another than we are? No, brother, they are a divided people—we are united; they quarrel about religion—we live in love and friendship; they drink strong water—have learned how to cheat—and to practise all the vices of the white men, which disgrace Indians, without imitating the virtues of the white men. Brother, if you are our well-wisher, keep away, and do not disturb us.

"Brother—We do not worship the Great Spirit as the white men do, but we believe that forms of worship are indifferent to the Great Spirit—it is the offering of a sincere heart that pleases him, and we worship him in this manner. According to your religion, we must believe in a Father and a Son, or we will not be happy hereafter. We have always believed in a Father, and we worship him, as we were taught by our fathers. Your book says the Son was sent on earth by the Father—did all the people who saw the Son believe in him? No, they did not; and the consequences must be known to you, if you have read the book.

"Brother—You wish us to change our religion for yours—we like our religion, and do not want another. Our friends (pointing to Mr. Granger, Mr. Parish, and Mr. Taylor) do us great good—they counsel us in our troubles—and instruct us how to make ourselves comfortable. Our friends the Quakers do more than this—they give us ploughs, and show us how to use them

They tell us we are accountable beings, but do not say we must change our religion. We are satisfied with what they do.

"Brother—For these reasons we cannot receive your offers—we have other things to do, and beg you to make your mind easy, and not trouble us, lest our heads should be too much loaded, and by and by burst."

Speech of Red Jacket.

[The occasion of the following speech, was, a white man had been murdered by an Indian at Buffalo, and the Indians were unwilling to deliver the perpetrator of the crime to our civil authority. Several meetings were held between them and the people of Canandaigua, for the purpose of reconciling them to the propriety and justice of surrendering him, to which, however, they at length reluctantly consented.]

"Brothers—Open your ears, and give your attention. This day is appointed by the Great Spirit to meet our friends at this place. During the many years that we have lived together in this country, good will and harmony have subsisted among us.

"Brothers—We have now come forward upon an unhappy occasion: we cannot find words to express our feelings upon it. One of our people has murdered one of your people. So it has been ordered by the Great Spirit who controls all events. This has been done: we cannot now help it. At first view, it would seem to have the effect of putting an end to our friendship; but let us reflect, and put our minds together. Can't we point out measures whereby our peace and harmony may still be preserved? We have come forward to this place, where we have always had a superintendent and friend to receive us, and to make known to him such grievances as lay upon our minds; but now we have none; and we have no guardian—no protector—no one is now authorized to receive us.

"Brothers—We therefore now call upon you to take

our speech in writing, and forward our ideas to the President of the United States.

"Brothers—Let us look back to our former situation. While you were under the government of Great Britain, Sir William Johnson was our superintendent, appointed by the king. He had powers to settle offences of this kind among all the Indian Nations, without adverting to the laws. But under the British government you were uneasy—you wanted to change it for a better. General Washington went forward as your leader. From his exertions you gained your independence. Immediately afterwards a treaty was made between the United States and the Six Nations, whereby a method was pointed out of redressing such an accident as the present. Several such accidents did happen, where we were the sufferers. We now claim the same privilege in making restitution to you, that you adopted towards us in a similar situation.

"Brothers—At the close of our treaty at Philadelphia, General Washington told us that we had formed a chain of friendship which was bright: He hoped it would continue so on our part: That the United States would be equally willing to brighten it, if rusted by any means. A number of murders have been committed on our people. We shall only mention the last of them. About two years ago, a few of our warriors were amusing themselves in the woods, to the westward of Fort Pitt: two white men, coolly and deliberately, took their rifles, travelled nearly three miles to our encampment, fired upon the Indians, killed two men, and wounded two children. We then were the party injured. What did we do? We flew to the treaty, and thereby obtained redress, perfectly satisfactory to us, and we hope agreeable to you. This was done a short time before President Adams went out of office. Complete peace and harmony was restored. We now want the same method of redress to be pursued.

"Brothers—How did the present accident take place? Did our warriors go from home, cool and sober, and commit murder on you? No. Our brother was in liquor, and a quarrel ensued, in which the unhappy accident happened. We would not excuse him on account of his being in liquor; but such a thing was far from his intention in his sober moments. We are all extremely grieved at it, and are willing to come forward and have it settled, as crimes of the same nature have been heretofore done.

"Brothers—Since this accident has taken place, we have been informed, that by the laws of this State, if a murder is committed within it, the murderer must be tried by the laws of the State, and punished with death.

"Brothers—When were such laws explained to us? Did we ever make a treaty with the State of New York, and agree to conform to its laws? No. We are independent of the State of New York. It was the will of the Great Spirit to create us different in colour. We have different laws, habits, and customs, from the white people. We will never consent that the government of this State shall try our brother. We appeal to the government of the United States.

"Brothers—Under the customs and habits of our forefathers, we were a happy people; we had laws of our own; they were dear to us. The whites came among us and introduced their customs; they introduced liquor among us, which our forefathers always told us would prove our ruin.

"Brothers—In consequence of the introduction of liquor among us, numbers of our people were killed. A council was held to consider of a remedy, at which it was agreed by us, that no private revenge should take place for any such murder—that it was decreed by the Great Spirit, and that a council should be called, to consider of redress to the friends of the deceased.

"Brothers—The President of the United States is called a great man, possessing great power—he may do what he pleases—he may turn men out of office—men who held their offices long before he held his. If he can do these things, can he not even control the laws of this State? Can he not appoint a commissioner to come forward to our country and settle the present difference, as we, on our part, have heretofore often done to him upon a similar occasion.

"We now call upon you, Brothers, to represent these things to the President, and we trust that he will not refuse our request, of sending a commissioner to us, with powers to settle the present difference. The consequence of a refusal may be serious. We are determined that our brother shall not be tried by the laws of the State of New York. Their laws make no difference between a crime committed in liquor, and one committed coolly and deliberately. Our laws are different, as we have before stated. If tried here, our brother must be hanged. We cannot submit to that. Has a murder been committed upon our people, when was it punished with death?

"Brothers—We have now finished what we had to say on the subject of the murder. We wish to address you upon another, and to have our ideas communicated to the President upon it also?

"Brothers—It was understood at the treaty concluded by Col. Pickering, that our superintendent should reside in the town of Canandaigua, and for very good reasons; that situation is the most central to the Six Nations, and by subsequent treaties between the State of New York and the Indians; and there are still stronger reasons why he should reside here, principally on account of the annuities being stipulated to be paid to our superintendent at this place. These treaties are sacred. If their superintendent resides elsewhere, the state may object to sending their money to him at a greater distance. We would therefore wish our superintendent to reside here at all events.

"Brothers—With regard to the appointment of our present superintendent, we look upon ourselves as much neglected and injured. When General Chapin and Captain Chapin were appointed, our wishes were consulted upon the occasion, and we most cordially agreed to the appointments. Captain Chapin has been turned out, however, within these few days. We do not understand that any neglect of duty has been alleged against him. We are told it is because he differs from the President in his sentiments on government matters. He has also been perfectly satisfactory to us; and had we known of the inention, we should most cordially have united in a petition to the President to continue him in office. We feel ourselves injured—we have nobody to look to—nobody to listen to our complaints—none to reconcile any differences among us. We are like a young family without a father.

"Brothers—We cannot conclude without again urging you to make known all these our sentiments to the President."

Speech delivered over the grave of Black Buffalo, principal Chief of the Teton tribe of Indians, by the Big Elk Maha Chief.

Do not grieve. Misfortunes will happen to the wisest and best men. Death will come, and always comes out of season. It is the command of the Great Spirit, and all nations and people must obey. What is past and cannot be prevented should not be grieved for. Be not discouraged or displeased, then, that in visiting your father here you have lost your chief. A misfortune of this kind may never again befall you, but this would have attended you perhaps at your own village. Five times have I visited this land, and never returned with sorrow or pain. Misfortunes do not flourish particularly in our path. They grow every where. (*Addressing himself to Governor Edwards and Colonel Miller.*) What a misfortune for me, that I could not have died this day, instead of the chief that lies before us. The trifling loss my nation would have sustained in my death would have been doubly paid for, by the honours of my burial—They would have wiped off every thing like regret. Instead of being covered with a cloud of sorrow, my warriors would have felt the sunshine of joy in their hearts. To me it would have been a most glorious occurrence. Hereafter, when I die, at home, instead of a noble grave and a grand procession, the rolling music and the thundering cannon, with a flag waving at my head—I shall be wrapped in a robe (an old robe perhaps) and hoisted on a slender scaf-

'old to the whistling winds, soon to be blown to the earth—my flesh to be devoured by the wolves, and my bones rattled on the plain by the wild beasts.

(*Addressing himself to Colonel Miller.*)

CHIEF OF THE SOLDIERS,—Your labours have not been in vain. Your attention shall not be forgotten. My nation shall know the respect that is paid over the dead. When I return, I will echo the sound of your guns

---

Speech of Red Jacket.

[In the summer of 1805, a number of the principal Chiefs and Warriors of the Six Nations, principally Senecas, assembled at Buffalo Creek, in the State of New York, at the particular request of the Rev. Mr. Cram, a Missionary from the State of Massachusetts. The Missionary being furnished with an Interpreter, and accompanied by the Agent of the United States for Indian affairs, met the Indians in Council, when the following talk took place.]

First, by the Agent.

"Brothers of the Six Nations—I rejoice to meet you at this time, and thank the Great Spirit that he has preserved you in health, and given me another opportunity of taking you by the hand.

"Brothers—the person who sits by me, is a friend who has come a great distance to hold a talk with you. He will inform you what his business is, and it is my request that you would listen with attention to his words."

MISSIONARY. "My friends—I am thankful for the opportunity afforded us of uniting together at this time. I had a great desire to see you, and inquire into your state and welfare; for this purpose I have travelled a great distance, being sent by your old friends, the Boston Missionary Society. You will recollect they formerly sent missionaries among you, to instruct you in religion, and labour for your good. Although they have not heard from you for a long time, yet they have not forgotten their brothers, the Six Nations, and are still anxious to do you good.

"Brothers—I have not come to get your lands or your money, but to enlighten your minds, and to instruct you how to worship the Great Spirit agreeably to his mind and will, and to preach to you the gospel of his Son Jesus Christ. There is but one religion, and but one way to serve God, and if you do not embrace the right way, you cannot be happy hereafter. You have never worshipped the Great Spirit in a manner acceptable to him; but have all your lives been in great errors and darkness. To endeavour to remove these errors, and open your eyes, so that you might see clearly, is my business with you.

"Brothers—I wish to talk with you as one friend talks with another: and if you have any objections to receive the religion which I preach, I wish you to state them; and I will endeavour to satisfy your minds, and remove the objections.

"Brothers—I want you to speak your minds freely; for I wish to reason with you on the subject, and, if possible, remove all doubts, if there be any on your minds. The subject is an important one, and it is of consequence that you give it an early attention while the offer is made you. Your friends, the Boston Missionary Society, will continue to send you good and faithful ministers, to instruct and strengthen you in religion, if, on your part, you are willing to receive them.

"Brothers—Since I have been in this part of the country, I have visited some of your small villages, and talked with your people. They appear willing to receive instruction, but as they look up to you as their elder brothers in council, they want first to know your opinion on the subject.

"You have now heard what I have to propose at present. I hope you will take it into consideration, and give me an answer before we part."

[After about two hours' consultation among themselves, the Chief commonly called by the white people Red Jacket, (whose Indian name is Sa-gu-yu-wha-hah, which interpreted, is *Keeper Awake*,' rose and spoke as follows:]

"Friend and Brother—It was the will of the Great Spirit that we should meet together this day. He orders all things, and has given us a fine day for our Council. He has taken his garment from before the sun, and caused it to shine with brightness upon us. Our eyes are opened, that we see clearly; our ears are unstopped, that we have been able to hear distinctly the words you have spoken. For all these favours we thank the Great Spirit, and HIM *only*.

"Brother—This council fire was kindled by you. It was at your request that we came together at this time. We have listened with attention to what you have said. You requested us to speak our minds freely. This gives us great joy; for we now consider that we stand upright before you, and can speak what we think. All have heard your voice, and all speak to you now as one man. Our minds are agreed.

"Brother—You say you want an answer to your talk before you leave this place. It is right you should have one, as you are a great distance from home, and we do not wish to detain you. But we will first look back a little, and tell you what our fathers have told us, and what we have heard from the white people.

"Brother—Listen to what we say.

"There was a time when our forefathers owned this great island. Their seats extended from the rising to the setting sun. The Great Spirit had made it for the use of Indians. HE had created the buffalo, the deer, and other animals, for food. HE had made the bear and the beaver. Their skins served us for clothing. HE had scattered them over the country, and taught us how to take them. HE had caused the earth to produce corn for bread. All this HE had done for his red children, because he loved them. If we had some disputes about our hunting ground, they were generally settled without the shedding of much blood. But an evil day came upon us. Your forefathers crossed the great water, and landed on this island. Their numbers were small. They found friends and not enemies. They told us they had fled from their own country for fear of wicked men, and had come here to enjoy their religion. They asked for a small seat. We took pity on them, granted their request; and they sat down among us. We gave them corn and meat; they gave us poison (alluding, it is supposed, to ardent spirits) in return.

"The white people had now found our country. Tidings were carried back, and more came amongst us. Yet we did not fear them. We took them to be friends. They called us brothers. We believed them, and gave them a larger seat. At length their numbers had greatly increased. They wanted more land; they wanted our country. Our eyes were opened, and our minds became uneasy. Wars took place. Indians were hired to fight against Indians, and many of our people were destroyed. They also brought strong liquor amongst us. It was strong and powerful, and has slain thousands.

"Brother—Our seats were once large and yours were small. You have now become a great people, and we have scarcely a place left to spread our blankets. You have got our country, but are not satisfied; you want to force your religion among us.

"Brother—continue to listen.

"You say that you are sent to instruct us how to worship the Great Spirit agreeably to his mind, and if we do not take hold of the religion which you white people teach, we shall be unhappy hereafter. You say that you are right, and we are lost. How do we know this to be true? We understand that your religion is written in a book. If it was intended for us as well as you, why has not the Great Spirit given to us, and not only to us, but why did he not give to our forefathers, the knowledge of that book, with the means of understanding it rightly! We only know what you tell us about it. How shall we know when to believe, being so often deceived by the white people?

"Brother—You say there is but one way to worship and serve the Great Spirit. If there is but one religion, why do you white people differ so much about it? Why not all agree, as you can all read the book?

"Brother—We do not understand these things.

"We are told that your religion was given to your forefathers, and has been handed down from father to son. We also have a religion, which was given to our forefa hers, and has been handed down to us, their children We worship in that way. It teaches us to be thankfu. or all the favours we receive; to love each other, and to be united. We never quarrel about religion.

"Brother—The Great Spirit has made us all, but HE has made a great difference between his white and red children. HE has given us different complexions and different customs. To you he has given the arts. To these he has not opened our eyes. We know these things to be true. Since HE has made so great a difference between us in other things, why may we not conclude that HE has given us a different religion, according to our understanding? The Great Spirit does right, HE knows what is best for his children; we are satisfied.

"Brother—We do not wish to destroy your religion, or take it from you. We only want to enjoy our own.

"Brother—We are told that you have been preaching to the white people in this place. These people are our neighbours. We are acquainted with them. We will wait a little while and see what effect your preaching has upon them. If we find it does them good, makes them honest, and less disposed to cheat Indians, we will then consider again of what you have said.

"Brother—You have now heard our answer to your talk, and this is all we have to say at present.

"As we are going to part, we will come and take you by the hand, and hope the Great Spirit will protect you on your journey, and return you safe to your friends."

As the Indians began to approach the missionary, he rose hastily from his seat and replied, that he could not take them by the hand; that there was no fellowship between the religion of God and the works of the devil.

This being interpreted to the Indians, they smiled, and retired in a peaceful manner.

It being afterwards suggested to the missionary that his reply to the Indians was rather indiscreet; he observed, that he supposed the ceremony of shaking hands would be received by them as a token that he assented to hat they had said. Being otherwise informed, he said ne was sorry for the expressions.

www.ingramcontent.com/pod-product-compliance
Lightning Source LLC
Chambersburg PA
CBHW022116300426
44117CB00007B/730